V&R

Studia Aarhusiana Neotestamentica (SANt)

Edited by
Eve-Marie Becker, Ole Davidsen, Jan Dochhorn,
Kasper Bro Larsen, Nils Arne Pedersen

Volume 2

Vandenhoeck & Ruprecht

Eve-Marie Becker/Jan Dochhorn/
Else Kragelund Holt (ed.)

Trauma and Traumatization in Individual and Collective Dimensions

Insights from Biblical Studies and Beyond

Vandenhoeck & Ruprecht

Bibliographic information published by the Deutsche Nationalbibliothek

The Deutsche Nationalbibliothek lists this publication in the Deutsche Nationalbibliografie; detailed bibliographic data available online: http://dnb.d-nb.de.

ISBN 978-3-525-53616-2

You can find alternative editions of this book and additional material on our Website: www.v-r.de

Typesetting by: Malte Rosenau
Printed and bound in Germany by CPI buchbücher.de, Birkach

Printed on non-aging paper.

Preface, Short Introduction and Acknowledgments

The present volume results from an international conference at Aarhus University (June 6-9, 2012) organized by the research sections of Old and New Testament studies, where scholars from the fields of Biblical exegesis, Classics, Patristics, the history of medicine, literary sciences, sociology, religious studies, psychology and psychiatry met in order to approach and discuss the phenomena of "Trauma and Traumatization in and Beyond Biblical Literature."

The focus of this highly interdisciplinary endeavor was placed on Biblical texts which—as eminent parts of ancient literature—were considered as cultural reservoirs pointing back in a historical sense to traumatization of either individuals or (religious) groups, containing traumatic experiences in a literary form or delivering them further in the sense of a 'cultural trauma.' The aim of the conference was two-fold. Firstly, by discussing the diverse papers presented by both Biblical scholars and researchers in the various fields of the humanities, social sciences and medicine, the conference wished to critically review existing trauma epidemiology and to broaden its empirical evidence historically, methodologically and terminologically. Secondly, the conference also wished to debate how far trauma studies could reasonably be applied to Biblical exegesis in order to enrich our understanding of Biblical texts as well as to establish how far 'Old' and 'New Testament' writings appear as crucial 'literary witnesses' to the experience, documentation and reprocessing of traumatization in history.

The editors have decided to arrange the publication of the various contributions into three sections: In the first section, trauma epidemiology is presented from a psychiatric point of view and applied—in the sense of a case study test case—to a core piece of ancient literature (history-writing). At the same time, the fruitfulness and limitations of trauma studies are discussed methodologically with regard to the instrument of 'retrospective diagnosis' as well as in their specific relation to Biblical exegesis. In the second and third sections, the phenomena of trauma and traumatization are presented on the basis of textual interpretations in "individual" as well as "collective" dimensions: Here, it may become evident how trauma and traumatization on the one hand affect the individual in a psychological or even somatic respect and, on the other hand, how trauma and traumatization relate to collectives or groups and ultimately become a trans-generational syndrome. While section two concentrates comparatively on literary examples of Old Testament literature (Job and Psalms), parabiblical literature from late antiquity, as well as 'orthonymous writers' from antiquity and modern times, such as Augustine and Thomas Bernhard, section three is divided into two parts: The first part covers phenomena of collective traumatization, ranging from the ancient Near East to modern Mexico, and the second part focuses specifically on textual material from the Old Testament / Hebrew Bible. This focus is based on the fact that trauma studies is currently concerned primarily with the field of the Old Testament / Hebrew Bible. For the time being, and due to the literary character of the texts—as well as the complicated and fundamentally ambiguous state of their chronological and relative dating—, many Old Testament / Hebrew Bible exegetes since the 1970s have included more literary interpretation than those of New Testament and classical antiquity. Thus, for some time, trauma studies has already served as a valuable scholarly approach in the field of Old Testament studies.

It is our hope that this collection of essays will impact on the reader in three ways: it may encourage Biblical scholars to approach common contemporary theories and methods of textual interpretation—such as trauma and traumatization—in order to facilitate interdisciplinary research in and beyond the humanities; it may encourage scholars from the humanities, as well as the social sciences and medicine, to consider Biblical interpretation as a valuable tool to better understand the individual as well as the collective psychic state in its social and cultural settings; finally, it may encourage scholars working specifically with traumatology to consider textual readings as an important means for enriching analytical expertise and cultural knowledge.

We would like to thank all who have supported this project from the very beginnings until the manuscript went to press: the Editor in Chief at Vandenhoeck & Ruprecht, Jörg Persch, for accepting this volume for SANt 2; Silke Hartmann for accompanying the entire editorial process; the former Dean for Theology, Associate Professor Dr. phil. Carsten Riis (d. December 8, 2013), for allocating generous funding for the conference—this volume is edited in his memory; the Vice Dean of Research of the Faculty of Arts and the Head of the Department of Culture and Society, Anne Marie Pahuus and Bjarke Paarup-Laursen, for participating in the conference; the "International Society for the Study of Deuterocanonical and Cognate Literature" (ISDCL) for its cooperation and financial support; PhD-student Erin J. Wright, research secretary Marlene Jessen and conference supporter Gitte Grønning Munk, as well as the students at the graduate course on "Trauma in the Book of Jeremiah" for their reliable organizational, administrative and technical help. We would also like to thank Malte Rosenau for his comprehensive editorial work. And, last but not least, we would like to thank all the contributors for their tremendous interest in this project and their kind and professional cooperation throughout the entire editorial process.

Aarhus, December 15, 2013

Eve-Marie Becker
Jan Dochhorn
Else Kragelund Holt

Contents

Part Two
Collective Dimensions

Part One
Individual and Existential Dimensions

Eve-Marie Becker

'Trauma Studies' and Exegesis

Challenges, Limits and Prospects

Abstract

This article reflects the origin, history and current state of "trauma studies" by discussing more detailed questions such as: speaking primarily as Biblical scholars, can or will we establish something like "trauma studies" in our fields of research? What could be the result or even the benefit of traumatology within theology, the humanities and cultural studies? There are several aspects of current trauma discourse demonstrating that the humanities and theology as well as Biblical exegesis in particular can and should contribute with essential observations and critical reflections based on what we could best call "cultural knowledge" and analytical expertise when interpreting textual traditions.

1. What Are 'Trauma Studies'?

'Trauma and traumatization' is an extensive field of research[1] that extends far beyond the boundaries of modern psychiatry, psychology and sociology. There is currently a growing interest in trauma studies among scholars in the diverse fields of theology,[2] religious studies, across the humanities and, in particular, in the literary sciences.[3] The approach to trauma and traumatization within these fields of research is based on the insight that studies in psychic mentality are crucially important to all academic disciplines that deal with the 'human' and the 'social' in their interaction within history, culture and religion. In that sense, trauma studies in the humanities and theology contribute to the historical and literary analysis of psychic mentality, which is, first and foremost, mediated through historical documents and literature.

Hereby, trauma studies focus on the aspect of disorder and vulnerability caused by external factors, such as human or natural violence, terror, viola-

1 Cf. lately: Alexander, *Trauma*.
2 Cf., for instance: Rambo, *Spirit and Trauma*.
3 Cf., for instance, recently: Modlinger and Sonntag, *Other People's Pain*.

tion, and so forth[4]. By investigating the psychic states of individuals and groups in history, theology and the humanities can widen the picture of the 'human' and its living conditions in the past and present[5]: While psychiatry and psychology base their analysis of the human psyche on a *contemporary* view of anthropology, a *historical* investigation enlarges our principal knowledge of psychic action and reaction tremendously. Thus, the interplay between psychology and psychiatry on the one hand and the humanities and theology on the other enriches both approaches to the 'human' in its socio-cultural setting. Here, interdisciplinarity is valuable to both parties.

How do the humanities and theology approach the field of trauma studies? In a general sense, historians such as Peter Burke claim that 'history' can only be constructed and reconstructed adequately when it takes into account socio-psychological and individual-psychological factors that determine historical contexts in a social as well as a biographical dimension.[6] To be more concrete from the point of view of Biblical exegesis and Classics: Mediterranean life in antiquity should also be explored from a psychological point of view.[7]

This evidently applies to the field of trauma studies,[8] both in an individual and a collective as well as a cultural sense.[9] For example, as scholars dealing with antiquity, we continuously investigate social groupings and certain socio-cultural and religious conditions that may cause traumatization for the individual as well as the collective.[10] Hereby, trauma studies specifically include the interpretation of religious experiences:[11] In combination with per-

4 It should be noted that, while completing this contribution, the "super typhoon Haiyan strikes the Philippines" (see: Samenow and McNoldy, "Super Typhoon"). This has provided numerous pictures that illustrate various forms of traumatic experience. Cf. FAZ-net: http://www.faz.net/aktuell/gesellschaft/philippinen-taifun-ueberlebende-sind-traumatisiert-12683155.html (cited 27 November 2013).

5 The philosopher Hans Blumenberg has suggested a detailed phenomenology of how to describe the 'human'; for instance, in its experience of pain: Blumenberg, *Beschreibung des Menschen*.

6 Cf. Burke, *History and Social Theory*.

7 Some previous work has been carried out in this field, either regarding psychology of religion or cultural anthropology: Cf., e.g.: Berger, *Historische Psychologie*; idem, *Identity and Experience*; Bilde, "Kognitive Dissonanzreduktion"; Türcke, *Jesu Traum*; Theißen, *Erleben und Verhalten*; Malina, *New Testament World*.

8 Cf. especially Andreas Mehl's, Alexandra Eckert's and Frank Ursin's contributions in this volume.

9 For this distinction and its implications for social theory, cf. recently: Eyerman, "Social Theory and Trauma." On 'cultural trauma' see: Alexander, "Toward a Theory."

10 Cf. J. Dietrich's contribution in this volume. Cf., e.g., also: Guldager Bilde, "Eschatological Currents." – This contribution is dedicated to the memory of my dear friend and colleague in Classical Archaeology at Aarhus University, Pia Guldager Bilde, who died, much too early, on January 10, 2013. She was planning to contribute to the 'Trauma Conference' in June 2012, but, due to serious illness, could not be present.

11 Cf. Theissen, *Psychological Aspects*.

sonality research in sociology[12] or psychology[13], we can reveal how the personal identity and the personal development of individuals—like Paul or Augustine[14]—can be violated by external stressors and thus become disordered, with huge consequences for the individual itself as well as the larger community.[15]

From here, it soon becomes evident how trauma studies can contribute to the historical understanding of the mental state of groups as well as individuals in a certain cultural and religious setting. Conversely, contemporary psychiatry may also profit from a broadened (i.e. historically enlarged picture) of the human psyche. At the same time, trauma studies themselves are rooted in a specific historical context and interrelated to various histories, to which we will now turn.

2. Trauma Discourse and Its Various 'Histories'

The contemporary interest in 'trauma and traumatization' is itself a historical phenomenon, since it is by no means only a modern invention. Even the terminology derives from ancient times, in both an etymological and a phenomenological sense:[16] In antiquity, the semantic field of τραῦμα (τρῶμα; lat.: *vulnus*) and its derivatives is well attested. According to Liddell, Scott and Jones, at this point, we have to consider a wide range of Greek lexemes:[17] "Trauma" and its derivatives primarily denote physical kinds of wounds and wounding. This is true of pagan literature from Herodotus' time onwards (*Hist.* 2.63), and it can also be observed later in the Septuagint writings.[18] Furthermore, Luke—who is the only New Testament author and one of the few earliest Christian writers[19] to make use of this terminology—conceives of trauma first and foremost in terms of physical wounding.[20] However, in Acts 19:16, he speaks of a wounding which was caused by a demon (τὸ πνεῦμα τὸ πονηρόν); here, the borderline between physical or somatic and psychic

12 Cf. e.g. Funder, *Studying Lives Through Time.*

13 Cf. Klessmann, "Identität des Paulus"; Thilo, "Paulus."

14 Cf., V. Burrus' contribution in this volume. – On Paul, see: Becker, "Person des Paulus."

15 See also below.

16 For a broader field of relevant trauma terminology in the Coptic language, cf. J. Dochhorn's contribution in this volume.

17 Τραῦμα, τραυματίζειν, τραυματίας, τιτρώσκω, τραυματεία, τραυματιαῖος, τραυματικός, τραυματισμός, τραυματοθεραπεύω, τραυματοποιός. Cf. Liddell et al., *Greek-English Lexicon*, 1799b, 1811a.

18 Τραῦμα, τραυματίζειν, τραυματίας: Gen 4:23; 34:27; Ex 21:25; Num 19:16, 18; 1 Sam 31:3; Ies 53:5 etc. – To the Hebrew equivalents cf.: Muraoka, *Two-Way Index*, 119.

19 Among the so-called Apostolic Fathers, see: Pol 2:1; Barn 5:2; 1 Clem 16:5.

20 Τραῦμα: Lk 10:34; τραυματίζειν: Lk 20:12; Acts 19:16.

kinds of wounding is evidently crossed. And already in Herodotus, τρῶμα could, in a wider sense, be understood as "defeat" (*Hist.* 1.18).

In various early Christian texts (such as 1 Clem 16:5 or Barn 5:2), trauma terminology is even constructed as a *theologoumenon*; in other words, it is applied to a Christological idea (ἐτραυματίσθη). What we read here is: 'Jesus is wounded (= traumatized) because of our sins' (διὰ τᾶς ἁμαρτίας) viz. 'Jesus was wounded (= traumatized) because of our ἀνομία'—the letter of Barnabas quotes Isaiah (53:5, 7) in particular. Should we think of a physical and/or a psychic wounding here? The terminology itself soon becomes an interpretive challenge. Already in Archaic and Classical Greece, we find some instances of what we might best call a 'metaphorical use of wounding' (trauma).[21] In the Septuagint writings, the verb τιτρώσκω in a passive form is also used explicitly for emotional, i.e. psychological, kinds of wounding.[22] Most interesting in this respect is Ct 5:8. The phrase: … ὅτι τετρωμένη ἀγάπης ἐγώ εἰμι, which refers to an inner wounding of the fictitious author, is formulated as a direct consequence of a wounding that was obviously caused externally, i.e. in a physical sense (Ct 5:7: … ἐπάταξάν με, ἐτραυμάτισάν με). A combining of somatic and psychic dimensions can also be observed in the Hellenistic world, beyond LXX-writings: In Diodorus Siculus (*Hist.* 17.112), the term τιτρώσκω (as participle passive) is even directly related to ψυχή. Trauma studies thus take their natural point of departure from the ancient world.[23]

Thus, we can by no means claim that it is only the *modern* pathological usage of 'trauma' and 'traumatization' in psychiatry and psychology that is oriented towards an inner wounding. Ancient authors were already making use of this terminology in various, partly metaphorical ways. Having said this, we should nevertheless admit that the analysis and treatment of an *inner wounding in a psychiatric and psychotherapeutic dimension* is certainly a result of the modern development of psychology and psychiatry, dating back to the mid and late 19th century.[24] Trauma studies in a contemporary sense are thus to be understood as a late result of what we might best call the modern 'history of psychology.'[25]

Interestingly enough, however, even here, where we meet the specialization of psychiatry in a modern sense, the focus on history and on a historical investigation of psychology is constant: It is in this context that the 'retro-

21 Cf. LSJ, 1799: regarding wine (Homer, *Od.* 21.293), love (Euripides, *Hipp.* 392), persons (Euripides, *Hipp.* 703) and examples (Plato, *Philb.* 13c).

22 Cf. Lust et al., *Greek-English Lexicon*, 2:477.

23 Cf., e.g.: Shay, "Combat Stress."

24 Cf. N. Metzger's contribution in this volume, with various references to, for instance: H. Oppenheim, J.-M. Charcot, and S. Freud/J. Breuer.

25 Cf. Löwe et al., "Geschichte."

spective diagnosis' appeared on the scene[26]—we could think, for instance, of Sigmund Freud's prominent essay on Leonardo da Vinci (1910).[27] At the same time—the beginning of the 20th century—, New Testament scholars were commenting in different, partly controversial, ways on how to apply—or not to apply[28]—'historical psychology' to eminent figures of earliest Christianity, and especially to Paul[29].

It is worthwhile keeping in mind the various reasons why theology and the humanities are indispensably involved in the studies of traumatology—we may even say that traumatology in medicine as well as in cultural studies can hardly escape from either historical or religious quests, since it always moves back and forth to the field of history in order to analyze how far the construction of our common past or 'history' is actually affected by the traumatic experience and its memorization, and to what extent the production of 'cultural artifacts'—especially literature, arts and music—in fact results from the transformation of an individual's or a group's traumatic experience. As well as this, trauma studies have to continuously reflect upon their own emergence and their precise role in the history of psychology and psychiatry.

Therefore, last but not least, there is another history related to traumatology. This becomes clear when we think back to how and when trauma studies came into being: The recent interest in traumatology takes its point of departure from the experiences of American soldiers during the Vietnam War and the psycho-somatic effects it had on them. Modern 'trauma studies' derive from here, in the sense that the aftermath of these war experiences and their psychological interpretations led to the introduction of the Post-Traumatic Stress Disorder (PTSD) diagnosis in the DSM-III in 1980 (s. also below).[30] Ever since, various previous or subsequent war experiences have been seen in the light of PTSD (e.g., 1948 Arab-Israeli War; Yom Kippur).[31]

26 Cf. also: Leven, "Ancient Facts"; to more recent applied historical psychiatry and psychology: Gottschalk and Bechtel, "Computerized Content Analysis"; Göttel-Leypold and Demling, "Persönlichkeitsstruktur."

27 Cf. Freud, *Eine Kindheitserinnerung.*

28 In his well-known book on the "Das Messiasgeheimnis in den Evangelien," William Wrede rejected psychologizing methods and instead voted for a literary and literary-historical interpretation of New Testament texts: Wrede, *Messiasgeheimnis,* 3–4.

29 Cf. to some degree, already: Cf. Deissmann, *Paulus,* 50; Pfister, "Entwicklung." – In more recent times: Bash, "Psychodynamic Approach."

30 Cf. Rubin et al., "Memory-Based Model."

31 Cf., e.g.: Rom, "Combat Stress Reactions"; Solomon and Mikulincer, "Combat Stress Reaction"; Solomon, *Combat Stress Reaction.*

3. The Quest for Definitions and Its Socio-Political Agenda

The interconnection of modern trauma studies with the Vietnam War can by no means be underestimated, since it guides the majority of how traumatology has been approached ever since: Psychiatric pathology, epidemiology and diagnosis are directly interrelated to social and cultural as well as juridical and economic issues; soldiers who, according to trauma-diagnosis, were traumatized by psychic incidents of the war could demand medical and psychotherapeutic treatment as well as economic compensation and reparation.

Traumatology, thus, is not only a matter of cultural studies: To a large extent, it is dependent on political recognition and social acceptance. This continues to be the case regarding current military conflicts and wars, such as the wars in Iraq and Afghanistan.[32] The interdependency of politics and sociology can be observed whether we appeal to history or to our own present time. First, victims of the Holocaust can now be better understood and eventually be treated and compensated in the light of trauma therapy. Thus, trauma studies can be said to shed light on the darkest chapter of European genocide. In this context, in the field of literature and literary theory, we can observe how the traumatic experience of historical concentration camp reality appears to be transformed into the aesthetics of world literature.[33] We therefore need to establish whether traumatization ultimately leads to the elimination of a victim's autobiography—for example, in the form of depersonalization—so that only literary means remain at hand, such as sarcasm, exaggeration and repetition, which may help to express the 'unsayable.'[34]

Secondly, current societies are now more sensitive when they raise the question of how the effects of World War II on soldiers, as well as civil victims[35] (especially refugees and children[36]), might have impacted on the psychic and cultural development of European societies in the second half the 20th century; and, more specifically, how various families have suffered, and may continue to suffer, from the psychic stress and somatic injury and violation caused by the war and post-war incidents. This, of course, becomes most evident in the field of so-called post-War and, more specifically, 'Holocaust

32 Cf., e.g.: Hummel, "Traumatisierte Soldaten." – Interestingly enough, the new German Defense Secretary, Ursula von der Leyen, who is a medical doctor, considers it one of her future socio-political responsibilities to take care of the various types of wounding, including PTSD, with which soldiers return home.

33 Cf., e.g., the works of Ruth Klüger, Professor em. of German Studies: Klüger, *Gelesene Wirklichkeit*. A recent interview with her was published in: *Frankfurter Allgemeine Zeitung* 273 (November 2013): 40. – Cf. in general: Selg, *Überleben in Auschwitz*.

34 Similar questions regarding the interrelation between 'traumatization' and literature were discussed frequently during the conference in Aarhus.

35 Cf. Berntsen, *Lidt skydning*. Cf. K. O'Connor's contribution, in this volume.

36 Cf., e.g.: Wendt et al., "Kinder des 2. Weltkrieges."

literature.'[37] In this context, we can think of the German-writing poet Paul Celan and his impressive poem "Todesfuge" (1948),[38] which is a well-known piece of 'Holocaust-lyrics.'[39] At the same time, a variety of literature was, and still is, heavily influenced by traumatic experience.[40] This fact is indeed intriguing. It indicates that 'trauma and traumatization' can clearly—beyond mere reflections on autobiography—have a stimulating effect on literature and literary history.[41]

Such an observation prepares the shift from an (auto-)biographical or existential conceptualization of trauma to its cultural dimensions, which are implied in its 'transgenerational communication.'[42] As a consequence, it can again act as a reading tool for ancient literature; read in this light, various parts of the Old Testament/Hebrew Bible appear as a literary adaption of traumatic experiences.[43] Conversely, the trauma-related process of producing literature can be seen as an essential cultural and religious strategy for coping with trauma, traumatization, PTSD and its socio-historical consequences.[44]

Finally, contemporary victims of political or sexual violence are also viewed against the criteria of trauma diagnosis. Such an analysis can be revealing in many ways, since it invites discussion about suppressive structures in modern societies and their later impact on politics, economy and culture.[45] In all of these cases where trauma studies can help to illuminate and explain psychic disorder, ethical questions appear on the scene: Should trauma diagnosis ultimately focus on the victim alone or also on the perpetrator? To what extent do trauma studies reveal 'guilt' and 'shame' on both sides? Will trauma studies help to better understand family history and thus have a liberating, or even a reconciling, function?

Alongside these considerations, there are other aspects related to trauma diagnosis that warrant our attention. In general, the PTSD criteriology, which has only recently been re-revised (DSM-V, May 2013),[46] also reveals itself as a highly ambivalent tool: In a diagnostic and an analytical sense, it does help to clarify psychic symptoms and work out psychiatric pathology and epide-

37 Cf., e.g.: Kansteiner, "Testing the Limits."

38 Cf. in: Celan, "Mohn und Gedächtnis" (1952); see the link to Paul Celan's own presentation of his poem: http://www.youtube.com/watch?v=gVwLqEHDCQE.

39 For the broad field of "Holocaust literature," see, for instance: Kremer, *Holocaust literature*; Patterson et al., *Encyclopedia of Holocaust literature.*

40 Cf. B. Meyer-Sickendiek's contribution on Thomas Bernhard's "Auslöschung," in this volume.

41 Cf. Neumann, "Schönheit des Grauens."

42 Cf. lately: Anastasiadis, "Transgenerational Communication."

43 Cf. K. Nielsen's, L. Stulman's and E. Boase's contributions, in this volume.

44 Cf. C. Frechette's contribution, in this volume.

45 Cf. R. Castro's contribution on contemporary Mexico, in this volume.

46 Further information is to be found at: http://www.dsm5.org/Pages/Default.aspx.

miology. However, at the same time, it also tends to be used (and eventually misused) as a political and juridical instrument that is defined by various social and economic interests, primarily in Western societies. In other words, traumatology itself can easily become a battlefield of its own where the definition and the authority of definition is already a matter of debate: Should one follow the DSM (= Diagnostic and Statistical Manual of Mental Disorders, ed. by the American Psychiatric Association) or the ICD-10 (= International Statistical Classification of Diseases and Related Health Problems, ed. by the WHO)[47] criteriology? How do scholars in the field list, determine and limit the symptoms of a 'Post-Traumatic-Stress-Disorder' concisely?

The traditional trauma phenomenology, when applied to PTSD- and trauma-diagnosis, mostly makes use of adjectives such as *uncontrollable, unpredictable, unscripted, immoral, un-sharable*, and *in-credible*. It is said that a trauma has biological as well as psychological effects,[48] and that it is possibly influenced and determined by pre- and peri-traumatic variables ('psychological risk factors').[49] A trauma affects the emotional as well as the intellectual part of the human brain. A PTSD appears as an 'intense emotional experience, a sense of detachment, de-realization, de-personalization, dissociative amnesia;[50] a re-experiencing of the traumatic event, and an avoidance of trauma-related stimuli.'[51] However, we can also identify further effects on the intellectual mind, such as violence imprinted on the mind, a loss of language, an emotional shutdown, or possibly a loss of faith and trust, which leads to a habit of latency.[52] Here, again, the interplay between trauma studies and social, as well as religious ethics proves to be highly relevant.

The basic assumption behind every attempt to define PTSD and 'trauma' is that it can be distinguished from "personal weakness." Accordingly, Chris Brewin (2003) has suggested the following definition of trauma and post-traumatic stress: "Victims of war, oppression, child abuse, marital violence, robbery, natural disaster or disaster of human origin, life-threatening accidents, and other overwhelming events have in common a mental and psychic response that is caused by the traumatic incident and has nothing to do with any personal weakness or vulnerability…."[53] However, the more detailed classification of PTSD has remained (and will remain) a constant matter of

47 Cf. World Health Organization, *ICD-10 Classification*. – For the distinction, cf. also: Maercker, "Symptomatik," 14–15.

48 Cf. Resick, *Stress und Trauma*, 91–107.

49 Ibid., 109–32.

50 Dorthe Berntsen highlights the fact that the dissociative amnesia claim is debatable, since it is supported by little empirical evidence.

51 Cf. R. Rosenberg's contribution, in this volume.

52 Cf. K. O'Connor's contribution, in this volume. – For more general aspects of latency in a cultural sense, cf. Gumbrecht, *After 1945*.

53 Brewin, *Posttraumatic Stress Disorder*, 1.

definition and dispute since the PTSD found its "formal recognition" in 1980.[54] As Dorthe Berntsen has identified, the revised DSM-V diagnosis for PTSD, for instance, leaves more room for considering the so-called predisposing factors, such as female gender and low socioeconomic status (SES).[55] Trauma studies thus look back on approximately 30 years of relatively intense research and discourse.

4. Prospects: Trauma Studies and Exegesis

Against this background, we may now ask the more detailed question: in the long run, can we or will we—primarily as Biblical scholars—establish something like 'trauma studies'? What could be the result or even the benefit of traumatology within theology, the humanities and cultural studies? There are several aspects of current trauma discourse which demonstrate that the humanities and theology can and should contribute with essential observations and critical reflections, which are based on—what we could best call—'cultural knowledge' and analytical expertise.

Firstly, as we established earlier, it is important to reflect critically upon when and how the trauma concept was established and what fields of studies are currently related to it; for example, historical psychology, post-colonial studies, gender studies,[56] and, more specifically, refugee studies. In other words, 'trauma studies' themselves are to be found at the intersection of various academic subjects, such as medicine, psychology, social sciences, theology, and the humanities. Thus, trauma studies build a bridge between diverse fields of research in and beyond university. Are trauma studies a useful heuristic instrument for strengthening interdisciplinary research? And, if so, how do we best proceed from here? The following volume identifies some potential answers to these questions.

Secondly, in theology and the humanities, we might discuss the sociocultural context in which trauma discourse is embedded as well as its sociopolitical implications and consequences: What is the historical, cultural, geographical and scientific context for establishing concepts of trauma-research? And what is the relevance of trauma research if 'only' ca. 10 % of contemporary (Western) society is in danger of being diagnosed with or developing trauma and PTSD? If we tend to 'collectivize' trauma heuristics, are we not in danger of finally dealing with a 'collective anxiety disorder'? Does trauma and traumatology ultimately become a postmodern, partly pessimistic 'world view' that reminds us of certain images already known from antiquity, such

54 Ibid., 2.
55 D. Berntsen in an e-mail comment on this contribution (December 5, 2013).
56 Cf. E. K. Holt's contribution, in this volume.

as the Nero *redivivus* myth?[57] How do we define the needs as well as the necessary limits of trauma phenomenology in our current political, social and religious discourse? It is not possible to provide answers to these questions here, but we should ensure that these questions are raised when discussing trauma research with scholars from medicine, psychology and the social sciences.

Thirdly, theology and the humanities can contribute extensively to the conceptualization and understanding of central patterns that are used in traumatology, such as 'memory,'[58] reconciliation, disaster,[59] personality and personal identity.[60] It is, for instance, highly debated in trauma studies whether it is the traumatic experience itself or the memorization of it that actually causes PTSD.[61] Similar questions regarding the construction of a history that is event-based and the role of memory within this process of construction have continuously been raised in theology and the humanities: How should we define an (traumatic) 'event' in the first place?[62] And how do trauma studies help to distinguish between the intellectual, emotional, and psychic dimensions of memory as a place for saving experience?

It is also possible to gain further insights into terminological or methodological distinctions. By examining how ancient figures such as Paul, Josephus or Augustine conceptualize their biography, we may on the one hand enrich our analytical tools for distinguishing between autobiographical and collective memory[63] and its transformation into cultural memory, and, on the other hand, we may sharpen our definition when analyzing the nature of an auto-biographical text as opposed to auto-fictional writing and how existential descriptions of trauma may vary from literary conceptualizations.

Finally, theology and the humanities will broaden the picture of how to define those "stressors" that occur over time or those that are connected to a particular point in time. Even if we assume that 'brain activity' from antiquity to today is more or less stable, we need to discuss whether the list of "stressors"—which cause trauma and affect PTSD—in ancient and modern societies is comparable.[64] On the one hand, we might argue for discontinuity here:

57 I would like to thank my colleague Jan Dochhorn for identifying this aspect during the conference. For a classification of redivivus-motifs in Biblical tradition, cf. Becker, "Elija *redivivus*."

58 Cf., e.g., Brewin, *Posttraumatic Stress Disorder*, 88ff.

59 Cf., e.g.: Keitel, "Art of Losing"; Berlejung, *Disaster and Relief Management*.

60 Cf., e.g., Brewin, *Posttraumatic Stress Disorder*, 63ff.

61 Cf., e.g.: Rubin et al., "Memory-Based Model." Cf. further reflections on this: Monroe and Mineka, "Mnemonic Model"; Berntsen and Rubin, "Contrasting Models."

62 Cf. Saur et al., "Ereignis." – To the concept of memory, cf., e.g.: Mendels, "Inscribed Memory."

63 Cf., lately: Olick, *Collective Memory Reader*.

64 Cf. the various (partly controversial) ideas in the contributions by R. Rosenberg and N. Metzger in this volume.

Paul's narrative accounts on, for instance, *peristaseis*, which he experienced regularly (e.g. 2 Cor 11:23ff.), are specifically bound to his situation as an ancient person, travelling around the Mediterranean and living according to the conditions of an apostate Diaspora Jew confronted with Roman imperial power. In many ways, Paul's living conditions are far removed from modern life and travel experience. This is mostly true when we look at the ecstatic dimensions of his 'personality.'[65]

On the other hand, we might look for continuity between ancient experiences of trauma and the modern world: In some sense, the implications and consequences of the temple destructions in 587 B.C.E. and 70 C.E. in Jerusalem[66] are quite similar to the destruction of the World Trade Center in New York on September 11, 2001. In both cases, the events of monumental destruction—caused by either war or terroristic attack—symbolize the loss of a core piece of national or cultural identity. We thus need to analyze more in detail if and how far trauma phenomenology can be used as a trans-historical instrument of understanding individual as well as collective experience of disaster, catastrophe and trauma.

Trauma studies, thus, open up space for interdisciplinary research, even though the objects of study may vary significantly: In psychiatry, it is first and foremost the individual victim who needs treatment; in sociology, it is the society which could be considered to be in danger of collectivizing trauma; in studies of history, we aim to identify the possible traumatic 'event,' which might have continued to impact on later generations. In the text-based humanities—such as Biblical Studies—, we start by reading and interpreting various texts: These texts either appear as historical or literary sources to and religious and cultural reflections on trauma and traumatization. They could also be literary constructs of traumatic experience. We thus need to investigate whether apocalyptic writings such as *4 Ezra* or *2 Bar* are *sources* for traumatic experience or *results* viz. products of traumatization. Similar questions arise in relation to the passion narrative (Mk 14-15) and its actual origin. They could also be discussed when reading Flavius Josephus' "Bellum Judaicum" in close affinity to its author's (auto-)biography.[67]

These various texts partly *result* from trauma, and partly aim at *overcoming* it, so as to perform a possible 'healing function,' either in a historical or in a contemporary sense.[68] However, in the end, we also need to admit that we

65 Cf. lately: Shantz, *Paul in Ecstasy*. – In a general sense cf.: Jeppesen and Bro Larsen, *Kognitionsforskning og eksegese*.

66 Cf. Flower, "Temple Destruction"; A. Reinhartz's contribution, in this volume.

67 Cf., lately: Varneda, "Early Empire," 327ff.

68 Cf. K. O'Connor's and L. Stulman's as well as C. Frechette's contributions, in this volume. – I would like to thank my colleague in psychology, Dorthe Berntsen, and my colleagues in Biblical exegesis, Jan Dochhorn and Else K. Holt, for their critical comments on and suggestions for this article.

will never know precisely how close ancient texts really are to certain traumatic experience and traumatization. Nevertheless, it could be the case that our scientific curiosity here proves to be even more important than the certainty about historical evidences: Ancient texts provide cultural reservoirs in which coping with pain, fear, wounding, guilt and shame is collected and expressed. To look for specific signs of trauma and traumatization will thus sharpen our exegetical optic, just as it will sharpen the general sensibility for dealing with trauma diagnosis. Therefore, it may be at precisely this point of analytical sensitivity that Biblical scholars could be of most assistance to psychiatrists and psychologists when dealing with both the diagnostic and the therapeutic complexity that arises when trauma and PTSD are described, defined, diagnosed and treated.

Bibliography

ALEXANDER, J. C. "Toward a Theory of Cultural Trauma." Pages 1-30 in: *Cultural Trauma and Collective Identity.* Edited by J. C. Alexander et al. Berkeley: University of California Press, 2004.

ALEXANDER, J. C. *Trauma: A Social Theory.* Cambridge: Polity, 2012.

ANASTASIADIS, A. "Transgenerational Communication of Traumatic Experiences." *Journal of Literary Theory* 6 (2012): 1-24.

BASH, A. "A Psychodynamic Approach to the Interpretation of 2 Corinthians 10-13." *Journal for the Study of the New Testament* 83 (2001): 51-67.

BECKER, E.-M. "Die Person des Paulus." Pages 128-34 in: *Paulus Handbuch.* Edited by F. W. Horn. Tübingen: Mohr (Siebeck), 2013.

—. "Elija *redivivus* im Markus-Evangelium? Zur Typologisierung von Wiederkehr-Vorstellungen." Pages 587-625 in: *Biblical Figures in Deuterocanonical and Cognate Literature.* Edited by H. Lichtenberger and U. Mittmann-Richert. Berlin: De Gruyter, 2009.

BERGER, K. *Historische Psychologie des Neuen Testaments.* 2d ed. Stuttgart: Katholisches Bibelwerk, 1991.

BERGER, K. *Identity and Experience in the New Testament*, Minneapolis: Fortress Press, 2003.

BERLEJUNG, A., ed. *Disaster and Relief Management: Katastrophen und ihre Bewältigung.* Tübingen: Mohr (Siebeck), 2012.

BERNTSEN D., and D. C. RUBIN. "Contrasting Models of Posttraumatic Stress Disorder: Reply to Monroe and Mineka (2008)." *Psychological Review* 115 (2008): 1099-107.

BERNTSEN, D. *Lidt skydning i gaderne tog vi ret roligt …: En psykologisk tematisering af erindringsbilleder fra Danmarks besættelse 1940-45.* Aarhus: Klim, 2005.

BILDE, P. "Kognitive Dissonanzreduktion in der Jesusbewegung: Ein sozialpsychologischer Beitrag zum Verständnis neutestamentlicher Texte." *Evangelische Theologie* 65 (2005): 118-35.

BLUMENBERG, H. *Beschreibung des Menschen.* Edited by M. Sommer, Frankfurt/Main: Suhrkamp, 2006.

BREWIN, C. *Posttraumatic Stress Disorder: Malady or Myth?* New Haven: Yale University Press, 2003.

BURKE, P. *History and Social Theory.* Cambridge: Polity Press, 1992.

CELAN, P. *Mohn und Gedächtnis.* Vol. 1 in: *Paul Celan: Gesammelte Werke.* Edited by B. Allemann. Frankfurt/Main: Suhrkamp, 1986.

Deissmann, A. *Paulus: Eine kultur- und religionsgeschichtliche Skizze*, Tübingen: Mohr (Siebeck), 1911.

Eyerman, R. "Social Theory and Trauma." *Acta Sociologica* 53 (2013): 41–53.

Flower, H. I. "Remembering and Forgetting Temple Destruction: The Destruction of the Temple of Jupiter Optimus Maximus in 83 B.C." Pages 74–92 in: *Antiquity in Antiquity*. Edited by G. Gardner and K. L. Osterloh. Tübingen: Mohr (Siebeck), 2008.

Freud, S. *Eine Kindheitserinnerung des Leonardo da Vinci*. 3d ed. Frankfurt/Main: Fischer, 2006.

Funder, D. C., et al., eds. *Studying Lives Through Time: Personality and Development*. Washington: American Psychological Association, 1993.

Gottschalk, L. A. and R. J. Bechtel. "Computerized Content Analysis of Writings of Mahatma Gandhi." *The Journal of Nervous and Mental Disease* 193 (2005): 210–16.

Göttel-Leypold, M., and J. H. Demling. "Die Persönlichkeitsstruktur des Paulus nach seinen Selbstzeugnissen." Pages 125–48 in: *Biographie und Persönlichkeit des Paulus*. Edited by E.-M. Becker and P. Pilhofer. Tübingen: Mohr (Siebeck), 2005.

Guldager Bilde, P. "Some Reflections on Eschatological Currents, Diasporic Experience, and Group Identity in the Northwestern Black Sea Region." Pages 29–45 in: *Meetings of Cultures Between Conflicts and Coexistence*. Edited by P. Guldager Bilde and J. H. Petersen, Aarhus: Aarhus University Press, 2008.

Gumbrecht, H. U. *After 1945: Latency as Origin of the Present*. Stanford: Stanford University Press, 2013.

Hummel, K. "Traumatisierte Soldaten: Durchs Rost gefallen." 5 pages. Cited 27 February 2014. Online: http://www.faz.net/aktuell/gesellschaft/traumatisierte-soldaten-durchs-rost-gefallen-1627578.html.

Jeppesen, K., and K. Bro Larsen, eds. *Kognitionsforskning og eksegese*. Collegium Biblicum Årsskrift 15 (2011). Cited 27 February 2014. Online: http://ojs.statsbiblioteket.dk/index.php/cb/issue/view/2164.

Kansteiner, W. "Testing the Limits of Trauma: The Long-term Psychological Effects of the Holocaust on Individuals and Collectives." *History of the Human Sciences* 17 (2004): 97–123.

Keitel, E. "The Art of Losing: Disaster Narrative." Pages 331–52 in: *Ancient Historiography and Its Contexts: Studies in Honour of A. J. Woodman*. Edited by C. S. Kraus et al. Oxford: Oxford University Press 2010.

Klessmann, M. "Zum Problem der Identität des Paulus: Psychologische Aspekte zu theologischen und biographischen Fragen." *Wege zum Menschen* 41 (1989): 156–72.

Klüger, R. *Gelesene Wirklichkeit: Fakten und Fiktionen in der Literatur*. Göttingen: Wallstein, 2006.

Kremer, S. L., ed. *Holocaust literature: An encyclopedia of writers and their work*. New York: Routledge, 2003.

Leven, K.-H. "'At Times These Ancient Facts Seem to Lie before me like a Patient on A Hospital Bed': Retrospective Diagnosis and Ancient Medical History." Pages 369–86 in: *Magic and Rationality in Ancient Near Eastern and Graeco-Roman Medicine*. Edited by H. F. J. Horstmanshoff and M. Stol. Leiden: Brill, 2004.

Liddell, H. G., R. Scott and H. S. Jones. *A Greek-English Lexicon*. 9th ed. with revised supplement. Oxford: Clarendon Press 1996.

Löwe, B. et al. "Geschichte einer politisch unerwünschten Diagnose: Die posttraumatische Belastungsstörung." *Psychotherapie, Psychosomatik, Medizinische Psychologie* 56 (2006): 182–87.

Lust, J., E. Eynikel and K. Hauspie. *A Greek-English Lexicon of the Septuagint*. 2 vols. Stuttgart: Deutsche Bibelgesellschaft, 1992–1996.

Maercker, A. "Symptomatik, Klassifikation und Epidemiologie." Pages 14–32 in: *Posttraumatische Belastungsstörungen*. Edited by A. Maercker. 3d ed. Heidelberg: Springer, 2009.

Malina, B. J. *The New Testament World: Insights from Cultural Anthropology*. 3d ed. Louisville, Ky.: Westminster John Knox, 2001.

Mendels, D. "Phases of Inscribed Memory Concerning the Land of Israel in Palestinian Judaism of the Second Century B.C.E." *Theologische Literaturzeitung* 138 (2013): 151–64.

Modlinger, M., and P. Sonntag, eds. *Other People's Pain: Narratives of Trauma and the Question of Ethics*. Bern: Peter Lang, 2011.

Monroe, S. M., and S. Mineka. "Placing the Mnemonic Model in Context: Diagnostic, Theoretical, and Clinical Considerations." *Psychological Review* 115 (2008): 1084–98.

Muraoka, T. *A Greek-Hebrew/Aramaic Two-Way Index to the Septuagint*. Leuven: Peeters, 2010.

Neumann, P. H. "Schönheit des Grauens oder Greuel der Schönheit? Über Celans ‚Todesfuge.'" Pages 93–99 in: *Zur Lyrik Paul Celans: Eine Einführung*. Edited by P. H. Neumann. 2d ed. Göttingen: Vandenhoeck & Ruprecht, 1990.

Olick, J. K., ed. *The Collective Memory Reader*. Oxford: Oxford University Press, 2011.

Patterson, D. et al., eds. *Encyclopedia of Holocaust Literature*. Westport, Conn.: Oryx, 2002.

Pfister, O. "Die Entwicklung des Apostels Paulus: Eine religionsgeschichtliche und psychologische Skizze." *Imago* 6 (1920): 243–90.

Rambo, S. *Spirit and Trauma: A Theology of Remaining*. Louisville, Ky.: Westminster John Knox, 2010.

Resick, P. A. *Stress und Trauma: Grundlagen der Psychotraumatologie*. Edited and translated by A. Maercker. Bern: Huber, 2003.

Rom, E. "Combat stress reactions during the 1948 war: A conspiracy of silence?" *Israel Affairs* 18 (2012): 645–51.

Rubin, D. C., D. Berntsen and M. Klindt Bohni. "A Memory-Based Model of Posttraumatic Stress Disorder: Evaluating Basic Assumptions Underlying the PTSD Diagnosis." *Psychological Review* 115 (2008): 985–1011.

Samenow, J., and B. McNoldy. "Super Typhoon Haiyan Strikes Philippines, among Strongest Storms Ever." *The Washington Post*. No pages. Cited 7 November 2013. Online: http://www.washingtonpost.com/blogs/capital-weather-gang/wp/2013/11/07/super-typhoon-haiyan-closes-in-on-philippines-among-strongest-storms-ever/.

Saur, M., E.-M. Becker, F. W. Graf, D. Hiller, H. Helbig, and P. Burger. "Ereignis." Pages 141–46 in: *Lexikon der Bibelhermeneutik: Begriffe – Methoden – Theorien – Konzepte*. Edited by O. Wischmeyer. Berlin: De Gruyter, 2009/2013.

Selg, P. *Überleben in Auschwitz: Elie Wiesel – Ruth Klüger – Ruth Elias – Primo Levi – Viktor Frankl*. Arlesheim: Ita Wegman Institut, 2010.

Shantz, C. *Paul in Ecstasy: The Neurobiology of the Apostle's Life and Thought*, Cambridge: Cambridge University Press, 2009.

Shay, J. "Learning About Combat Stress from Homer's Iliad." *Journal of Traumatic Stress* 4 (1991): 561–79.

Solomon, Z., and M. Mikulincer. "Combat Stress Reaction, PTSD and Social Adjustment: A Study of Israeli Veterans." *Journal of Nervous and Mental Disease* 175 (1987): 277–85.

Solomon, Z. *Combat Stress Reaction: The Enduring Toll of War*. New York: Plenum, 1993.

Theissen, G. *Erleben und Verhalten der ersten Christen: Eine Psychologie des Urchristentums*. Gütersloh: Gütersloher Verlagshaus, 2007.

Theissen, G. *Psychological Aspects of Pauline Theology*. Edinburgh: T & T Clark, 1987.

Thilo, H.-J. "Paulus: Die Geschichte einer Entwicklung psychoanalytisch gesehen." *Wege zum Menschen* 37 (1985): 2–14.

Türcke, C. *Jesu Traum: Psychoanalyse des Neuen Testaments*. Springe: Klampen, 2009.

Varneda, P. V. "The Early Empire." Pages 315–62 in: *Political Autobiographies and Memoirs in Antiquity*. Edited by G. Marasco. Leiden: Brill, 2011.

Wendt, C., S. Freitag, and S. Schmidt. "Wie traumatisiert sind die Kinder des 2. Weltkrieges? Der Zusammenhang von Alter bei Flucht und Vertreibung und aktuellen posttraumatischen Belastungssymptomen." *Psychotherapie, Psychosomatik, Medizinische Psychologie* 62 (2012): 294–300.

World Health Organization. *The ICD-10 Classification of Mental and Behavioural Disorders: Clinical Descriptions and Diagnostic Guidelines.* 267 pages. Cited 17 February 2014. Online: http://www.who.int/classifications/icd/en/bluebook.pdf.

Wrede, W. *Das Messiasgeheimnis in den Evangelien: Zugleich ein Beitrag zum Verständnis des Markusevangeliums*, Göttingen: Vandenhoeck & Ruprecht, 1901.

Raben Rosenberg

Trauma and Mental Disorders: A Biomedical Approach

Abstract

Concepts of traumas in modern medicine and psychiatry are shortly presented focusing on descriptive usage and nosological (disease) entities, including acute stress reaction and post-traumatic stress disorder. Then theories of traumas within modern neuroscience are presented, e.g. within current medical science with its naturalistic conception of man. Structural and functional aspects of traumatic events on the brain as well as treatment by means of psychotherapy and drugs are shortly described. Finally, the naturalistic frame of reference in relation to man's reaction to traumas is transgressed advocating a hermeneutic approach to trauma including reflection on the relevance of religion for modern neuroscience.

Trauma as a Descriptive Concept

Trauma is a concept frequently used in clinical medicine and psychiatry but with different meanings and theoretical implications. The most simple usage of trauma in clinical medicine refers to all events that compromise the integrity of the structure and physiology of the body—typically arising suddenly. In this sense trauma is identical to an injury to the body, for instance when exposed to a traffic accident leading to fractures of limbs, contusions of organs or in the worst case death. The list of injuries to the body is very long, including a variety of disease etiologies: infectious, hormonal, toxic, metabolic, cellular dysfunctions, etc. In a broad sense, the focus of clinical medicine is the characterization of pathophysiology and treatment with restoration of normal functioning by elimination of the trauma, i.e. the causes of disease.

The close relation between trauma and integrity of the body is indeed implied by the Greek noun and verb related to trauma. According to the Louw-Nida Lexicon:

- τραῦμα: the condition resulting from being severely hurt or wounded – 'wound.'
- τραυματίζω: to hurt or wound, normally resulting in some mark or permanent scar on the body – 'to hurt, to wound.'

Similar meaning is also found in the the New Testament:

- προσελθὼν κατέδησεν τὰ τραύματα αὐτοῦ – "he went to him and bandaged his wounds." (Lk 10:34)
- οἱ δὲ καὶ τοῦτον τραυματίσαντες ἐξέβαλον – "they wounded him, too, and threw him out." (Lk 20:12)

In mental health settings, trauma is equivalent to events to the individual that lead to suffering, dysfunction of cognition, emotional and behavioral disturbances or eventually mental disorders with loss of autonomy or social functioning.

The international American classification system, 4th edition of Diagnostic and Statistical Manual of Mental Disorders (DSM-IV), delineates traumas as

> Traumatic events that are experienced directly include, but are not limited to, military combat, violent personal assault (sexual assault, physical attack, robbery, and mugging), being kidnapped, being taken hostage, terrorist attack, torture, incarceration as a prisoner of war or in a concentration camp, natural or manmade disasters, severe automobile accidents, or being diagnosed with a life-threatening illness. For children, sexually traumatic events may include developmentally inappropriate sexual experiences without threatened or actual violence or injury.

In daily usage traumas probably most often refer to such dramatic or catastrophic incidents. However, a large body of research has shown that traumatic events may be much more subtle, including a variety of common daily events such as changes of life due to marriage, divorce, new jobs, new accommodation etc. Therefore, in modern theories of mental health trauma is often substituted by concepts, such as stressors, or various life events all characterized by leading to psychic or social dysfunction of the individual with low quality of life or to mental or somatic illnesses. Thus, in relation to mental health it is important to conceive traumatic events on a graduated scale from mild to moderate stressors in one end of the spectrum to catastrophic events that will lead to reaction in almost all people in the other end.

In conclusion, traumas represent a variety of significant threats to the integrity of the individual seen as a whole person.

Trauma as Nosological (Disease) Entities

The importance of traumas in relation to mental health has been known for centuries, and today international classification of mental disorders, i.e. the American Diagnostic and Statistical Manual of Mental Disorders (DSM-IV) and the European International Classification of Diseases (ICD-10), agrees on the delineation of several disorders that represent reactions to traumatic events. According to ICD-10, distinction is made between three different reactions:

- *Acute stress reaction*
  - Exposure to an exceptional mental or physical stressor.
- *Post-traumatic stress disorder*
  - Exposure to a stressful event or situation (either short or long lasting) of exceptionally threatening or catastrophic nature, which is likely to cause pervasive distress in almost anyone.
- *Adjustment disorders*
  - Exposure to identifiable psychosocial stress—not of an unusual or catastrophic type.

For acute stress reaction and post-traumatic stress disorder (PTSD), the traumatic event is of exceptional or catastrophic nature whereas adjustment disorders are reactions to more subtle stressors.

The clinical phenomenology of *acute stress reaction* involves a series of psychological changes:

- Intense emotional experience
- Sense of detachment, absence of emotional responsiveness
- De-realization
- De-personalization
- Dissociative amnesia
  - Re-experiencing the traumatic event with flashbacks, intruding thoughts and images
- Avoidance of trauma-related stimuli

Luckily, most acute stress reactions have very limited time length, typically disappearing after 8–24 hours. However, extensive empirical evidence shows that acute trauma can lead to persistent stress reaction, now classified as post-traumatic stress disorder (PTSD) with the following defining symptoms (shortly abridged, see table 1):

A. The person has been exposed to a traumatic event in which both of the following have been present:
(1) the person experienced, witnessed, or was confronted with an event or events that involved actual or threatened death or serious injury, or a threat to the physical integrity of self or others
(2) the person's response involved intense fear, helplessness, or horror.

B.	**The traumatic event is persistently re-experienced in one (or more) of the following ways:**
(1)	recurrent and intrusive distressing recollections of the event, including images, thoughts, or perceptions.
(2)	recurrent distressing dreams of the event.
(3)	acting or feeling as if the traumatic event were recurring (includes a sense of reliving the experience, illusions, hallucinations, and dissociative flashback episodes, including those that occur upon awakening or when intoxicated).
(4)	intense psychological distress at exposure to internal or external cues that symbolize or resemble an aspect of the traumatic event.
(5)	physiological reactivity on exposure to internal or external cues that symbolize or resemble an aspect of the traumatic event.
C.	**Persistent avoidance of stimuli associated with the trauma and numbing of general responsiveness (not present before the trauma), as indicated by three (or more) of the following:**
(1)	efforts to avoid thoughts, feelings, or conversations associated with the trauma
(2)	efforts to avoid activities, places, or people that arouse recollections of the trauma
(3)	inability to recall an important aspect of the trauma
(4)	markedly diminished interest or participation in significant activities
(5)	feeling of detachment or estrangement from others
(6)	restricted range of affect (e.g., unable to have loving feelings)
(7)	sense of a foreshortened future (e.g., does not expect to have a career, marriage, children, or a normal life span)
D.	**Persistent symptoms of increased arousal (not present before the trauma), as indicated by two (or more) of the following**:
(1)	difficulty falling or staying asleep
(2)	irritability or outbursts of anger
(3)	difficulty concentrating
(4)	hypervigilance
(5)	exaggerated startle response
E.	**Duration of the disturbance (symptoms in Criteria B, C, and D) is more than one month.**
F.	**The disturbance causes clinically significant distress or impairment in social, occupational, or other important areas of functioning.**

Table 1: DSM-IV Criteria for Post-traumatic Stress Disorder.

The intense emotional reaction may compromise the functional integrity of emotions, cognition and behavior leading to dissociative symptoms such as feeling that the surrounding world and personal identity have been changed in an uncanny and frightening way or that emotions may disappear. The concepts of de-realization and de-personalization comprise such reactions.

In PTSD the person has lost control of the trauma in the sense that the traumatic event causes significant distress by intruding the consciousness at any time of the day, or it may appear in dreams and nightmares. The organism is put in a state of hyper-arousal and behavioral changes with avoidance of any activity that may give associations to the trauma, often leading to social dysfunctions in family and work settings. Unfortunately, the course may be chronic. To give an example:

> A 30-year-old bank clerk became victim of a dramatic and violent bank robbery during which she suddenly was facing the robber who turned his pistol towards her demanding "all her money." She froze, and although she could hear the demanding voice of the robber, she was paralyzed expecting to be shot. Afterwards she remembered that although this reaction probably only lasted for less than a minute, she had an experience of time stopping and she felt everything was unreal. She behaved calmly and handed over the money to the robber who then immediately ran away. Then she experienced severe anxiety and distress, she continued to cry even when she returned to her home with her husband and two children. She was unable to go back to work and was on sick leave during the next month. Still she did not improve, had severe nightmares and during the day had frequent flashbacks of the robbery. She was unable to concentrate, had memory problems, and towards her children and husband she had frequent outbursts of anger followed by self-reproaches. Visiting crowded supermarkets, she felt very uneasy and dizzy, and eventually isolated herself in her home.

The great variability in how people react to traumatic events is well-known. The reaction is determined by several factors, including the intensity and nature of the trauma, individual vulnerability due to genetic factors and mental vulnerability caused by previous life experiences as well as a variety of social and cultural factors. Accordingly, the prevalence of PTSD differs widely in different studies across the world.[1]

This complicated causal net has the important implication that trauma must be seen in both an individual and cultural context. As stated in the invitation to this conference: "Thus, psychiatry meets the Humanities (e.g. history, art, religion) as well the social science and politics. Since traumata affect nearly all areas of social and cultural life, reflection upon them as well as developing the ability to overcome them goes beyond pure medical science."

In the following a short presentation will be given on trauma conceived in

1 National Institute for Clinical Excellence, *Post-traumatic Stress Disorder.*

modern psychiatry, e.g. pure medical science with its naturalistic conception of man, and theories based on neuroscience[2]. However, I will transgress this frame of reference by advocating a hermeneutic approach to trauma including some thoughts on the relevance of religion for modern neuroscience in relation to people's reaction to traumas.

Trauma and Neuroscience

Why do traumas have such great impact on human mental life? And why may a transient trauma lead to incapacitating disease despite the fact that the body was not hurt, and the person survived and could return to the usual daily activities?

To answer such questions, modern neuroscience analyses trauma in an evolutionary frame of reference,[3] studying the interaction between the human organism and its environment with focus on brain mechanisms and other biological processes in the body.[4]

The driving force in evolution is optimization of fitness. It is the survival of the individual and its ability to produce offspring for the future. Accordingly, a variety of adaptive processes leading to increased fitness, have been developed during the evolution of man, reactions to traumas being essential ones. Several homeostatic mechanisms can be identified. Important bodily mechanisms involve regulation of the inner milieu of the organism, e.g. temperature, blood pressure, appetite, sleep and sexual reproduction. A variety of behavioral functions have important adaptive value for the organism, the most important perhaps being the fight or flight function of anxiety: the individual is immediately activated when exposed to a dangerous situation. But anxiety is not solely a mental phenomenon but a reaction of the organism as a whole, and includes a specific phenomenology (e.g. subjective conscious experiences), bodily symptoms, cognition and behavior. The basic neurobiology of anxiety is fairly well characterized including the interaction between emotions and cognition.

Figure 1 (p. 36) illustrates important areas in the brain.[5] The limbic system situated deep in the brain is the major emotional module with amygdala as a center for anxiety, and the frontal lobes are the most important area for a variety of cognitive processes that help clarify the nature of the dangerous situation and give meaning to the traumatic events.[6] Cognition also includes

2 Yudofsky and Hales, *Textbook of Neuropsychiatry.*
3 Gluckman et al., *Principles.*
4 Rauch et al., "Neurocircuitry Models"; Lanius,"Complex Adaptations."
5 LeDoux, *Emotional Brain*; Dalgleish, "Emotional Brain."
6 Shin et al., "Amygdala."

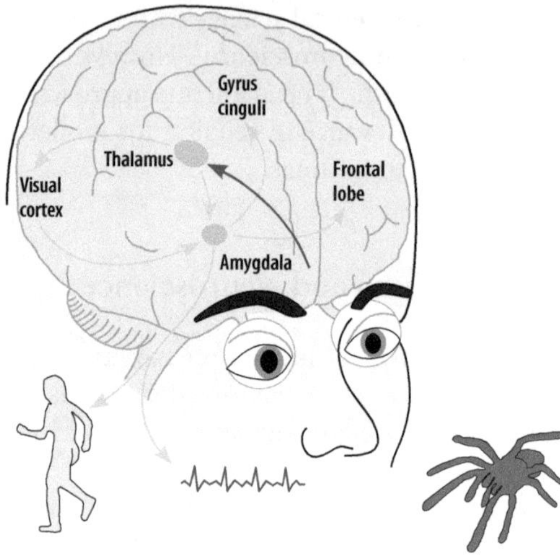

Figure 1: Fear and Brain activation (modified after LeDoux). A fear signal immediately stimulates amygdala in the limbic system leading to activation of emotions and the body for fight-or-flight reactions. The signal is perceived (visual cortex) and analysed (frontal cortex). In gyrus cinguli emotion, cognition and behavior are integrated.

the retrieval of memories from previous experiences, personal values etc. There is good evidence that a certain part of the brain, the anterior cingulate gyrus, has a specific role for the interaction of cognition and emotion.[7]

In case of traumatic events of longer duration, several other processes are activated, the most important being increased release of a major stress hormone, e.g. cortisol.

Clarification of various circuits of fear and its firmly biological roots can help explain why it is so difficult to overcome irrational fears, and why reactions to trauma may persistently change so many functions of the body. As Sah and Westbrook express: "Blame it on the specific neural circuits, hardwired in the brain that controls fear, recognition and fear renewal, even when fear has seemingly been overcome."[8] Similarly, substantial evidence suggests that the long-term consequences of stressors on the body are due to dysregulated stress in the body, especially disturbance of cortisol production.

Thus, there is good evidence to conclude that the sensitivity for traumatic events is due to the importance of our brain's fear and danger detection systems with low thresholds intended to guarantee the survival of the individual. Interestingly, our basic biology has not changed during the last 40,000 years in deep contrast to our social lives. We live in social structures and societies of extreme complexity compared to past times when we lived as hunters in

7 Etkin et al., "Emotional Processing."
8 Sah and Westbrook, "Circuit of Fear," 589.

small groups of humans. As it is often expressed: today, there is a mismatch between our basic biology and our environment.[9] In our modern society we are often exposed to traumas. When traumas are excessive or catastrophic to the individual, there is a significant risk of developing very distressing symptoms such as severe anxiety, derealisation and depersonalisation as the upper limits of our danger systems are bypassed. Similarly, when exposed to long-term mild or moderate stressors, we may develop depression, indicating that our biological homeostatic mechanism has been insufficient.

Many of these adaptive systems can be identified in mammals, but humans gain distinction by special cognitive abilities that give the possibility not only to react appropriately to specific traumatic events, but also to reflect on life and to see traumas in the frame of reference of the individual person. This brings a whole new dimension to traumas and documents that a much broader theoretical approach is needed than basic neurobiology. However, our ability to reflect on traumas often leads to unnecessary and excessive worrying about health, money, family, or work.

Trauma and Treatment

The basic attitude in neuropsychiatry is that traumatic events impede the integrity of the individual, and when they have led to symptoms or disabilities with low quality of life, treatment should be given to reinstall the integrity of the body. Today, treatment options include psychological[10] and pharmacological treatments.[11]

Cognitive therapy is an evidence-based treatment of several anxiety disorders and is based on both learning and cognitive theories. A well-known mechanism for developing and sustaining anxiety is classical conditioning in the Pavlovian sense. Almost any non-harmful event can be conditioned to lead to future anxiety when the non-harmful event is co-occurring with a harmful event, such as noise or punishment. With this knowledge, an important treatment technique is exposure *in vivo* where the individual is exposed to the traumatic situation in a graduated way until the anxiety disappears.[12] Similarly, cognitive restructuring involving processes from information and psycho-education to social skill training is also an important method, giving the individual the option to react to future traumatic events in a more balanced and non-pathological way.

9 Gluckman et al., *Principles*.
10 Cozolino, *Neuroscience*.
11 National Institute for Clinical Excellence, *Post-traumatic Stress Disorder (PTSD)*.
12 Breedlove et al., *Biological Psychology*.

Anxiolytic and antidepressant drugs are also options in the treatment of acute stress and PTSD and are based on comprehensive theories of the cellular and molecular events underlying anxiety and fear reactions. Essentially drugs interact with the chemical messengers, the neurotransmitters, that transfer the electrical signal from one cell to another, thereby normalizing synaptic dysfunctions.[13] A variety of neurotransmitters exist, and GABA (gamma-hydroxybuturate), noradrenalin and serotonin are among the most important for our reactions to traumas. Psychotherapy and drugs may be combined, indicating that monism is the assumption of modern neuroscience, e.g. body and mind are of similar nature—in fact identical. Indeed, man is a whole person.

This short presentation of the current conception of trauma in modern psychiatry illustrates that trauma is conceived in a naturalistic frame of reference focusing on causal factors and brain mechanisms studied by neurobiological and neuropsychological methods. Reactions to traumas often cause various forms of dysfunctions and are accordingly considered as mental disorders that require therapeutic endeavors. The main purpose of treatment is to normalize dysfunction of the brain by chemical (drugs) or psychological interventions. Research is driven by the epistemiology of empiricism intending to lead to nomothetical knowledge.

Despite the modern therapeutic methods, a significant number of people do not respond sufficiently, and to them trauma is an event that significantly or dramatically changes their way of life, especially the quality of life. Traumas inevitably involve important existential themes to the individual, and a need to conceive humankind in a much broader perspective, e.g. psychiatry has to meet the humanities.

Trauma in a Hermeneutic View

Despite the importance of neuroscience and a medical conception of disease, man is not just a complicated biological machine. Humans have essential abilities not found in other mammals such as a distinctive experience of being a self with specific identity, reflection on his own life and executive functions in relation to conscious planning, controlling and changing his behavior. In other words, humans are equipped with autonomy and responsibility for their lives.[14]

In treatment within a naturalistic frame of reference, there is little interest in reflecting on the specific meaning of the trauma for the individual person

13 Charney et al., *Neurobiology.*

14 Wulff et al., *Philosophy.*

and the need for the person to integrate the trauma in its own horizon of understanding to be able to live in a future with significantly changed premises due to the trauma. What is needed is a hermeneutic approach with strong links to the humanities (e.g. history, art, literature and religion) as well as the social sciences.

In the 19th century, the grand neurologist Charcot studied "Grande hysterie," e.g. patients with marked dissociative neurological symptoms without evident somatic causes. Patients demonstrated gross sensory and motoric dysfunctions (loss of sensation and paralyses) that could not be explained by anatomical lesions. The father of psychoanalysis Sigmund Freud (1856–1939) attended Charcot's lectures and clinical demonstrations, and this inspired him to see both mental and certain somatic symptoms as expression of unconscious psychic conflicts through the influence of various defense mechanisms. In other words, symptoms were not just symptoms but had a specific meaning for the individual person.[15]

A detailed characterization of trauma in a psychoanalytical theoretical setting is beyond the purpose of this paper but psychoanalytical thinking has had a strong influence on psychiatry with domination in Europe in 1940–1970. By giving an in-depth psychological explanation for reactions to traumatic events, the therapy focused on emotional working through of unconscious processes that were brought to consciousness during the therapeutic intervention, including interpretation of dreams, slip of tongues etc.

The scientific nature of psychoanalytic thinking in psychiatry has been heavily disputed for instance by the philosopher Karl Popper (1902–1994), but the German psychoanalyst Alfred Lorenzer (1922–2002) has strongly advocated that psychoanalysis belongs to the hermeneutic tradition with specific concepts and theories for both normal psychology and psychopathology.[16] Psychoanalytic theories have in recent years lost their impact on mainstream psychiatry for a variety of reasons, the most important being the lack of empirical evidence for therapeutic efficacy and the lack of interest to relate psychoanalytic concepts and theories in neuroscience. Personally, I find the psychoanalytic hermeneutic activity too restricted as it is so closely confined to specific psychoanalytic theories.

In our book Philosophy of Medicine[17] we have introduced part of the thinking of Søren Kierkegaard (1813–1855), especially in relation to anxiety and the conception of man as an autonomous person, and we have advocated for the need to include his non-naturalistic approach in modern medicine, thereby giving it "a humanistic face." We also directed medicine to the thinking of several continental philosophers, e.g. Martin Heidegger (1889–1976),

15 On Freud and the history of medicine, see Nadine Metzger's article in this volume.

16 Lorenzer, *Wahrheit*.

17 Wulff et al., *Philosophy*.

Hans-Georg Gadamer (1900–2002) and Jürgen Habermas (born 1929) for a broader understanding of man and disease phenomena.

I would like to give a personal example of the importance of seeing traumas in a hermeneutic perspective within the realms of the individual by shortly presenting my late father's reactions to his deportation to the KZ camp Theresienstadt in 1943–45. This period of his life started dramatically with his unsuccessful attempts to flee by boat to Sweden. In the harbor of Gilleleje north of Copenhagen, the Nazis captured the boat transporting a group of Jews just after their departure from the quay, and all were transferred to the uncertain future in Theresienstadt. My father has given many reports from his daily life in the camp and several dramatic episodes where he was quite sure that his life was near an end. Luckily, he survived the war and returned home in April 1945 when, on the day of his arrival, he married my mother and immediately continued his university studies to be a medical doctor the following year. Compared to several other members of his family, he was indeed very lucky. Most members of his mother's family did not return from Auschwitz.

The message of the story is that these traumatic events had an immense impact on my father's life, and nearly everything that were to happen or did happen to him was seen through the special lens that his stay in Theresienstadt had created before his eyes. His golden rule was to get the best out of life, never let misfortune pervade him and to fight against injustice. Furthermore, to qualify his children for their future life through education and also expecting them to work hardly because life is by no means just a matter of course and can disappear instantaneously. His whole horizon of understanding had been significantly changed. For my father the deportation to Theresienstadt became an essential existential theme throughout his life. It was not just a trauma.

Religion and Faith as "Cure"

An excellent example of understanding trauma in a religious perspective is the book of Job. It is hard to imagine worse traumas than Job experienced when hit by severe disease and losing his family and livestock. How can a deeply religious man understand why God treats his servant in such a way? In Job's long dialogues with his friends, a series of themes is discussed again and again with increasing intensity and often also despair, dramatically showing Job's attempts to understand God's action towards Job and his suffering. Job tries to understand what he has done to deserve such a fate. Why is he suffering without evident reason? Why are some ungodly people happy until their death? This is just a few examples of questions that people may ask in their efforts to understand why they have been hit by an unjust and incomprehensible fate. For religious people some of the answers may be given by religious reflections *ad modum* Job and his friends even if the final end will not be as happy as that of Job to whom seven sons and three daughters as well as significant amounts of cattle were given, and furthermore a very long and happy life: Job died at the age of 140 and full of days.[18]

וַיהוָה שָׁב אֶת־שְׁבִית אִיּוֹב בְּהִתְפַּלְלוֹ בְּעַד רֵעֵהוּ וַיֹּסֶף יְהוָה אֶת־כָּל־אֲשֶׁר לְאִיּוֹב לְמִשְׁנֶה׃

And the LORD restored the fortunes of Job when he had prayed for his friends; and the LORD gave Job twice as much as he had before. (Job 42:10 NRSV)

In the invitation to this conference it is stated that biblical and para-biblical literature plays an important role as it reflects more than 2500 years of coping with traumatic incidents (e.g. temple destruction, exile, exodus, wars, passion narratives, martyrdoms, persecutions), and thus provides a substantial contribution to our understanding of trauma in both historic and modern contexts.

I do not intend to suggest that biblical reflection *ad modum* Job is just another therapeutic technique, but as stated in the invitation to strongly recommend a much broader approach in daily clinical work in our therapeutic attitude towards traumas.[19] Let us benefit from the many different sources to understand man's suffering due to traumatic events.

Conclusion

In daily clinical settings, psychiatrists are often confronted with PTSD patients who have not obtained significant improvement by traditional psychiatric treatment with psychotherapy and drug and who have to continue their life in a meaningful way. It is my suggestion to neuroscience that traumas and PTSD should be seen in a much broader perspective under the inspiration of history, art, literature and religion and my claim that patients may benefit significantly from this approach—both in their social functioning and in their quality of life.

Similarly, there is a clear and important message to scholars within the theology, humanities and social sciences. The impact of traumas—man-made or natural ones—cannot be understood without seeing man as a whole, e.g. as a psychobiological unity, the function of which also requires substantial neuroscientific knowledge.

18 On reading the book of Job from the perspective of trauma, see Kirsten Nielsens article in this volume.

19 Cf. Christopher Frechette's article in this volume.

Bibliography

American Psychiatric Association. *Diagnostic and Statistical Manual of Mental Disorders.* Washington: American Psychiatric Association, 1994.

Breedlove, S. M., N. V. Watson, and M. R. Rosenzweig. *Biological Psychology.* Sunderland, Mass.: Sinauer, 2010

Charney, D. S., E. J. Nestler, and B. S. Bunney. *Neurobiology of Mental Illness.* New York: Oxford University Press, 2001.

Cozolino, L. J. *The Neuroscience of Psychotherapy: Building and Rebuilding the Human Brain.* New York: Norton, 2002.

Dalgleish, T. "The Emotional Brain." *Nature Reviews of Neuroscience* 5(7) (2004): 583-89.

Etkin, A., T. Egner, and R. Kalisch. "Emotional Processing in Anterior Cingulate and Medial Prefrontal Cortex". *Trends in Cognitive Science* 15(2) (2011): 85-93.

Gluckman, P., A. Beedle, and M. Hanson. *Principles of Evolutionary Medicine.* Oxford: Oxford University Press, 2009.

Lanius, R. "Complex Adaptations to Rraumatic Stress: From Neurobiological to Social and Cultural Aspects." *American Journal of Psychiatry* 164(11) (2007): 1628-30.

LeDoux, J. *The Emotional Brain.* New York: Simon & Schuster, 1996.

Lorenzer, A. *Die Wahrheit der psychoanalytischen Erkenntnis. Ein historisch-materialistischer Entwurf.* Frankfurt/Main: Suhrkamp, 1988.

National Institute for Clinical Excellence. *Post-traumatic Stress Disorder (PTSD): The Management of PTSD in Adults and Children in Primary and Secondary Care.* No pages. Cited 17 February 2014. Online: http://publications.nice.org.uk/post-traumatic-stress-disorder-ptsd-cg26.

Rauch, S. L., L. M. Shin, and E. A. Phelps. "Neurocircuitry Models of Posttraumatic Stress Disorder and Extinction: Human Neuroimaging Research-Past, Present, and Future". *Biological Psychiatry* 60(4) (2006): 376-82.

Sah, P., and R. F. Westbrook. "The Circuit of Fear." *Nature* 454 (2008): 589-90.

Shin, L. M., S. L. Rauch, and R. K. Pitman. "Amygdala, Medial Prefrontal Cortex, and Hippocampal Function in PTSD." *Annals of the New York Academy of Sciences* 1071 (2006): 67-79.

World Health Organization. *The ICD-10 Classification of Mental and Behavioural Disorders. Diagnostic Criteria for Research.* Geneva: World Health Organization, 1993.

Wulff, H. R., S. A. Pedersen, and R. Rosenberg. *Philosophy in Medicine, an Introduction.* 1st ed. Oxford: Blackwell Scientific Publications, 1986.

Yudofsky, S. C., and R. E. Hales. *The American Psychiatric Publishing Textbook of Neuropsychiatry and Behavioral Neurosciences.* Arlington, Va.: American Psychiatric Publishing, 2008.

Nadine Metzger

Railway Spine, Shell Shock and Psychological Trauma

The Limits of Retrospective Diagnosis

Abstract

Psychological trauma and traumatization are concepts of the late 19th century. Prior to this, we have to consider that people not only *used* different explanatory systems to describe their inner workings but the available systems *shaped* experiences as well. Under these premises, how are we to grasp historical trauma and traumatization?

Psychological Trauma, and especially Post-traumatic Stress Disorder, are medical and/or psychological concepts. Even though the term "trauma" is used frequently outside strictly medical and psychological practice, it was a medical concept long before it entered everyday language and commonplace usage. "Trauma" as a term for psychological occurrences was first used in the late 19th century, while the term "Post-Traumatic Stress Disorder" did not appear until 1980. Both are new concepts in the context of the long history of medicine.

Besides writing the history of medical concepts such as trauma and PTSD, historians of medicine have delved into the methodological problems inherent to their research.[1] In both these areas, medical history has a lot to offer for any study of psychological mechanisms in the past.

One of the epistemological problems frequently encountered in the course of medico-historical research, and therefore methodologically addressed, is

1 The history of trauma and traumatization falls directly into the field of study and competence of medical history. In general, medical historians study the history of all aspects of illness and health, body, patients and medical practitioners of all kinds, health care, medical research and the social and cultural concept of all things medical. Like all historians, we too work with a multitude of different approaches to our subject matter, for example social history, cultural history or the history of ideas. Thematic introductions to the history of medicine in English include Bynum et al., *Western Medical Tradition;* Porter, *Benefit to Mankind*; current methodological approaches are discussed in Hofer and Sauerteig, "Kulturgeschichte der Medizin"; Eckart and Jütte, *Medizingeschichte*; some fundamental and still valid thoughts on the relationship with current medicine can be found in Temkin, "Medical History" [1946].

retrospective diagnosis.[2] Retrospective diagnosis means the identification of illnesses of the past, for example as documented in ancient sources, with the names of modern diseases. A classic example of retrospective diagnosis is the tendency to diagnose famous men of the past with illnesses defined by modern medicine: a common example of this is the frequent claim of Julius Caesar supposedly suffering from severe migraines.[3] The problems with this claim are numerous; not only are the textual sources not specific in their descriptions of the symptoms, they are not written by physicians and usually cater to a very special need in the textual composition. To identify an illness after 2000 years based on such meager evidence does not comply with current professional standards in medical diagnostics. From a historical standpoint, how does it help us to know that Julius Caesar supposedly suffered from migraines? Will it change how we interpret the Rubicon episode? Is it not more interesting to ask why Caesar was portrayed as suffering from bodily ailments and by whom, and what exactly this meant for his contemporaries?

The study of trauma and traumatization in the past touches upon the same dilemma: can the modern medical concept of Post-traumatic Stress Disorder help us in understanding the past? Are "trauma" and "traumatization" applicable to experiences of humans regardless of their culture or epoch?[4]

The Psyche Being Shaped by Prevalent Concepts

In his small early volume *Maladie mentale et psychologie* from 1954, Michel Foucault calls psychology a "general relationship modern man has established with himself."[5] The reciprocal quality of psychology, he emphasizes here, is constitutional and affects the historian of psychological phenomena in a significant way: the fact that we imagine our inner workings with the help of concepts from modern psychology might influence exactly those in-

2 Specifically discussed in Leven, "Krankheiten"; Leven, "Retrospective Diagnosis"; Arrizabalaga, "Retrospective Diagnosis"; Eckart and Jütte, *Medizingeschichte*, 329–31. On the social construction of medical knowledge in general see Jordanova, "Social Construction"; Lachmund and Stollberg, "Social Construction of Illness." Awareness of the problem can be seen as early as in Fleck, "Wissenschaftliche Tatsache" [1935], 165–90; Temkin, "Medical History" [1946], 99–100.

3 As repeatedly claimed by numerous self-help books and even physicians riding the proverbial historical hobbyhorse, see for example Jones, "Great Pains," 627.

4 These questions have been raised before: Young, "Memory Sciences," *Harmony of Illusions*, 3–10; Jones and Wessely, "War Syndromes."

5 Foucault, *Maladie mentale*, 103: "… ce rapport général que l'homme occidental a établi voici bientôt deux siècles de lui-même à lui-même."

ner workings to a significant degree.[6] This is the reason why mental and psychosomatic illnesses are especially bound to their cultural context.[7]

We, as men and women of the 21st century, socialized by Western culture, picture a distinct psyche, a separate entity from our body, which can be harmed in an analogue way. We distinguish an unconscious part from consciousness, and sometimes we speak of our conscience as another distinct part of this inner system. We are aware of certain psychological mechanisms; we explain human behavior in psychological terms. Trauma and traumatization belong to the multitude of psychological concepts we use frequently in everyday speech to describe and explain the inner workings of ourselves or others.

Unnoticed, however, these readily available psychological models and concepts—patterns of thinking and explaining—shape our experiences. The fact that our reactions and feelings are culturally bound at least to some degree becomes clear when we consider inter-cultural differences in mental disease. A whole field of research, cross-cultural psychiatry, is devoted to the phenomenon that much of our Western psychology cannot be applied to the inner workings of people from a different cultural background.[8] This can cause severe problems for psychiatrists who find themselves confronted with people suffering from conditions impossible to grasp and to cure in Western medical terms. Our Western psychology describes the psyche of people who have grown up and been shaped by those concepts, and may utterly fail with people from other cultures.

Of course, this is not only true of cultures from different places in our present world, but from a historical perspective as well. The example of late 19th century trauma concepts as elaborated in this paper will show exactly that. We can *not* assume that people in historical times functioned the same as we do nowadays. We have to keep in mind that many concepts which we employ as a matter of fact to make sense of ourselves did not exist in earlier times. People then had their own models which might seem very strange to the modern researcher, and which we must reconstruct painstakingly from the sources without any guarantee that we are right.[9]

6 Similarly to the question of the cultural impact on psychological phenomena with many examples of psychological changes observed in different centuries, see for example Stolberg, *Homo patiens*, 215–60.

7 Universally acknowledged in the field of History of Psychiatry since at least the late 1980s, see, for example, Rousseau and Porter, "Natural History"; Pressman, "Mental Illness"; Stolberg, *Homo patiens*, 217–18.

8 Cross-cultural psychiatry: Stolberg, *Homo patiens*, 216–18; special issue "New Approaches to Culture-bound Mental Disorders" of *Social Science and Medicine* 21 (1985): 163–228.

9 Some examples of many convincing approaches by medical historians include Duden, *Geschichte*; Porter, "Social Perspective"; Stolberg, *Homo patiens*.

In short: we cannot assume without questioning that people in ancient times experienced "psychological trauma" the way we do. Furthermore, even if the basal mechanisms stay the same through time, everything we know about historical individuals is channeled into text—language-shaped, interpreted, explained and put into their own historical frame of reference by the authors. The written word is shaped by its historical socio-cultural background.

The Early History of Psychological Trauma[10]

Conventionally, the history of psychological trauma is taken to begin with the railway spine.[11] In 1866, the London surgeon John Eric Erichsen (1818–1896) published his book on a burning issue of the time: railway accidents and resulting injuries.[12] These were widely discussed by contemporaries and welcome fodder for newspapers and pamphlets. In the eyes of mid to late 19th century people, railway accidents were both especially dangerous and increasing in numbers. The train's destructive force and uncontrollable velocity were seen as symbolic for modern times and the industrial age.[13]

But Erichsen's book not only dealt with this hot topic of the time, it also served a special purpose: for some years, railway companies had been forced by law to compensate anyone injured in a railway accident. This led to numerous court cases, and increasing numbers of physicians were being asked to testify about subjects' real or fraudulent health problems and whether these were directly caused by the accident.

10 In the medical history of psychological trauma, fundamental work was done by Fischer-Homberger, *Traumatische Neurose*; idem, "Medizingeschichte." In English-speaking history of psychiatry, the topic picked up momentum in the 1990s, resulting in the excellent international essay collection edited by Micale and Lerner, *Traumatic Pasts*. Medical Anthropology contributed the partly historical, partly ethnographic book by Young, *Harmony of Illusions*, which sparked intense discussion, especially in the US context. These seminal works may both be recommended as introductory literature to the topic and the methodological perspective of medical history.

11 E.g. Fischer-Homberger, *Traumatische Neurose*, 7; Young, *Harmony of Illusions*, 13; Thomann and Rauschmann, "Posttraumatische Belastungsstörung," 105–8; Seidler and Eckart, "Psychotraumatologie," 9; Seidler, "Geschichte der Psychotraumatologie," 4.

12 Erichsen, *Railway*. In fact, Erichsen himself rejects the term 'railway spine' for his concept as absurd, but, nevertheless, this is the name under which the concept was discussed from then on. For Erichsen and the railway spine, trains and accidents, see Fischer-Homberger, *Traumatische Neurose*, 16–23, 36–48; Young, *Harmony of Illusions*, 13–19; Caplan, "Trains and Trauma"; Harrington, "The Railway Accident."

13 The significant symbolism of trains and railway accidents during this time may lead to the interpretation that the trauma concept itself is expressive of modernity, as followed up by the excellent collection of Micale and Lerner, *Traumatic Pasts*, explicated esp. pp. 10–11.

Erichsen's book also describes fractures of bones etc., but it is especially known for his concept of the railway spine—a typical occurrence in railway accident survivors he observed. These patients suffer from mostly unlocalized symptoms such as tiredness, dizziness, headaches, faulty sensual impressions, fear and pain. In his opinion, these symptoms were caused by concussions of the spine—and only slight jolts and jerks could cause severe troubles in the spine: microfractures and chronic inflammation of the spinal cord.

Clearly, this concept of the railway spine is purely somatic in its nature. Other than being caused by an accident, Erichsen's concept has virtually nothing to do with psychological trauma. The patient's spine is hurt, therefore they show a variety of previously unlocalized symptoms. So why is this episode conventionally placed at the beginning of a history of trauma concepts?—It is symptomatic for the difficulties modern medicine has with ailments which cannot be localized in the body or were not caused by something tangibly material.[14] Therefore, the history of trauma concepts in modern medicine is always closely bound to somatic causation theories.

Some twenty years later, Erichsen's work was continued by a German neurologist who brings us somewhat closer to our own idea of psychological trauma. Similarly to Erichsen's context, accident insurance had been introduced in Germany some years earlier, and thus the need arose for physician expert witnesses. Medical interest in long-term effects of accidents was at its highpoint. Hermann Oppenheim (1857-1919) observed and described numerous cases of railway invalids who sported similarly varied and unlocalized symptoms to those observed by Erichsen.[15] Spasms, uncontrollable tremors, temporary palsy and paralysis of the legs, fainting, sexual dysfunction, sleep disorders, stammering—the symptoms described are numerous. They all have in common the fact that they could not be localized or somatically explained.

Oppenheim did not believe in Erichsen's aetiological hypothesis of concussions of the spinal cord.[16] Medicine had moved on and agreed that the mental capacities of the spinal cord had been greatly overestimated by physicians of Erichsen's generation. Another category of disease offered itself to Oppenheim: he coined the syndrome "traumatic neurosis." "Neurosis" was a general term for any neurological illness which could not yet be localized in

14 Fischer-Homberger, "Medizingeschichte," 268-69.

15 Oppenheim, *Traumatische Neurosen*. Then, Oppenheim was a physician at the Charité Hospital in Berlin. The patient files from which his conclusions are drawn and whose case stories are cited in the book are still existent and are part of research projects by the Charité Institute for Medical History, see Hess and Mendelsohn, "Cases and Series," 300-303.

16 He mentions Erichsen as the first to describe the railway spine in detail, but cannot agree with his explanation, Oppenheim, *Traumatische Neurosen*, 1-2. It might be due to Oppenheim's reference to Erichsen as the starting point of the medical discussion of these phenomena that our histories today also start with Erichsen.

the body of the sufferer.[17] However, this does not make "neurosis" a psychological ailment—the key factor is "not yet localized": physiologists at the end of the 19th century were sure that future research would reveal both afflicted body part and precise somatic causation of neuroses.[18] Oppenheim suggested cautiously that traumatic neurosis might be due to dysfunctions in certain regions of the cerebral cortex.[19]

Nevertheless, Oppenheim allowed for shock and agitation, the so-called "mental factor," being partly responsible for the ailment—if not as single cause, then as a catalyst for the fully-fledged neurosis he describes.[20]

The idea of "mental factors" being responsible for diseases was problematic in late 19th century medicine. Oppenheim was very soon entangled in several fierce disputes with colleagues who refuted the concept of traumatic neurosis on exactly these grounds:[21] the experience of shock and intense fear in railway and other accidents could not be responsible for the resulting neurosis—because how could it be explained that only some accident survivors develop symptoms while others stay perfectly healthy? The sufferers must surely have had some dormant neurological disorder or a hereditary disposition towards such ailments which the shocking accident then triggered. Therefore, it was not the accident which was to blame for the following illness, but rather the poor prior bodily condition of the patient. Another problem for which Oppenheim was assailed was that he could not distinguish honest sufferers of traumatic neurosis from perfectly healthy malingerers: not only were the symptoms easy to feign, but the lack of observable somatic evidence did not meet the standards of medical theory in the early 1890s.

Obviously, Oppenheim's opponents and their arguments were quite beneficial to the financial interests of insurance and railway companies. On the other hand, psychological mechanisms which Oppenheim claimed to be the cause simply did not fit into the medical paradigm of the time. It is not surprising at all that after some intense refutations, traumatic neurosis was excluded from professional discourse and no longer mentioned in neurological

17 Fischer-Homberger, *Traumatische Neurose*, 26–29; May-Tolzmann, *Neurose*. Eulenburg, *Real-Encyclopädie*, 12:167: "… diejenigen Formen von Nervenerkrankungen …, die eine pathologisch-anatomische Definition und Localisirung *zur Zeit* nicht zulassen." [emphasis in original]

18 Fischer-Homberger, "Medizingeschichte," 268–69.

19 Oppenheim, *Traumatische Neurose*, 127: "… cerebrale functionelle Störungen, die ihren Sitz aller Wahrscheinlichkeit nach in der Grosshirnrinde haben und die Psyche, sowie die Centren für Motilität, Sensibilität und Sinnesfunction betreffen."

20 Oppenheim, *Traumatische Neurosen*, 123–29.

21 Dening, "Oppenheim"; Fischer-Homberger, *Traumatische Neurose*, 56–77; Kloocke et al., "Psychische Ereignisse," 77–79; Seidler and Eckart, "Geschichte der Psychotraumatologie," 4–6, Thomann and Rauschmann, "Posttraumatische Belastungsstörung," 110–13.

and psychiatric journals. Only outside medicine, for example in popular encyclopedias, did the concept of traumatic neurosis remain in circulation.[22]

More than 25 years later, Oppenheim sensed another chance for his traumatic neurosis.[23] During World War I, he proposed the concept again to explain the puzzling number and intensity of war neuroses—known in English by the term shell shock—which demanded a medical explanation. Just as 25 years before—and on much the same grounds—his concept was refuted. This ultimately led to the German post-war legislation that sufferers from shell shock had no claim to an invalid's pension.[24]

While German medicine insisted on somatic causes of diseases,[25] medical research in other countries moved in directions more promising for the eventual development of the idea of psychological trauma. One of the more experimental methods popular with neurologists was hypnosis.[26] The center of learning in this field was Paris, where Jean-Martin Charcot (1825-1893), the so-called "Napoleon of neuroses," demonstrated his cutting-edge research

22 See the comprehensive evaluation of German professional journals since 1889 by Kloocke et al., "Psychische Ereignisse," 77-81. Surprisingly, some German neurologists reinterpreted Oppenheim to their own liking—such as Binswanger, *Hysterie*, 78-79, who agrees with Oppenheim that physical injury of the nerves ("Molecularschädigung der centralen Nervenelemente") is responsible for traumatic neurosis. Purely psychological causation of neurosis is rejected by Binswanger, p. 80.

23 Oppenheim, "Krieg." Analyses of the German wartime discussion centered on Oppenheim's renewed suggestion include Lerner, "Traumatic Neurosis," and Dening, "Oppenheim," 468-74.

24 There are numerous works on shell shock and the subsequent medical challenge in the countries affected. As an introduction for Germany see Eckart, "Kriegsgewalt und Psychotrauma"; Lerner, "Traumatic Neurosis"; Lerner, *Hysterical Men*. Austria: Hofer, *Nervenschwäche*, 185-375. France: Roudebush, "Battle of Nerves"; Michl, *Im Dienste des "Volkskörpers,"* 181-271. Great Britain: Winter, "Shell-Shock"; Leese, "British Shellshock Treatment"; Leese, *Shell Shock*. Italy: Bianchi, "Psychiatrists, Soldiers, and Officers." At this point it should be noted that human reactions to war experiences take on different medical forms; classical shell shock symptoms were especially common in World War I, but seldom occurred in wars after that. Very few soldiers in the Second World War suffered from great bodily tremors as had been the case 25 years before, with their psychotraumatic reactions seeming to have been in the form of internal ailments, such as intestinal problems without somatic aetiology. Since then, major wars have each brought forth their own symptoms, e.g. Gulf War Syndrome, while PTSD is closely connected to the suffering of Vietnam veterans, see Jones and Wessely, "War syndromes"; Thomann and Rauschmann, "Posttraumatische Belastungsstörung," 113-19.

25 A exemplary discussion of the German stand on traumatic causation in the case of hysteria is provided by Binswanger, *Hysterie*, 72-80, who rejects purely psychological causation of neurosis in favor of predisposition or invisible physical damage to the nerves, while attributing only an additional trigger character to shock.

26 For hypnosis during Charcot's times see Ellenberger, *Discovery of the Unconscious*, 111-20; Gauld, *A History of Hypnotism*, 297-318.

into hysteria and other neuroses in weekly public lectures.[27] Hysteria,[28] once perceived as an affliction of the female reproductive organs, was known to lead to a wide variety of bodily and behavioral symptoms such as spasms, palsy, chronic pain, respiratory distress, dizziness, headaches and fainting without somatic causes, along with more general complaints like excessive weeping, laughing fits, chronic telling of falsehoods and melodramatic behavior.

Charcot, whose work is pivotal to the history of hysteria, not only described hysteria in men for the first time—thereby significantly softening the traditional link between the disease and female sexual organs[29]—but also *proved* by means of hypnosis that ideas alone, immaterial ideas, could lead to somatic symptoms in hysterical persons. Under hypnosis, he told the test subject to display a certain symptom after being woken up—and once brought back from hypnosis, the patient displayed this specific bodily symptom without remembering why. By these means, Charcot convinced his audience that experiences, non-somatic psychological occurrences, could play a part in shaping the symptoms of hysteria.[30]

In Charcot's opinion, however, this only worked with people already afflicted with hysteria or having a dormant disposition towards it or other neuroses. For him, in fact, only hysterics were susceptible to hypnosis. Therefore, experiences or intense emotions only led to symptoms and illness in hysterical persons, not in the general population.[31] This is still far from the modern idea of psychological trauma.

In the early 1890s, the young neurologist Sigmund Freud (1856-1939) experimented with the kind of hypnosis he had seen when visiting Charcot in Paris. Together with his older colleague Josef Breuer (1842-1925), he found in his hysteria patients an astonishing connection between their specific present symptoms and certain traumatic experiences of the past. These experiences were not only shocks from occurrences such as railway accidents, but

27 Charcot's public lectures in which he describes his cases are published as Charcot, *Maladies du système nerveux*. For Charcot see Ellenberger, *Discovery of the Unconscious*, 89-101; Micale, *Hysterical Men*, 117-21; a critical account of Charcot's work on hysteria is Didi-Huberman, *Invention of Hysteria*.

28 Hysteria is one of the most well-researched and controversial illnesses of the 19th century. For more on the topic see Gilman, *Hysteria beyond Freud*; Micale, *Approaching Hysteria*; Scull, *Hysteria*; Nolte, *Gelebte Hysterie*.

29 For male hysteria see Micale, *Hysterical Men*, and Charcot, *Maladies du système nerveux*, 3:249-369.

30 The experiment is described in Oppenheim, *Traumatische Neurosen*, 6. For ideogenic hysteria with mention of the experiment see Charcot, *Maladies du système nerveux*, 3:334-36.

31 For Charcot's position in the development of the idea of psychological trauma see Micale, "Jean-Martin Charcot and *les névroses traumatiques*"; Fischer-Homberger, *Traumatische Neurose*, 105-28.

in most cases intense emotional disturbances like an engagement broken by the groom-to-be, the death of a loved one or sexual abuse.[32]

It must be noted that this was Freud as a young doctor, before he had written his Dream Interpretation. He had not yet formulated his concept of psychoanalysis. There is no notion of children's sexual development and no formed concept of the unconscious.[33] For those amongst us who are socialized by modern Western culture, the idea of the unconscious is so very deeply ingrained in our way of thinking that it is fundamental to the way we explain and perceive the inner workings of ourselves and of others. It is difficult to imagine a time without the concept. But in the early 1890s, the concept of the unconscious was still in the making.

Freud and Breuer, like Charcot, drew on the concept of hypnosis to explain certain observations in their patients. Both were convinced that people susceptible to hypnosis had something resembling a split memory: some things they remembered only under hypnosis, other things only while awake. When the patient was awake, the hypnosis part could only make itself heard by causing the appearance of inexplicable hysterical symptoms. This split between the two memories was complete: only under hypnosis could the patient remember the reasons why those symptoms occurred—and the traumatic experience or thought which caused them must have happened in a hypnosis-like state. It must be noted, though, that it is generally not the traumatic event itself which triggers hysteria at the moment it occurs. Retrospective reflection on the event while in the described hypnosis-like state brought forward the unsolvable inner conflict responsible for hysterical symptoms. Day-dreaming and an over-active imagination could easily lead to such states. Some people were more prone to them than others—mostly women, frequent sufferers of hysteria. But there was a cure: by moving the traumatic memory from the hypnotic part to the awake part, thereby retroactively working through all the "normal" emotions attached to the traumatic experience, the physician could cause the symptom to disappear.[34]

Freud and Breuer pushed these mechanisms into the center of hysteria depiction—most cases of hysteria were caused by traumatic experiences or traumatic thoughts.[35] Here, at least, we have arrived at the notion of a purely psychological trauma producing severe somatic and behavioral symptoms in the sufferer.[36] However, this was not to last. Ten years later, Freud would re-

32 Freud and Breuer, "Hysterische Phänomene," 28-29. For Freud's and Breuer's collaboration and eventual dissolution see Sulloway, *Freud*, 91-109, 115-40, 151-54.

33 For details see May-Tolzmann, *Freuds frühe klinische Theorie*, 20.

34 Freud and Breuer, "Hysterische Phänomene," esp. 35-37, 39-41.

35 Ibid., 29.

36 The term "psychic trauma" is used and defined this way first in Freud and Breuer, "Hysterische Phänomene," 29, they continue: "Als solches [= psychisches Trauma] kann jedes Erlebnis wirken, welches die peinlichen Affekte des Schreckens, der Angst, der Scham, des

ject the idea as a whole that hysteria patients had suffered traumatic experiences which caused their illness. His subsequent psychoanalytical model would only allow for suppressed wishes to cause hysteria and other neuroses.[37]

This change in Freud's attitude is especially controversial because it involves the topic of sexual abuse. As mentioned previously, Freud and Breuer, in their joint works of the early 1890s, acknowledged sexual abuse during childhood or in adulthood as a traumatic experience able to cause hysterical symptoms.[38] This was quite revolutionary for their time and resulted from them actually listening to what their patients under hypnosis had to say. Of course, sexual abuse of children was discussed in a wider public context at the time, but it was mostly nannies, governesses and other servants who were accused of "seducing" previously innocent children, mostly boys.[39] Freud and Breuer introduced other attackers: fathers, brothers, other close family members, husbands.[40] While Breuer was open for other possible traumata, Freud soon focused on sexual abuse as *the* single cause of hysteria and other neuroses. In 1896, he wrote with conviction that every hysterical woman had suffered sexual abuse in her childhood—most likely at the hands of her brother or other close family members.[41]

It is not surprising that this hypothesis did not meet with approval from his physician colleagues. His first presentation to Viennese physicians received a "frosty response"[42] and his publication did not fare better. Hysteria was a very common affliction and his hypothesis logically led to a general

psychischen Schmerzes hervorruft." Compare Sulloway, *Freud*, 104-14, 140-46, who emphasizes the physiological reasonings underlying Freud's trauma hypothesis.

37 More on his changing attitudes below. Accounts of Freud himself describing the development retrospectively can be found in Freud, "Selbstdarstellung," 54-60, and Freud, "Geschichte," 55-56.

38 Not as early as in the short article Freud and Breuer, "Hysterische Phänomene," but their case studies and separately written theoretical papers in "Studien über Hysterie" from 1895 all include sexual assault as a traumatic experience. For Breuer's explicit statements on a sexual etiology see Freud and Breuer, *Hysterie*, 265-66, for Freud see Freud and Breuer, *Hysterie*, 273, 275.

39 Schmersahl, *Medizin und Geschlecht*, 243-45; Fischer-Homberger, "Medizingeschichte," 275-78.

40 Breuer: Sexual abuse by husbands most common cause for neuroses in women, Freud and Breuer, *Hysterie*, 265; Freud: family members, Freud and Breuer, *Hysterie*, 152-53, 292. Freud talks more explicitly about sexual abuse by close family members in his works "Ätiologie der Hysterie" and "Weitere Bemerkungen über die Abwehr-Neuropsychosen," both published in 1896. Freud was reluctant in publicly naming fathers as attackers, but was convinced of their guilt, as a later letter to Fließ (Sept. 1897) shows, Freud, *Briefe an Wilhelm Fließ*, 283. Cf. Esterson, "Psychoanalytic History," 342, who doubts that Freud thought about fathers that early on.

41 Freud, "Ätiologie der Hysterie," 439, 442-46.

42 Letter to Fließ, Freud, *Briefe an Wilhelm Fließ*, 193: "Eine eisige Aufnahme." On reception of his theories see Schmersahl, *Medizin und Geschlecht*, 245, 247-48.

suspicion of countless respected family men. And, very early on, Freud became cautious himself—he discovered contradictions in some patients' accounts and wondered if it was not he himself as a hypnotist who had suggested tales of sexual abuse in his patients—keeping in mind the problematic dynamic between hypnotist and the hypnotized.[43] Having had doubts for many years, in 1905/06 he finally revised his theory, stating that their reports of sexual abuse had not been real occurrences, but rather wishful fantasies on part of his female patients whose suppressed sexual desires were released in this way.[44] Here, finally, the eventual psychoanalyst's model of how the human psyche works surfaces.[45]

While this u-turn by Freud is still hotly debated among feminists and psychoanalysts, let it simply be stated that it took about 70 years for sexual abuse to be pulled out of the closet once more. Feminists broached the issue in the 1970s, and thanks to them, sexual abuse is now a recognized traumatic experience which can lead to post-traumatic reactions.[46]

Evaluation of the Historical Account

The early history of psychological trauma as presented above shows that the formulation of a specific medical concept depends to a large degree on external factors. In the case of 19th century railway accidents, compensation and insurance legislation initially sparked certain medical research—while the social issues and financial interests attached shaped the medical stand on

43 In fact, as early as September 1897, Freud entrusts Fließ with his change of mind regarding the seduction theory. Freud, *Briefe an Wilhelm Fließ*, 283–84. Freud's doubts and final rejection of the "Verführungstheorie" is evaluated very differently depending on the perspective of the historian: a feminist perspective can be found in Schmersahl, *Medizin und Geschlecht*, 241–53; psychoanalytical background informs May-Tolzmann, *Freuds frühe klinische Theorie*, 44–56, and underlies Leys, *Trauma*; for a medico-historical account see Fischer-Homberger, "Medizingeschichte," 275–79; idem, *Traumatische Neurose*, 74–80. Much uproar was caused by Masson, *Assault on Truth*, who accuses Freud of abandoning assaulted women and siding with the perpetrators. A both critical and historically sound answer to Masson is Israëls and Schatzman, "Seduction theory." Freud's lasting retrospective interpretation of the seduction theory episode is problematized by Esterson, "Psychoanalytic History."

44 Published in Freud's "Drei Abhandlungen zur Sexualtheorie" (1905) and "Meine Ansichten über die Rolle der Sexualität in der Ätiologie der Neurosen" (1906).

45 In fact, the most important psychoanalytical doctrines are not possible within the framework of Freud's early seduction theory, as Anna Freud declared retrospectively, Fischer-Homberger, "Medizingeschichte," 278.

46 Fischer-Homberger, "Medizingeschichte," 290–91; Lerner and Micale, *Traumatic Pasts*, 4–6. It should be noted that many of the short overview articles on the history of psychological trauma focus solely on (male) railway accident victims and soldiers, e.g. Seidler and Eckart, "Psychotraumatologie"; Priebe et al., "Trauma und Psyche."

things. To be successful in the medical community, an illness concept must be compatible with the prevailing state of society at the time.

On the scientific level, the formulation of medical concepts is determined by the explanatory systems available. The huge influence of the modern medical paradigm on Erichsen and Oppenheim becomes clear above: illnesses are illnesses of the body, they have a certain location in the body and are caused by clearly discernible material effects. If precise explanations are not possible using present medical means, they will be in the future. Likewise, the concepts are bound, even in their details, to the current state of research: Erichsen's picture of the properties of the spinal cord only works in his immediate time, while Oppenheim drew upon the easily available concept of neurosis. Charcot and Freud used the mechanics of hypnotism to describe their observations. They did not yet have the modern concept of the psyche with its unconscious part at their disposal, but nevertheless formulated an inherently logical concept within a contemporarily available explanatory system.

But this was obviously not enough. The early history of psychological trauma as presented here is marked by the failure of most of the concepts which we perceive as important steps towards our contemporary notion of psychological trauma. At least in the medical community, both traumatic neurosis and Freud's sexual traumatization theory failed completely. Even under extraordinary circumstances, such as the numerous shell shocked soldiers in World War I, the psychological causation of disease did not receive a second chance from German physicians. They stayed focused on somatic aetiology, and the word "trauma" continued to mean physical injuries.

It must be acknowledged that none of the concepts presented actually describe psychological trauma as it is conceived in the 21st century. This early history of the concept of psychological trauma is retrospective and focuses on aspects comparable to our contemporary concept in past medical science without an exact fit. Even Freud's acknowledgement of sexual abuse being able to cause hysterical symptoms—by far the closest to our own concept—is founded upon a hypnosis model of memory and is restricted to people with a disposition to abnormal mental states. There is no psychological trauma in late 19th century medicine, only tiny steps in that direction.

This raises several questions.

Medicine in the late 19th century shows a significant lack—or at least strong rejection—of concepts which allow for intense experiences to cause health problems. Does this mean that it was not known in the 19th century and before that intense experiences might cause severe ailment?

Is it legitimate to use our *modern* concept of psychological trauma to describe historical concepts which are clearly different? How do we deal with historical times in which the concept of psychological trauma did not yet exist? Must we restrict ourselves to the contemporaneous explanatory models rather than speaking about "psychological trauma"?

The following section outlines some thoughts on these questions raised. By now, we have already embarked on the second part of the paper, the debate on retrospective diagnosis of the modern concept of psychological trauma. I will concentrate on two main arguments: first, I will highlight the difference between medical concepts and describable wider phenomena. Then I will broach the issue of historically changing concepts of body, psyche and medical etiology, thus not being a safe anchor for the historian's journey through time.

Psychological Trauma is a Modern Concept

Not unexpectedly, everyday experience gave people some ideas about intense experiences or emotions causing health problems long before the 20th century. This could be the conviction that seeing shocking scenes or certain persons would endanger the health of an unborn child or the expectant mother,[47] or perhaps the *vague phenomenon* of emotional hardships causing illness, which was referred to frequently. There are numerous examples of this in literature from the late 19th century.[48]

At the same time, medicine was at least suspicious, if not downright rejecting, of non-material causes for illness, while non-medical people acknowledged the possibility that intense negative feelings could make people ill and ultimately cause their death. These ideas are mostly vague, and a detailed explanation of the mechanics in such cases is not attempted here. It is possible that the idea not only arose from observation, but that older concepts of pre-modern medicine were still prevalent among the general population.

In fact, pre-modern medicine, or humoral pathology, did not have any problems with emotions and experiences causing bodily harm. This was due

47 The first part of Schott, "Das psychische Trauma," is dedicated to trauma-like mechanisms in pre-modern medicine. In the second part, Schott describes the conditional prerequisite of hypnosis theory for the formulation of psychological trauma as we know it.

48 Typical quotes include (a random selection): "To the shock of this horror the womanly spirit of Madame de la Tour succumbed; she fell into a decline and died soon after." (C. D. Warner, Baddeck And That Sort of Thing, 1874, travel account) – "But imprisonment, disgrace and indignation had consumed the strength of the ill-used man as a worm eats into cedar wood, and he fell into a decline and died." (Georg Ebers, The Sisters vol. 1, 1880, historical romance). – "As time went on, the treatment she had received from the recreant lover preyed upon her mind so that she fell into a decline in the summer of 1835.... There were those of her friends who said that she died of a broken heart, but the doctors called it 'brain fever.'" (W. Whipple, The Story of Young Abraham Lincoln, 1915, biography).

to their model of the human body which included mind, emotions and impulses as integral parts.[49] Unlike in modern medical thought, there was no division between the material body and immaterial psyche, no division between somatic and psychological diseases, and certainly no demand that pathological states be materially visible to the doctor's eyes or instruments. The four bodily humors, the mixture of which determined health or illness, were stirred by all kinds of internal and external influences, be it food intake or physical exercise, the seasons or the time of day, the astrological situation or emotional turmoil. At the same time, the humors and their mixtures were the carriers of emotions: too much black bile made people melancholic, while phlegm made them slow and dense. Similarly, conditions such as fear and paranoia could be explained: strong and dark steam from black bile rose from the stomach to the brain, there clouding reason and causing incorrect perceptions of the world.[50]

In this pre-modern medical model of the human condition—I try to avoid the misleading word "body" because, as we have seen, the model encompasses more than merely the "body"—there is no distinction between what we would call somatic or psychological causes of disease. Any concepts surrounding the term "psychological" are not applicable here.[51]

This explains why medical histories of psychological trauma conventionally start in the second half of the 19th century: the whole idea of psychological trauma only works in the context of modern medicine and its distinction between the somatic and the psychological. The medical technical term "trauma," traditionally used to denote physical injury, is transfered from somatic medicine to the new field of psychology—while still being viewed along the lines of the traditional usage. With the psychological trauma, it is not the skin of the unhurt body which is punctured, but rather the entirety of the psyche which is injured. This parallel construction of bodily and psychological trauma can only occur on the grounds of the division between body

49 For the question of the purely somatic look of pre-modern medicine on madness and psychological functions see in more detail, for example, Porter, "Social Perspective," esp. 54-67, and Stolberg, *Homo patiens*, 222-32. Both authors not only characterize the pre-modern model but describe the first steps towards the idea of a discreet "psyche" in at least some schools of early psychiatry since around 1800—soon crushed by the lasting orientation of 19th century psychiatry along the lines of "scientific" somatic medicine. For the historical changes undergone by the mind/body problem see Rousseau and Porter, "Natural History," on medicine esp. 23-24, 33-34.

50 For humoral pathology with an emphasis on psychological functions see Klibansky et al., *Saturn und Melancholie*, 39-54, 110-24.

51 Similarly Schott, "Das psychische Trauma," 42.

and psyche conceptualized by modern medicine and psychology. [52] At the same time, it is an integral part of our everyday contemporary Western thinking because we are formed by those concepts.

Conclusions

Throughout European history, there always seem to have been ideas suggesting that intense emotions can influence one's health. However, *medical concepts* change very much over time and are tightly bound to contemporaneous explanatory systems. The concept of "psychological trauma" is closely connected to modern medicine and psychology. Accordingly, the terms "trauma" and "traumatization" are exclusively defined in modern conceptualization.

The more specific a concept is and the more it relies on larger explanatory systems (like medicine), the more specific it is to its socio-cultural background. Post-traumatic stress disorder, as a recent concept of psychiatry, might be the right answer for our times, but could change. It can tell us only about this point in time. Therefore, modern medical concepts are problematic when applied to historical contexts. This is especially true for psychological and psychiatric concepts: while the materiality of broken bones should be the same in every time and place, ailments of the soul, such as madness and psychosomatic phenomena, are culture-bound to a very large degree. Concepts of modern psychology and psychiatry in particular are therefore misleading when applied to historical findings.

Even if we use retrospective diagnosis to name and classify historic psychological phenomena, this might not tell us much else. If we identify Erichsen's railway spine as a misguided attempt at explaining PTSD, what more is there to say about it? Is it not much more interesting to attempt to understand historical suffering in the terms of the historical time in question, and in terms of the protagonists' own explanations, assessments and subsumptions according to their world view?

Of course, as historians, we rely on our modern language and our modern thinking to study the past. It is important to open up new questions and new perspectives in historiography. Therefore, we need modern concepts to unlock new ways of thinking about the past. The important thing is to keep in mind which concepts are ours and which are historical, and to be conscious about the limits of their usage.

52 Stolberg, *Homo patiens*, 248–56, discusses the historicity of "trauma" from an entirely different angle but with the same result: he shows how in different historical times, similar "traumatic" experiences lead to different somatic responses (and culture-specific illnesses) in the sufferers.

As I have tried to show here, specific *medical* concepts such as post-traumatic stress disorder are problematic when applied to make sense of historical accounts. However, they can help the historian in realizing what ways of thinking and explaining separate us from those people featured in historical accounts. In most cases, furthermore, those medical concepts are used to explain more general observations, for example the fact known to people in every European epoch that intense feelings and experiences can influence one's health. It is advisable to follow such *more vague phenomena* through time, and to regard the different medical conceptual attempts at an explanation as being changing varieties, none more true than any other.

Outside historiography, there are some circumstances in which retrospective diagnosis might be beneficial. Ancient texts might be read by non-historians from the perspective of their own present needs, for example in counseling or pastoral care, to help sufferers of PTSD to find help by reading biblical accounts of comparable experiences. As a poet, one could write a creative reworking of an ancient tale. Many other practical applications are conceivable, but academic students of trauma-like phenomena in the past need to consider the problem of retrospective diagnosis.

Bibliography

ARRIZABALAGA, J. "Problematizing Retrospective Diagnosis in the History of Disease." *Asclepio* 54 (2000): 51-70.

BIANCHI, B. "Psychiatrists, Soldiers, and Officers in Italy During the Great War." Pages 222-52 in *Traumatic Pasts: History, Psychiatry, and Trauma in the Modern Age 1870-1930*. Edited by M. S. Micale and P. Lerner. Cambridge: Cambridge University Press, 2001.

BINSWANGER, O. *Die Hysterie*. Vienna: Hölder, 1904.

BYNUM, W. F., A. HARDY, S. JACYNA, C. LAWRENCE, and E. M. TANSEY. *The Western Medical Tradition: 1800-2000*. Cambridge: Cambridge University Press, 2006.

CAPLAN, E. "Trains and Trauma in the American Gilded Age." Pages 57-77 in *Traumatic Pasts. History, Psychiatry, and Trauma in the Modern Age 1870-1930*. Edited by M. S. Micale and P. Lerner. Cambridge: Cambridge University Press, 2001.

CHARCOT, J. M. *Leçons sur les maladies du système nerveux faites à la Salpêtrière*. Edited by D. M. Bourneville. 3 vols. Paris: Delahaye & Lecrosnier, 1872-1887.

DIDI-HUBERMAN, G. *Invention of Hysteria: Charcot and the Photographic Iconography of the Salpêtrière*. Translated by Alisa Hartz. Cambridge, Mass.: MIT Press, 2003.

DUDEN, B. *Geschichte unter der Haut: Ein Eisenacher Arzt und seine Patientinnen um 1730*. Stuttgart: Klett-Cotta, 1987.

ECKART, W. U. "Kriegsgewalt und Psychotrauma im Ersten Weltkrieg." Pages 85-105 in *Verletzte Seelen. Möglichkeiten und Perspektiven einer historischen Traumaforschung*. Edited by G. H. Seidler and W. U. Eckart. Gießen: Psychosozial, 2005.

ECKART, W. U., and R. JÜTTE. *Medizingeschichte: Eine Einführung*. Cologne: Böhlau, 2007.

ELLENBERGER, H. F. *The Discovery of the Unconscious: The History and Evolution of Dynamic Psychiatry*. New York: Basic Books, 1970.

ERICHSEN, J. E. *On Railway and other Injuries of the Nervous System*. London: Walton & Maberly, 1866.

ESTERSON, A. "The Mythologizing of Psychoanalytic History: Deception and Self-Deception in Freud's Accounts of the Seduction Theory Episode." *History of Psychiatry* 12 (2001): 329-52.

EULENBURG, A. *Real-Encyclopädie der gesammten Heilkunde.* 26 vols. 3d ed. Vienna: Urban & Schwarzenberg, 1894-1901.

FISCHER-HOMBERGER, E. *Die traumatische Neurose: Vom somatischen zum sozialen Leiden.* Bern: Huber, 1975.

FISCHER-HOMBERGER, E. "Zur Medizingeschichte des Traumas." *Gesnerus* 56 (2001): 260-94.

FLECK, L. *Entstehung und Entwicklung einer wissenschaftlichen Tatsache: Einführung in die Lehre vom Denkstil und Denkkollektiv.* Frankfurt/Main: Suhrkamp, 1994.

FOUCAULT, M. *Maladie mentale et psychologie.* Paris: Presses Universitaires de France, 1962.

FREUD, S. "Zur Ätiologie der Hysterie." [1896] Pages 423-59 in *Sigmund Freud: Gesammelte Werke. Band I: Werke aus den Jahren 1892-1899.* Edited by A. Freud et al. London: Imago, 1952.

—. "Zur Geschichte der psychoanalytischen Bewegung." [1914] Pages 43-113 in *Sigmund Freud. Gesammelte Werke. Band X: Werke aus den Jahren 1913-1917.* Edited by A. Freud et al. London: Imago, 1946.

—. "Selbstdarstellung." [1925] Pages 33-96 in *Sigmund Freud. Gesammelte Werke. Band XIV: Werke aus den Jahren 1925-1931.* Edited by A. Freud et al. London: Imago, 1948.

—. *Briefe an Wilhelm Fließ 1887-1904.* Edited by J. M. Masson. Frankfurt/Main: Fischer, 1986.

FREUD, S., and J. BREUER. "Über den psychischen Mechanismus hysterischer Phänomene." [1893] Pages 27-41 in *Studien über Hysterie.* By S. Freud and J. Breuer. Frankfurt/Main: Fischer, 1991.

FREUD, S., and J. BREUER. *Studien über Hysterie* [1895]. Frankfurt/Main: Fischer, 1991.

GAULD, A. *A History of Hypnotism.* Cambridge: Cambridge University Press, 1992.

GILMAN, S. L., H. KING, R. PORTER, G. S. ROUSSEAU, and E. SHOWALTER. *Hysteria Beyond Freud.* Berkeley: University of California Press, 1993

HACKING, I. "Memory Sciences, Memory Politics." Pages 67-87 in *Tense Past: Cultural Essays in Trauma and Memory.* Edited by P. Antze and M. Lambek. New York: Routledge, 1996.

HARRINGTON, R. "The Railway Accident: Trains, Trauma, and Technological Crises in Nineteenth-Century Britain." Pages 31-56 in *Traumatic Pasts: History, Psychiatry, and Trauma in the Modern Age 1870-1930.* Edited by M. S. Micale and P. Lerner. Cambridge: Cambridge University Press, 2001.

HESS, V., and A. MENDELSOHN. "Cases and Series: Medical Knowledge and Paper Technologies, 1600-1900." *History of Science* 48 (2010): 287-314.

HOFER, H.-G. *Nervenschwäche und Krieg: Modernitätskritik und Krisenbewältigung in der österreichischen Psychiatrie (1880-1920).* Vienna: Böhlau, 2004.

HOFER, H.-G., and L. SAUERTEIG. "Perspektiven einer Kulturgeschichte der Medizin." *Medizinhistorisches Journal* 42 (2007): 105-41.

HOLDORFF, B. "The Fight for 'Traumatic Neurosis', 1889-1916: Hermann Oppenheim and his Opponents in Berlin." *History of Psychiatry* 22 (2011): 465-76.

ISRAËLS, H., and M. SCHATZMAN. "The Seduction Theory." *History of Psychiatry* 4 (1993): 23-59.

JONES, E., and S. WESSELY. "War Syndromes: The Impact of Culture on Medically Unexplained Symptoms." *Medical History* 49 (2005): 55-78.

JONES, J. M. "Great Pains: Famous People with Headaches." *Cephalalgia* 19 (1999): 627-30.

JORDANOVA, L. "The Social Construction of Medical Knowledge." *Social History of Medicine* 8 (1995): 361-81.

KLIBANSKY, R., E. PANOFSKY, and F. SAXL. *Saturn und Melancholie: Studien zur Geschichte der Naturphilosophie und Medizin, der Religion und der Kunst.* Frankfurt/Main: Suhrkamp, 1990.

KLOOCKE, R., H.-P. SCHMIEDEBACH, and S. PRIEBE. "Psychische Ereignisse - organische Interpretationen: Traumakonzepte in der deutschen Psychiatrie seit 1889." *Gesnerus* 67 (2010): 73-97.

LACHMUND, J., and STOLLBERG, G. *The Social Construction of Illness: Illness and Medical Knowledge in Past and Present*. Stuttgart: Franz Steiner, 1992.

LEESE, P. "'Why Are They Not Cured?' British Shellshock Treatment During the Great War." Pages 205-21 in *Traumatic Pasts: History, Psychiatry, and Trauma in the Modern Age 1870-1930*. Edited by M. S. Micale and P. Lerner. Cambridge: Cambridge University Press, 2001.

—. *Shell Shock: Traumatic Neurosis and the British Soldiers of the First World War*. New York: Palgrave, 2002.

LERNER, P. "From Traumatic Neurosis to Male Hysteria: The Decline and Fall of Hermann Oppenheim, 1889-1919." Pages 140-71 in *Traumatic Pasts: History, Psychiatry, and Trauma in the Modern Age 1870-1930*. Edited by M. S. Micale and P. Lerner. Cambridge: Cambridge University Press, 2001.

—. *Hysterical Men: War, Psychiatry, and the Politics of Trauma in Germany, 1890-1930*. Ithaca, N.Y.: Cornell University Press, 2003.

LEVEN, K.-H. "Krankheiten: Historische Deutung versus retrospektive Diagnose." Pages 153-85 in *Medizingeschichte: Aufgaben, Methoden, Perspektiven*. Edited by N. Paul and T. Schlich. Frankfurt/Main: Campus, 1998.

—. "'At Times These Ancient Facts Seem to Lie Before Me Like a Patient on a Hospital Bed': Retrospective Diagnosis and Ancient Medical History." Pages 369-86 in *Magic and Rationality in Ancient Near Eastern and Graeco-Roman Medicine*. Edited by H. F. J. Horstmanshoff and M. Stol. Leiden: Brill, 2004.

LEYS, R. *Trauma: A Genealogy*. Chicago: Chicago University Press, 2000.

MASSON, J. M. *The Assault on Truth: Freud's Suppression of the Seduction Theory*. New York: Farrar, Straus and Giroux, 1984.

MAY-TOLZMANN, U. "Die Verwandlung der Neurose in der Zeit um 1900." *Zeitschrift für psychoanalytische Psychotherapie* 15 (1993): 39-55.

—. *Freuds frühe klinische Theorie, 1894-1896: Wiederentdeckung und Rekonstruktion*. Tübingen: Diskord, 1996.

MICALE, M. S. *Approaching Hysteria: Disease and Its Interpretations*. Princeton: Princeton University Press, 1995.

—. "Jean-Martin Charcot and *les névroses traumatiques*: From Medicine to Culture in French Trauma Theory of the Late Nineteenth Century." Pages 115-39 in *Traumatic Pasts: History, Psychiatry, and Trauma in the Modern Age 1870-1930*. Edited by M. S. Micale and P. Lerner. Cambridge: Cambridge University Press, 2001.

—. *Hysterical Men. The Hidden History of Male Nervous Illness*. Cambridge, Mass.: Harvard University Press, 2008.

MICALE, M. S., and P. LERNER, eds. *Traumatic Pasts: History, Psychiatry and Trauma in the Modern Age, 1870-1930*. Cambridge: Cambridge University Press, 2001.

MICHL, S. *Im Dienste des "Volkskörpers": Deutsche und französische Ärzte im Ersten Weltkrieg*. Göttingen: Vandenhoeck & Ruprecht, 2007.

NOLTE, K. *Gelebte Hysterie: Erfahrung, Eigensinn und psychiatrische Diskurse im Anstaltsalltag um 1900*. Frankfurt/Main: Campus, 2003.

OPPENHEIM, H. "Der Krieg und die traumatischen Neurosen." *Berliner Klinische Wochenschrift* 52 (1915): 257-61.

—. *Die traumatischen Neurosen nach den in der Nervenklinik der Charité in den letzten 5 Jahren gesammelten Beobachtungen*. Berlin: Hirschwald, 1889.

PORTER, R. "Barely Touching: A Social Perspective on Mind and Body." Pages 45-80 in *The Languages of Psyche: Mind and Body in Enlightenment Thought*. Edited by G. S. Rousseau. Berkeley: University of California Press, 1990.

—. *The Greatest Benefit to Mankind: A Medical History of Humanity.* Hammersmith, London: Fontana, 1999.

Pressman, J. D. "Concepts of Mental Illness in the West." Pages 59-85 in *Cambridge World History of Human Disease.* Edited by K. F. Kiple. Cambridge: Cambridge University Press, 1993.

Priebe, S., M. Nowak and H.-P. Schmiedebach. "Trauma und Psyche in der deutschen Psychiatrie seit 1889." *Psychiatrische Praxis* 29 (2002): 3-9.

Roudebush, M. "A Battle of Nerves: Hysteria and its Treatments in France During World War I." Pages 253-79 in *Traumatic Pasts: History, Psychiatry, and Trauma in the Modern Age 1870-1930.* Edited by M. S. Micale and P. Lerner. Cambridge: Cambridge University Press, 2001.

Rousseau, G. S., and R. Porter. "Introduction: Towards a Natural History of Mind and Body." Pages 3-44 in *The Languages of Psyche: Mind and Body in Enlightenment Thought.* Edited by G. S. Rousseau. Berkeley: University of California Press, 1990.

Schmersahl, K. *Medizin und Geschlecht: Zur Konstruktion der Kategorie Geschlecht im medizinischen Diskurs des 19. Jahrhunderts.* Opladen: Leske & Budrich, 1998.

Schott, H. "Das psychische Trauma in medizinhistorischer Perspektive: Von Paracelsus bis Freud." Pages 41-55 in *Verletzte Seelen: Möglichkeiten und Perspektiven einer historischen Traumaforschung.* Edited by G. H. Seidler and W. U. Eckart. Gießen: Psychosozial, 2005.

Scull, A. T. *Hysteria: The Biography.* Oxford: Oxford University Press, 2009.

Seidler, G. H. "Einleitung: Geschichte der Psychotraumatologie." Pages 4-10 in *Posttraumatische Belastungsstörungen.* Edited by A. Maercker. Heidelberg: Springer, 2009.

Seidler, G. H., and W. U. Eckart. "Einleitung: 'Psychotraumatologie,' eine Disziplin im Werden." Pages 7-25 in *Verletzte Seelen: Möglichkeiten und Perspektiven einer historischen Traumaforschung.* Edited by G. H. Seidler and W. U. Eckart. Gießen: Psychosozial, 2005.

Stolberg, M. *Homo patiens: Krankheits- und Körpererfahrung in der Frühen Neuzeit.* Cologne: Böhlau, 2003.

Sulloway, F. J. *Freud. Biologie der Seele: Jenseits der psychoanalytischen Legende.* Cologne: Maschke, 1982.

Temkin, O. "An Essay On the Usefulness of Medical History for Medicine." [1946] Pages 68-100 in *The Double Face of Janus and Other Essays in the History of Medicine.* By O. Temkin. Baltimore: Johns Hopkins University Press, 1977.

Thomann, K.-D., and M. Rauschmann. "Die 'posttraumatische Belastungsstörung': Historische Aspekte einer 'modernen' psychischen Erkrankung im deutschen Sprachraum." *Medizinhistorisches Journal* 38 (2003): 103-38.

Winter, J. "Shell-Shock and the Cultural History of the Great War." *Journal of Contemporary History* 35 (2000): 7-11.

Young, A. *The Harmony of Illusions: Inventing Post-traumatic Stress Disorder.* Princeton: Princeton University Press, 1995.

—. "Memory Sciences, Memory Politics." Pages 89-102 in *Tense Past. Cultural Essays in Trauma and Memory.* Edited by P. Antze and M. Lambek. New York: Routledge, 1996.

Kirsten Nielsen

Post-traumatic Stress Disorder and the Book of Job*

Abstract

Ronnie Janoff-Bulman lists three types of fundamental assumptions: *The world is benevolent. The world is meaningful. The self is worthy.* The same assumptions are found in the book of Job. According to Janoff-Bulman traumatised people experience "shattered assumptions." Job's experiences shatter the fundamental assumptions that he has made about *God*. It is further shown that Roberts Carroll's claim that *dissonance gives rise to hermeneutic* aids in understanding that the book of Job is an example of hermeneutic activity coming to terms with cognitive dissonance in a literary form.

The purpose of this article on Post-traumatic Stress Disorder and the book of Job is to demonstrate how studies of PTSD can contribute to an understanding of the book of Job. My starting-point is Ronnie Janoff-Bulman's book *Shattered Assumptions*, published in 1992. In the introductory chapter, *Our Fundamental Assumptions*, she describes how we normally perceive human existence. We are equipped with what she calls:

> a conceptual system, developed over time, that provides us with expectations about the world and ourselves. This conceptual system is best represented by a set of assumptions or internal representations that reflect and guide our interactions in the world and generally enable us to function effectively.[1]

Ronnie Janoff-Bulman lists three types of such assumptions about the world and ourselves:

> The world is benevolent.
> The world is meaningful.
> The self is worthy.[2]

These fundamental assumptions help to ensure that under normal circumstances our everyday life can pass without major problems. But if people are exposed to violent events such as war, violence, natural disasters, and such-

* Translated by Edward Broadbridge.

1 Janoff-Bulman, *Shattered Assumptions*, 5.

2 Ibid., 6.

like, they will experience how these assumptions do not correspond to reality. The world has shown itself as evil, meaningless, unreasonable.

Immediately after stating the three fundamental assumptions Janoff-Bulman mentions the book of Job, and affirms that generation after generation has been fascinated by this work. She concludes:

> The attention this biblical story has received reflects the deeply disturbing nature of seemingly unwarranted human suffering; the attention it has received reflects our unwitting acceptance of the three fundamental assumptions.[3]

In fully agreeing with this assessment I wish here to look more closely at *how* these fundamental assumptions are formulated in the book of Job.

Fundamental Assumptions in the Book of Job

The book of Job is a literary masterpiece. We do not know the author. What we have to deal with is a text about a man called Job, his friends and his God. Job and his friends have been brought up to follow classical wisdom and its optimistic view of existence. The world was created by God, and the world is a good place for good people. This is made clear in the introduction to the book of Job, where we read how God has blessed the righteous, devout Job with a large family and great wealth (Job 1:1–3). This corresponds very well with Janoff-Bulman's first example of a fundamental assumption: "The world is benevolent."

The second, "The world is meaningful," also appears in the book of Job. Both Job and his friends assume that God rewards those who do good and punishes those who do evil. The friends make this abundantly clear when they try to convince Job that his misfortune is God's just punishment (Job 8:1–7; see also Prov 10:28–29). And the same assumption lies behind Job's complaint about God's injustice. It is because he expects God to *bless* the righteous that he reacts so vehemently to the misfortunes which strike him undeservedly.

Also the third assumption: "The self is worthy" is found in the book of Job. Job is convinced that it is possible to be a righteous person and that indeed he himself is an example of just such a person (cf. Job 29). The author underlines this when he writes that in the end God acknowledges that Job's complaints are justified. Job is indeed, and will continue to be, a pious, honorable man, and this is further emphasized when God finally turns his fate around, so that Job receives the blessings that are his due.

3 Ibid., 6.

Janoff-Bulman's three fundamental assumptions thus help us to see the assumptions that underlie the book of Job.

Shattered Assumptions in the Book of Job

According to Janoff-Bulman, these fundamental assumptions help to make everyday life *work* for us. But major problems arise when people experience violent, traumatic events. For it turns out that our fundamental assumptions do not correspond to reality. Traumatized people experience what Janoff-Bulman calls "shattered assumptions."[4] And that is precisely what happens in the book of Job. Early in the story misfortunes suddenly rain down on Job. Though unable to see any reason why, Job loses his cattle, his servants, his sons and daughters, and finally his health and his good name (Job 1:13–19; 2:7–10). No longer is the world benevolent and meaningful. And even though he continues to think of himself as a worthy man, his associates think otherwise.

To begin with, Job accepts what is happening, but from ch. 3 onwards he begins to accuse God of punishing him for no reason. The charge only makes sense on the fundamental assumption which Job has so far held that God is just and repays good with good and evil with evil. This belief is supported by the words of his friend Elifaz: "Consider now: Who, being innocent, has ever perished? Where were the upright ever destroyed?" (Job 4:7), or as Elihu says, "He does not keep the wicked alive but gives the afflicted their rights. He does not take his eyes off the righteous" (Job 36:6). Job's experience proves something else, however, and he must therefore draw the conclusion: "It is all the same; that is why I say, 'He destroys both the blameless and the wicked!'" (Job 9:22; cf. also Job 10:6–7; 27:1–2).

What Job experiences is clearly 'shattered assumptions.'

Reinterpretation of Previous Assumptions

In the second part of her book Janoff-Bulman examines the consequences of a traumatic experience and underlines that traumatized people react with "intense fear, terror, and helplessness."[5] For the essence of traumatic experi-

4 Ibid., 52: "These traumatic events do not produce the psychological equivalent of superficial scratches that heal readily, but deep bodily wounds that require far more in the way of restorative efforts. The injury is to the victim's inner world. Core assumptions are shattered by the traumatic experience."

5 Ibid., 49.

ence is "the abrupt disintegration of one's inner world."[6] How then does life continue for such traumatized people? Janoff-Bulman lists a number of ways, including one that we shall concentrate on here: namely, how they reinterpret *previous* assumptions. This is a difficult process, for they are faced with a massive dilemma. Janoff-Bulman describes it thus:

> The victim is stuck between two untenable cognitive-emotional choices: preexisting assumptions that are no longer viable in describing the world and oneself and new assumptions that not only involve a total reworking of prior views, but are themselves extremely negative and threatening.[7]

This is the dilemma that Job is facing. He is unwilling to give up his belief in a just God, but his experiences belie this trust. When he is faithful to God, as we read in the prologue, it is because the question of God's righteousness is not under discussion. Job justifies his acceptance of his misfortunes with the argument that God is the creator and can therefore both give *and* take. Job therefore makes the following confession:

> Naked I came from my mother's womb,
> And naked I shall depart!
> The Lord gave and the Lord has taken away;
> May the name of the Lord be praised. (Job 1:21)

So at first Job does not consider whether God's giving and taking is part of his righteousness. He avoids asking the unpleasant question about God's justice and chooses instead to react by singing praises to his creator God.[8] But already in his first real speech (Job 3) he radically revises this way of relating to God. He curses the day that he was born, and follows up with an accusation that God has treated him unjustly! In so doing Job changes genre. No longer is he singing a song of praise. Now he wishes to take the matter to court, and his tone is correspondingly a combination of complaint and accusation.

Through her research Ronnie Janoff-Bulman has established that we humans are extremely conservative about our fundamental assumptions.[9] This too is clearly the case with Job's friends, who believe that his sufferings are God's righteous punishment. Yet Job too wishes to *retain* his faith in a just God. So the process of interpreting his new insights causes him pain and induces angst.

Ronnie Janoff-Bulman distinguishes between traumatizing acts that are caused by one or more people with malicious intention, and natural disasters,

6 Ibid., 63.
7 Ibid., 93.
8 Cf. the tendency to deny reality as a step towards re-establishing the previous existence. Cf. ibid., 96–101.
9 Ibid., 26–45.

for which no one is responsible. There is no *intention* behind natural disasters, she says, and that is why we are seized with great insecurity when they come. Suddenly the world seems less controllable. Nor do traumatized people accept any personal *responsibility* for a natural disaster. However, when violence against a person is deliberate, victims often question themselves: Could they have acted otherwise and avoided the attack? Were they themselves in some way to blame for the attack?[10]

If we apply Janoff-Bulman's observations to the book of Job, it becomes clear that Job is facing a double catastrophe. Like modern man, he experiences an impotence in the face of natural disasters. He cannot control the world, nor can he insure himself against misfortune by living a righteous life—as classical wisdom would have it. But worse is to follow. Job is convinced that the misfortunes that strike him come from a malicious God who is deliberately trying to destroy him. In Job's case we meet both the experience of a world that is uncontrollable *and* the conviction that a spiteful God is behind it. Job therefore experiences not only great insecurity but also a dreadful angst. And yet. The belief that it is God who is causing his downfall does not persuade Job to admit any guilt of his *own*!

Job is now forced to deal with his negative experiences. One of the ways in which he does so is to supplement them with other insights. Janoff-Bulman examines the various ways of coming to terms with traumatic experiences,[11] but she does not include the type that Job employs: holding firm to his hope in God.[12] In Job 16:19 he says that he has a witness in heaven, an advocate to whom he can turn. And further on we read the following:

I know that my Redeemer lives,
and that in the end he will stand upon the earth.
And after my skin has been destroyed,
yet in my flesh I will see God;
I myself will see him with my own eyes—I, and not another.
How my heart yearns within me! (Job 19:25-27)

Job thus holds firm to both sides of God's being. He has not lost hope in God, yet nor has he given up complaining against him.

10 Ibid., 76-83.

11 Ibid., 93-114.

12 There is no mention of ‚God' in Janoff-Bulman's Subject Index, only ‚Acts of God', which is used about natural disasters behind which there lies no intention. Only in a few places is God mentioned: "Belief in a God who rewards a moral existence also reflects belief in a meaningful world, despite the fact that direct control does not rest with the individual performing the deeds but rather with a God responsible for making the ultimate judgment about one's outcomes" (Ibid., 11). See also her mention (pp. 137-138) of the ways in which various religions attempt to give meaning to suffering.

A further important step for Job in working through his experiences is the address from God that we read in chapters 38–41. Here it is not Job but God himself who takes the floor. God describes the created world as an ordered cosmos. But in the midst of this cosmos there is nevertheless room for two great beasts of chaos, Behemoth and Leviathan. In God's perspective these chaotic powers are part of creation, of the world he has created, and therefore he retains his power over them. This is new information for Job. But for us readers there is a sense of déjà vu over this depiction of the great beasts of chaos to whom God has granted a certain amount of latitude, but on whom he has also set limits. The same is true of Satan, as we meet him in the prologue. Both he and the beasts of chaos have a scope within which to work, but God still holds ultimate power. This opens up for the possibility that not everything that happens in the world is just.[13]

Moreover, God's address actually fulfills Job's wish to see God face to face in a legal action. As we have seen, Job employs the genres of both lament/complaint and accusation in his plea. And both demand a response from God. The plaintive asks for God's help and expects God to send an oracle of salvation. Legal action requires that both parties are present and that the judge gives his ruling. And this is indeed what happens in the book of Job: God appears and Job's meeting with him becomes more important than the actual legal proceedings. And in the event, Job simply humbles himself before God and confesses:

My ears had heard of you
But now my eyes have seen you.
Therefore I despise myself and repent
In dust and ashes. (Job 42:5–6)

As readers we might imagine that nothing has changed. Job has repented and has gone back to his original fundamental assumptions of God's righteousness and the world as being good and meaningful. However, in the epilogue a change occurs. God asserts that in contrast to his friends Job has spoken the *truth*. In other words God declares that indeed he has not treated Job fairly. For Satan can make his presence felt and the beasts of chaos can create disorder. Thus God admits that Job is right to complain. But we never learn what this means for Job's fundamental assumptions. For from now on Job is silent. We are only told that he intercedes for his friends, and that "the Lord made him prosperous again and gave him twice as much as he had before" (Job 42:10).

The book ends almost like a fairy-tale, but readers are left with the question: Did Job *really* change his fundamental assumptions about God and the

13 Cf. Nielsen, *Satan*, 69–71 and 92–99.

world? Is his humble reaction also an expression of a deep realization? Or does his meeting with the mighty God mean that his reflection is suspended in favor of awe? And one further question: Is this just about Job and his experiences? By way of answer we must turn to certain observations on the phenomenon of 'cognitive dissonance'.

Cognitive Dissonance

In his book *When Prophecy Failed* Old Testament scholar Robert Carroll has analyzed the concept of cognitive dissonance. As the title suggests, the book deals with the consequences for a prophecy that did *not* come to pass. Cognitive dissonance is very closely associated with what Ronnie Janoff-Bulman calls shattered assumptions. But where Janoff-Bulman examines phenomena and people in the present, Carroll works with the texts of the past. His research material resembles more the book of Job than Janoff-Bulman's studies of traumatized people nowadays.

One of the most important results of Carroll's studies in prophecy is that the experience of cognitive dissonance gives rise to hermeneutic activity. He writes:

> The important principle for this study is *dissonance gives rise to hermeneutic.* That is, the experience of dissonance forced individuals or groups to reinterpret their basic material or the contemporary events so as to avoid dissonance.[14]

Carroll demonstrates in his book how cognitive dissonance has led to hermeneutic activity in the form of reinterpretation of prophetic oracles, and from there to literary activity.[15] In my view, the book of Job is also an example of hermeneutic activity coming to terms with cognitive dissonance. The author of the book of Job works with the general human experience of cognitive dissonance and the consequent reinterpretation of previous assumptions. And the consequence takes a *literary form.* Whether the author's purpose was to deal with his *own* experiences of cognitive dissonance, or whether he is dealing with collective experiences in continuation of the destruction of Jerusalem and the Babylonian exile we cannot know. But what we do have is a work of literature, the book of Job, which we can use to interpret our *own* existence. From this perspective it becomes less important whether the person Job, when he hears God agreeing with him, actually reaches a greater understanding of who and what God is. Nor does it matter whether his meeting with God is more important for him than the question of God's righteousness.

14 Carroll, *Prophecy Failed*, 110.

15 This corresponds to the need for traumatized people to talk about the traumatic event (Janoff-Bulman, *Shattered Assumptions*, 108–110).

Under all circumstances we are dealing here with *models* for how a traumatic experience can be worked through. This can happen through further reinterpretation of the fundamental assumptions concerning God or through a religious experience; the one does not exclude the other. Which of these possibilities seems the most convincing is up to readers to decide. For it is the readers' task, depending on their own life experience of cognitive dissonance to determine what can carry them on through life. Job's answer is silence, and that hands over the floor to us, the readers.

Conclusion

Carroll points to the hermeneutic activity that follows from cognitive dissonance. The book of Job is a good example of a literary treatment of this. Certain fundamental experiences are made available to others who must go through the painful process of revising their image of God.

The results that Ronnie Janoff-Bulman has achieved in her studies of Post-traumatic Stress Disorder are also a help for us biblical scholars in studying the book of Job. Her demonstration of the three fundamental assumptions can lead us to see how the book of Job builds on such assumptions.

Moreover, by comparing the book of Job with Janoff-Bulman's descriptions of the struggle of traumatized people to re-create a meaningful existence, we gain an insight into where the emphasis lies in the biblical book. It is striking that Job does not complain about the loss of his children, and that the writer at no point indicates that the new children whom Job acquires can in any way replace the dead ones. The book of Job deals first and foremost with the fundamental assumptions that Job has made about *God*. And it is here that Job's assumptions are shattered.

For those who wish to include God in their interpretation of life the book of Job still offers a relevant message as to how we can deal with new experiences, draw in other perspectives, and move on with our lives, whether we have had what modern psychologists define as traumatic experiences, or we are dealing with religious qualms.

For it is not only traumatized people who experience how their image of God may crack in the meeting with reality. If that image is limited to an idea of a good and loving father who always looks after his children and protects them against all evil, it will sooner or later prove inadequate.[16] And here a work such as the book of Job demonstrates how it is possible to reinterpret fundamental assumptions without giving up a fundamental trust in God.

16 In this context it is interesting to note that the name 'Job' means 'Where is father?' Cf. Nielsen, *Satan*, 99.

Bibliography

Janoff-Bulman, R. *Shattered Assumptions: Towards a New Psychology of Trauma*. New York: The Free Press, 1992.

Carroll, R. P. *When Prophecy Failed: Receptions and responses to failure in the Old Testament prophetic traditions*. London: SCM Press, 1979.

Festinger, L., H. W. Riecken, and S. Schachter. *When Prophecy Fails: A Social and Psychological Study of a Modern Group that Predicted the Destruction of the World*. Minneapolis: University of Minnesota Press, 1956.

Nielsen, K. *Satan: The Prodigal Son? A Family Problem in the Bible*. Sheffield: Sheffield Academic Press, 1998.

Christopher G. Frechette

Destroying the Internalized Perpetrator

A Healing Function of the Violent Language against Enemies in the Psalms

Abstract

Violent language against enemies in the Psalter has proven nettlesome for good reason. Addressing to God wishes for the harm of one's enemies can all too easily be interpreted as license to engage in actual violence, and even the voicing of such wishes in prayer can be interpreted to imply a misanthropic character in God. However, such interpretations are as unnecessary as they are disturbing. In this essay, I propose to identify a healing function for the violent language against enemies in the Psalms, a function that can be accessed without harming anyone. In order to articulate a paradigm for such a healing function, I draw upon a model employed in therapeutic treatment intended to foster healing for trauma survivors. This model supplements reinterpretation of traumatic experience with a symbolic, safe, and controlled expression of intense anger resulting from that experience.

Introduction

One does not have to turn many pages in the Psalter before finding descriptions of God harming, or being asked to harm, persons or groups that are presented as deserving it. In modern scholarship, a common overarching designation for such adversaries is "the enemies." Whether acting as adversaries toward the individual speaker or the people of Israel as a collective, the enemies are presumed to have acted unjustly and thus also to have offended God. It is reasonable to suppose that the ancients who recited the psalms at least in some cases would have associated the psalmist's descriptions of the violent fate of the enemies with actual persons upon whom they wished such a fate. Yet, we may also consider the psychological function of reciting the prayers that contain descriptions of God enacting harm against enemies. It is this psychological function upon which I focus here. Specifically, I propose that praying psalms that contain imagery of God destroying perpetrators of injustice could have a healing function for people who have been traumatized.

Among contemporary disciplines, trauma and its effects are approached from various perspectives. Drawing on the theoretical works of Judith Herman, a professor of psychiatry, and Peter Levine, a psychologist, I will employ the concept of trauma broadly to refer to an experience of being overwhelmed and terrified that leaves specific types of profound and lasting changes within the victim. I will also discuss three fundamental tasks in the process of recovery from being traumatized. This broad manner of defining trauma and recovery allows for the identification of a resonance between what contemporary psychology has identified as the experience and effects of trauma and particular descriptors in the psalms. It further provides a framework for proposing a healing function for the violent language against enemies.

Of the effects of traumatization, particularly relevant here is the way in which being traumatized by someone confuses the victim's moral compass and can impress deep within the person—often out of consciousness—the felt sense that he or she deserves to be mistreated. This felt sense of worthlessness and abandonment is intimately linked to the lingering memory of the perpetrator, and because of the emotional intensity of the trauma, this tandem tends to persist in affecting the survivor's interpretation of his/her ongoing experience, producing injurious meaning. For this reason, I refer to this combination of memory and belief as the "internalized perpetrator." I propose that the recitation of prayers that include descriptions of God enacting or being asked to enact harm against enemies, sometimes in violent detail, could have a healing effect on trauma survivors both in the ancient world and today.[1] Such healing does not depend in any way upon actual harm being done to anyone. Dramatic and emotionally intense depictions of God acting against the enemies have significant capacity to confront the deeply embedded memory of the violation and the beliefs spawned by it and to impress upon the survivor that both are wrong. In other words, they can advance the work of destroying the "internalized perpetrator."

I first address hermeneutical issues that arise for interpreting the violent imagery against the enemies in the psalms. I proceed by showing how the language describing the enemy's activity and the resulting experience of the speaker resonate with traumatic experience. I then discuss how the violent imagery against the enemies can be understood to address the psychological effects of trauma. I illustrate my discussion with passages from Psalms 9–10, which form a single acrostic, and from Psalm 18.

1 In proposing a healing function, I do not imply a removal of all effects of traumatization. Rather, I argue for particular ways in which ritualized recitation of these psalms could contribute to the task of remembering and grieving the traumatic experience (see discussion below).

Hermeneutical Considerations: Safety, Justice, and Healing

The framework within which biblical texts depicting justified violence are interpreted is of crucial importance. Those who interpret such texts in the context of the faith communities that presume them to be revelatory must attend also to the challenging task of arguing for how they ought or ought not to be employed. Such texts have been used in dangerous ways in the past, and the community has a responsibility to educate people as to their proper use. For instance, it may seem obvious that using biblical texts describing the ban (חֵרֶם), the practice of total destruction of a population, as a license to kill people is wrong. Yet, the massacre of indigenous populations by Christian colonizers is but one example of the horrific use of such texts.[2]

Many Christian interpreters of psalms that seek violence against enemies have tended to construe them as wishing actual harm and so have found them radically at odds with New Testament teaching, with its presumption against enacting violence and revenge. Erich Zenger observed among Christian theologians a common hermeneutical strategy for coming to terms with such passages. They see the function of such texts as a negative one: the violent images against enemies in the psalms serve best to highlight the superiority of New Testament teaching.[3]

But Zenger argued for a different hermeneutic, one that interprets the language of enmity in the psalms as poetic speech, the primary function of which is to plea to God for justice; and he emphasized the necessity of educating contemporary audiences regarding God's activity as judge in the Bible.[4] Broadly speaking, God's judgment is on behalf of the victims of injustice

2 For instance, in the mid-sixteenth century, the Dominican bishop Bartolomé de las Casas argued against using Deuteronomy 7 and the book of Joshua to justify such massacres (*In Defense*, 105–12). John Collins has recounted a number of horrific cases in which the biblical ban has been used to justify violence, and he observes that behind them lies the problematic tendency of people to use the Bible to confer an aura of certitude on any position that it can be construed to support (Collins, *Does the Bible*).

3 "The theological problem of the 'psalms of violence' has its full impact where there is an attempt to reconcile the (real or supposed) alien feeling of these psalms with their canonical and biblical quality by granting some positive function to their very strangeness. This usually is accomplished by use of an underlying dialectic metaphor that appears in several variations.... The 'strangeness' of the Old Testament in contrast to the message of the justifying grace of the New Testament became, in reality, a dialectical principle of Lutheran dogmatic theology for a whole series of influential authors .... They have in common an adherence to the canonical Old Testament and its salvific significance for Christians as well, although *e contrario*—that is, according to them Christians discover in the Old Testament the 'old' human being also present in themselves as long as and whenever they do not believe in the message of Christ" (Zenger, *God*, 16–17).

4 Ibid., 63–76. Zenger explained that contrary to popular perception, the biblical notion of God as judge is neither vindictive nor misanthropic. In modern languages, "vengeance" connotes personal retaliation or actions stemming from uncontrolled emotions as distinct

and for the purpose of restoring things as they should be; the wicked are to be confronted in their injustice in a way that they may honor justice through their repentance.[5] In this interpretive framework, Zenger emphasizes that to those who are oppressed the psalms against enemies afford hope and strength for resistance and for holding fast to their human dignity, even when it is being trodden under foot.[6] Psalm 9:3–11 illustrates this point:

When my enemies turned back,
they stumbled and perished before you.
For you have maintained my just cause;
you have sat on the throne giving righteous judgment.
You have rebuked the nations,
you have destroyed the wicked;
you have blotted out their name forever and ever.
The enemies have vanished in everlasting ruins;
their cities you have rooted out;
the very memory of them has perished.
But the LORD sits enthroned forever,
he has established his throne for judgment.
He judges the world with righteousness;
he judges the peoples with equity.
The LORD is a stronghold for the oppressed,
a stronghold in times of trouble.
And those who know your name put their trust in you,
for you, O LORD, have not forsaken those who seek you.
Sing praises to the LORD, who dwells in Zion.
Declare his deeds among the peoples.[7]

By confronting God in an emphatic way with their situation of suffering, these psalms help people to live with the paradoxical situation of believing in a God of justice who allows such injustice.[8] I will take up in detail this func-

from legal means of dealing with offenses; by contrast, God's enacting vengeance (נקם) guards against human emotional excess and seeks to restore order (ibid., 71). The monograph on the meaning and function of the root נקם by Hendrik Peels supports this position (Peels, *Vengeance*, reference courtesy of Brent Strawn). The appeal to God in these psalms depends on the presupposition that God is personally touched by injustice, and is even called into question by it (Zenger, *God*, 71). By anticipating a response from God, these psalms challenge assumptions that God is static (ibid., 74). Zenger emphasized that the psalms are poetic prayers open to many different actualizations (ibid., 76). The images of vengeance in the psalms may have different functions in different contexts, but generally speaking, they confront us with the reality of violence in our world, and especially the perpetrators of violence; they also confront the people who pray them (ibid., 84–85).

5 Ibid., 64.

6 Ibid., 65.

7 All English translations of biblical texts are from the NRSV.

8 Zenger, *God*, 66.

tion of using dramatic imagery to come to terms with the suffering that results from being violated and develop it by interpreting these psalm texts in light of the experience of trauma survivors and the process by which they can recover.

The interpretive framework that I propose relies on the following insight from contemporary psychology echoed by Judith Herman: for the victims of violence, healing of injuries to their sense of identity and dignity can occur without respect to any aspect of the fate of the actual perpetrator of the violence.[9] Thus, to propose a healing function for the ritualized recitation of violent imagery against the enemies one ought not to give the slightest impression that people should intend that their adversaries be harmed in any way. The recovery process of trauma survivors *may* be helped by the perpetrator's being held accountable by the criminal justice system, acknowledging the wrong done, or making restitution. However, as explained below, the only *necessary* role that the perpetrator has in the survivor's recovery process is a symbolic one. For ancient Israelites as well as modern victims of violent crime, it may seem as if one could find peace only when one's assailant is punished. However, one's recovery from trauma does not depend on the perpetrator's acknowledging the wrong, making restitution, or being punished.

Traumatic Experience and Its Resonance in the Psalter

Many descriptions of the psalmist's experience of (corporate or individual) self and enemies in relationship to God resonate with contemporary descriptions of how trauma is perceived and of how it affects the self-perception of those who survive it. It is therefore useful here to draw upon contemporary descriptions of both the way trauma is perceived and its lasting effects on the survivor's emotions and cognition.

In the words of Peter Levine: "Trauma occurs when we are intensely frightened and are either physically restrained or perceive that we are trapped. We freeze in paralysis and/or collapse in overwhelming helplessness."[10] Judith Herman describes trauma as occurring when one is overwhelmed and rendered helpless, when action is of no avail, and it results in feelings of intense fear, helplessness, loss of control, and threat of annihilation: "Traumatic events produce profound and lasting changes in physiological arousal, emotion, cognition, and memory."[11] Perceptions of self and world are also profoundly affected: "Traumatic events destroy the victim's fundamental assumptions about the safety of the world, the positive value of the self, and the

9 See below the summary of Herman's discussion of revenge and compensation fantasies.

10 Levine, *Unspoken*, 48.

11 Herman, *Trauma*, 33–34.

meaningful order of creation."[12] Among the feelings that, long after the events of the trauma, may continue to be brought about by these changes are anxiety, fear, helplessness, and shame. These feelings occur in connection with beliefs about the self as being utterly abandoned, worthless, and in cases where the trauma occurs at the hands of a perpetrator, deserving of, or somehow responsible for, the mistreatment.[13] Such beliefs function as what psychologists call "core beliefs" or "schemas" in that they remain largely unconscious and serve as interpretive frames that generate thoughts and emotions by filtering one's experiences.[14] To illustrate, when Sue walks by Bill without acknowledging him, he feels rejected and pained as a result of interpreting the event through the core belief, unconscious to him at that moment, that he lacks value.

Trauma may occur in a single event, but chronic trauma occurs in a situation of captivity, such as imprisonment or domestic child abuse.[15] Chronic trauma produces much more complex and often more intractable symptoms than does a single traumatic event.[16] Trauma severely damages the victim's capacity to relate to others with trust, and God is implicated; this damage is more severe in cases of chronic trauma, in which the victim has repeatedly experienced the perpetrator as omnipotent.[17] Survivors of chronic trauma often carry particularly intense justifiable rage within themselves, and they are likely to direct it at those whom they perceive to have had the power to help them but did not, and especially at God.[18] Domestic child abuse can lead to deformations of personality development that leave the abused child without normal capacities for emotional self-regulation and emotional self-soothing.[19] The resulting compromised ability to experience safety and comfort develops in concert with deeply embedded beliefs that the child is fundamentally unacceptable, bad, abandoned, alone, and unworthy of love and respect.[20]

12 Ibid., 51.

13 Cf. ibid., 101-3.

14 The idea that "core beliefs" or "schemas" give rise to thoughts and emotions is foundational for the influential form of psychotherapy initially developed independently by Aaron T. Beck and Albert Ellis, and which later became known as cognitive behavioral therapy (CBT) (Hofmann, *Modern*, 1-4).

15 On repeated trauma as occurring in captivity, see Herman, *Trauma*, 74-86; on the syndrome of chronic trauma, ibid., 86-95.

16 Ibid., 86-87.

17 Ibid., 51-56, 93-94.

18 Ibid., 94-95.

19 Ibid., 106-7.

20 Whether as a result of physical abuse or emotional neglect, the deformations of personality development resulting from childhood trauma are similar: "The abused child is unable to form inner representations of a safe, consistent caretaker. This in turn prevents the development of normal capacities for emotional self-regulation. The fragmentary, idealized

We may assume that ancient Israelites who prayed the psalms would have experienced in a variety of circumstances something akin to trauma as I have described it. The resonance between traumatic experience and the language in the psalms that describes the situation of the speaker with respect to the enemies suggests that addressing situations of trauma was one function of these prayers. Of that language, I list here a number of descriptors of the enemies, of their actions, and of the speaker's resulting experience. The Psalter contains more than 100 different expressions that specify who the "enemies" are and what they do.[21] Although some of these expressions are rather general, many resonate with traumatic experience in that they describe actions by which the enemy overwhelms and terrorizes the speaker, or threatens to do so. Such actions include: to lurk or lie in wait,[22] to pursue or persecute,[23] to ensnare in a trap or pit,[24] to surround,[25] to overpower,[26] to seize,[27] to terrify,[28] to oppress,[29] to tear apart,[30] and to devour (people).[31] Psalm 10:7-10 (discussed below) employs several such terms:

Their mouths are filled with cursing (אָלָה) and deceit (מִרְמוֹת) and oppression (תֹּךְ);
under their tongues are mischief (עָמָל) and iniquity (אָוֶן).
They sit (ישב) in ambush (מַאְרַב) in the villages;
in hiding places they murder (הרג) the innocent (נָקִי).
Their eyes stealthily watch (צפן) for the helpless (חֶלְכָה);
they lurk (ארב) in secret (מִסְתָּר) like a lion in its covert;
they lurk (ארב) that they may seize (חטף) the poor (עָנִי);
they seize the poor and drag them off (משך) in their net.
They stoop (דכה), they crouch (שחח),
and the helpless fall (נפל) by their might.

images that the child is able to form cannot be evoked to fulfill the task of emotional soothing. They are too meager, too incomplete, and too prone to transform without warning into images of terror" (ibid., 106-7).

21 Othmar Keel has identified and analyzed 94 different designations of enemies that occur in nominal or participial form in the psalms of individual lament and praise (Keel, *Feinde*, 93-131). In addition to the terms in his list, I would include verbs that describe the actions of the psalmist's adversaries; of the verbs I cite below, only four are included in Keel's list: רדף חרף אבל שׂמח; the substantive עָרִיץ is also included there, but not the verb ערץ.

22 ארב Pss 10:9; 59:4; צפן Pss 10:8; 56:7.

23 רדף Pss 7:2, 6; 31:16; 35:3; 69:27; 71:11; 109:16; 119:84, 86, 150, 157, 161; 142:7; 143:3; דלק Ps 10:2.

24 פעל / עשׂה שַׁחַת Pss 7:16; 9:16; טמן רֶשֶׁת / פַּח Pss 9:16; 31:5; 35:7, 8; 140:6; כון רֶשֶׁת Ps 57:7.

25 סבב / נקף Pss 17:9, 11; 18:6; 22:13, 17; 49:6; 55:11; 59:7; 88:18; 109:3; 118:10, 11, 12; 140:10.

26 אמץ מִן Pss 18:18; 142:7.

27 תפשׂ Pss 10:2; 71:11.

28 ערץ Pss 54:5; 86:14.

29 לחץ Pss 56:2; 106:42; ענה Ps 89:23; 94:5.

30 טרף Pss 7:3; 17:12; 22:14.

31 אכל Pss 14:4; 27:2; 53:5; 79:7.

In addition, many terms describing the actions of the enemies indicate that they threaten to diminish the speaker's sense of dignity: חרף taunt (Pss 42:11; 44:17; 55:13; 89:51; 102:9; 119:42); לעג mock, deride (Pss 22:8; 80:7); בזה despise (Ps 22:7); and שמח rejoice (over the speaker's misfortune) (Pss 35:15, 19, 24; 38:17).

Such expressions of ridicule articulate the psalmist's perception that the adversary's violent actions are linked to a strong negative assessment of the psalmist's dignity and value.

Recovery and the Recitation of God's Violent Acts against the Enemies

According to Herman, three fundamental tasks in the process of recovery from trauma are: establishment of safety, remembering and grieving the trauma, and reconnecting with ordinary life.[32] The function of violent imagery against the enemies in the Psalms that I am proposing presumes that some sense of safety has been established, but it also cultivates a sense of safety while facilitating *affective engagement* and *reinterpretation of the traumatic events*, both of which are necessary aspects of remembering and grieving.

Remembering and grieving must be done in a way that is at once safe and affectively engaged, allowing for the discharge of rage in a safe way. Traumatic events give rise within the victim to interpretations of the events and beliefs regarding the self that are injurious. For instance, the survivor may believe that the violation was morally acceptable or that he/she in some way deserves such treatment. Remembering and grieving must include reinterpretation that confronts such injurious beliefs and addresses the damage done to the survivor's fundamental sense of dignity.[33] However, the injurious beliefs are not easily dislodged. Although they continuously give rise to interpretations of experience that are harmful, as are "core beliefs" (discussed above), these beliefs are largely hidden from awareness. Moreover, the intensity of feelings associated with the traumatic events makes the interpretations and beliefs that arise from them resistant to confrontation. Any attempt to explain them away in merely intellectual terms has little hope of succeeding. Retelling and reinterpretation of the traumatic events and associated beliefs require attentive, empathetic listeners and engagement of the intense feelings associated with the events.[34] Survivors of trauma carry intense justifiable

32 Herman, *Trauma*, 155.

33 Ibid., 178.

34 Of the survivor's retelling of traumatic events, Herman observes: "The recitation of facts without the accompanying emotions is a sterile exercise, without therapeutic effect" (ibid., 177).

rage, which is particularly acute in survivors of chronic trauma. Here *rage* refers to an emotional state without implying harmful expression. Processing this rage must be done in a way that is safe, controlled, and integrated into the full retelling and reinterpretation of the traumatic events.

Here, one must distinguish between a revenge fantasy and a safe, controlled expression of rage. Survivors of trauma may attempt to relieve their anxiety by circumventing a detailed remembering of the trauma and the intense feelings associated with it. To do this, they may fixate on a fantasy that the situation can be made right simply by either exacting revenge from the perpetrator, forgiving the perpetrator, or gaining compensation for the damage sustained. Yet, such fantasies are counterproductive because each avoids the difficult work of coming to terms with the effects of the trauma.[35] Revenge fantasies are often a mirror image of the trauma; they envision doing to the perpetrator what was done to the victim. The victim imagines that actually inflicting violence on the perpetrator will both restore her/his sense of power and force the perpetrator to acknowledge having acted wrongfully and harmfully. However, such fantasies make things worse: they may be as frightening and intrusive as the original trauma, and they may exacerbate the victim's sense of degradation. Herman observes that people who actually commit acts of revenge do not succeed in getting rid of post-traumatic symptoms but rather suffer the most severe and intractable disturbances. The psychological research thus demonstrates that actual revenge whether enacted or contemplated in fantasy does not achieve the intended goal: relief.

By contrast to a revenge fantasy, a safe, controlled expression of rage is directed at the perpetrator *symbolically* and does not intend actual harm. Moreover, it does not become a fixation but occurs as a phase in a recovery process that does not circumvent but rather affectively engages in remembering and reinterpreting the trauma.[36] The safe, controlled expression of rage carried out in the presence of those who can provide emotional support and a moral compass for the survivor can be a crucial component of the recovery process. Amanda Curtin, a therapist who specializes in therapy groups for adults seeking healing from the present effects of childhood trauma, considers rage work an essential phase of the recovery process. She offers the following four observations:

(1) Feelings of a desire for retaliation in response to being violated are normal and should not be shamed, repressed, or denied.

35 The following summarizes the explanation of Herman, *Trauma*, 189.

36 Concerning the usefulness of a safe expression of rage, Hermann observes: "During the process of mourning, the survivor must come to terms with the impossibility of getting even. As she vents her rage in safety, her helpless fury gradually changes into a more powerful and satisfying form of anger: righteous indignation" (ibid., 189).

(2) The expression of rage is to be done in a way that is safe for everyone involved and conducted in a manner consistent with the person's value system; the perpetrator is to be made present symbolically but is not to be physically present; nor is any fantasy of actually harming the perpetrator to be cultivated.

(3) The rage that survivors carry can be released, but this cannot be done simply by writing or talking; there must be a physical component.

(4) It is important that the expression of rage be witnessed by the therapy group.[37]

In order to preserve the sense that such enactments do not countenance any harm to the actual perpetrator, it may be helpful to liken them to a blend of theatrical and courtroom performance intended to express physically, emotionally, and rationally that the violation was wrong.

The violent imagery of the psalms can contribute to a process of safe, affectively engaged remembering and grieving of trauma that includes a reinterpretation of injurious beliefs. The psalms presuppose that God is more powerful than the perpetrator and that God is confronting the enemies in order to establish a just world in which the speaker can feel safe and valued. The dramatic imagery of the psalms offers affective resonance with the actual memories of the person, especially with feelings of being overwhelmed and terrorized. Yet, it does this while at the same time affirming that God provides a safe haven. It may evoke disturbing memories, but since the language of the psalms is poetic and not specific to the individual's actual trauma, it can allow the survivor to let the details surface gradually and in a way that is not overwhelming. Reciting the psalms liturgically makes concrete their authoritative and revelatory character. To the degree that the survivor regards the Psalms as such, they evoke the community of faith as a collective witness that the violation was wrong and that God opposes it.

Psalms 9–10 demonstrate how the psalmist juxtaposes assurances of God's care for the wellbeing and dignity of the psalmist alongside petitions for help that describe the terror posed by the enemies' threats. The division of Pss 9-10, originally a single psalm, into separate psalms corresponds to a shift in tone. Psalm 9 gives thanks and praise to God for protecting the psalmist against enemies (see vv. 3–11 quoted above). Psalm 10 mostly petitions God for help against present oppressors (see vv. 7–10 quoted above), and it concludes by expressing confidence in God: "O Lord, you will hear the desire of the meek; you will strengthen their heart, you will incline your ear to do justice for the orphan and the oppressed, so that those from earth may strike terror (ערץ) no more" (Ps 10:17–18).

37 Curtin, "Childhood."

As noted above, the survivor's greatest contempt is often reserved for passive bystanders to the trauma. Survivors often regard God either as a bystander for having allowed the violation to occur, or as having intended it. In either case, such interpretation may include the conclusion that God did so because God does not value the survivor. By voicing protestation over divine inaction, some of the very psalms that appeal to God as advocate for the speaker may also affirm the validity of the deep sense of anger towards God that trauma survivors may feel.[38] For instance, returning to Ps 10: "Why, O LORD, do you stand far off? Why do you hide yourself in times of trouble? … Rise up, O LORD; O God, lift up your hand; do not forget the oppressed" (Ps 10:1, 12).

The language by which one appeals to God to intervene or affirms that God responds to the violation of the speaker has the capacity to alter an interpretation that God does not value the victim. Depictions of God as passionately angry on behalf of the survivor, such as those in Ps 18:2–20 (NRSV 18:1b–19), may be particularly effective in this regard. Note that before describing the psalmist's terror and the violent imagery of the divine rescue, this psalm establishes in vivid terms that God assures the speaker's safety and dignity.

I love (רחם) you, O LORD, my strength (חֵזֶק).
The LORD is my rock (סֶלַע), my fortress (מְצוּדָה), and my deliverer (פלט),
my God, my rock (צוּר) in whom I take refuge (חסה),
my shield (מָגֵן), and the horn of my salvation, my stronghold (מִשְׂגָּב).
I call upon the LORD, who is worthy to be praised,
so I shall be saved (ישׁע) from my enemies (אֹיֵב).
The cords of death encompassed (אפף חֶבְלֵי־מָוֶת) me;
the torrents of perdition assailed (בעת נַחֲלֵי בְלִיַּעַל) me;
the cords of Sheol entangled (סבב חֶבְלֵי שְׁאוֹל) me;
the snares of death confronted (קדם מוֹקְשֵׁי מָוֶת) me.
In my distress (צַר לִי) I called upon the LORD;
to my God I cried for help.
From his temple he heard my voice,
and my cry to him reached his ears. (Ps 18:1b–6)

38 Craig Broyles has observed a correlation between petitions arising from situations perceived as involving (violent) death or imminent death and language of protest against God. Among the roughly 65 lament psalms in the Psalter, Broyles has distinguished 21 (including Pss 9-10) that include expressions that may be regarded as voicing protest against God, which he calls "God-laments": "Most God-laments are expressions of complaint regarding God's disposition or action, which the psalmists in their distresses interpret as being indifferent or hostile" (Broyles, *Conflict*, 40, see n. 7 for a listing of these 21 psalms). Broyles notes a high correlation between God-laments and descriptions of distresses in terms of images of death or perceived imminent death, national catastrophe, and murderous social violence (ibid., 83–99).

In the evocative imagery of these opening verses, the psalm first establishes the protective regard of God for the psalmist. Then, it expresses how the enemies have overwhelmed and terrorized the speaker, a situation that prompts God's angry response on the speaker's behalf, depicted in violent imagery that blends aspects of warrior and thunderstorm:

Then the earth reeled and rocked;
the foundations also of the mountains trembled and quaked,
because he was angry (חרה לו) (Ps 18:7).

Nine verses of violent imagery portray such things as fire and smoke blasting from God's nose and mouth, a rain of fiery coals, and the shooting forth of arrows and lightning. Then, the scene concludes with an interpretation of the aim of God's violent actions in it: to express tender and effective protection for the psalmist. These verses include a description of the perpetrator's actions that expresses how they overwhelmed and terrorized the speaker.

He reached down (שׁלח) from on high, he took (לקח) me;
he drew me out (משׁה) of mighty waters.
He delivered (נצל) me from my strong enemy (אֹיֵב עָז),
and from those who hated (שׂנא) me;
for they were too mighty (אמץ מִן) for me.
They confronted (קדם) me in the day of my calamity (אֵיד);
but the LORD was my support (מִשְׁעָן).
He brought me out into a broad place (מֶרְחָב);
he delivered (חלץ) me, because he delighted (חפץ) in me. (Ps 18:16–19)

Such a passionate response may have been anticipated by the psalmist even when the descriptions of or petitions for divine action are terse, as for instance, in these verses: "The wicked (רָשָׁע) shall depart to Sheol, all the nations that forget God" (Ps 9:17). "Break (שׁבר) the arm of the wicked (רָשָׁע) and evildoers (רַע); seek out their wickedness (רֶשַׁע) until you find none" (Ps 10:15). Furthermore, the violent images against the enemies presuppose that God is more powerful than the perpetrator and is the ultimate arbiter of right and wrong. Thus, these images confront any perception that the perpetrator is omnipotent and controls meaning, a perception echoed when the psalmist portrays the enemy acting as if immune from divine justice, as in Ps 10:3–4: "For the wicked (רָשָׁע) boast of the desires of their heart, those greedy for gain curse and renounce the LORD. In the pride of their countenance the wicked say, 'God will not seek it out'; all their thoughts are, 'There is no God.'"

The harm of the enemies that is envisioned in the psalms in many cases includes the bringing of their own violent actions back upon them. However, such images differ from the revenge fantasy discussed above in that it is not the victim but God who is envisioned as the agent enacting them. For example, note the following:

The nations have sunk (טבע) in the pit that they made (עשׂה שַׁחַת);
in the net that they hid (טמן רֶשֶׁת) has their own foot been caught (לכד).
The Lord has made himself known, he has executed judgment;
the wicked are snared (נקשׁ) in the work of their own hands. (Ps 9:15–16)

In arrogance the wicked persecute (דלק) the poor (עָנִי)
let them be caught (תפשׂ) in the schemes (מְזִמָּה) they have devised (חשׁב). (Ps 10:2)

To summarize, it is the dramatic depiction of God as responsive to the victim's cries for help, as passionately angry over the violation of the victim, and as capable of stopping the violation by defeating the enemy that give restorative power to the violent imagery of the psalms. This dramatic imagery can confront beliefs that the survivor has been abandoned by God and that the perpetrator's disrespect of the victim reflects the survivor's true worth. It is the symbolic expression of the violent imagery against the enemies that has healing potential. Thus, in contemporary usage, any feelings of rage at the perpetrator or envisioning his/her destruction are to be framed not as acts of "getting even" or as in any way associated with the contemplation of actual violence against anyone. Rather, I propose that the intense drama here functions within a phase of the recovery process to counter the intensity with which injurious interpretations and beliefs have taken root in the survivor of trauma. In this way, it contributes to the compelling interpretation that the actions of the enemy and the injurious beliefs spawned by them are wrong. Thus, it is the nefarious power of these memories and beliefs over the survivor, what I am calling the "internalized perpetrator," that is being destroyed.

Bibliography

Broyles, C. C. *The Conflict of Faith and Experience in the Psalms: A Form-Critical and Theological Study*. Sheffield: JSOT, 1989.

Casas, Bartolomé de las. *In Defense of the Indians: The Defense of the Most Reverend Lord, Don Fray Bartolomé de las Casas, of the Order of Preachers, Late Bishop of Chiapa, against the Persecutors and Slanderers of the Peoples of the New World Discovered across the Seas*. Translated and edited by S. Poole. DeKalb, Ill.: Northern Illinois University Press, 1992.

Collins, J. J. *Does the Bible Justify Violence?* Minneapolis: Fortress, 2004.

Curtin, A. "Childhood Reparenting and Grief Groups: For Adults Who Want to Heal from Childhood Experiences That Are Still Affecting Them," in preparation.

Herman, J. L. *Trauma and Recovery*. Rev. ed. New York: BasicBooks, 1997.

Hofmann, S. G. *An Introduction to Modern CBT: Psychological Solutions to Mental Health Problems*. Malden, Mass.: Wiley-Blackwell, 2012.

Keel, O. *Feinde und Gottesleugner: Studien zum Image der Widersacher in den Individualpsalmen*. Stuttgart: Katholisches Bibelwerk, 1969.

Levine, P. A. *In an Unspoken Voice: How the Body Releases Trauma and Restores Goodness.* Berkeley, Calif.: North Atlantic Books, 2010.

Peels, H. G. L. *The Vengeance of God: The Meaning of the Root NQM and the Function of the NQM-Texts in the Context of Divine Revelation in the Old Testament.* Leiden: Brill, 1995.

Zenger, E. *A God of Vengeance? Understanding the Psalms of Divine Wrath.* Translated by L. M. Maloney. Louisville, Ky.: Westminster John Knox, 1996.

Jan Dochhorn

Peter's Daughter: A Case Story from Late Antiquity

Abstract

The apocryphal story about Peter's daughter is preserved in only one Coptic codex from the fourth or fifth century, Papyrus Berolinensis 8502 (generally labelled BG). My main concern is to describe how this text depicts a person as a religious role model who, in the eyes of a "modern majority," would primarily require medical or psychiatric assistance. By being ill, Peter's daughter functions as a role model that enables the reader to take part in cultural innovation. Through the inspiration of her example, the reader can learn to think unconventionally about God and thereby to understand life in a new fashion. What seems to be a disadvantage can be an advantage, what seems to demonstrate that God does not take care can demonstrate the opposite. Things are not as they appear to be.

1. Introduction

Traumatizing events can result in a corporal affliction that would ordinarily be viewed as a disadvantage, both by the one suffering from the symptoms and the society to which the afflicted person belongs. In this article I want to present an ancient Christian text dealing with the daughter of the apostle Peter which offers a different understanding of a post traumatic corporal affliction (I deliberately avoid the diagnostic term *post traumatic stress disorder* [PTSD] because it might be too narrow to cover the symptoms described in this text).[1] This narrative about Peter's daughter belongs to a genre I call parabiblical literature because it takes up characters and narrative constellations pertaining to the biblical world and thereby presupposes that a narra-

1 The diagnosis PTSD does not include somatic diseases, but somatic diseases can be comorbid with PTSD, cf. Tagay et al., "Trauma." For the history of the concept PTSD, cf. Löwe et al., "Geschichte." For a critical view on the discourse, cf. Freyberger and Kuwert, "Posttraumatische Belastungsstörung," who state that on the one hand there is a tendency to regard even the birth of a child as potentially traumatic and that on the other hand the victims of Socialism in Germany (especially the 250,000 political prisoners in the former GDR) have nearly no chance to be assessed as traumatized (and thereby entitled to claim compensation). Cf. the short description of the diagnosis PTSD in Freyberger and Kuwert, "Posttraumatische Belastungsstörung," 270, which only includes symptoms pertaining to behaviour (including hypervigilance), but no corporal symptoms.

tive world which can be labelled biblical already exists.[2] The aim of this article is not primarily a diagnosis classifying the symptoms described in our text, which would exceed the limits of my professional knowledge and beyond that be of little benefit for a person who in any case has been dead for more than 1900 years and whose existence was probably restricted to literature. My main concern is to describe and discuss how this text depicts a person as a religious role model who, in the eyes of a "modern majority," would primarily require medical or psychiatric assistance.

2. The Case

The apocryphal story about Peter's daughter is preserved in only one Coptic codex from the fourth or fifth century, Papyrus Berolinensis 8502 (generally labelled BG)[3], which contains four tractates. Three of them (the *Gospel of Mary*, the *Apocryphon of John*, the *Sophia of Jesus Christ*) are conventionally categorized as Gnostic[4] whereas the religious identity of the fourth and last of them, the story about Peter's daughter, probably is different. In the codex, the story found on pages 128–141 (according to the original pagination of the codex) is named "the Act of Peter" (ⲧⲉⲡⲣⲁⲝⲓⲥ ⲙⲡⲉⲧⲣⲟⲥ).[5] Two decisive pages are missing in the middle of the text. Apart from that the story is preserved nearly complete.[6]

The manuscript context of our story shows that it obviously was interesting for readers belonging to the Gnostic "margins" of Christianity. This fits well with the fact that according to the testimony of Augustine this story was

2 For the term "parabiblical literature," cf. Dochhorn, "Literatur," especially 291–300. In that article I only discuss parabiblical literature associated with the Old Testament; here I deal with a parabiblical text related to the New Testament. The term "parabiblical" does not imply that the authors or the readers of parabiblical writings regarded them as not being canonical or that a fixed corpus of canonical writings existed at all. Concerning the story about Peter's daughter discussed here we can conclude from a reference to it made by Augustine (cf. notes 7 and 13) that the Manichaeans obviously accepted it as authoritative but criticized a narrative similar to it which is regarded by mainstream Christianity as canonical, namely Acts 5:1–11.

3 For the date of the origin of the codex, cf. Schmidt, *Petrusakten*, 2, who assigns the handwriting palaeographically to the fourth or fifth century C.E. Cf. also Robinson, "Codicological Analysis," 36–45. Robinson states that in terms of codicology BG is similar to the Nag Hammadi codices but of a little later origin. This fits well with the assessment of the palaeographical data by Schmidt (who did not know the Nag Hammadi Codices).

4 Cf. Röwekamp, "Maria Magdalena"; idem, "Johannes-Literatur," 372; idem, "Sophia Jesu Christi."

5 For a critical edition with English translation and introduction, cf. Brashler and Parrott, "Act of Peter"; cf. also Schmidt, *Petrusakten* 1–7.

6 Pages 133–34 are missing; cf. Brashler and Parrott, "Act of Peter," 484.

known to the Manichaeans.[7] However, codices preserving a text do not necessarily represent the author's own milieu. As a matter of fact, there is evidence in Christian literature that this story was read by Christians as well: Jerome mentions that the *Acts of Peter* (which he terms περιόδοι) know of a wife and a daughter of Peter, the *Acts of Phillippus* retell the basic elements of our story, and the *Acts of Nereus and Achilleus* take up the initial episode attributing to Peter's daughter the name Petronilla.[8] Obviously this text was read by Christians. And it was read not only in Coptic but also in Greek and Latin (cf. the Greek *Acts of Philippus* and the testimonies presented by Latin authors such as Jerome and Augustine). This makes it plausible to suggest that the text was originally composed in Greek. Therefore, hereafter I will name this text *Praxis Petrou* (cf. the Coptic header ⲧⲉⲡⲣⲁⲝⲓⲥ ⲙⲡⲉⲧⲣⲟⲥ). We can leave open the often debated question of whether the *Praxis Petrou* was originally an episode of the oldest *Acts of Peter* which are partially preserved in Latin by the famous Codex Vercellensis CVIII.1 (saec. VII).[9]

The story runs as follows: after Peter has healed many sick people, one man in the crowd surrounding him dares to ask him[10] why he does not heal his daughter, who looks nice and believes in God but lies in the corner with one half of her body paralyzed (BG 128,1–129,8). Smiling a bit, Peter heals his daughter and commands her to walk around[11] in order to show that God is

7 Cf. Augustine, *Adim.* 17 (ed. Zycha, *Aureli Augustini,* 170). Augustine's testimony is cited by Schmidt, *Petrusakten,* 14 in Latin and translated by Schneemelcher, "Petrusakten," 248.

8 Concerning these texts cf. Schmidt, *Petrusakten,* 15–20.

9 The assumption that the *Praxis Petrou* preserved in BG 128–41 belongs together with the *Actus Vercellenses* is the standard view first proposed by Schmidt, "Petrusakten," 21–25; cf. Brasher and Parrott, "Act of Peter," 474–75. Schneemelcher cites the testimony of Augustine as evidence for this view (p. 248). However, Augustine mentions our story along with another story about the daughter of a gardener (see below and notes 13; 14; 28; 29) which is not preserved by the *Actus Vercellenses,* just as is the case with our story. It would have been better if Augustine had cited it along with a story from the *Actus Vercellenses.* A thesis contrary to the standard view and regarding the *Praxis Petrou* as an independent composition written after the legalization of Christianity in 312 by Galerius is proposed by Molinari, *"I never knew the Man"*; cf. Molinari, "Attacking Carl Schmidt's Theory." For some further discussion about this theme, cf. note 37. For an edition of the *Actus Vercellenses,* cf. Lipsius, *Acta Petri.* There exist several romances narrating episodes of Peter's life; they are generally of later origin than the *Acts of Peter* preserved by the *Actus Vercellenses,* cf. Röwekamp, "Petrus-Literatur," 566–68.

10 In the *Acts of Nereus and Achilleus* the one who puts this question to Peter is Titus, cf. Schmidt: Petrusakten 16. Perhaps an original TIC has been transformed to TITOC in the Greek text of the story about Peter's daughter, before this story was taken up by the *Acts of Nereus and Achilleus.* Here, we can detect a tendency to "biblicize" apocryphal tradition, cf. the following notes.

11 In the *Acts of Nereus and Achilleus* Peter commands his daughter to serve him and the people (Schmidt, *Petrusakten,* 16), cf. the story about the healing of Peter's mother-in-law in Mk 1:29–31 par. Perhaps this storyteller wanted to set a specific Petrine link. Here as well, the story about Peter's daughter is enriched with biblical flavour (see the preceding

not unable to heal her (BG 128,8–130,18). After that, he commands his daughter to go back to her corner[12] and to be paralyzed again since that would be better for her and for him (BG 130,18–131,9). The crowd weeps and asks Peter to revise his decision (131,9–11), but Peter tells a story which explains why her affliction is better for her and him (131,12–140,13). Peter recounts that when his daughter was born, in a dream the Lord revealed to Peter that a great temptation had been born to him and that his daughter would smite many souls as long as her body was not disabled. Peter does not take the dream seriously, but in fact, when his daughter was about ten years old, many people were tempted by her (131,12–132,11). This was especially the case of a rich man, Ptolemaios, who observed Peter's daughter bathing with her mother and asked her mother to allow him to marry her daughter (132,11–18). She declined (132,19), and here the tale is interrupted as two leaves of the codex are missing here (133–134). From Augustine's testimony, and the following context, we can conclude that in these passages Ptolemaios kidnapped Peter's daughter and that she was paralyzed following a prayer by Peter.[13] In BG 135,1–17 we read that Peter and his wife found their daughter paralyzed at the door of their house and praised God for he had preserved her from pollution, impurity and corruption and that she therefore should remain in the same condition. Peter continues with the story of Ptolemaios (135,17–139,17): Ptolemaios first became blind because of shedding many tears and considered hanging himself (135,17–136,10). However, when staying alone he saw a great light and heard a voice saying to him that he should not have tried to defile somebody whom he should have regarded as his sister since they had become one Spirit (136,10–137,12)[14] and that he would learn

note). However, the command to a person healed from a disease to walk around is already biblical, cf. Mk 2:9; Joh 5:8; Acts 3:6 and chapter 3 of this article.

12 In the *Acts of Nereus and Achilleus*, Peter's daughter goes back to her "pallet" (*grabatum*; Schmidt, *Petrusakten*, 16). Like somebody else suffering her disease in the bible (she is paralytic; see below) she lies on a "pallet" (κράββατος); cf. Mk 2:4, 9. Cf. the preceding note.

13 Augustine objects to Manichean critique of the story about Ananias and Sapphira in Acts 5:1–11 with the argument that the Manichaeans appreciate the story "I have mentioned about the apostle Thomas and the daughter of Peter himself who was made a paralytic by the prayer of her father and the daughter of the gardener who was killed by the prayer of the same Peter" (*illud, quod de apostolo Thoma commemoravi, et ipsius Petri filiam paralyticam factam precibus patris et hortulani filiam ad precem ipsius Petri esse mortuam*), cf. Augustine, *Adim.* 17 (ed. Zycha, *Aureli Augustini,* 170).

14 Here, it is apparently presupposed that Ptolemaios was a Christian. The same is presumed of the male deceiver in the story about the daughter of the gardener cited by Pseudo-Titus (lines 92–93), which with a certain degree of probability originally belonged to the same work as our story (not necessarily the *Acts of Peter*; cf. note 9): *Inruit homo uinctus* fidelis *in domum eius senis conmorari perdiditque puellam et ambo nusquam conparuerunt* ("A man, *believing in God* but overcome [by desire] forced entry into the house of this old man [scil. the gardener], in order to have intercourse and corrupted this maiden. Neither was

everything in the house of Peter (137,12–17). Having been transported to Peter's house by his servants, he told Peter his story and saw everything through the eyes of his body and his soul (137,17–138,10). At that moment, many believed in Christ and he granted them the gift of God (138,10–15). After that, Ptolemaios died and went back to Christ (138,16–19). Before his death, he transferred a piece of land to Peter's daughter since by her he had become a believer of God (138,19–139,6).[15] Peter, however, sold the land and did not withhold anything of the profit (139,6–139,17).[16] Peter concludes his story by an exhortation to "the servant of God" to be aware that God provides what is good for everyone of us while we think that he does not take care of us (139,18–140,6). Then he invites "all brothers" to mourn and to be awake and to pray (140,7–13). After that he gives bread to the crowd and goes back to his house (140,13–141,6).

To a certain degree, this story can be read as an example of symptoms following a traumatizing event: something bad happens to Peter's daughter and, as a consequence, she is partially paralyzed.[17] However, not everything fits this line and more can be said about this story, exceeding the limits of a psychiatric view on the matter:

- The traumatizing event itself remains unclear, and thus exactly who experienced it is likewise unclear. The primary reason for this fact is the loss of precisely those two pages in the codex which virtually certainly reported what happened to Ptolemaios and Peter's daughter. More important, however, is something else: words associated with harm and injury are quite often used in the passages preserved, but never with regard to what Peter's

ever seen again" [for the text see De Bruyne, *Epistula Titi*, 50]). Cf., however, the following note.

15 Here Ptolemaios seems to be depicted as someone who was converted to the Christian faith by his experience. However, that does not fit with BG 137,4–12 where the text seems to imply that Ptolemaios was already a Christian when he tried to defile Peter's daughter; see the preceding note.

16 Here we encounter a motive known from a biblical narration about Peter, cf. the story about Ananias and Sapphira in Acts 5:1–11 who privatize a part of the money they got as a the price for a property they sold and were punished for that with death (after Peter had predicted their fate). Our story aims at integrating biblical reminiscences—not only here, see note 11, chapter 3 and note 35. Molinari supposes that the *Praxis Petrou* describes Peter as not withholding anything from the profit of his sale in order to oppose contemporary church leaders who behaved in another way (cf. Molinari, *"I Never knew the Man,"* 174), but I do not think that the story does enough in order to present Peter as a role model here. It seems more likely that this motive simply belongs to a strategy of setting biblical links.

17 Lameness or weakness of muscles can be a consequence of traumatization, cf. Tagay et al., "Trauma," 202 (Tab 2): In a group of 483 patients (178 not traumatized; 256 traumatized; 49 with PTSD) 7% of the persons that were not traumatized, 14% of those traumatized without PTSD and 39% of those traumatized with PTSD suffered from these symptoms.

daughter suffered (e.g. by Ptolemaios). What we have instead concerns what others (men) suffered by her: in BG 132,1–3 Peter is informed by a dream that his daughter will smite a good many souls (ⲥⲛⲁϣⲱⲱϭⲉ ⲛϩⲁϩ ⲙ̄ⲯⲩⲭⲏ), and in 135,19–136,10 Ptolemaios is the one who suffers the emotional consequences of the bad event; he is described as somebody who "strikes his heart" (ⲉϥϯ ⲉϩⲟⲩ̄ ϩⲙ ⲡⲉϥϩⲏⲧ)[18] and considers hanging himself. If anyone suffers from something that may remind us of PTSD, it is Ptolemaios.[19] Concerning Peter's daughter herself, we can conclude from the thanksgivings of Peter and his wife after they had found her paralyzed that God had thereby preserved her from defilement. Here, Peter's daughter plays a passive role. However, in other passages, her healthy body is described as a safety hazard for other people (132,1–11), and she is the one by whom Ptolemaios became a believer in God (139,4–5). For the most part, she plays an active role in our story, and obviously she was paralyzed in order to have a less dangerous body. We have good reason to ask whether it was really Peter's daughter who is regarded as being traumatized in this story, if we are allowed to apply this modern term to an ancient text.

- Nevertheless, our story openly states that Peter's daughter is ill (cf. the word ϣⲱⲛⲉ in 131,3–4).[20] One half of her body (from the nails to the head) is ⲥⲏϭ (129,4). This word is the qualitative of the verb ⲥⲱϭ and is equivalent to the Greek παραλυτικός, παραλελυμένος (lame, paralyzed)[21]; cf. Mark 2:1–12 where Jesus and Acts 8:7; 9:33 where Peter heals persons that suffer from this disease[22]. Her general condition is described by the word ⲥⲟϣⲧ (129,5) which is best rendered by "disabled" as it is mainly used in the sense of being in many respects prevented from activity.[23] The

18 For the meaning of this phrase, cf. Crum, "ϯ ⲉϩⲟⲩⲛ," *Coptic Dictionary,* 395. Brashler and Parrot, "Act of Peter" translate "he was smitten in his heart" (p. 485, 487); Schmidt, *Petrusakten* "er ging in sich" (p. 9).

19 However, tears alone, even many tears, do not suffice for a PTSD diagnosis. For the symptoms of PTSD cf. Freyberger and Kuwert, "Posttraumatische Belastungsstörung," 270.

20 For the meaning of ϣⲱⲛⲉ cf. Crum, *Coptic Dictionary,* 570 (citing Coptic texts translated from Greek sources that read, for example, νοσεῖν and ἀσθενεῖν).

21 Cf. Crum, "ⲥⲱϭ," *Coptic Dictionary,* 388. A precise definition of what is meant by this Coptic word resp. the Greek terms παραλυτικός or παραλελυμένος exceeds the limits of this article; for an older attempt to describe what is meant by paralytics in biblical sources cf. Winer, *Biblisches Realwörterbuch,* 2:225–27. Important is a parallel in 1 Macc 9:55, where somebody who is paralyzed is neither able to do anything nor to speak (cf. note 23).

22 The word ⲥⲏϭ is also the translation for παραλυτικός in Mk 2:3 (sah), cf. Aranda Pérez, *San Marcos,* 28.

23 Cf. Crum, "ⲥⲱϣⲧ," *Coptic Dictionary,* 377. Cf. also the parallel in 1 Macc 9:55 where paralysis and disability are combined: Ἐν τῷ καιρῷ ἐκείνῳ ἐπλήγη Ἄλκιμος, καὶ ἐνεποδίσθη τὰ ἔργα αὐτοῦ, καὶ ἀνεσφράγη τὸ στόμα αὐτοῦ, καὶ παρελύθη καὶ οὐκ ἠδύνατο ἔτι λαλῆσαι λόγον καὶ ἐντείλασθαι περὶ τοῦ οἴκου αὐτοῦ ("At that moment Alkimos was smitten, his

opposite of her "disabled" state is represented by the phrase ⲙⲟⲧⲛ̄ ⲉ- which mainly denotes that somebody can do something easily (129,12).[24] Apparently her most important lack is the ability to move, and it is in this connection that Peter commands her to walk around—in order to demonstrate that, in principle, God was in a position to heal her. Something she does not lack is obviously attractiveness: the one who asks Peter concerning her asserts that she looks "nice" (ⲥⲁⲓⲏ)! Her social position seems to be ambiguous: she lies in a corner which might point to social isolation[25], but on the other hand people know that she believes in God and thereby shares with others the highest value propagated in our story. Beyond that, she is labelled "servant of God," and that is also the designation of the one Peter appeals to in the concluding section of his story: Peter's daughter is a role model. Ultimately, it is evident that her suffering does not entail any segregation.

- For a modern reader, it seems counterintuitive that Peter (by God's power) is able to heal his own daughter but—after demonstrating that this is possible in principle—decides to let return her to her former condition. However, we would not understand this story correctly if we explained this irritation by a fundamental cultural gap between our values and the values of the culture represented by the text: Peter's behaviour is counterintuitive for his public as well. The whole story starts with a question posed by someone who simply shares the majority values of our own times: why do you—who help others– not help your own daughter? And the reaction of the crowd when Peter decides to let her return to her former place and sit down paralyzed corresponds to the same values. It is the aim of this story to contradict these values and to introduce others which do not match conventional expectations. And that means that this story aims at cultural innovation, respectively new ways of thinking and behaviour, and the role model is someone who needs medical help and can in principle be healed, but who is better off remaining sick.
- What are the new values propagated by this story? It ends with an appeal to the "servant of God", who can be identified with the reader who should indirectly identify himself with another "servant of God", namely the

works were hindered and his mouth was closed, and he was paralyzed and was no longer able to say a word or to order his household"), cited from Kappler, *Maccabaeorum liber I*, 105.

24 Cf. Crum, "ⲙⲧⲟⲛ," *Coptic Dictionary*, 194.

25 The term "corner" can bear connotations of political or social unimportance, cf. Bauer, "γωνία," *Wörterbuch*, 336, §2, who cites Acts 26:26 (the matter the Gospel deals with has not happened in a corner) and Plato, *Gorg*. 485d (where living in a corner together with children is opposed to living on the Agora where honourable men interact with one another).

daughter of Peter (the Coptic word for "servant" is in both cases ϩⲙ̄ϩⲁⲗ, both feminine [ⲧⲉϥϩⲙ̄ϩⲁⲗ] and masculine [ⲡϩⲙ̄ϩⲁⲗ]). And this appeal begins with a theological statement: God watches over those who are his and he prepares what is good for "each one" (ⲡⲟⲩⲁ ⲡⲟⲩⲁ) of them whereas we think that he does not take care of us. Here we find a structure that resembles the main idea of the preceding narrative. There is also something counterintuitive in God's behaviour: what we can conclude about it gives the impression that he neglects us, but things are not what they seem to be. In fact, he does what is good, and he does it with regard to each individual; the Coptic phrase ⲡⲟⲩⲁ ⲡⲟⲩⲁ has distributive meaning[26] and stresses that God takes care of each individual and his special needs. In the case of Peter's daughter, this means that her disability appears to be bad and seems to indicate that God does not care for her, yet in fact her handicap is good for her and for others (as has been explicitly stated in BG 131,4) and is a result of God's special concern for her individual needs (cf. BG 135,10–14). The theological implication is: we are expected to think unconventionally if we want to understand God, and according to that, Peter behaves unconventionally in the whole story by not healing his daughter and by giving thanks to God when he found her paralyzed.

- Unconventional is also what "we" (the collective addressed after the theological statement) should do in accordance with our new knowledge of God. The first word that describes the new behaviour to which Peter exhorts us is "to mourn" (ϩⲏⲃⲉ); after that we read words describing normal Christian activity (to be awake, to pray; cf. 1 Thess 5:6, 17). Christianity starts with unconventional behaviour which does not look like salvation, but we have already learned that things are not as they seem.

- The new message exposed by the *Praxis Petrou* presupposes a conviction which is neither disputed nor emphasized but important for the logic of our story. The good enabled by God for Peter's daughter in an unconventional way consists of protection from defilement. Cf. BG 135,1–17, where Peter and his wife thank God for protecting their daughter from defilement after they have found her paralyzed in front of their house. Here the presupposition lies in the notion that defilement is something bad. What precisely is meant? Does the story encompass a negative view on every kind of sexual activity? The story line of the *Praxis Petrou* seems to indicate something else: its climax is an abduction of Peter's daughter by Ptolemaios which at first appears to be successful but is in fact unsuccessful with regard to its final aim, namely a sexual intercourse which—as we can conclude from the basic characteristics of the phenomenon of abduction

26 Cf. Till, *Koptische Grammatik*, 64–65 (§109).

marriage well known from Mediterranean societies—would enable Ptolemaios to marry Peter's daughter.[27] It is sexual intercourse in this special situation—an abduction enabling a man to marry a maiden—that is regarded as defilement in our story, and it does not seem to be important whether or not the maiden consents to this intercourse. A parallel can be found in a story about Peter and the daughter of a gardener which has already been mentioned in footnotes and probably belonged to the same composition as the *Praxis Petrou* (cf. notes 9; 13; 14). This other story also deals with an abduction marriage, but here the maiden appears to have consented to sexual intercourse. The girl's father, a gardener, asks Peter to pray for something good for his daughter. Peter prays and the daughter dies. The father complains (for which he is strongly criticised by the narrator), and Peter calls the daughter to life again. The next day a man comes to her, defiles her and they are never seen again.[28] It would have been better for her if she had remained dead.[29]

That our story is concerned with the avoidance of sexuality has sometimes been overemphasized in the research discussion: There has been suggested that our story supports an Encratitic view[30] admonishing sexu-

27 The term abduction marriage designates bride robbery which is a well-known practice in traditional societies and also in ancient Mediterranean societies. It is generally regarded as being illegal, but in social reality not invariably deemed unacceptable. The unacceptability is normally not concerned with the issue of whether or not the maiden consents to the robbery; instead, the main point lies in the fact that a contract concerning marriage and its financial consequences (dowry, bridal gift etc.) are avoided or annihilated. Cf. Grubbs, "Abduction Marriage," 61–64; Kuefler, "Marriage Revolution." There is an edict of Constantine in Codex Theodosianus 9.24.1 which prescribes high penalties for abduction marriage (cf. the articles mentioned). One may suppose that the *Praxis Petrou* belongs in the ideological context of this edict insofar as here abduction marriage is presented as a problem; cf. Molinari, *"I Never Knew the Man,"* 173–77, who cautiously presents the edict as evidence for his proposal to date the *Praxis Petrou* in the 4th century (cf. note 9).

28 This story is known from the letter of Pseudo-Titus, cf. the sentence cited in note 14: *Inruit homo uinctus fidelis in domum eius senis conmorari perdiditque puellam et ambo nusquam conparuerunt* ("A man, believing in God but overcome [by desire] forced entry into the house of this old man [scil. the gardener] in order to have intercourse, and corrupted this maiden. Neither was ever seen again"). It is difficult to imagine something other than that the daughter of the gardener and the deceiver lived together by mutual consent afterwards and that the narrator does not accept that.

29 Cf. Pseudo-Titus, line 83–96 according to De Bruyne, *Epistula Titi,* 50.

30 The term Encratitic is derived from the term ἐγκρατῖται used in patristic sources (e.g. Irenaeus, Clement of Alexandria) for a sect which abstained from marriage, meat and wine in the second century (supported not at least by Tatian), cf. Lampe, "ἐγκρατῖται," *Patristic Greek Lexicon,* 404. In secondary literature it is often used in a broader sense in order to designate (more or less) radical asceticism in Early Christianity, cf. Völker, "Enkratiten," which might be paradigmatic for the use of the term Encratitic/Encratists in modern research.

al abstinence in general.[31] However, it is only a particular kind of sexuality that is divinely discouraged here; we do not read anything about a general illegitimacy of sexuality (otherwise Peter would not have a wife and a daughter). Here our story differs from stories told in the section concerning the martyrdom of Peter in the *Actus Petri cum Simone* preserved by the Codex Vercellensis CVIII.1 (saec. VII), where the reason for Peter's martyrdom is the fact that—through the preaching of Peter—some women were motivated to refuse sex with their influential husbands.[32] We can, however, state a closer relationship to the story about the daughter of a gardener. Both stories use a strategy of counterintuitivity (the crowd around Peter has to learn why illness is good for Peter's daughter and the gardener does not understand that death which appears to be bad for his daughter is in fact good for her) and both stories seem to be less strict concerning sexuality than the final sections of the *Actus Petri cum Simone*. And, not least, sex is not the primary concern of these two stories: they presuppose rather than defend the notion that a special kind of sexual intercourse (connected to abduction marriage) is a shame, and mainly aim at presenting the idea that God provides what is good for people—who do not always understand the good will behind events.

3. Discussion

Applying a modern concept like PTSD to an ancient text is a complicated task. It presupposes that a diagnostic concept reflects something in reality and that this aspect of reality exists across cultural and historical boundaries. OT researchers have, e.g., tried to diagnose PTSD in the case of Saul (and other diseases as well), a debate that is astonishing for anyone who has been instructed by German scholars to assume complicated source critical problems in the Books of Samuel.[33] However, that such diagnoses on characters of ancient literature are not necessarily far-fetched or that they can be successfully applied in modern society—at least as a public discourse—may be demonstrated by a project called the "Theater of War," sponsored by a US $ 3.7

31 Cf. Schmidt, *Petrusakten*, 25, who stresses the Encratitic moment both in our text and in the *Actus Vercellenses* and Brashler and Parrott, "Act of Peter," 475 (with a modest critique of this view).

32 Cf. *Actus Petri cum Simone* 30-41. This passage is also attested in Greek; for the Latin and Greek text, cf. Lipsius, *Acta Petri*, 78-103. The motif of the apostle whose preaching attracts married women who subsequently avoid sexual activity with their husbands is not attested elsewhere in the *Actus Petri cum Simone* (neither in the *Praxis Petrou* and the story about the daughter of the gardener).

33 Cf. Williams and le Roux, "Malady." Typical for a source critical access to the book of Samuel is Rudnig, *Davids Thron*.

million Pentagon grant. In this case, actors read, for example, Sophocles's *Ajax* and *Philoctetes* in order to help traumatized soldiers cope with trauma and their own pains of coming home, as it confronts them with the realisation that their problems are quite normal for human beings. The "Theater of War" attracted more than 20,000 spectators (soldiers and their families) in 2009–2010. Here a modern diagnosis applied to characters belonging to the literature of the distant past is used for therapeutic purposes in the present.[34] However, the textual treatment of the fate of Peter's daughter is not comparable to the character development of Ajax or other warriors suffering from emotional afflictions in Classic literature. We have only some words pointing to lameness and disability. The reason lies in the literary purposes of the *Praxis Petrou*: nearly everything in this story shows that the narrator primarily aims at presenting Peter's daughter as suffering from a "biblical" affliction, and for this purpose detailed diagnostic material is not relevant. Peter's daughter is paralyzed, like biblical persons healed by Jesus and Peter, and she is temporarily healed by the command to walk around which is also well known from the Bible (cf. Mk 2:9; Joh 5:8; Acts 3:6).[35]

Something that is not known from biblical stories about the healing of paralyzed or lame persons is the information that the lameness of Peter's daughter is partial paralysis. A partial paralysis also occurs in *Actus Petri cum Simone* 2, where Paul causes a woman who had sexual intercourse with the

34 Concerning the "Theater of War," cf. Kamieński, "Helping the Postmodern Ajax 398." The actual facebook presentation of the "Theater of War" mainly announces readings of the book of Job, see https://www.facebook.com/TheaterOfWar (visited on 15/12/2013). Cf. also a passage from an announcement of the Vassar college (http://info.vassar.edu/news/announcements/2013-2014/131103-theater-of-war.html; visited on 15/12/2013): "The dramatic reading of Ajax will be followed by a panel discussion including two veterans, a military family member, and a clinical psychologist—all of whom are from the local area. A facilitated town-hall style audience discussion will conclude the program. The Ajax Greek tragedy serves as a centerpiece because it timelessly and universally depicts the visible and invisible wounds of war. By presenting this play to mixed military and civilian audiences, the hope is to de-stigmatize psychological injury, increase awareness of post-deployment psychological health issues, disseminate information regarding available resources, and foster compassion and understanding. To date, there have been over 225 Theater of War performances attended by over 50,000 military service members, veterans, and their families." For an access to Homer inspired by experiences of modern war cf. also Shay, "Learning about Stress from Homer's Illiad." Correlating the afflictions of modern and Illiadic and ancient Greek veterans is typical of the work of Jonathan Shay, cf. Shay, *Achilles in Vietnam.*

35 For the biblicisms in our story cf. BG 139,6–139,17 where Peter does not withhold anything from the proceeds accruing from the sale of a field his daughter had inherited from Ptolemaios (cf. Acta 5 and note 16). Even more biblical motives appear in the version of the first episode of our story presented by the *Acts of Nereus and Achilleus*; cf. notes 10, 11, 12.

wrong man to be smitten with such a disability.[36] Perhaps this disability had the connotation of being a punishment for wrongful sexual activity; in our story it would not be a punishment but rather a means of prevention. In every case, these two stories have a motif in common, which could indicate that the *Praxis Petrou* originally belonged to the oldest *Acts of Peter* attested by the *Actus Petri cum Simone*, but perhaps the explanation is sufficient that oral traditions about Peter could belong to the same or similar milieux of production and transmission.[37] However, this motif does make the "case" of Peter's daughter more accessible to a modern diagnosis either. And it is even more improbable that many people will experience with Peter's daughter what American soldiers experience when confronted with distressed heroes of antiquity, namely that their feelings (or corporal diseases) are "quite normal."

But perhaps this lack of normality is the point which makes our story interesting for a more general assessment in terms of cultural science or anthropology. By being ill, Peter's daughter functions as a role model that enables the reader to take part in cultural innovation. Through the inspiration of her example, the reader can learn to think unconventionally about God and thereby to understand life in a new fashion. What seems to be a disadvantage can be an advantage, what seems to demonstrate that God does not take care can demonstrate the opposite. Things are not as they appear to be. It is in this sense that the broader cultural context of our story can be recog-

36 Cf. Lipsius, *Acta Petri,* 46: Paul says to Rufina: *Rufina, non tamquam digna accedis ad altarium dei, surgens a latere non mariti sed moechi* ("Rufina, not as somebody who is worthy do you come near to God's altar because you had had intercourse—not with your husband but with an adulterer"). After that he announces that Satan will throw her down before everybody, and then the symptoms from which she suffers are described: *Et confestim Rufina a sinistra parte a capite usque ad ungues pedum contorminata cecidit. Cui nec potestas data est loquendi: lingua enim eius obligata est* ("And suddenly Rufina fell down, lame from the head till the nails of her feet; and she was not able to speak, because her tongue was bound"). Cf. the symptoms of a paralyzed one described in 1 Macc 9:55. The phrase "from the head to the nails" also occurs in the *Praxis Petrou*, cf. BG 135,8-9.

37 I feel uncertain concerning the question of whether the *Praxis Petrou* belongs to the same composition as the *Actus Vercellenses* (cf. note 9). I am not willing to exclude that there existed oral stories about Peter which could have been independent of the oldest *Acts of Peter* but to some degree similar to those stories we read in the *Actus Vercellenses*. Possibly the *Praxis Petrou* and the story about the daughter of the gardener represent such story telling. Should this scenario be acceptable, I would also leave the question open of whether the *Praxis Petrou* should be dated later or earlier than the *Actus Vercellensis* (cf. the thesis of Molinari who stresses the differences between the *Praxis Petrou* and the *Actus Vercellenses* and proposes that the *Praxis Petrou* was composed in the 4th century C.E.; not all his arguments are convincing, cf. note 16). On oral traditions concerning the apostle John that probably preceded the written records of the *Acta Johannis,* cf. Dochhorn, "Überlegungen," 321.

nized. Even if Encratism may be the wrong designation for the ideological background of the *Praxis Petrou*, it cannot be denied that a tendency to avoid sex plays a role in our text. However, this tendency was crucial for the ascetic movement that became more and more important in Paganism and Christianity in late antiquity.[38] And along with our story asceticism shared a strategy of redefining values: asceticism is nothing without abstention—abstention from something that is normally regarded as beneficial. However, what is normal is to be left behind for the sake of something of higher value. The story about Peter's daughter thereby pertains to a strategy of social behaviour that was innovative in this period. By being sick, Peter's daughter is a promoter of cultural innovation.

Cultural heroes can be described as sick and conversely sick persons can be portrayed as cultural heroes. The reason might be that both innovation and disability are patterns of behaviour that ordinary people tend to avoid. In modern times a good example is to be found in a (post-) romantic view of poets and artists where they are at once depicted as both a cultural *avantgarde* and as outsiders (entailing both emotional and corporal diseases).[39] In late antiquity we can detect this tendency in connection with asceticism (which was a very avantgardistic phenomenon in these times).[40]

38 For a collection of sources pertaining to Christian asceticism cf. Rouët de Journel and Dutilleul, *Enchiridion Asceticum*. For secondary literature, cf. the bibliographical data in Altaner and Stuiber, *Patrologie*, 17-18; 538 and Villadsen, *Nordisk Patristisk Bibliografi*, 1:310-14.

39 Cf. Benn, "Genie und Gesundheit," 84-89. Benn writes about Schopenhauer: "Wäre Schopenhauer nicht der neurotisch schwer gefesselte Mann gewesen, schreibt ein Analytiker, hätte er sich einer Analyse unterzogen, seine Metaphysik trüge ein anderes Gesicht – nämlich ein behaglicheres, gemütlicheres, hausväterchenhaftes, angenehmes Gesicht, so wünschte er. Oben spendet er Drüsen und unten Hormone: mit dem Hinterlappen nivelliert er die Exzentrik, mit dem Vorderlappen führt er den Debilen zum Gesangbuch empor – mit einem Wort: es gibt kein Schicksal mehr, die Parzen sind als Directricen bei einer Lebensversicherung untergekommen, im Acheron legt man eine Aalzucht an, die antike Vorstellung von dem Furchtbaren des Menschen wird bei der Eröffnung der Hygieneausstellung stehend und unter allgemeiner Teilnahme … in tiefer Ergriffenheit auf ihren Normalgehalt zurückgeführt." For a similar view on the poet, cf. Jung, "Psychologie und Dichtung," 114-20. Interesting is the comparison between the gentleman and the poet on p. 116: both are actors of a collective psychology, the former of the one created by society, the latter of the one represented by the collective unconciousness (which, like society, is transpersonal). The consequence for the poet is that his personality is influenced by powers which can conflict with the necessity of conducting a normal life (p. 117).

40 In this regard, a parallel to Peter's daughter might be found in a story about Melchisedech of probably Jewish origin that described Melchisedech as somebody who before meeting Abraham lived as a wild man in social isolation on Mount Tabor, reacting in this manner to the loss of his whole family. Melchisedech's stay on Mount Tabor may remind us of traumatization. However, the story itself calls Melchisedech a "man of God." And Christian monks and pilgrims read this story and perhaps took his stay on Mount Tabor as a role model for an eremitic life. A church was built for him on Mount Tabor—one that still exists today. On the text of the Historia de Melchisedech, cf. Dochhorn, *Historia de Mel-*

Bibliography

Altaner B., and A. Stuiber. *Patrologie: Leben, Schriften und Lehre der Kirchenväter.* Freiburg: Herder, 1993.

Aranda Pérez, G. *El Evangelo de San Marcos en Copto Sahídico: Texto de M 569 y aparato crítico.* Madrid: C.S.I.C.,1988.

Bauer, W. *Griechisch-deutsches Wörterbuch zu den Schriften des Neuen Testaments und der frühchristlichen Literatur.* Edited by K. Aland and B. Aland. 6th ed. Berlin: De Gruyter, 1988.

Benn, G. "Genie und Gesundheit." Pages 84-89 in *Gottfried Benn: Essays / Reden / Vorträge.* Vol. 1 of *Gottfried Benn: Gesammelte Werke in vier Bänden.* Edited by D. Wellershoff. 5th ed. Stuttgart: Klett-Cotta, 1986. Repr. from *Der Querschnitt* 10 (1930): 574-77.

Böttrich, C. *Geschichte Melchsedechs.* Jüdische Schriften aus hellenistisch-römischer Zeit. New Series 2. Gütersloh: Gütersloher, 2010.

Brashler, J., and D. M. Parrott, eds. "The Act of Peter. BG 4: 128,1-141,7." Pages 473-93 in *Nag Hammadi Codices V,2-5 and VI with Papyrus Berolinensis 8502,1 and 4.* Edited by D. M. Parrott. Leiden: Brill, 1979.

De Bruyne, D., ed. "Epistula Titi, Discipuli Pauli de Dispositione Sanctimonii." *Revue Bénédictine 37* (1925): 47-72.

Crum, W. E. *A Coptic Dictionary.* Oxford: Oxford University Press, 1939. Repr., with a foreword by J. M. Robinson. Eugene, Oreg.: Wipf & Stock, 2005.

Dochhorn, J. "Die Historia de Melchisedech (Hist Melch): Einführung, editorischer Vorbericht und Editiones praeliminares." *Le Muséon* 117 (2004): 7-48.

—. "Jüdisch-alexandrische Literatur? Eine Problemanzeige und ein Überblick über diejenige Literatur, die potentiell dem antiken Judentum entstammt." Pages 285-312 in *Alexandria.* Edited by T. Georges, F. Albrecht and R. Feldmeier. Tübingen: Mohr (Siebeck) 2013.

—. "Ist die Apokalypse des Johannes ein Text des Christentums der Asia? Einige Überlegungen." Pages 299-322 in *The Rise and Expansion of Christianity in the First Three Centuries of the Common Era.* Edited by C. K. Rothschild and J. Schröter. Tübingen: Mohr (Siebeck), 2013.

Grubbs, J. E. "Abduction Marriage in Antiquity: A Law of Constantine and its Social Context." *Journal of Roman Studies* 79 (1989): 59-83.

Freyberger, H. J., and P. Kuwert. "Posttraumatische Belastungsstörung: Konzeptualisierung als Krankheit der (Post-) Moderne." *Psychotherapeut* 3 (2003): 269-75.

Jung, C. G. "Psychologie und Dichtung (1930)." Pages 97-120 in C. G. Jung, *Über das Phänomen des Geistes in Kunst und Wissenschaft.* Vol. 15 of C. G. Jung, *Gesammelte Werke.* Olten and Freiburg: Walter 1971.

Kamieński, Ł. "Helping the Postmodern Ajax: Is Managing Combat Trauma through Pharmacology a Faustian Bargain?" *Armed Forces & Society* 39 (2013): 395-414.

Kappler, W., ed. *Maccabaeorum liber I.* Septuaginta. Vetus Testamentum Graecum Auctoritate Academiae Litterarum Gottingensis Editum 9,1. 3d ed. Göttingen: Vandenhoeck & Ruprecht, 2008.

Kuefler, M. "The Marriage Revolution in Late Antiquity: The Theodosian Code and Later Roman Marriage Law." *Journal of Family History* 32 (2007): 343-70.

Lampe, G. W. H. *A Patristic Greek Lexicon.* Oxford: Clarendon, 1961.

Lipsius, R. A., ed. *Acta Petri, Acta Pauli, Acta Petri et Pauli, Acta Pauli et Theclae, Acta Thaddaei* Vol. 1 of *Acta Apostolorum Apocrypha.* Edited by R. A. Lipsius and M. Bonnet. Leipzig: Mendelssohn, 1891.

chisedech, on the transmission of the Historia de Melchisedech among monks and the church on Mount Tabor, cf. Böttrich, *Geschichte Melchisedeks,* 29-51 (reception of the *Hist Melch*); 156-57 (about the church, including a photo).

Löwe B., P. Henningsen, and W. Herzog. "Geschichte einer politisch unerwünschten Diagnose: Die posttraumatische Belastungsstörung." *Psychotherapie, Psychosomatik, Medizinische Psychologie* 56 (2006): 182-87.

Molinari, A. L. *"I never knew the Man": The Coptic Act of Peter (Papyrus Berolinensis 8502.4)*. Québec and Leuven: Peeters, 2000.

—. "Augustin, Contra Adimantum, Pseudo-Titus, BG 8502.4 and the Acts of Peter: Attacking Carl Schmidt's Theory of an Original Unity Between the Act of Peter and the Acts of Peter." Pages 426-47 in *The Society of Biblical Literature 1999 Seminar Papers* 38. Chico, Calif.: Scholars Press, 1999.

Robinson, J. M. "Codicological Analysis of Nag Hammadi Codices V and VI and Papyrus Berolinensis 8502." Pages 9-45 in *Nag Hammadi Codices V,2-5 and VI with Papyrus Berolinensis 8502,1 and 4*. Edited by D. M. Parrott. Leiden: Brill, 1979.

Rouët de Journel, M. J., and J. Dutilleul. *Enchiridion Asceticum: Loci SS. Patrum et Scriptorum Ecclesiasticorum ad Ascesim Spectantes*, Freiburg: Herder, 1929.

Röwekamp, G. "Maria Magdalena (Evangelium)." Page 485 in *Lexikon der antiken christlichen Literatur.* Edited by S. Döpp and W. Gerlings. 3d ed. Freiburg: Herder, 2002.

—. "Petrus-Literatur." Pages 565-56 in *Lexikon der antiken christlichen Literatur.* Edited by S. Döpp and W. Gerlings. 3d ed. Freiburg: Herder, 2002.

—. "Johannes-Literatur." Pages 372-73 in *Lexikon der antiken christlichen Literatur.* Edited by S. Döpp and W. Gerlings. 3d ed. Freiburg: Herder, 2002.

—. "Sophia Jesu Christi." Page 647 in *Lexikon der antiken christlichen Literatur.* Edited by S. Döpp and W. Gerlings. 3d ed. Freiburg: Herder, 2002.

Rudnig, T. *Davids Thron: Redaktionskritische Studien zur Geschichte von der Thronnachfolge Davids.* Berlin: De Gruyter, 2006.

Schmidt, C. *Die alten Petrusakten im Zusammenhang der apokryphen Apostelliteratur nebst einem neuentdeckten Fragment untersucht.* Leipzig: Hinrichs, 1903.

Schneemelcher, W. "Petrusakten." Pages 2:243-89 in *Neutestamentliche Apokryphen in deutscher Übersetzung.* Edited by W. Schneemelcher and E. Hennecke. 2 vols. 5th ed. Tübingen: Mohr (Siebeck), 1989.

Shay, J. "Learning about Stress from Homer's Illiad." *Journal of Traumatic Stress* 4 (1991): 561-79.

—. *Achilles in Vietnam: Combat Trauma and the Undoing of Character.* New York: Athenaeum, 1994. Repr., New York: Scribner, 2003.

Tagay, S., S. Herpertz, M. Langkafel, and W. Senf. "Trauma, posttraumatische Belastungsstörung und Somatisierung." *Psychotherapie, Psychychosomatik, Medizinische Psychologie* 54 (2004): 198-205.

Till, W. C. *Koptische Grammatik (Sahidischer Dialekt).* 2d ed. Leipzig: Enzyklopädie, 1961.

Villadsen, H. *Nordisk Patristisk Bibliografi.* Vol. 1. Copenhagen: Books on Demand, 2011.

Völker, W. "Enkratiten." Page 169 in vol. 2 of *Die Religion in Geschichte und Gegenwart.* Edited by H. Gunkel und L. Zscharnack. 6 vols. 2d ed. Tübingen: Mohr (Siebeck), 1928.

Williams, G. P., and M. le Roux, "King Saul's Mysterious Malady." *HTS Teologiese Studies* 68, No. 1 (2012). 6 pages. Cited 17 February 2014. Online: http://dx.doi.org/10.4102/hts.v68i1.906.

Winer, G. B., *Biblisches Realwörterbuch zum Handgebrauch für Studirende, Kandidaten, Gymnasiallehrer und Prediger.* 2 vols. 2d ed. Leipzig: Reclam, 1833-1838.

Zycha, I., ed. *Sancti Aureli Augustini de utilitate credendi, de duabus animabus, contra Fortunatum, contra Adimantum, contra epistulam fundamenti, contra Faustum.* Corpus scriptorum ecclesiasticorum latinorum 25,1. Prague: Tempsky, 1891.

Virginia Burrus

“Nec sanabatur vulnus illud meum” (Conf. 6.15)

Trauma, Time, and Voice in Augustine’s *Confessions*

Abstract

This essay explores resonances of contemporary trauma theories with Augustine’s account of his own unhealable wound in *Confessions* 6.15. A passage often remarked upon for its surprising brevity and seeming detachment from the larger narrative may, nonetheless, offer a window onto significant aspects of *Confessions* as a whole, including such key issues as narrativity, temporality, sin, shame, salvation, and voice.

Nec sanabatur vulnus illud meum, quod prioris praecisione factum erat, sed post fervorem doloremque acerrimum putrescebat, et quasi frigidius, sed desperatius dolebat.

And it was not healed, that wound of mine, which had been made by the amputation of my former lover, but after a raging fever and a most piercing pain it putrefied, and it continued to hurt, as if the pain were duller, but more hopeless (Augustine, *Conf.* 6.15).

A wound that will not heal; a wound that is not physical but can only be described as if it were; a wound that is mine and also another’s; a wound that both refuses and demands narration; a wound from which I am always departing, to which I was never really present; a wound that *is* the incomprehensible pain of departure itself—this is Augustine’s wound. It is also the wound of contemporary trauma theory, as it happens. Of course, it is misleading to speak of trauma theory as if it were a monolith, rather than a lively field of interdisciplinary conversation and contestation that often offers more questions than answers.[1] Are certain kinds of events inherently traumatic, equatable with catastrophe or disaster, for example? Or is it only the nature of the response to an event that renders it traumatic after the fact, so to speak, so

1 As Cathy Caruth puts it, “Indeed, the more we satisfactorily locate and classify the symptoms of PTSD, the more we seem to have dislocated the boundaries of our modes of understanding—so that psychoanalysis and medically oriented psychiatry, sociology, history, and even literature all seem to be called upon to explain, to cure, or to show why it is that we can no longer simply explain or simply cure” (Caruth, “Introduction,” 3–4).

that the traumatic event is always, paradoxically, *post traumatic*, as well as deeply subjective? If trauma is defined less by an event itself than by how that event is experienced, is a traumatized response pathological, and if so, in what sense? What is the relation of the traumatizing event to truth or knowledge—alternately, to fiction or fantasy—if it is only ever experienced belatedly and imperfectly? Can traumatic experience, notoriously resistant to representation, be shared with others or transmitted across generations? Should it be? Finally, what kind of response does trauma call for? Such questions will prove suggestive for this reading of the wound in Augustine's *Confessions*, a reading that attempts not to psychoanalyze the author (I hasten to say) but rather to analyze the literary text.[2] As we shall see, a passage often remarked upon for its surprising brevity and seeming detachment from the larger narrative may, nonetheless, offer a window onto significant aspects of *Confessions* as a whole.

1. Trauma, Narrative, and Time

The passage in question occurs in Book 6. There Augustine narrates his mother's arrival in Milan when he is thirty years old and in a quandary over the course his life should take. What constitutes true happiness? What school of philosophical or religious thought offers the greatest insight on that question? Should he continue to pursue a prestigious career in the city or withdraw to the countryside to follow a life of intellectual study and conversation with friends? Entwined in these questions is another: *Should he marry?* A governor's appointment is not out of the question for a man of Augustine's talent and ambition, and a wealthy wife is the perfect complement to such a post: indeed, "this will be the full measure of desire," as Augustine puts it. He rationalizes: "many great men worthy of imitation have been dedicated to the pursuit of wisdom *cum coniugibus*"—alongside marriages. A few lines later, he adds: "For I thought I would be excessively unhappy if I were deprived of the embraces of a woman" (6.11). Marriage is a topic of particular debate between himself and his friend and disciple Alypius. "Indeed, Alypius prevented me from taking a wife," Augustine professes; Alypius does so on the grounds that this would compromise their own pursuit of a life dedicated to the shared love of wisdom. Augustine, however, continues to make the case that marriage is not necessarily at odds with such a life. Again, he adds an ap-

2 I would here distinguish my approach from that of Kim Power, whose exploration of "the connections between his experience and his theology" surfaces evidence of Augustine's "unacknowledged grief" and "denial" of loss in this passage (Power, *Veiled Desire*, 9, 102–3). My own interest lies not with Augustine's personal psychological trauma but rather with his literary and theological inscription of traumatic experience as such.

peal to sexual pleasure, referring to "the delights of my habit, to which, if the honest name of marriage should be added, [Alypius] should not need to wonder why I was not able to despise that life." Yet Augustine goes on to confess that the conventional life of marriage and child-rearing does not in fact draw him; rather, he is captive to the "habit of satisfying insatiable desire" (6.12).

It comes as something of a surprise when Augustine reports immediately thereafter: "*Et instabatur inpigre, ut ducerem uxorem*: And it was swiftly pressed that I take a wife." Precisely by implying narrative continuity, the use of the conjunction *et* here underlines discontinuity: we have not been prepared for such sudden and energetic action. Moreover, the agency behind this action is initially masked by the impersonal form of the verb. But not for long: "I asked, I was promised, *with my mother especially exerting herself* ..." (6.13). Monica's desire that Augustine marry is closely linked with her desire that he receive baptism, as he tells it; presumably she is seeking a catholic wife for her son. Augustine subsequently repeats the initial narrative line and elaborates the outcome, now piling on passive and impersonal verbs in such a way as to muffle not only Monica's agency but also, and especially, his own: "It was pressed nonetheless, and the girl was asked for, her age being almost two years short of marriageable, and because she pleased, she was awaited" (6.13). Augustine has very nearly evacuated himself from the text altogether: *instabatur, petebatur, expectabatur*. He does not act; at most, he is acted upon. This is, perhaps, the first hint of trauma.

Another connective *et* bridges a shift of topics in the next chapter, albeit with slightly less disjunctive effect in the overall context of Book 6: "*Et multi amici agitaveramus animo*: And we many friends deliberated...." An arrested agency is restored. The subject of the friends' deliberations is, once again, the way of life to be pursued. Several of them make plans to withdraw from society and live communally on a rural estate; the plans are quite specific. However, "after it began to be thought about, whether the girls [*mulierculae*], whom others already had and we wanted to have, would allow this, what was well formed dissolved in our hands and was shattered and discarded. Thence we returned to our sighs and groans and wanderings ..." (6.14). With Augustine's engagement deferred and the friends' utopian dreams thwarted by "little women," Book 4's suspense within indecision is preserved. Augustine is drawn by both the life of marriage and the life of study in a community of like-minded men, and however much he protests otherwise, these do not seem entirely compatible. As a result, he is not able to will either option wholeheartedly.

This stasis is interrupted—but by no means resolved—by the brief narrative that brings us, in the penultimate chapter of Book 6, to the scene of Augustine's wounding. This scene is as unexpected as is the account of his engagement to marry, albeit a direct consequence of his engagement. It opens thus: "Meanwhile my sins were multiplying, and when she with whom I was accustomed to share a bed was torn from my side, as a hindrance to marriage, my heart, where she cleaved, was cut and wounded and drew blood." Augustine goes on to relate that the woman returns to Africa, vowing to lead a celibate life and leaving behind the son she has borne with him. He himself is unable to follow her example and instead takes a new lover, thereby continuing the sexual habit that draws him inexorably, as if forced by an armed guard, toward the "kingdom of uxoriousness," as he puts it. "And it was not healed, that wound of mine, which had been made by the amputation of my former lover, but after a raging fever and a most piercing pain it putrefied, and it continued to hurt, as if the pain were duller but also more hopeless" (6.15). We now recognize that the unnamed woman who is torn from Augustine's side has been a ghostly presence haunting prior chapters of Book 6, when Augustine refers to his inability to forego "the embraces of a woman" (6.11) and references the "delights of his habit.... of satisfying insatiable desire" (6.12)—pleasures that have little to do with the pursuit of an advantageous marriage to a wealthy heiress, even if Augustine has seemed to conflate the two.

Augustine's trauma, the wound in his *Confessions*, thus arrives without narrative preparation or anticipation or any form of effective contextualization; moreover, it produces no results, narratively speaking. The closing chapter of Book 6 returns to the question of true happiness, carnal delights, and the pleasures derived from friendship with men, with which the book has been concerned all along; chapter 15 could be excised without leaving any detectable gap.

The account of wounding does, however, catapult us backward in narrative time to another dense, disjunctive, and elusive moment. Although readers of *Confessions* will not meet Augustine's lover again, we have met her once before, at the beginning of Book 4: "In those years I had someone, not one known by the union that is called lawful, rather one whom a wandering ardor, lacking prudence, tracked down, but one, nonetheless, to whom I also kept the faith of the (marriage-)bed, in whom indeed I could prove by my own example what the difference is between the constraint of a marital agreement that is contracted for the sake of descendants and the pact of libidinous love, where an offspring may be born even against our wish, although once born it compels one to love it" (4.2.2). This complex memory is embedded—very nearly buried—in Augustine's description of his experiences as a rhetoric teacher in Carthage; there it seems to arrive belatedly, as Augustine's own chronological cues suggest that this relationship must have begun in his student days, lasting some thirteen years. Retrieved from the context of Book 4, the passage lends a degree of depth to the loss later recounted in Book 6. Still, it may be too much to say that it gives the loss a proper *past*: we know so little; we understand even less. Augustine had *someone*, both less and more than a wife; she bears no proper name, defies social classification. It is that *someone* who is torn from his side. The wound will not heal; nor will he speak of it again.

If this trauma has neither an articulated past nor an anticipated future, it might seem to perform the very temporal fragmentation that *Confessions* apparently attempts to overcome through its extended narrative performance. Indeed, although ostensibly placed in their proper chronological order and context, these shards of memory—*Conf.* 6.15 and 4.2—refuse both order and context. To borrow Cathy Caruth's words, for the reader they are "experienced too soon, too unexpectedly"; as a result they can only be revisited belatedly.[3] They puncture the narrative flow, breaking out of time and thereby giving oblique witness to affective intensities that exceed the logic of cause and effect and evade explanation. Neither past nor future nor present, but rather manifest as a strangely *absent presence*, trauma wounds time itself. In this, it both mimics and shadows eternity.

2. Trauma and the Other

The wound in Augustine's text disrupts temporality in another way, by relocating itself in the mythical timescape of the biblical text, as Danuta Shanzer has shown.[4] The "one" is torn from his side (*a latere*) like Eve from Adam, in a violent replay of Genesis 2:21-22—"he took one of his ribs"—that is also a perverse reversal of Genesis 2:24: "therefore, a man leaves his father and mother and cleaves (*adhaerebit*) to his wife, and they become one flesh." In a contemporaneous treatise, *On the Good of Marriage* (401), Augustine presents the bond between Adam and Eve in Paradise explicitly as a model for marriage: "The first natural bond of human society is husband and wife. And God did not make them singly and join them as if from alien births but created the one from the other, further signifying the power of their conjunction in the side (*latere*) from which she was drawn (*detracta*) and formed" (1.1). In *Confessions*, however, the primeval bond is implicitly the model for his relationship with the one who evokes his libidinous love. Mere marriage "contracted for the sake of descendants" pales in comparison. Those who were joined and rejoined as one flesh are now cut apart at the very site of their cleaving, and this trauma is not only Augustine's. *It is hers too.*

3 Caruth, *Unclaimed Experience*, 4.
4 Shanzer, "*Avulsa a latere meo.*"

In a reading of Freud's analysis of Tasso's retelling of the tale of the Crusader Tancred (who unwittingly kills his beloved Clorinda), Caruth notes that this becomes "the story of the way in which one's own trauma is tied up with the trauma of another."[5] Admittedly, the wound of the other, the "very possibility and surprise of listening to another's wound,"[6] remains merely implicit in Augustine's text, carried by one spare, ascetic line: "And she went back to Africa, vowing to you that she would not know another man, my natural son from her having been left with me." Yet it is she who has suffered the violence of amputation as much as he, she who has, moreover, been *cut off*, vowing not to know another *(alium)*, while he lives on to take another *(aliam)* to his bed. The silence that settles around the recounting of the woman's departure thus speaks louder than the words; it speaks of what cannot be spoken.[7] As Caruth puts it, there is in trauma an oscillation "between the story of the unbearable nature of an event and the story of the unbearable nature of its survival."[8] Augustine survives to tell the doubled tale, but only in the barest strokes.

Beyond that, Augustine's trauma, relocated to the Genesis narrative and thus placed at the beginning of salvation history, becomes the trauma of all humankind, written not only to be read and acknowledged, but also to be appropriated by others. After all, "history, like trauma, is never simply one's own" but "is precisely the way we are implicated in each other's traumas," notes Caruth.[9] Indeed, there is no limit to our mutual implicatedness—to our ability to wound and be wounded.

3. Trauma, Sin, and Shame

On this reading, human existence itself becomes a kind of wounding, the irrecoverable loss of an imagined seamless connection.[10] This trauma, origi-

5 Caruth, *Unclaimed Experience*, 8.

6 Ibid.

7 Cf. Shoshanna Felman's reading of Albert Camus's recounting of his witness of a woman jumping from a bridge: "Silence here is not a simple absence of an act of speech, but a positive avoidance—and erasure—of one's hearing, the positive *assertion* of a deafness, in the refusal not merely to know but to *acknowledge*—and henceforth respond or *answer to*—what is being heard or witnessed." Ultimately, however, "Camus succeeds in giving to the very silence of a generation—and to the very voicelessness of history—the power of a *call*: the possibility, the chance, of our *response-ability*" (Felman, "The Betrayal of the Witness," 183, 203).

8 Caruth, *Unclaimed Experience*, 7.

9 Ibid., 24.

10 Cf. Eric Sean Nelson's interpretation of Martin Heidegger's understanding of the traumatic, "shattered" character of *Dasein* in and as resistance and differentiation; the question

nating with Adam's birthing of Eve and replayed in every subsequent birth, comes to be bound up with sin and shame, for Augustine. "My sins were multiplying," he has told us, echoing Sirach 23:3. But what are those sins? Faced with the pain of his lover's forced departure, "I procured another," he confesses. He adds that the habit that he thereby feeds will eventually lead him to marriage. In other words, he craves what he cannot have: love without end, love without loss. This hopeless craving is the wound that festers, even as the pain grows duller; and this festering is itself equated with the state of sin. As he puts it elsewhere, "a wound with pain is better than painless putrescence"; Jesus' flesh was wounded but did not putrefy, as he further observes (On the Nature of the Good 20). Nor, we might add, did Adam's: as the biblical text records, God "closed up the flesh" (Gen 2:21). Yet what lures Augustine is not the unity of humanity in Adam—for that is a unity without relationality—but the unity of Adam and Eve and, by extension, the unity of all individuated creatures. A unity in woundedness, then—albeit a woundedness that resists putrefaction, that is receptive to healing. However, his own wound festers still: the craving remains; he cannot grieve and let go. That is to say, sin will not let him go; rather, it returns again and again, possessing him against his will, with the relentless force of habit.

For Augustine, this sin is strongly linked with shame. At a crucial point, he addresses his God as follows: "You turned me back to reflect upon myself, taking me from behind my own back, where I had up to now placed myself …; and I beheld and abhorred myself, nor could I find any place to flee from myself.… I was most vehemently confused by a horrible shame" (8.7). There is also a traumatic character to shame itself, and for Augustine we are always already marked by that trauma of shame, by that falling, by that departure.[11]

4. Trauma and Salvation

Is there ever healing for the one who has suffered trauma? In Book 10, Augustine proclaims to his god, "Behold, I do not hide my wounds: you are the physician, I the sick one; you are compassionate (*misericors*), I miserable (*miser*)." Despite having invoked the figure of the physician, Augustine depicts himself not as healed but as suspended amidst both joy and suffering, seeking in vain a "middle place" where he is tortured neither by desire for prosperity nor by fear of adversity. In the meantime, he survives; he endures. "You com-

becomes "how to respond to violence and the trauma that it invokes.… Could being wounded call forth a reply that recognizes its wounded character, letting the wound appear as wound even in the case of the potentially irrevocable traumatic wound?" (Nelson, "Traumatic Life," 197, 199).

11 See also my *Saving Shame*.

mand that we endure these things, not that we love them," he quips. "No one loves what one endures, even if one loves to endure" (10.28). His hope lies with God's *misericordia*—God's capacity to witness the misery of others, to take that misery to heart. Augustine begs that he might become responsive to this divine love, this holy affection, and in so doing that he might be released from his craving. But he is not there yet (10.29). Later in this same book, he proclaims, "Frequently I feel that my wounds are healed by you rather than not inflicted on me." Whatever healing may come, he remains wounded, mired in habit: "Here I am able to be and not want it, there I want to be but am not able, miserable in both places" (10.40). This, mind you, is *after* his so-called "conversion."

At such moments (and there are many such in *Confessions*) Augustine seems to gesture toward something like the theology of trauma recently articulated by Shelly Rambo. When triumphalist soteriologies fall short in the face of trauma's persistence, theology itself may become the practice of witnessing to what *remains after* trauma, suggests Rambo—witnessing to the wound that cannot be healed, but witnessing also to the surprising power of endurance, the inexplicable capacity for survival, the stubborn persistence of a movement toward life, precisely in the midst of death and devastation. "Perhaps the divine story is neither a tragic one nor a triumphant one but, in fact, a story of divine remaining, the story of love that survives," writes Rambo. "It is a cry arising from the abyss."[12]

5. Trauma and Voice

Confessions is a very long prayer. It is also a very long exercise in the immensely tricky process of arrogating voice—that is, of laying claim to the improbable right to speak. Augustine effects this by inhabiting the voice of scripture—above all the Psalms—and by borrowing the authority of his divine addressee; in so doing, he also exploits the tensive relation between trauma and voice—the "cry arising from the abyss," as Rambo has it,[13] "the speech delivered by the other's wound," "an address that remains enigmatic yet demands a listening and a response," in the words of Caruth.[14] Crying from the abyss, Augustine addresses God as his witness, beseeching divine *misericordia*, demanding a listening ear. Yet the wound itself remains strangely inarticulable, manifest in mere fragments of narrative, as we have seen. "In those years I had someone...." "My heart, where she cleaved, was cut and wounded and drew blood. And she went back to Africa.... Nor was it healed, that

12 Rambo, *Spirit and Trauma*, 172.
13 Ibid.
14 Caruth, *Unclaimed Experience*, 8-9.

wound of mine...." Scholars have been quick to fill in the narrative gaps with speculation, urging readers to see how "normal" and indeed unremarkable Augustine's relational configurations were. From a social historical perspective, this is no doubt accurate, and yet from a literary perspective it misses the mark. Augustine writes the loss of his love as traumatic, not least in the withholding of its story.

This withholding stands in stark contrast to his recounting of the death of a beloved friend in Book 4 of *Confessions*—the same book where he introduces the woman to whose bed he is faithful, as if already intimating loss through such narrative proximity. There Augustine describes the symptoms of his grief for his friend at some length. "Only weeping was sweet to me," he recalls, "and it succeeded my friend in the affections of my soul" (4.4.9). He marvels at the tenacity with which he cleaves to his own mourning. "How is it that sweet fruit is plucked from the bitterness of life—to lament and to weep and to sigh and to complain?" (4.5.10). Unable to answer his own question, he contents himself with confessing his condition: "I was miserable, and every soul bound by the friendship of mortal things is miserable; it is torn to pieces when it loses them, and then feels a misery with which it is already miserable even before it loses them." If "the friendship of mortal things" inevitably entails loss, grief is sweet in the face of loss because it appears to be the one thing that cannot be lost. Prolonging his mourning, he tries to halt the march of time. Tears are a frozen mirror in which he preserves the image of his friend. Citing (and exceeding) Horace (*Carm.* 1.3.5-8), he can imagine them as two halves of one soul, virtually indistinguishable: "and therefore life horrified me, because I did not want to live as a half" (4.6.11). His soul is now "cut and bleeding" (4.7.12).[15]

Ultimately, he attempts to replace his friend with others, renewing his pretense that *they* will live forever. "Having loved one who would die as if he would not die," he finds himself prolonging the "great fiction and long lie": friends might die, "but the fiction did not die." The fiction of immortality lives on because Augustine cannot bear to relinquish the pleasures of friendship: "to speak and to laugh with one another, to yield to each other willingly; to read pleasant books together, to joke and to be serious together; sometimes to disagree without rancor, as one would with oneself, with the rare discord seasoning the more usual accord; to teach or to learn things from one another, to long impatiently for those who are absent, to welcome those who arrive with joy..."; such acts and gestures "set our hearts aflame like kindling

15 Shanzer, "*Avulsa a latere meo*," 158, notes the parallel with the account of his parting with the woman, which leaves the place of cleaving in his heart "cut and wounded and trailing blood" (6.15.25), but she also emphasizes differences: the wound left by his friend's death was "treated neutrally and eventually healed," unlike the one left by the woman's departure.

and make one out of many." "This is what is loved in friends," he concludes (4.8.13-4.9.14).

The parallels with his account of the departure of the woman—the imagery of a wounded heart or soul, the attempt to replace the beloved with others—throw the differences into stark relief. The narration of his friendship, loss, and grief takes up five long chapters in Book 4 and is skillfully integrated into the larger concerns of that book. Indeed, his description of his feelings about his friend is as verbose and performatively passionate as his description of his feelings about the woman is constrained and concise. They were friends less than a year, yet Augustine has no trouble grieving. And when he eventually comforts himself with other friendships, this proves effective. He experiences loss and suffering but not *trauma*. This wound is healed.[16]

In contrast, the power of the traumatic inscription of the woman's departure in Book 6 lies as much in what it does not say as in what it does. Its faltering silences beseech our own compassionate listening, in the face of an unplumbable mystery—a wounding of comprehension itself. "A human being is a great deep (*grande profundum*)," notes Augustine in Book 4; "his hairs are more easily counted than are his affects and the movements of his heart" (4.14). In Book 10 he professes, "I will confess therefore what I know of myself, and I will confess what I do not know of myself" (10.5). Traumatic narrative is always a site of ignorance more than of knowledge. As Caruth puts it, "it is always the story of a wound that cries out, that addresses us in the attempt to tell us of a reality or truth that is not otherwise available. This truth, in its delayed appearance and its belated address, cannot be linked only to what is known, but also to what remains unknown in our very actions and our language."[17]

6. Trauma as Point of Departure

It would perhaps be too much to claim that *Confessions* as a whole is a traumatic text. Yet I have tried to suggest that the unhealable wound in the text is, in its very brevity and detachment, revealing of the whole. As Burcht Pranger has argued brilliantly, narrative time in *Confessions* is non-linear and elusive, yielding unfathomable moments "at once eternal and intermittent and as such both sweeter and grimmer than can ever be grasped."[18] Traumatic expe-

16 See also Augustine's account of his grief for his mother in Book 9: "My soul was injured (*sauciabatur*) and life, which had been made one from mine and hers, was torn to pieces (*dilaniabatur*).... But my heart was now cured from that wound (*sanato corde ab illo vulnere*) ..." (9.12-13).

17 Caruth, *Unclaimed Experience*, 4.

18 Pranger, "Augustine and the Return of the Senses," 66-67.

rience, in its break with linearity, its paradoxical conjunction of immediacy and evasiveness, and its fearsome dance with eternity, participates powerfully, albeit darkly, in such a temporality. In so doing it also conveys something of the Augustinian understanding of sin while pointing toward a chastened theory of salvation. Indeed, for Augustine sin holds us in its grip like a trauma, possessing us against our will, persisting no matter what we will—the unhealable wounding of desire that cannot tolerate loss, and is always therefore lost, departing from itself, displaced from its own presence. If trauma also points the way toward salvation, the way is not that of healing as usually construed, but is rather the way of endurance, of survival, the modest miracle of living on, in the midst of pain—one's own, others'—and with openness to possibility. But this can only happen if, somehow, there are ears to hear the voice of the trauma, speaking what remains nonetheless unspeakable and incomprehensible—speaking with wounded speech, then. "I had someone...." "My heart ... was cut and wounded and bleeding. And she went back.... My wound did not heal ..." A departure, and a departure from the departure: this is where we will always return, the point from which we will depart, again and again.

Bibliography

Burrus, V. *Saving Shame: Martyrs, Saints, and Other Abject Subjects*. Philadelphia: University of Pennsylvania Press, 2008.

Caruth, C. "Introduction." Pages 3-12 in *Trauma: Explorations in Memory*. Edited by C. Caruth. Baltimore: Johns Hopkins University Press, 1995.

—. *Unclaimed Experience: Trauma, Narrative, and History*. Baltimore: Johns Hopkins University Press, 1996.

Felman, S. "The Betrayal of the Witness: Camus' *The Fall*." Pages 165-203 in *Testimony: Crises of Witnessing in Literature, Psychoanalysis, and History*. Edited by S. Felman and D. Laub. New York: Routledge, 1992.

Nelson, E. S. "Traumatic Life: Violence, Pain, and Responsiveness in Heidegger." Pages 189-204 in *The Trauma Controversy*. Edited by K. Brown Golden and B. G. Bergo. Albany, N.Y.: State University of New York Press, 2009.

Power, K. *Veiled Desire: Augustine on Women*. New York: Continuum, 1996.

Pranger, M. B. "Augustine and the Return of the Senses." Pages 53-67 in *Seeing the Invisible in Late Antiquity and the Early Middle Ages*. Edited by G. de Nie, K. F. Morrison and M. Mostert. Turnhout: Brepols, 2005.

Rambo, S. *Spirit and Trauma: A Theology of Remaining*. Louisville, Ky.: Westminister John Knox, 2010.

Shanzer, D. "*Avulsa a latere meo*: Augustine's Spare Rib: *Confessions* 6.15.25." *Journal of Roman Studies* 92 (2002): 157-76.

Burkhard Meyer-Sickendiek

Trauma and Sarcasm in Modern Austrian Literature

Thomas Bernhard's Novel "Extinction"

Abstract

My paper tries to explain why a trauma-theory is so important for a better understanding of modern literature, especially if we focus on the Austrian literature of the 20th century. Thomas Bernhard's last novel Extinction is regarded as an example for that traumatic kind of reminiscence that Sigmund Freud described in "Beyond the Pleasure Principle." My paper examines the relation of biography and rhetoric in Bernhard's last novel and presents two very important concepts for modern Austrian literature in general and Bernhard's novels in particular: the first is the concept of trauma as a central category in biography beyond the pleasure principle; the second is the concept of sarcasm, which is just as central for rhetoric on this side of the pleasure principle. Trauma and sarcasm—according to my theory—describe the common area of Bernhard's writings and are of special import for his novel Extinction.

My paper tries to explain why a trauma-theory is so important for a better understanding of modern literature, especially if we focus on the Austrian literature of the 20th century. This importance can be explained by the certain kind of rhetoric that characterizes this modern Austrian literature ever since the famous Karl Kraus. This rhetoric could easily be characterized by the main aspect of the traumatic experience, given by Sigmund Freud in *Beyond the Pleasure Principle*, the important and fundamental essay from 1920. The definition is known and even used up to our times: Excitations from the external world that are powerful enough to penetrate the protective shield of an individual person are experienced as traumatic. I guess that every reader of modern Austrian literature knows about these kinds of experiences Freud described it in this essay:

> We shall designate as traumatic those excitations from outside strong enough to break through the shield against stimuli. I believe the concept of trauma requires this characterization with respect to an otherwise effective barrier to stimuli. An event like an external trauma certainly produces a huge diszurbance in the energy opera-

tions of the organism and sets in motion all means of defense. Simultaneously, though, the pleasure principle is incapacitated for the time being.[1]

The most important home of literature "strong enough to break through the shield against stimuli" in the 20th century was certainly Austria. Staging the ugly and the disgusting has been a central topic in modern literature ever since Charles Baudelaire's poetry, it played its role in German expressionism and has found unparalleled representation in Austrian literature in the 20th century. To redefine or completely undo the limits of the aesthetic tolerability might well be called characteristic of Austrian literature. Think, for instance, of the bloody installations of performance artist Hermann Nitzsch, the cruelly brutal films of Michael Hanekes, the scatological imagery in the theatre pieces of Werner Schwab or the dramatic choreography of Johann Kresnik; and don't forget the deliberately ugly depiction of petty Austrian bourgeois in Manfred Deix' caricatures. Now complete that list with the tradition of the "anti-Heimatroman" beginning in the 1960s: Hans Lebert's "Die Wolfshaut" (1960), Thomas Bernhard's complete oeuvre from "Frost" (1963) up to "Auslöschung," "Extinction" (1986), Peter Handke's "Hornissen" (1966), Franz Innerhofer's "Schöne Tage" (1974), Josef Winkler's trilogy "Das wilde Kärnten" (1879–1982) as well as "Der Leibeigene" (1990) or Elfriede Jelinek's prose up to and including "Die Kinder der Toten" (1997): You will find it difficult to come up with a comparable accumulation of such sinister, terrifying and cruel imaginations in other nations' literature. Austria is identified as an angst-ridden atmosphere that conveys a latent threat of violence built from Catholicism, xenophobic hatred and a partially hidden, partially overt National Socialist ideology; these themes appear relatively constantly in what is a collection of otherwise widely differing novels. Thomas Bernhard's texts provide an unsurpassable plethora of examples: "A hate-love for Austria is, ultimately, the key to all that I write." he explained in an interview.[2] If this ambiguous emotion makes Bernhard see nothing but "ugliness and stench"[3] in his literary treatment of Austria, this approaches a fixation that is interesting not least from a psychoanalytical point of view: after all, this Austria-bashing does continue from "Frost" (1963) right through to "Extinction" (1986).

1 Freud, *Beyond the Pleasure Principle*, 70.
2 "Haßliebe zu Österreich ist letztlich der Schlüssel zu allem, was ich schreibe." In: Dreissinger, *Katastrophe*, 112.
3 "Häßlichkeit und Gestank" (ibid.).

Thomas Bernhards Novel "Extinction"

Thomas Bernhards Novel "Extinction" reminds me of that compulsive repetition of certain actions and experiences marked by 'unpleasure' that Sigmund Freud described in "Beyond the Pleasure Principle": An unconscious effort to repeat past circumstances, even if or especially if they were first experienced as extremely unpleasant, destructive or hurtful and stay that way when they are experienced again. The parallel, however, runs deeper than that. Starting with this repetition compulsion, that seems to oppose the pleasure principle, Freud goes on to develop a dichotomy of instincts in those that affirm life (called "Eros") and those that oppose them, summarized in the so-called "death instinct." While the life instinct expresses the organism's effort to reproduce itself in other living organisms, i.e. to repeat its life ad infinitum and not to die, the death instinct represents the wish to return to the inorganic calm that precedes birth, i.e. to end life in order to recreate the long-lost inorganic state from which all life came. Anyone who has read Thomas Bernhard's last great novel "Extinction" will recognize this in the novel's essential intention:

> The only thing my mind is set on is the title: Extinction. For my report serves only to extinguish that which it describes, extinguish everything I connect with Wolfsegg and everything that Wolfsegg is, everything, Gambetti, do you understand what I'm saying, actually, really everything.[4]

It is in these words that the first-person narrator Josef Murau tells his pupil Gambetti about the opus he's planning; its creation is referred to several times in the course of the novel. This makes the structure of "Extinction" similar to that of other texts by Thomas Bernhard that focus on their own creation: in "Das Kalkwerk" ("The Lime Works") from 1970 the protagonist plans a study by the name of "On hearing," in "Beton" ("Concrete") from 1982 we witness the narrator Rudolf's failure to compose a treatise on the composer Mendelsohn Bartholdy, and in "Der Untergeher" ("The Loser") from 1983 the first-person narrator is constantly developing and discarding an essay "On Glenn Gould." What distinguishes "Extinction" from the others is that the theme and the intention of the opus mentioned within the text is basically congruent with those of the novel itself. This obviously self-referential constellation not only allows us to surmise that "Extinction" is one of the few completed 'studies' to be mentioned in Bernhard's texts; but it also enables us to interpret this 'extinction' by following Murau's description of his own re-

4 "Das einzige, das ich schon endgültig im Kopf habe, ist der Titel Auslöschung, denn mein Bericht ist nur dazu da, das in ihm Beschriebene auszulöschen, alles auszulöschen, das ich unter Wolfsegg verstehe, und alles, das Wolfsegg ist, alles, Gambetti, verstehen Sie mich, wirklich und tatsächlich alles." (Bernhard, *Auslöschung*, 199).

port in the text itself. For if there should be any need for further proof of the novel's similarity to the report that Murau plans, we find it in two more terms that Murau uses and that have been used in turn to describe the novel "Extinction": "Anti-autobiography" is one; and "the art of exaggeration" is the other. This hands us two more categories central to our understanding of the text; and it also names two general themes that are combined in "Extinction" and that I intend to examine more closely on the following pages. I would like to start by establishing that extinction confronts the relation of biography and rhetoric. However, literary criticism has yet to clearly define what that relation is actually about, for the terms anti-autobiography and art of exaggeration enjoy a rather contradictory relationship in the first place.

Murau believes unlimited exaggeration and the stylization of a "great master of survival" to be the only chance for an "Existenzüberbrückung," an "existential bridging": "The art of exaggeration, (in order) to bear existence, I said to Gambetti, to make existence possible."[5] So if this exaggeration is meant to make existence bearable, can it also serve to extinguish existence, i.e. to destroy Wolfsegg's "Herkunftskomplex," his "complex of origin"? And whose existence is supposed to be extinguished anyway? Does "Extinction" tell of two separate existences? One that narrates and one that is narrated, one that extinguishes—and becomes possible due to exaggeration –, and one that is to be extinguished? And how can we find clear terms to describe all this, what categories might we use to understand this ambiguous process of extinguishing and facilitating existence? I will return to Freud for a closer examination and focus on an economy that is central to "Beyond the Pleasure Principle" and might help us to explain the complex entanglement of extinction and facilitation of existence. This economy encompasses invalidating the pleasure principle on the one hand and reactivating it on the other. Between these extremes, I plan to examine the relation of biography and rhetoric and present two concepts I deem immensely useful for any discussion involving Bernhard: The first is the concept of trauma as a central category in biography beyond the pleasure principle; the second is the concept of sarcasm, which is just as central for rhetoric on this side of the pleasure principle. Trauma and sarcasm—according to my theory—describe the common area of Bernhard's writings and are of special import for his novel "Extinction."

5 "Übertreibungskunst, [um] die Existenz auszuhalten, habe ich zu Gambetti gesagt, sie zu ermöglichen." (Bernhard, *Auslöschung*, 612).

On Trauma

The term "trauma" comes from the Ancient Greek and is usually translated as "wound"; it refers to a certain kind of wound that keeps re-opening.[6] It describes the physical consequences of a major blow. Psychic trauma is a term used to describe the effect on a person of an extremely stressful life event. An "overwhelming experience"[7] or an external event that is outside the range of usual human experience and that would be markedly distressing to almost anyone. Transferred to psychology, trauma refers to a confrontation with an incident that took place in reality and to which the individual felt exposed, vulnerable and helpless. The usual mechanisms of defense and of assimilation are unsuccessful. The individual is overcome by a flood of stimulus, resulting in a kind of shock with which it cannot cope.[8] I'll gonna refer to a psychoanalytic definition, cause this is the most important one in the humanities.[9] In "Beyond the Pleasure Principle," Freud tried to conceptualize the common traumatic neurosis as the result of an extensive breach of the shield against stimuli, as we quoted already in the beginning. Pretty important is the fact that Freuds psychoanalytic view of the traumatic neurosis is not identical to the most simplistic form of the shock theory, as Freud points out.[10] While the latter attributes the essence of shock to direct damage, Freud focusses on the certain condition of the shock:

> And we still attribute importance to the element of fright. It is caused by lack of any preparedness for anxiety, including lack of hypercathexis of the systems that would be the first to receive the stimulus. Owing to their low cathexis those systems are not in a good position for binding the inflowing amounts of excitation and the consequences of the breach in the protective shield follow all the more easily.[11]

Jean Laplanche has given a general description of Freud's understanding of trauma, which varied significantly over the course of Freud's career: "An event in the subject's life, defined by its intensity, by the subject's incapacity to respond adequately to it and by the upheaval and long-lasting effects that it brings about in the psychical organization"[12] The famous "repetition compulsion" serves to reestablish the traumatic incident in order to bind the stimulus flood or to find an outlet and so to revalidate the pleasure principle. The same function governs repetition in dreams and repetitive symptoms. This is

6 Scaer, *Trauma Spectrum*; Schönfelder, *Wounds and Words*.
7 Van der Kolk et al., *Traumatic Stress*.
8 Peitzman et al., *Trauma Manual*.
9 Cf.: Robson, *Writing Wounds*; Bennett, *Empathic vision*; Caruth, *Unclaimed Experience*; Garloff, *Words from Abroad*.
10 See: Freud, "Beyond the pleasure principle," 37.
11 Ibid., 31.
12 Laplanche et al., *Language*, 465–69.

pretty important, cause Freud now has to admit a contradiction concerning his earlier theory of dreams. Neurotic dreams are an exception to the rule that the dream is the fulfillment of a wish:

> The fulfilment of wishes is, as we know, brought about in a hallucinatory manner by dreams, and under the dominance of the pleasure principle this has become their function. But it is not in the service of that principle that the dreams of patients suffering from traumatic neuroses lead them back with such regularity to the situation in which the trauma occurred. We may assume, rather, that dreams are here helping to carry out another task, which must be accomplished before the dominance of the pleasure principle can even begin.[13]

Because this form of repetition is connected with extreme displeasure, Freud concludes that there is a mental layer, a basic instinct, that precedes the antithesis of pleasure and displeasure and which he names the death instinct, as mentioned before. This drive is identified as "to reduce, to keep constant or to remove internal tension due to stimuli"[14]; which is why it becomes the essential motor for the repetition compulsion of traumatized patients in the economic model. For if the trauma is understood as "excitations from outside which are powerful enough to break through the protective shield"[15], threatening to destroy the human organism, the constant repetition of this traumatic experience—in the dreams of patients suffering from war neuroses, for instance—is an attempt at abolishing this extreme "stimulus tension" that created the trauma in the first place; and finally, to revalidate the pleasure principle, which "seems actually to serve the death instinct"[16], as Freud says.

So does "Extinction" speak of such a trauma? Not directly it doesn't, at least not of an authentic case, if authenticity can even enter the question as far as Bernhard is concerned: for the text is no less an expression of an (unauthentic and above all extremely childish) exaggeration. His own traumatic childhood experiences are told in another text, in the last part of the five volumes of his biographical narrative prose in "The Child": Bernhard's mother was forced to give the infant in care with a woman who "stored foster children below deck" on a fishing smack in Rotterdam. And yet the childhood described in this autobiographical text is in many ways similar to the one told in "Extinction." In "The Child" the enormously labile boy is on a futile search for direction between the fits of his mother ("awful devil's child") and the caring administrations of his grandfather, who brings him up according to the principles of a mental anarchism; in "Extinction," we find a similar relation between Murau and his beloved anarchistic uncle Georg and the extremely

13 See: Freud, "Beyond the pleasure principle," 32.
14 Ibid., 55-56.
15 Ibid., 35.
16 Ibid., 63.

tyrannous, mean and evil-spirited mother. Again, the mother's fits are in the foreground; remember, for instance, her cussing ("you are inhuman," p. 267) and young Murau's punishment for reading too long in Jean Paul's "Siebenkäs" in his parents' library:

> The real punishment was that I wasn't allowed to leave my room for three days, my mother had locked the door and left me without any kind of food for the whole of the three days. I had sat down at my table and done nothing for the whole three days but to cry. Outside my door, my sisters kept running up and down the hall and constantly shouted Siebenkäs, Siebenkäs, Siebenkäs in highest schadenfreude.[17]

You might read these and several other passages in the novel as traumatic experiences—in a rather wide sense of the word, no doubt. For one thing, it is the relation with the mother, as in "The Child," that is described as traumatic. That this mother is not only deeply convinced of National Socialism, but at the same time systematically betraying her husband with archbishop Spadolini, isn't even the real reason for Murau's identification of his mother with "evil personified" (p. 569) when he extensively remembers his childhood. Instead, it is her systematical penalizing of young Murau that dominates the memory of his mother. This, in turn, is probably founded in the fate of the unwanted child: "For my whole life, she accepted me as something she never wanted, and she kept referring to me that way, at any opportunity, and often called me *the most superfluous child you can imagine.*"[18] Her permanent distrust is symptomatic for this mother-child-relationship and makes it impossible for her to even begin to understand her son or to show the least of the respect for him he would naturally deserve as her child. This expresses itself in numerous unjustified punishments and accusations that by necessity make the mother seem "ruthless, inhumane, even atrocious."

So in this sense, one can interpret Murau's intent to "extinguish" his origin and family as an attempt in the terms of Freud's economy to rebalance the extreme "penetrations of his protective shield" during his childhood with an "abolishment of the inner stimulus tension" which marks the death instinct. This might explain the awkward idea of the "Extinction" of the "complex of origin Wolfsegg." But such an interpretation does nothing but copy the novel unto a representation of psychoanalytic theory and does it no justice. Nor

17 "Die eigentliche Bestrafung hatte darin bestanden, daß ich drei Tage nicht mehr aus meinem Zimmer herausgehen durfte, meine Mutter hatte es abgesperrt und mich die ganzen drei Tage ohne jegliche Nahrung gelassen. Ich hatte mich an meinen Tisch gesetzt und die ganzen drei Tage nichts anderes getan, als geheult. Vor der Tür liefen die ganze Zeit meine beiden Schwestern hin und her und schrieen ununterbrochen in höchster Schadenfreude *Siebenkäs, Siebenkäs, Siebenkäs.*" (Bernhard, *Auslöschung*, 268).

18 "Lebenslänglich betrachtete sie mich als unerwünscht und sie stellte mich auch immer nur als unerwünscht hin, gleich bei welcher Gelegenheit, bezeichnete mich auch oft als *das überflüssigste Kind, das man sich vorstellen kann.*" (ibid., 290).

does it deal with the question of the novel's rhetoric, which in fact contradicts this psychoanalytic reading. The essential rhetoric tool of this extinction or negation is, after all, exaggeration; but exaggeration above all marks the fact that it wasn't really meant like that, that the extreme qualities of the description are owed to a certain rhetoric which makes the description worse than the described really was. Doesn't that mean that exaggeration as a rhetorical technique, if marked as such, serves rather to depotentize that traumatization which characterizes Murau's relationship with Wolfsegg and which triggers the extinction we've been discussing? If the "anti-autobiography" that Murau plans to write next for his adored uncle Georg deal with "an awful Wolfsegg with awful human beings" (A 197), doesn't that constitute a first obvious exaggeration? Isn't that in fact a misjudgement? The whole set of awfulness that is described in "Extinction": The Austrian state and its enduring national socialist and catholic disposition; the likewise awful and contemptible family—"my mother is disgusting, my sisters are too, the father's weak, my brother is a fool, they all are idiots": isn't all this an expression of exaggeration?

The Art of Exaggeration

The text provides us with two more characterizations of the "art of exaggeration," which allow us a further differentiation of these questions which are of extreme importance for Thomas Bernhard's prose. They concentrate on the paradoxical aspects of the exaggeration, the bridging and the possibility or destruction of the individual's existence:

> "In order to make things understandable, we have to exaggerate, is what I had said to him, only exaggeration makes things graphic, even the danger of being called a fool doesn't disturb us once we've reached a certain age. There is nothing better than being named a fool in old age. The greatest bliss I know is that of the aged fool, who can follow his foolishness in total independence.... It is foolishness that makes us happy, is what I said to Gambetti."[19]

Murau refers his art of exaggeration to the figure of the fool, prominent in Austrian literature at least since Johann Nestroy. This makes the riddle sketched above seem more approachable. Firstly, it affirms the rhetoric or ironic dimension of the text, i.e. it ascribes constant relevance to a distinction

19 "Um etwas begreiflich zu machen, müssen wir übertreiben, hatte ich zu ihm gesagt, nur die Übertreibung macht anschaulich, auch die Gefahr, daß wir zum Narren erklärt werden, stört uns in höherem Alter nicht mehr. Es gibt nichts Besseres, als in höherem Alter zum Narren ernannt zu sein. Das höchste Glück, das ich kenne, ist das des Altersnarren, der gänzlich unabhängig seinem Narrentum nachgehen kann.... Das Narrentum ist es, daß uns glücklich macht, habe ich zu Gambetti gesagt." (ibid., 128–29).

of proposition and meaning. But secondly, it allows us to describe Murau's traumatic experiences not as a contradiction of the rhetoric hyperbole, but as its equivalent. For the figure of the fool that Murau identifies with explains that all the descriptions of his early childhood experiences and all of the gruesomeness they involve are created from the point of view of a new, quasi-foolish existence. The first existence was associated with the unhappy place of Wolfsegg, the second connects to the happiness of the aged fool. The constellation is consciously ambiguous and elucidates the whole text's ambivalence: The content is fraught with extreme displeasure, the form in which it is described however is pleasant, in as much as it expresses the fool's happiness or can lead to such happiness by means of exaggeration.

It is astonishing how much alike this rhetoric is to the deconstructive rhetoric of Paul de Man; the irony in Bernhard's novel creates the same form of a duplicated first ego that de Man described in "The Rhetoric of Temporality" by referring to examples from Baudelaire, Schlegel, E.T.A. Hoffmann and Stendal. Murau possesses the ironic competence of reduplicating his ego that de Man believes to be the basis of all irony whatsoever. De Man quotes Baudelaire: "Almost no one can laugh at his own fall, unless he is a philosopher, a man who has acquired, through habit, the ability to double himself rapidly and look on as a disinterested spectator."[20] De Man concludes: "Ironic language divides the subject into an empirical ego that lives in an unauthentic state and another ego that existes only in the form of language and that claims knowledge of this lack of authenticity."[21] This reduplication seems to take place in "Extinction," in the course of the same ironic structure of the novel that we found in connection with the term "exaggeration." So exaggeration, distortion and caricature aren't limited to that well known means of literary satire, simply rendering the criticism of Wolfsegg (pars pro toto for all of Austria) "understandable" and "graphic." Instead, the exaggeration leads to a reduplication of the ego in a way that we have yet better to understand, which makes it possible to disconnect Murau from his first existence in Wolfsegg and to extinguish that first existence. The happy fool ironically recounts his or someone's unhappy childhood and extinguishes it in the process, a feat both foolish and pleasant: "This however, I had said to Gambetti, is in turn a pleasant me, the thought of my self-disintegration and extinction."[22]

20 De Man, "Rhetoric," 211-12. In Baudelaires text it's like that: "Le comique, la puissance du rire est dans le rieur et nullement dans l'objet du rire. Ce n'est point l'homme qui tombe qui rit de sa propre chute, à moins qu'il ne soit un philosophe, un homme qui ait acquis, par habitude, la force de se dédoubler rapidement et d'assister comme spectateur désintéressé aux phénomènes de son moi." (Baudelaire, *Œuvre complètes*, 2:370).

21 De Man, "Rhetoric," 214.

22 "Das allerdings, hatte ich zu Gambetti gesagt, ist mir wieder ein angenehmer Gedanke, meine Selbstzersetzung und Auslöschung." (Bernhard, *Auslöschung*, 296).

This is a first step towards analyzing the relation of biography and rhetoric, of memory and exaggeration; a relation that structures extinction. If we read the text's irony not as a difference of proposition and intent in the sense of the classical rhetoric, but in the neo-rhetoric, deconstructivist sense of Paul de Man's double ego, the double telos of Murau's artful exaggeration—to allow for existence and to extinguish it—appears not as a contradiction, but as a mark and an effect of such irony. And yet I would like to replace de Man's concept of irony with yet another model that I deem more relevant for the phenomenon of the double ego. In considering the ambivalent construction of pleasure and displeasure, of happy foolishness and unhappy memory, which are the two essential elements of this reduplication, we can offer a more narrow description of this irony: Sarcasm. Only in the category of sarcasm can we adequately subsume that violent disposition that we found on the level of memory in dealing with Murau's traumatic experiences. The relationship between the narrator and the narrated, or rather: between the extinguishing and the extinguished ego is sarcastic in a very specific sense of the word.

Sarcasm as a Traumatizing Kind of Rhetoric?

Sarcasm is a concept of Ancient rhetoric, it goes back to the Greek and the Byzantine schools of rhetoric and is conserved in the Roman rhetorician Quintilian's lore of the trope. An element of Quintilian's extensive treatise on tropes in his *Institutio Oratoriae*, sarcasm belongs to one of four forms of irony taken from the Greek tradition.[23] I will refer to a classical definition of this rhetoric figure, directed at arguably the most famous image of sarcastic irony: The scene of the crucifixion. Crucified Jesus is being mocked, not only by the soldiers, but by the leading priests, the masters of law and the council elders. "If thou be the king of the Jews, save thyself." we read in Luke (23:35 KJV). In Anthony Blackwell's "An introduction to the classics. With an essay, on the nature and use of those emphatical and beautiful figures which give strength and ornament to writing" (1719) we find a definition of sarcasm that corresponds to this same image: "When a dying or a dead Person is insulted with Scoffs and ironicall Tardness 'tis is usually called a sarcasm."[24] Thus sarcasm is close to the forms of black or macabre humor, which often refers to the dying or the dead and prompts a bitter response. According to Blackwell's definition, the mocking words of the Roman soldiers epitomize sarcasm;

23 Quintilian, *Inst.* 8.6.57 (Winterbottom, 2:83).
24 Blackwall, *Introduction*, 179.

their uttering is sarcastic since it replaces any sympathy for the dying with mockery and *schadenfreude*.[25]

Now isn't that what the fundamental plot of "Extinction" is all about? Doesn't it revolve around that very same rhetorical figure? 46-year-old private scholar and author Franz Josef Murau, from Austria, living in Rome, receives a telegram from his two sisters reporting the fatal accident of his parents and his brother. He does not in any way respond with sadness, *au contraire*! The memory engendered by the impending journey to the funeral in Upper Austria and to the family estate in Wolfsegg is essentially a mockery of the dead. In fact, the text closely associates the concept of mockery and ridicule, these essential elements of sarcasm, with the idea of his familiy's "extinction": "I had only ever wanted this one photo of my brother that made him so ridiculous, is what I had said to Gambetti once, I had wanted a ridiculous brother, a funny one, as I wanted ridiculous parents and funny little sisters, just their mocking faces, Gambetti, that's the truth."[26] Not sadness nor sympathy, but hatred and *schadenfreude* make Murau's response to the report of their death, his reaction is not least explainable by a feeling of resentment. Which is why the portraits of his family members in "Extinction" serve the purpose of emphasizing an absolute ridiculousness; of depicting them as laughably grotesque. Take, for instance, Murau's description of his parents' photographs, which he takes out in order to aid his memory: the parents, Murau tells us, "make but a pitiful, in no way a good impression, ridiculous, comical, getting onto the train for Dover at Victoria station in London."[27] In the same sense, his sisters' photograph freezes their "mocking faces"—a picture that renders the real existence of his sisters no longer imaginable. Murau understands this as an expression of his "meanness, shamelessness, lack of character": "I only had to open the desk drawer in order to revel in my impossible sisters' mocking faces, is what I had said to Gambetti once, to revel in my parents' ridiculousness, in my brother's unhappy stance, strengthening myself in a moment of weakness by taking their pictures from the drawer and finding in this meanness, I must say it: calm."[28]

25 Meyer-Sickendiek, *Literarischer Sarkasmus*, 561–63.

26 "Ich hatte immer nur dieses eine, ihn lächerlich darstellende Foto von meinem Bruder haben wollen, hatte ich einmal zu Gambetti gesagt, ich hatte einen lächerlichen Bruder haben wollen, einen komischen, wie ich lächerliche Eltern haben wollte, komische, keine Schwestern, nur ihre spöttischen Gesichter, Gambetti, das ist die Wahrheit." (Bernhard, *Auslöschung*, 248).

27 "nur einen erbärmlichen, keinerlei guten Eindruck, einen lächerlichen, einen komischen, wie sie auf dem Victoriabahnhof in London den Zug nach Dover besteigen." (ibid., 246).

28 "Gemeinheit, Unverschämtheit, Charakterlosigkeit": "Ich brauchte immer nur die Schreibtischlade aufzumachen, um mich an meinen unmöglichen Schwestern mit ihren spöttischen Gesichtern zu weiden, hatte ich einmal zu Gambetti gesagt, um mich an der Lächerlichkeit meiner Eltern, an der unglücklichen Haltung meines Bruders zu weiden, mich dadurch zu stärken in einem Schwächeanfall, indem ich die Fotos aus der Schreibtischlade

Summary

At the center of the rhetoric-ironic level of this novel we found Bernhard's well known figures of exaggeration and repetition coupled with a rhetoric of rendered ridicule, that encompasses almost all those persons associated with the complex of origin that is Wolfsegg. My interest here was the motivation of this extreme intent for an "Extinction" and destruction that focuses not on Murau's family, but on his own existence and ruin: "I am in fact about to dissect Wolfsegg and those that are my own and to disintegrate, to destroy, to extinguish them and to take apart myself in the process."[29] I attempted to retrace this idea of extinction by ridicule that is found in Murau's extreme sarcasm to a previous history. You might call it an attempt at a kind of economy in Freud's sense, centered on a repetition compulsion that Freud observed, among others, in war neuroses. The repetition compulsion serves to re-establish the traumatic incident with the aim of binding the flood of stimuli or to find an outlet and thereby re-invalidate the pleasure principle. It is the reactivated pleasure principle connected to the description of unpleasant and awful experiences that create the impression of sarcasm in this novel. It is difficult to distinguish cause and effect in between the fields of trauma and sarcasm, i.e. to answer the question whether it is the traumatic experiences that lead to the sarcastic irony or whether it is the sarcastic irony that makes the novel's contents appear traumatic. What is important, however, is to recognize this mixture as an essential element of Bernhard's rhetoric. When Murau gives his family's estate to the Israeli Cultural Community of Vienna, which is lead by his "brother in spirit" Rabbi Eisenberg, he commits more than a political feat; he inflicts the greatest possible hurt, the worst meanness on his family and his own sisters that he can achieve. So what remains in the end is not nothing, but rather—comparable to Elias Canetti's "Die Blendung," "Auto da Fé"—the lustful and foolish laughter of Murau, a *schadenfreude*, a *joy of damage*, in the word's truest sense.

Bibliography

Baudelaire, C. "On the Essence of Laughter." Pages 140–61 in: *The Painter of Modern Life and Other Essays*. Translated and edited by J. Mayne. New York: Da Capo, 1964.

—. *Œuvres complètes*. 7 vols. Paris: Callman-Lévy, 1868–1870.

herausnehme und betrachte und mich in dieser Gemeinheit, muß ich sagen, beruhige." (ibid., 249).

29 "tatsächlich bin ich dabei, Wolfsegg und die Meinigen auseinanderzunehmen und zu zersetzen, sie zu vernichten, auszulöschen und nehme mich dabei selbst auseinander, zersetze mich, vernichte mich, lösche mich aus." (ibid., 199).

BENNETT, J. *Empathic Vision: Affect, Trauma and Contemporary Art.* Stanford: Stanford University Press, 2005.

BERNHARD, T. *Auslöschung: Ein Zerfall.* Frankfurt am Main: Suhrkamp, 1986.

BLACKWALL, A. *An Introduction to the Classics: With an Essay, on the Nature and Use of those Emphatical and Beautiful Figures which give Strength and Ornament to Writing.* London, 1718. Repr., New York: Garland, 1971.

CARUTH, C. *Unclaimed Experience. Trauma, Narrative and History.* Baltimore: Johns Hopkins University Press, 1996.

DREISSINGER, S., ed. *Von einer Katastrophe in die andere: 13 Gespräche mit Thomas Bernhard.* Weitra: Bibliothek der Provinz, 1992.

FREUD, S. *Beyond the Pleasure Principle.* Edited by T. Dufresne and translated by G. C. Richter. Peterborough, Ontario: Broadview, 2011.

—. "Beyond the Pleasure Principle." Pages 7-64 in vol. 18 of *The Standard Edition of the Complete Psychological Works of Sigmund Freud.* Edited and translated by J. Strachey. 24 vols. London: Hoghart, 1956-1974.

GARLOFF, K. *Words from Abroad: Trauma and Displacement in Postwar German Jewish Writers.* Detroit: Wayne State University Press, 2005.

LAPLANCHE, J., and J. B. PONTALIS. *The Language of Psycho-Analysis.* Translated by D. Nicholson-Smith. New York: Norton, 1967.

PEITZMAN, A. B., et al. *The Trauma Manual: Trauma and Acute Care Surgery.* 3d ed. Philadelphia: Lippincott, Williams & Wilkins, 2007.

ROBSON, K. *Writing Wounds: The Inscription of Trauma in Post-1968 French Women's Life-Writing.* New York: Rodopi, 2004.

SCAER, R. C. *The Trauma Spectrum: Hidden Wounds and Human Resiliency.* New York: Norton, 2005.

SCHÖNFELDER, C. *Wounds and Words: Childhood and Family Trauma in Romantic and Postmodern Fiction.* Bielefeld: Transcript, 2013.

DE MAN, P. "The Rhetoric of Temporality." Pages 187-228 in *Paul de Man. Blindness and Insight: Essays in the Rhetoric of Contemporary Criticism.* Edited by W. Godzich. 2d ed. Minneapolis: University of Minnesota Press, 1983.

MEYER-SICKENDIEK, B. *Was ist literarischer Sarkasmus? Ein Beitrag zur deutsch-jüdischen Moderne.* Paderborn: Fink, 2009.

VAN DER KOLK, B. A., A. C. MCFARLANE, and L. WEISAETH. *Traumatic Stress: The Effects of Overwhelming Experience on Mind, Body, and Society.* New York: Guilford, 1996.

WINTERBOTTOM, M., ed. *M. Fabi Quintiliani institutionis oratoriae libri duodecim.* Oxford Classical Texts. 2 vols. Oxford: Oxford University Press, 1970.

Part Two
Collective Dimensions

Roberto Castro and Joaquina Erviti

A Society Undergoing Trauma*

Criminal Violence in Mexico and the Search for Justice and Hope

Abstract

Is Mexico suffering a cultural traumatization process, according to Alexander's terms? The paper aims to provide the initial elements required to ponder this question, starting with the enormous crisis of violence and criminality currently sweeping the nation. The first section of this paper will aim to describe two concepts; that of cultural trauma, as defined by Alexander, and that of social suffering, as defined by Kleinman. The second section of this paper will offer a brief description of the process of violence which Mexico is currently experiencing. Special attention will be paid to the crisis of femicides in Ciudad Juárez, the war against drugs, as directed by Mexico's government, and the increase in crimes such as kidnapping and extortion observed in recent years. The third part of this paper will analyze the main coping strategies which the Mexican population has turned to in order to attempt to process the immense pain caused by this situation. We highlight the different manifestations that this process has created among social actors; a process in which the construction, or not, of a social trauma is at play. Popular protest movements are analyzed as mechanisms against the inefficiency of the judicial system in this country. We will look at the role of religion and popular folklore as coping mechanisms along with the strategy to maintain a policy of silence in order to minimize the magnitude of this tragedy as implemented by much of the Mexican media and also the current government, which took power in December of 2012. This paper will conclude by stating that the origins of this situation may go as far back as the 1970s and by defining the yet uncertain character of the current struggle to define this crisis as a cultural trauma.

This paper is centered on the huge social suffering the people of Mexico have been experiencing in recent years. A major social crisis has arisen due to an unprecedented increase in violence originally related to the dispute among different drug cartels throughout the national territory, but which now involves factors other than drug trafficking. Crimes such as extortion, kidnap-

* We are very grateful to Anna Shildrick for translating both the presentation delivered at Aarhus and this chapter into English.

ping and the like have dramatically increased in recent years. More than 90,000 persons were killed in the previous government's "war against crime." (2006-2012). At least 10,000 of the dead remain unidentified. There are also thousands of missing and displaced people due to violence. The main question we want to address here is how Mexican people are coping with this pain. What role does popular religion play, and what other cultural and sociological resources do Mexican people seem to be resorting to in order to process all this suffering? To answer this question, the first part of this paper will describe the concepts of cultural trauma and social suffering in order to allow us to develop the analysis based on those concepts presented in the rest of the paper. In the second section, we shall describe the process of violence that Mexico is currently experiencing. In the third section, we will analyze the principle coping strategies which the Mexican population has turned to in order to attempt to process the immense pain caused by this crisis. We will highlight the social struggle that exists between various actors and arenas as to whether to construct, or not, a cultural trauma from this situation. This paper will conclude by examining the current crisis of violence and crime in Mexico in relation to recent history (wherein we will identify one of its principal causes) and in relation to the immediate future in order to establish whether the current crisis will succeed or not in being construed as a cultural trauma.

1. Social Suffering and Trauma Theory

The concept of trauma involves at least two levels of analysis. On the one hand, we may speak of trauma in psychological terms: "psychic trauma occurs when a sudden, unexpected, overwhelming intense emotional blow or a series of blows assaults the person externally. Traumatic events are external, but they quickly become incorporated into the mind."[1] This is primarily a naturalistic approach, which suggests that trauma emerges from painful situations or experiences. In regard to this approach, Alexander opposes the concept of *cultural trauma* which essentially emphasizes the active and deliberate process of social construction which different communities undergo.[2] The process consists of defining a certain painful experience as a cultural crisis and then redefining the collective identity. This redefinition may be carried out through what Alexander calls "cultural work," which consists of speeches, rituals, marches, meetings, plays, movies, and storytelling of all kinds.[3] The process of constructing a cultural and social trauma requires, among other

1 Terr, *Too scared to cry*, 8
2 Alexander, *Trauma.*
3 Ibid., 4.

things, carrier groups (i.e. collective agents of the trauma process), the development of a new master narrative, and institutional arenas within which this new narrative may develop. For the purposes of this paper, we will focus on the legal and scientific arenas. We sustain that it is relevant to examine both levels of analysis (psychoanalytic and cultural) to gauge the traumatic consequences that a crisis of violence and security, such as that currently prevalent in Mexico, can have on a country's inhabitants. In this context we may also take into account Kleinman's concept of social suffering. Phenomena often associated with the concept of social suffering and collective pain may manifest as afflictions such as hunger and poverty, war, violence, insecurity, epidemics, enforced migrations, and various forms of structural violence.[4] But an often overlooked and more devastating dimension of pain and suffering exists as a consequence of a crisis such as Mexico's; one that affects thousands more than those who are killed and injured. It is a dimension that reflects the resulting emotional turmoil of grief for the murder or disappearance of a loved one, anger at seeing the one's security taken away, outrage at the atrocity of the attacks, the impotence and fear stemming from the absolute impunity that abounds, the thirst for revenge barely contained by a spirit of institutional loyalty that still survives in many victims and their relatives, and the search for physical and spiritual explanations that give meaning to the pain experienced.[5]

This is the essence that we give to the concept of social suffering in the pages that follow. Our premise is that Mexican society is immersed in a vast process of social suffering. This national insecurity crisis affects all levels of society, not only the direct victims themselves, but in fact all sectors of the population in so many ways.

2. The Violence and Insecurity Crisis in Mexico

2.1 Femicide in Ciudad Juárez

Ciudad Juárez is a city located in northern Mexico on the U.S. border. It is a city of approximately 1,515,000 inhabitants which boasts a large number of industries dedicated to the assembly of U.S. goods. The reason for setting up their companies on Mexican soil, of course, is that labor is much cheaper in Mexico.

In 1993, a series of murders of women began to be reported in Ciudad Juárez. These were acts characterized by extreme cruelty to the victims. In the

4 Kleinman et al.
5 Salazar, "Entre la ley y el miedo."

early years, the pattern consisted of the victims' disappearance. But as of the year 2000, the bodies of the previously missing women began to turn up on vacant lots, on streets, or in the desert surrounding the city. All the victims showed evidence of having been sexually attacked with ferocity, of being mutilated, and dismembered.

From January 1993 to November the 30th, 2012, the total number of femicides in the city had amounted to 1,348. An average of 67 each year. More than 5 a month. Around one per week.[6]

State action has been particularly deficient in the investigation of these cases. The State has failed dramatically in the administration of justice. In some cases, innocent scapegoats have been blamed after undergoing a process of torture.[7] Furthermore, several self-confessed murderers have been released arbitrarily. Other cases have remained unsolved, with no-one arrested, no-one sentenced.

In recent years, one case gained international visibility. In 2001, three women were murdered in what became known as the Cotton Field case. The American Court of Human Rights condemned the Mexican State in 2009 for violating its duty to investigate these cases and to ensure access to justice and judicial protection.[8]

In short, for over 20 years, Ciudad Juárez has come to represent the epitome of a double-sided problem that has hit this country: violence and impunity. In 2008, in the context of the war on drugs declared by the federal government (see following section), a war between two drug cartels began: the Sinaloa Cartel, the strongest in the country, which controls the western drug trafficking route to the U.S.A. and the Juárez cartel, which for decades had controlled that same route. Ciudad Juárez became Mexico's most dangerous city.[9] The abundant testimonies of its own people, ethnographic research undergone onsite, along with extensive reputable media reports all document the overwhelming terror that has fallen on the region.[10]

2.2 The Failure of the War on Drugs

In late 2006, upon taking power the former president Felipe Calderón, the Mexican government began what it called the "war against organized crime."

6 Personal communication from Julia E. Monárrez, specialist in the field.
7 Villamil, *Ciudad Juárez*.
8 IACHR, *Case of González v. Mexico*.
9 Del Bosque, "El lugar más peligroso de México".
10 Documentaries such as *Missing Young Woman*, and films such as *Backyard*, based on true stories, serve well to illustrate the reality.

This was a public policy designed to crack down on gangs and cartels involved in drug trafficking.

Due to inadequacy, lack of preparation or outright corruption on behalf of the police force, the government based its strategy mainly on the highly controversial use of the army within cities and the countryside. In some cities it has become commonplace to see armed confrontations between the army and criminals on the streets. This has resulted in a significant number of "collateral casualties." Another common scene is that of clashes between rival gangs and the mass execution of innocent people. For instance, in January 2010, also in Ciudad Juárez, a group of gunmen raided a private party and fired indiscriminately into the crowd, leaving 16 young people dead and 14 wounded. This event, known as the massacre of Villa Salvacar, had a worldwide impact[11,12]

Furthermore, it has become commonplace to hear of the appearance of executed, decapitated and mutilated corpses openly abandoned in public places. This is not only a matter between members of rival gangs. Such acts are demonstrations of power that are full of symbolism. For example, in September de 2011 the Sinaloa cartel (from western Mexico) entered the territory of the "Zetas" (a drug cartel from the east of Mexico), leaving behind 40 bodies by a main interstate crossing. In November later that year, the "Zetas" responded by leaving 42 corpses on the streets of two cities in enemy territory.[13] Over the 6 years of Calderón's time in office, the escalating violence reached unprecedented levels in the country's history. The death toll from this war stands at over the 90,000 victims (an average of 21 per day);[14] of those, only 47,000 were "executions," i.e. deaths related directly to organized crime;[15] the number of people missing stands at more than 20,000;[16] the number of people displaced and fleeing the violence is over 1,600,000,[17] and the number of people injured is also extremely high. The homicide rate, which had been decreasing steadily between 1982 and 2006, began to increase sharply after 2007. In just five years, the rate increased by more than 700%, and in fact returned to levels previously seen 30 years ago.[18] Organized crime has had a particularly painful effect on illegal migrants traveling from Central America and South-east Mexico to the U.S. in search of better oppor-

11 Malkin and Thompson, "In Mexico, promises do little."
12 Spiegel Online, "Massaker in Drogenhochburg."
13 Mexico has a population of 117 million inhabitants (CONAPO, "Proyecciones de Población"). The figures presented may be seen as rather low, given the size of the population. However, the scale of the impact of the violence on Mexican society is enormous.
14 CIDAC, *8 Delitos primero.*
15 Guerrero and Herrera, "Matan a 21 cada día."
16 Propuesta Cívica, *Bases de datos.*
17 Parametría, "México y sus desplazados."
18 Hijar, "Tras la evidencia."

tunities. They often travel "free-ride" on the roof of a freight train, popularly known as "the Beast," which runs from the Guatemalan border to the U.S. border.[19] Accidents often occur, resulting in the loss of an arm or leg, or death, especially if a person falls under the train. But losing a limb is the lesser danger, in comparison to others that await them on their journey. The "Zetas" have control of the territory along the entire train route. Women testify to taking birth control measures before embarking on their perilous journey, "just in case the Zetas rape them." Others beg their assailants not to hurt them.[20] It is also known that people traveling in these conditions are liable to be abducted, forcibly recruited into the ranks of the Zetas, extorted and killed. In August, 2010, in San Fernando, Tamaulipas, the bodies of 72 migrants (58 men and 14 women) originating from Guatemala, Honduras, El Salvador, Brazil and Ecuador were found. They were executed because they refused to join the ranks or pay the ransom that the Zetas demanded.

A notable increase in civilian human rights violations has been observed alongside the deployment of the army and navy to fight organized crime in the streets. Such abuse by the military has been widely documented on both a national[21,22,23] and international level.[24] In a letter from the organization called Human Rights Watch to the incoming president of Mexico, on December 11, 2012, the institution stated: "During the administration of President Felipe Calderón, Human Rights Watch was able to provide solid evidence to support the theory that military and police officers in five states not only routinely resorted to torture tactics to extract confessions and information from detainees, but have also participated in numerous cases of enforced disappearances and executions. Virtually none of these crimes have been formally investigated and tried, despite the weight of evidence to suggest that public servants are involved. The patterns of abuse seen throughout the accounts of the victims and witnesses, as well as official data collected from interviews with court, public safety and human rights officials, all show that these are not isolated cases. On the contrary, they are examples of the spread of abusive practices displayed by the security forces in the war against organized crime in Mexico."[25] The strategy of "security" implemented by Calderon's government was woefully misguided.[26] Not only did it fail to combat or-

19 Sistiaga, "Las víctimas americanas."
20 García, "'No nos hagan sufrir.'"
21 Díaz, "Dos años."
22 Castellanos, "En Michoacán."
23 Martínez, "Mejoran las leyes."
24 GTDFI, "Desapariciones forzadas."
25 HRW, "Carta al Presidente."
26 A large number of political analysts agree with the opinion that Calderón's war on crime proved to be counterproductive and a failure. See, for example *Nexos* Nos. 405, 407, 409, 410 and 420, and Volpi, "Iatrogenia y antifragilidad."

ganized crime, but violent crime and other forms of criminal activity increased significantly. The cartels, under pressure from the government's strategy, opted to diversify operations and turn to alternative avenues of crime, such as kidnapping and extortion, to offset the losses suffered under this war against crime. The effect of the government's policy was, in fact, counterproductive.

This offers us an explanation as to why, in addition to violence between different cartels deriving from the disputed territories, and the corresponding violence exerted against the population, other crimes such as human trafficking, kidnapping and extortion, are affecting thousands of people. A recent study carried out by a state university estimates that each year there are ten thousand cases of human trafficking in Mexico; 99% for sexual exploitation purposes; 95% women; half of them taken to the United States and Canada and some European countries. [27] The vast majority of trafficked women are kidnapped and forced into prostitution. The families never hear from the victims again.

The incidence of kidnapping has grown dramatically since 2005. In 2010 there were just over 8,640 recorded kidnappings in the country,[28] yet it is suggested that in fact the real number of kidnappings in 2012 may range instead around 21,000.[29]

A common occurrence in today's Mexican society, the everyday citizen is subject to receiving threatening phone calls in which the voice on the line claims to have kidnapped a family member. It is known that many such calls are made by inmates from inside the prisons around the country, in a bid to obtain a sum of money «in exchange for the freedom" of the alleged victim. By means of radio spots, authorities warn people about these calls. Similarly, extortion is common practice, especially in the north of the country. Business owners are threatened with violence if they do not pay out large sums of money. Cooperation means being able to continue to function as a business, or at least, to avoid a violent encounter. In August 2011, a casino in the city of Monterrey was burned down in broad daylight in retaliation for the refusal of the owners to pay the amount they were asked for. The event killed 52 people, most of them housewives, retired or elderly, and dozens more were injured in the attack.

Fear has become an ever-present feeling for many people across the country. This fear governs many of Mexico's inner-city practices (and also those in small towns and rural areas, many of which are abandoned). For example, a growing number of neighborhoods and estates across many cities around the country have closed off access points with gates and surveillance teams. Giv-

27 Kumar, *Perspectivas*.
28 Ch. and Rivera, "¡Es el secuestro, señores!"
29 ICESI, *Análisis*.

en the state's inability to provide security, citizens have been forced to "privatize" their immediate residential areas and establish their own rights of access. Similarly, it is estimated that the number of Mexican citizens who dare to wear jewelry outside the home decreased by 55% in recent years, while the number of people leaving the home to go jogging in public places decreased by 25%.[30] Also in decline is the number of people who go out at night, who carry cash or credit cards, who take a walk, who take a taxi directly from the street, etc.[31] On the increase, the use of armored cars can be noted among the higher socio-economic groups.[32]

It is clear that Mexico is experiencing an extremely complex situation. The femicides reported in Ciudad Juárez in 1993 were perhaps the first clear signs of a process of social disintegration that was emerging across various parts of the country. The rise of crime in Mexico is directly linked to its context of a weak judicial system, whose institutions are infiltrated by organized crime. This institutional weakness is accompanied by public distrust of the authorities and hence a lack of "culture" of reporting crime. According to recent studies, for every 100 crimes committed in Mexico in 2010, only one was punished.[33] There is a "sense of practicality" in this country, which makes it inadvisable to report crime. Not only is it highly unlikely that the reported crime be translated into concrete action on behalf of the authorities (as these numbers previously mentioned illustrate), but there is also a high risk that the authorities themselves are involved in the crime.

In short, slaughter after slaughter, tragedy after tragedy, death after death, the Mexican people have suffered a great deal of pain in recent years. We're neither talking about political nor ethnic violence (in the traditional sense), nor war between two countries. Mexico's experience is different from all other forms of violence and suffering that have been studied in various contexts[34,35]. So how are people facing all of this?

30 CIDAC, *8 Delitos primero.*
31 Baranda, "Restringen mexicanos actividades."
32 Vera, "El blindaje del miedo."
33 Rivera, "Los números rojos."
34 Das et al., *Violence and Subjectivity.*
35 Kleinman et al., *Social Suffering.*

3. Coping Strategies and the Battles on the Process of Trauma Making

3.1 Civil Society's Fight against Crime

In March 2011, a young student named Juan Francisco Sicilia was killed along with six of his friends in Cuernavaca. His father, the Mexican Catholic poet Javier Sicilia, has since initiated the largest public protest against the lack of security and the escalating violence in the country's history. He created the "Movement for Peace with Justice and Dignity" (MPJD), which has brought together a number of victims of violence and impunity, and has received widespread social sympathy. The movement demands the country's demilitarization, a change in strategy in the fight against organized crime, and the end of impunity.

This movement, as one of several carrier groups we have identified, represents one form of expression that this country has found in response to the rising tide of violence and insecurity: that of collective organization and a peaceful but firm challenge to the authorities. Its members have toured the country and the U.S., sometimes organizing marches. They succeeded in forcing the former President of the republic himself to hold public dialogues with them, in which they openly objected to government strategy. One positive result from these discussions was the adoption of the Victims of Violence Law, proposed by the movement.[36] As stated by Alexander, it is the cultural classification of the empirical manifestations of collective trauma which have entered the legal realm. By implementing a specific law for the victims of violence, the distribution of responsibility and punishment, along with the process of compensation, becomes institutionalized. Thus, the process takes a step further in the recognition, by all participants of the phenomenon around which the cultural trauma is constructed.

What we want to emphasize here is that one of the options that some sectors of the country have found useful in harnessing the enormous suffering brought on by the crisis of violence we are experiencing, is indeed public protest and collective organization. Yet, in some extreme cases, protests have culminated in the murder of relatives seeking justice. The most dramatic example, but only one of many, is the case of Marisela Escobedo, who attempted to bring her daughter's murderer to justice. In the face of the ineffectiveness of the authorities, she alone sought and found him. In a trial that caused a national outcry, the accused confessed to the crime, was acquitted and subse-

36 Despite promising to approve it, Calderón eventually decided to veto the Victims of Violence Law. This was considered another offence to an already damaged population due to violence. The government of Mexico's new president, Peña Nieto, has enacted this legislation immediately.

quently released by a court case that became entangled in legal technicalities. Marisela appealed against the outcome but the murderer was freed. Thereafter, Marisela maintained a permanent protest against the state and federal authorities and claimed to be the subject of death threats. In December 2010, Marisela was killed at the state government's palace gates while protesting. The Pan-American Commission on Human Rights reports that approximately 61 human rights defenders were killed in Mexico between 2006 and 2011.[37]

Other organizations with the characteristics of carrier groups have emerged in recent years as a result of the violence and impunity that prevails in the country. One of the most famous is "Bringing Our Daughters Home": a civil organization founded by the family and friends of women and girls missing or murdered in Ciudad Juárez and the state of Chihuahua. Another is "United Forces for Our Missing Ones" in the State of Coahuila, an association that demands the return of their missing loved ones at the hands of the armed forces themselves. In other states, civil organizations fighting for the same purpose, to claim their right to bury their dead, have also emerged.[38] This public response mirrors the pain experienced by thousands of people whose loved ones suddenly disappear, increasingly over time feared dead, and the overwhelming suspicion that the authorities (the police, judges, the justice system) are in collusion with criminals.[39]

3.2 The Memorial and the Victims of Violence Law: Chronicle of a Conflict

A further example of the struggle that has unfolded between the government and civil organizations to determine the character of the collective pain generated as a result of the countless victims of the war against drug crime refers to a proposal made by the movement for Peace with Justice and Dignity (MPJD) to build a Memorial to the victims of this war. The proposal referred to the construction of a monument that would honor the memory of the victims of violence and become established as a reference point that would allow the many affected people to be commemorated. It was, indeed, a step in the right direction to advancing the construction of the cultural trauma, as proposed by Alexander.

37 CIDH, "Segundo Informe."

38 For example, Unidos por los Desaparecidos [United for Missing Persons] from Baja California, Asociación Esperanza contra las Desapariciones Forzadas y la Impunidad [Hope against Impunity and Missing Persons Association]; and Asociación Ciudadana contra la Impunidad [Civil Association against Impunity], all from the state of Baja California.

39 Mendoza, "El derecho a sepultar."

Initially, the government accepted the proposal. Later, the government argued that the Memorial should also include the soldiers killed in the process. The government finally commanded that the Memorial be located in Campo Marte, a military facility in Mexico City. The civil organizations openly protested, rejecting the decree: "We came to tell you that this site perpetuates imposition and nonsense; we came to tell you that this is not the place to heal the pain of the whole country, and it is not the place to convene our memories, our stories and our tears," read Tania Ramirez, from "Children of Mexico," an organization created by children of missing persons detained by federal agents during the period of the dirty war. "A monument as forgetful and irresponsible as this will not heal our wounds (…) wearing our pain on our sleeves and here on the grounds of an army that has been an ally of horror and directly responsible on countless occasions, is outrageous."[40]

To date, and with a new government initiating its term of office in December 2012, the Memorial has yet to be inaugurated and is still under serious dispute between both parties. This issue clearly represents a struggle to define the significance of the monument which ultimately echoes the meaning of the war on crime launched by the previous federal government and the pain that it has caused.

3.3 Other Coping Mechanisms

A highly popular coping mechanism is, of course, popular religion. Mexico is a country with deep religious roots. In a context of violence, fear, and doubt, popular religion serves to provide answers, to comfort its followers, and to provide meaning, significance and certainty to people's lives. It also provides a meaningful answer to the concept of death.[41] The fear of death and the prevalent uncertainty in the face of such an elevated risk of becoming a victim is calmed by the belief in life after death, the belief that a peaceful heaven, reined by justice and happiness for the innocent exists, just as hell and eternal punishment for the guilty.

We may then question what role the two most important totems of this nation play in society. How do they serve as a resource to process the pain, uncertainty and fear that have resulted from this security crisis which we are experiencing? The first refers to the Virgin of Guadalupe, a variant of the Virgin Mary who, according to popular tradition, appeared before an Aztec Indian in the sixteenth century, and is one of the axes of the Mexican reli-

40 Turati, "Protestan contra Memorial."

41 A number of priests have reported a significant increase in the number of special weekly prayer services requested by families of kidnap victims (Barrón and Menchaca, "Llega a misas dolor de plagios").

gious psyche[42,43]. Devotion to the Virgin of Guadalupe supersedes devotion to other central figures of Catholicism, such as Jesus Christ himself, throughout large segments of the population.[44,45]

Devotion to the Virgin of Guadalupe reaches its peak on December 12, the day of her commemoration. Thousands of people join in pilgrimage swarming to the temples to worship and beg, asking for her help and protection, seeking her intercession before God. This devotion to the Virgin and other saints is accompanied by the use of medals, holy cards, and other good luck charms which are used as protective amulets.

This sense of devotion and religious identity is furthermore expressed through the people's enormous faith in and admiration for the Pope, which principally resulted from the enormous popularity that Pope John Paul II enjoyed in this country. Pope Benedict XVI, on his recent visit to Mexico, was received by the multitudes at every public event and cheered incessantly by millions of faithful followers hoping for a word of encouragement: a clear sign of the faith of the people in the face of such violent times for their country. Just days before the Pope's visit, Javier Sicilia—the founder of the MPJD—traveled to Rome to deliver a letter to the Pope petitioning him to address the problem of violence, and to offer comfort to the Mexican people in such times of suffering.[46] The Pope's response was dishearteningly tepid, rather abstract and distant.[47] Like many other institutions in this country, the Church also failed, and has often failed under such circumstances.

The second central totem in Mexico is death itself. Much has been said of the special relationship between the Mexican people and the concept of death. Octavio Paz[48] and several others writers have spoken of the lighthearted and humorous tone in which Mexicans celebrate their dead. Yet recent studies have shown that this is an invented tradition which emerged along with the modern Mexican state.[49] Moreover, beyond the colorful festivities related to the world renowned Day of the Dead, so well promoted for

42 Wolf, "Virgin of Guadalupe."
43 Lafaye, *Quetzalcoatl.*
44 Taylor, "Virgin of Guadalupe."
45 Napolitano, "Virgin of Guadalupe."
46 Sicilia, "De christiano a christiano."
47 In one of his homilies he simply said: "We said, 'A pure heart, create for me, O God' (Ps 50:12) during the responsorial psalm. This exclamation shows us how profoundly we must prepare to celebrate next week the great mystery of the passion, death and resurrection of the Lord. It also helps us to look deeply into the human heart, *especially in times of sorrow as well as hope, as are the present times for the people of Mexico* and of Latin America." (italics added). No additional reference was made to the problem of violence in Mexico. http://www.vatican.va/holy_father/benedict_xvi/homilies/2012/documents/hf_ben-xvi_hom_20120325_ leon_en.html.
48 Paz, *Labyrinth of Solitude.*
49 Lomnitz, *Death and the Idea of Mexico.*

the tourist population, the fact is that the Mexican people continue to suffer, as all humans do, the solitude that death, grief, and pain bring.

In recent years, Mexico has seen a rise in worship of both "la Santa Muerte" (Holy Death), and to "alternative/peripheral/deviant" saints such as Jesus Malverde.[50,51] The Santa Muerte is an image of death, which is revered as a saint. Initially, such practice was directly related to drug traffickers and assassins, as the worship of and sacrifices offered to the Santa Muerte derived from requests to give the criminals the courage to kill, to not fear death.[52]

However, its cult has spread to other sectors of the population, to those who call on la Santa Muerte to ask for all kinds of help, from gaining employment, improving health, to finding protection from the prevailing wave of violence and insecurity. This form of worship is not recognized by the Catholic Church. However, the way in which it has come to be revered is based on Catholic rituals. The rise of worship of la Santa Muerte is possibly related, at least partially, to the inability of Mexican institutions—the state as well as the Church—to bring justice and comfort to the thousands of victims of crime in Mexico.[53]

Finally, a new wave of music has appeared; "narcocorridos," a sub-genre of the popular Mexican "corridos," most popular in the north of Mexico and in the U.S.A.[54,55] The "corridos" are Mexican folk songs which emerged during the Mexican Revolution between 1910 and 1921, and which were sung to celebrate the heroes, their battles and the heroic deeds of the era. Naturally, this new genre exists to exalt heroism within the world of the drug cartels. This increasingly popular music celebrates the world of drug trafficking and its principal drug lords, and promotes a new system of values that tends to legitimize, albeit in a rather passive manner, the lifestyle and aspirations associated with organized crime.[56]

3.4 Silence: A Power Strategy

In recent years, a variety of power related coping strategies have also emerged. One such mechanism is the "Agreement for Information of Violence Coverage," signed by over 700 media organizations from around the country, in March of 2011. This agreement seeks to limit the propaganda effect that

50 Creechan and de la Herran García, "Without God or Law."
51 Price, "Of bandits and saints."
52 Castaneda, *La Santa Muerte.*
53 Gil Olmos, *La Santa Muerte.*
54 Astorga, "Los corridos de traficantes de drogas."
55 Simonett, "Narcocorridos."
56 Wald, *Narcocorrido.*

widespread dissemination of news about violence may incur, since criminal gangs were using this diffusion in their favor. This is illustrated by the behavior of the gangs, who usually leave written messages to their enemies next to a pile of corpses. They trust that the contents of these messages will be disseminated by the media. This diffusion, say those who signed the agreement, is helping to spread terror and, eventually, to limit freedom of expression. A form of self-censorship has thus been imposed.[57]

Barely a month after the signing of the agreement, there was a second slaughter in San Fernando. This time 193 people were killed. The impact of the slaughter on public opinion, however, was much weaker than the previous event. It is unclear whether this was due to the effect of the controlled censorship imposed by the media, or perhaps the result of the inability of the people to comprehend such a tragedy. Perhaps it was a combination of both.

Mexico's new government under the presidency of Enrique Peña Nieto, who took office on December 1, 2012, has adopted an entirely different communication strategy from the previous government's and has chosen to avoid discussing the issue. While acknowledging the seriousness of the problem, the current government's strategy aims to place other relevant issues on the public agenda and to downplay the problem of insecurity.

This is surely yet another expression of the ongoing struggle to define the "true" nature of Mexico's problem: a period of social suffering to be recognized as, and to be transformed into a cultural crisis and hence a cultural trauma; or perhaps, at the other extreme, a period of increased criminal activity that must be understated and controlled in order to be able to get on with other business.

4. Final Remarks

Several recent studies show that it is possible to trace one of the many causes of Mexico's current social breakdown back to the decade of the 1970s.[58,59] The seventies boasted the valuable mass incorporation of women into the labor market (including the formal labor market, although more frequently in the informal labor market), many of whom were housewives, and the sole carers of children, a phenomenon which in turn was the result of various economic and cultural changes that had accumulated across the country.

57 Yet the number of deaths of journalists also increased and some claimed a lack of support from the trade unions or the great capitals of the media who were the ones who had signed the agreement (Borbolla, "Van 67 periodistas asesinados").

58 Jusidman and Almada, *La realidad social.*

59 Jusidman and Marín, *El colapso de la economía.*

This incorporation of women into paid work undoubtedly constituted the exercising of a basic human right as well as a major triumph for the feminist agenda. However, the change was not supported by state policy releasing women from their domestic chores and child rearing duties. The state did not actively promote the co-responsibility of men, nor did it create a widespread system of childcare centers to take over care of children during women's working hours. The state thought and acted with a classic patriarchal style of logic: «Someone else will take care of those tasks.» The result was the well known dilemma of women working the double or triple shift, bringing with it the emergence of a generation of neglected children who grew up without a clear sense of social belonging, no sense of limits in relation to others, without a clear notion of the importance of a lifetime of hard work. Other causes of the security crisis that Mexico is experiencing have to do with the breakdown of institutions and the state's inability to clearly differentiate the criminal groups from the public servants such as the police, judges, and prosecutors among others. This is further complicated, of course, by the booming drugs market in the United States and Mexico. This has given rise to the forming of criminal gangs that fight to the death to control markets and trafficking routes.

Mexico is experiencing a huge rise in the number of human rights violations; the result of an erroneous security strategy promoted by the previous government under Calderon, and which is accompanied by total impunity. Very few cases are ever investigated, sanctioned, or solved. Consequently, Mexico is being traumatized by high levels of violence, criminality and death not seen in decades. We can clearly see the struggle that has unfolded around this phenomenon to define its «true» character, as either a real and lasting trauma, or as simply a temporary and minimal crisis. Arguably, the various coping strategies that we have mentioned, to which the population is turning today, constitute a variety of efforts to interpret and find a sense of understanding of this new reality, to rebuild the social fabric, or to build new forms of community—civil, religious, political, emotional, etc.—that provide shelter and protection. Sociologically, it is possible to identify several of these coping mechanisms as clear signs of a cultural traumatization process currently underway in this country. Alongside the question of how long civil society in Mexico will take to return to a level of normality (once the true character of this trauma is defined), the big questions are which will be the most appropriate sources to keep the hopes of our people alive, and how can we ensure an end to impunity and forge a legal path to achieve justice for all.

Bibliography

ALEXANDER, J. C. *Trauma: A Social Theory*. Cambridge: Polity, 2012.

ASTORGA, L. "Los corridos de traficantes de drogas en México y Colombia" [Drug Traffickers' corridos in Mexico and Colombia]. *Revista Mexicana de Sociología* 59 (1997): 245–61.

BARANDA, A. "Restringen mexicanos actividades por miedo al delito: Temen inseguridad y cambian hábitos" [Mexicans restrict activities out of fear of crime. Fear of insecurity forces a change of habits]. *Reforma* 6853 (28 September 2012): 2.

BARRÓN, F., and A. MENCHACA. "Llega a misas dolor de plagios" [Churches feel the pain of abductions]. *Reforma* (23 September 2012): 10.

BORBOLLA, L. A. "Van 67 periodistas asesinados durante el sexenio" [67 journalists killed so far this current presidential term]. *El Universal* (17 July 2012). Cited 17 February 2014. Online: http://www.eluniversal.com.mx/notas/859648.html.

CASTANEDA, K. P. *La Santa Muerte, protectora de los hombres* [The Holy Death: Defender of Men]. Mexico: Instituto Nacional de Antropologia e Historia, 2008.

CASTELLANOS, F. "En Michoacán, las fuerzas federales arrasan parejo" [Federal police in Michoacán clean up the streets]. *Proceso* 1868 (2012): 20–22.

CH., RAFAEL, and M. RIVERA. "¡Es el secuestro, señores!" [It's the kidnapping, gentlemen!]. *Nexos* 412 (2012): 21.

CIDAC (Centro de Investigación para el Desarrollo). *8 Delitos primero [8 Offences first]*. Mexico: CIDAC, 2012.

CIDH (Comisión Interamericana de Derechos Humanos). "Segundo Informe sobre la Situación de las Defensoras y los Defensores de los Derechos Humanos en la Américas" [Second Report on the Situation of Human Rights Defenders in the Americas]. Cited 17 February 2014. Online: http://www.oas.org/es/cidh/defensores/docs/pdf/defensores2011.pdf.

CONAPO (Consejo Nacional de Población). "Proyecciones de Población 2010–2050." No pages. Cited 17 February 2014. Online: http://www.conapo.gob.mx/es/CONAPO/Proyecciones.

CREECHAN, J. H., and J. DE LA HERRAN GARCÍA. "Without God or Law: Narcoculture and Belief in Jesus Malverde." *Religious Studies and Theology* 24 (2005): 5–57.

DAS, V., A. KLEINMAN, M. RAMPHELE, and P. REYNOLDS, eds. *Violence and Subjectivity*. Berkeley: University of California Press, 2000.

DEL BOSQUE, M. "El lugar más peligroso de México" [The most dangerous place in Mexico]. *Nexos* 413 (2012): 34–42.

DÍAZ, G. L. "Dos años … y la culpa se desvanece" [Two years … and the guilt starts to fade]. *Proceso* 1868 (2012): 17–19.

GARCÍA, J. DE DIOS. "'No nos hagan sufrir,' piden mujeres migrantes a delincuentes" ["'Don't hurt us,' migrant women beg of offenders"]. *Milenio Semanal* (12 march de 2012): 26–32.

GIL OLMOS, J. *La Santa Muerte. La Virgen de los Olvidados* [The Holy Death. The Virgin of the Forgotten]. Mexico: Debolsillo, 2010.

GTDFI (Grupo de Trabajo de las Naciones Unidas sobre las desapariciones forzadas o involuntarias). "México / Desapariciones forzadas: grupo de expertos de la ONU hace amplias recomendaciones a las autoridades." No pages. Cited 17 February 2014. Online: http://www.ohchr.org/SP/NewsEvents/Pages/DisplayNews.aspx?NewsID=10909&LangID=S.

GUERRERO, H., and R. HERRERA. "Matan a 21 cada día" [21 killed each day]. *Reforma* (30 November 2012): 8.

HIJAR, M. "Tras la evidencia de la violencia contra las mujeres: un análisis de los homicidios" [In search of evidences of violence against women: an analysis of homicides]. Pages 134–310 in *Estudio Nacional sobre las Fuentes que producen y Reproducen la violencia contra las mujeres*. [A national study on the sources that produce and reproduce violence against women]. Edited by F. Riquer and R. Castro. Mexico: CONAVIM (Comisión Nacional para prevenir y erradicar la violencia contra las Mujeres), 2012. Cited 4 May 2014. Online: http://

www.conavim.gob.mx/work/models/CONAVIM/Resource/103/1/images/EstudiosNacionalesTomo1Volumen1.pdf.

HRW (Human Rights Watch). "México: Carta al Presidente Enrique Peña Nieto." No pages. Cited 17 February 2014. Online: http://www.hrw.org/es/news/2012/12/11/mexico-carta-al-presidente-enrique-pena-nieto.

IACHR (Inter American Court of Human Rights). *Case of González et al. ("Cotton Field") v. Mexico: Judgment of November 16, 2009.* Cited 17 February 2014. Online: http://www.corteidh.or.cr/docs/casos/articulos/seriec_205_ing.pdf.

ICESI (Instituto Ciudadano de Estudios sobre la Inseguridad). *Análisis de la séptima encuesta nacional sobre inseguridad [Analysis of the seventh national survey on insecurity]. ENSI-7/2010.* Mexico: ICESI, 2011.

Jusidman, C., and H. Almada. *La realidad social de Ciudad Juárez* [The Social Reality in Ciudad Juárez]. Ciudad Juárez: Universidad Autónoma de Ciudad Juárez, 2007.

Jusidman, C., and O. Marín. *El colapso de la economía del cuidado en Ciudad Juárez* [The collapse of the care service economy in Ciudad Juárez]. Draft, 2012.

Kleinman, A., V. Das, and M. Lock. "Introduction." *Daedalus* 125 (1996): xi–xx.

Kleinman, A., V. Das, and M. Lock, eds. *Social Suffering.* Berkeley: University of California Press, 1997.

Kumar, A. *Perspectivas del tráfico de personas en México* [Perspectives on human trafficking in Mexico]. Monterrey: UANL, 2012.

Lafaye, J. *Quetzalcoatl and Guadalupe: The formation of Mexican national consciousness, 1532-1815.* Chicago: University of Chicago Press, 1976.

Lomnitz, C. *Death and the Idea of Mexico.* New York: Zone Books, 2005.

Martínez, M. "Mejoran las leyes; aumentan abusos" [Laws improve: abuse increases]. *Enfoque* (Reforma) No. 966 (11 November 2012): 4-9.

Malkin, E., and G. Thompson. "In Mexico, promises do little to ease a city's pain." *The New York Times* (16 March 2010). No pages. Cited 17 February 2014. Online: http://www.nytimes.com/2010/03/17/world/americas/17juarez.html.

Mendoza, N. "El derecho a sepultar" [The right to bury]. *Nexos* 411 (2012): 34-39.

Napolitano, V. "The Virgin of Guadalupe: a nexus of affect." *Journal of the Royal Anthropological Institute* 15 (2009): 96-112.

Parametría. "México y sus desplazados." No pages. Cited 17 February 2014. Online: http://www.parametria.com.mx/DetalleEstudio.php?E=4288.

Paz, O. *The Labyrinth of Solitude.* New York: Grove, 1961.

Price, P. L. "Of Bandits and Saints: Jesús Malverde and the Struggle for Place in Sinaloa, Mexico." *Cultural geographies* 12 (2005): 175-97.

Propuesta Cívica. *Bases de datos sobre personas desaparecidas en México 2006-2012.* No pages. Cited 17 February 2014. Online: http://desaparecidosenmexico.wordpress.com.

Rivera, M. "Los números rojos" [The numbers in red]. *Nexos* 410 (2012): 19.

Salazar, P. "Entre la ley y el miedo" [Between the law and fear]. *Nexos* 411 (2012): 30-33.

Sicilia, J. "De cristiano a cristiano" (From Christian to Christian). *Proceso* 1846 (2012): 13-14.

Simonett, H. "Narcocorridos: An Emerging Micromusic of Nuevo L.A." *Ethnomusicology* 45 (2001): 315-37.

Sistiaga, J. "Las víctimas americanas de 'la bestia" [American victims of 'The Beast']. *El país semanal* 1849 (2012): 36.

Spiegel Online. "Massaker in Drogenhochburg: Blutbad bei Jugendparty in Mexiko." No pages. Cited 17 February 2014. Online: http://www.spiegel.de/panorama/justiz/massaker-in-drogenhochburg-blutbad-bei-jugendparty-in-mexiko-a-675136.html.

Taylor, W. "The Virgin of Guadalupe in New Spain: An Inquiry into the Social History of Marian Devotion." *American Ethnologist* 14 (1987): 9-33.

Terr, L. *Too Scared to Cry: Psychic Trauma in Childhood.* New York: Harper & Row, 1990.

TURATI, M. "Protestan contra Memorial a víctimas de violencia" [Protests held against victims of violence memorial]. *Proceso* 1847 (November 2012): 26-27. Cited 17 February 2014. Online: http://www.proceso.com.mx/?p=326224.

VERA, R. "El blindaje del miedo" [The shield of fear]. *Proceso* 1874 (2012): 16-18.

VILLAMIL, J. *Ciudad Juárez. El doble Crimen a las Mujeres* [The double crime against women]. *Proceso Edición Especial* 34 (2012).

VOLPI, J. "Iatrogenia y antifragilidad" [Iatrogenesis and anti-fragility]. *Reforma* 6932 (16 December 2012): 12.

WALD, E. *Narcocorrido: A Journey into the Music of Drugs, Guns, and Guerrillas*. New York: Harper Collins, 2001.

WOLF, E. "The Virgin of Guadalupe: A Mexican National Symbol." *Journal of American Folklore* 71 (1958): 34-39.

Jan Dietrich

Cultural Traumata in the Ancient Near East*

Abstract

The issues of disaster and trauma form a new perspective in anthropological research and have been investigated more deeply in recent years. This article focuses on the question of how cultural trauma, in difference to disaster, can be defined and, more deeply, on presenting some important examples of "real" cultural traumata in the Ancient Near East—in contrast to the ornate poetry so typical for the ancient cultures when speaking about disasters. Therefore, this article tries to identify instances of traumata that are not celebrated openly in high literature, but that display elements of haunting and perhaps even psychic mechanisms like, e.g., repression or reaction formation. In this way, three examples for cultural traumata in the Ancient Near East will be presented here: from Anatolia, the *Plague-Prayers of Muršili II*, from Mesopotamia, the *Death of Sargon II*, and from Ancient Egypt, the *Revolution of Akhenaten*.

Cultural Traumata: Aspects and Terminology

The difficulties involved in trying to use a psychoanalytic concept in relation to ancient peoples and cultures are clear and well documented. Trauma as a psychoanalytical concept holds that a person can be overwhelmed by disastrous events, which disturb his or her character in a way that continues to damage or destroy his or her psychic resilience and frustration tolerance. Although such experiences ingrain themselves neurotically in a person's character, those affected can attempt to expel them by repressing the wounding experiences into their unconscious. Nevertheless, these unreconciled traumatic experiences repeatedly re-emerge from the unconscious in disguised forms, ready to haunt the traumatized.

This psychoanalytic concept of trauma is not easily applied to ancient cultures (though both fields of research may regard themselves as hermeneutical sciences) because there is simply no possibility for the peoples of ancient times to lie down on the Freudian couch. This becomes even more difficult when we discuss not only texts, but also the "hard facts" of archaeology. As the biblical archaeologist from the University of California, Aaron A. Burke,

* I wish to thank Sarah Jennings (Aarhus) for improving my English.

identifies: "While the emotional, physical, and psychological trauma is not without significance, such elements of the experience are largely inaccessible to the archaeological study of ancient populations."[1]

If we look more closely at the Greek term τραῦμα, we are led back to the verb τιτρώσκω ("to wound, injure, damage") and find the original meaning of τραῦμα as "wound; damage; defeat (in war); leak (of ships)."[2] To use an example, in the literal sense of "wound," the Apis bull can die of his thigh wound (ἐκτοῦτρώματος) after Cambyses stabs him (Herodotus, *Hist.* 3.29). But τραῦμα can also be used more figuratively, and can indicate defeats in battle as disastrous events in war; for example, the Persian τρῶμα (disaster) at Marathon (*Hist.* 6.132), or the Laconian τρῶμα (disaster) at Thermophylae (*Hist.* 8.66). In this way, disasters and catastrophes can be termed and remembered as τραῦματα in Greek sources. Therefore, as well as its literal meaning as "wounds," traumata can also be regarded as "disastrous events," not only for single people, but for whole groups and nations; events that remain part of the cultural memory.

What about terms from the Ancient Near East? Unfortunately, we do not have terms from here that can be equated with the Greek term τραῦμα. In Akkadian, the term *miḫṣu* can not only mean "wound," but also the attack of a disease, a demon, or an army, and, when used together with the words *qaqqadu* ("head") or *pānu* ("face"), can also mean military defeat (*miḫiṣ qaqqadi; miḫiṣ pani*), thereby pointing to disastrous military events.[3] Since disastrous defeats are implied here, one might even include other terms that focus on strong military defeats or other disastrous events, such as Akkadian *karašû* ("catastrophe; annihilation; slaughter") or *šaḫluqtu* ("catastrophe; disaster").[4] In Ancient Egyptian sources, there are of course words for "wound" (e.g. *wbn.w*) and words that describe times of distress (e.g. *qnj*). However, I am unaware of any that comprise both the literal meaning "wound" and a metaphorical meaning, which indicates disastrous events (except perhaps *snj-mnt*, which describes catastrophic times of need that pace the land similar to illness and sorrow[5]). In other cases, terms for disaster do not etymologically imply events that have already been stricken (such as wounds) but *forthcoming* events. Here, terms like *jyt* ("the coming [events]; mischief") and *ḫprt* ("the future [events]") may include disastrous connotations.[6]

1 Burke, "Coping," 266.
2 Cf., e.g., Frisk, *Wörterbuch*, 905.
3 Cf. "miḫṣu," *CAD* 10.2:61.
4 Cf. Schaudig, "Erklärungsmuster," 425.
5 Cf. also *jꜣdt* resp. *jdw* meaning "illness" and "distress; calamity" (Goedicke, "Seuche," 918).
6 Cf. Morenz, "Bedeutungsentwicklung."

This brief overview of historical terms suggests that we cannot achieve a modern, scientific understanding of trauma by relying exclusively on ancient terms. In this article, I wish to examine more closely historical sources that show 1. disastrous events that are, 2. recalled in cultural memory, 3. in a way that reveals wounds not reconciled over time, but that are, 4. often hidden, explained away, rationalized, or domesticated and neutralized in other ways,[7] for example, by psychic mechanisms of repression, transference, rationalization, or reaction formation. I call this phenomenon *cultural trauma*. By developing this notion of cultural trauma, we can provide historical research with a non-orthodox concept of trauma (free from its traditionally narrow clinical and sexual definitions), which we can apply to the study of ancient cultures.[8] Cultural trauma shall not only be defined as a disastrous event—by itself, this is insufficient, since "societies can experience massive disruptions that do not become traumatic"[9]—but as a catastrophe that continues to be recalled in cultural memory in such a way that its wounds are (either directly or indirectly) revealed and not healed by time. Although we cannot offer the ancient peoples a rest on the Freudian couch in order to unveil their veiled, traumatized, and unconscious character traits, we might at least touch upon some of these "character traits" when looking for Ancient Near Eastern sources that show cultural trauma as described above.

The term "cultural trauma" includes a constructivist approach. This means that disasters and catastrophes may be either "real" or "invented," but, in either case, they are always culturally constructed: "the traumatizing event is always a cultural construction."[10] In this way, both realism and constructivism are recognized as appropriate approaches in combination with each other.[11] Invented or "constructed disasters" may have traumatic effects because they have the potential to heavily influence and wound later generations. Even the "real" disaster has to be further "invented" and imagined as traumatic, since the disaster's naked reality by itself can never traumatize a collective culturally; this only occurs when it is included in the cultural memory's ways of remembering. An example of this is the Babylonian exile of the Jews. Historically, this event was probably less devastating than the Old Testament texts portray (in 2 Chr 36:21, the Judean Land is described as

7 For this cf. Sztompka, "Cultural Trauma," 457, and below.

8 Concerning psychoanalytical theories, I tend to agree with the perspectives and approaches of the so-called 'non-orthodox Neo-Freudians', such as Erich Fromm, Karen Horney, or Harry Stack Sullivan, who emphasize the importance of the inter-personal relationships and the cultural and social circumstances as main influences on the self. Concerning psychoanalysis, I believe it is their approach that fits best into cultural historical research (on Erich Fromm's approach to religion in this regard cf. Dietrich, "Religion").

9 Alexander, "Cultural Trauma," 10.

10 Sztompka, "Cultural Trauma," 457.

11 For a constructivist approach cf. Alexander, "Cultural Trauma."

empty and completely in ruins). However, the historical destruction of Jerusalem was constructed as an immensely devastating trauma, and this trauma was remembered in the cultural history of the Jewish people. Therefore, my final definition of cultural trauma conforms partly, though not entirely, with Jeffrey Alexander, who identifies that: "Cultural trauma occurs when members of a collectivity *feel* they have been subjected to a horrendous event that leaves indelible marks upon their group consciousness, marking their memories forever and changing their future identity in fundamental and irrevocable ways."[12]

However, there is a problem with a solely constructivist approach to cultural trauma: when leaving aside the unconscious and its mechanisms (especially the repression of experiences) and focusing solely on the constructivist perspective, there remains no distinction between disaster and trauma. This is problematic, because the exact concept of trauma risks becoming meaningless. Alongside trauma studies, there has also been a lot research carried out on disaster studies in recent years. Disasters are also defined as culturally constructed phenomena, since there is no catastrophe in nature, but only in culture. In his narration, *Man in the Holocene*, Max Frisch observes that, "only human beings can recognize catastrophes, provided they survive them; nature recognizes no catastrophes."[13] It is no catastrophe if a meteorite collides with the planet Jupiter, and Mount Vesuvius does not fear its own eruption. Disasters only become disasters because of their impact on human society and their cultural interpretation as disasters. Therefore, we need a *differentium specificum* when talking about trauma alongside catastrophe/disaster. In this way, we should also be able to avoid the excessive use of the term trauma. As Erich Fromm claims, "Today people talk of a real trauma because they missed the train or had some disagreeable experience somewhere. A trauma is by definition an event which goes beyond the charge which the human nervous circuit can tolerate. Since the person cannot tolerate the trauma the trauma has created a deep disturbance. But most traumata in this sense are very rare [...]."[14]

I want to mention two aspects here. Firstly, the perspectives associated with catastrophe and trauma are different. With catastrophe, the perspective focuses on the disastrous events and their impacts on society (an outside-view); whereas, with trauma, the perspective focuses on the psychic and cultural wounds, and the severe mental injuries that disasters create (an inside-view). Secondly, and to be combined with the inside-view, trauma "resists simple comprehension."[15] Trauma does not simply represent disastrous

12 Alexander, "Cultural Trauma," 1. Cf. Sztompka, "Cultural Trauma," 455.

13 Frisch, *Man in the Holocene*.

14 Fromm, "Therapeutic Aspects," 49–50.

15 Caruth, *Unclaimed Experience*, 6.

events in the mentalities of people, but their "very incomprehensibility."[16] It is precisely this incomprehensibility that enables us to include psychic mechanisms of non-orthodox psychoanalytic theory in cultural-anthropological and historical research on trauma. Within his constructivist account of trauma, Piotr Sztompka identifies one aspect that returns, at least in part, to a psychoanalytical understanding of trauma: humans dealing with cultural trauma, he claims, may interpret traumatic events by "hiding, explaining away, rationalizing or in other ways domesticating or neutralizing the occurrences which objectively, potentially, may be traumatizing."[17] In contrast to the concept of disaster, such specific psychic mechanisms, such as repression, transference, rationalizing, or reaction formation, could be considered when looking for historical sources in the Ancient Near East, in which we might find at least glimpses of cultural trauma; even though, as we have already noted, we are not able to offer the ancient cultures a lie down on the Freudian couch.[18]

Disasters or Traumata?

I shall now introduce some texts that show the effects of disaster on culture (and that should, therefore, be considered within a disaster volume[19]), but that do not reveal much about cultural traumata in the sense we described above. This is the case for texts I call *high literary disaster-texts* in Ancient Egypt and Mesopotamia. These texts describe disastrous events in such a way that these events are being retold and even stylized as disastrous in cultural memory. Quite often, these texts use a literary *topos* called *inverted world, world upturned* or *world turned upside down*.[20] The most important and well-known texts to be mentioned here are the following:

- Mesopotamian: Curse of Agade; City-Laments; the Esagil-Chronicle[21]
- Egyptian: Admonitions; Man Tired of Life; Eloquent Peasant; Khakheperreseneb

16 Caruth, *Unclaimed Experience*, 6.

17 Sztompka, "Cultural Trauma," 457.

18 When trying to identify psychic mechanisms, we are not implying the existence of universal anthropological formations (such as the drive of the Libido or the Oedipus complex), but simply stating the existence of similar psychic mechanisms (such as repression, transference, rationalization, even sublimation etc.), although these may lead to very different historical formations.

19 Cf., e.g., Berlejung, *Disaster*.

20 Cf. the overview by Kruger, "Disaster."

21 One could also include the lamenting literatures, *Sumerian Job*, *Babylonian Theodicy*, and *ludlul bēl nēmeqi*, since, like the book of Job, they are ornate poetry.

The *Curse of Agade* was written during the prosperous times of the 3d Dynasty of Ur (ca. 2100–2000 B.C.). This "tendentious composition,"[22] written as ornate poetry, explains how, one hundred years earlier, Enlil of Nippur destroyed Agade by turning the Guteans against the Mesopotamians. The text even ends with a "doxology glorifying the destruction of Agade." This sentence reads: "Agade is destroyed—hail Inanna!" (line 281).[23]

It appears to be similar with the Mesopotamian City Laments and the case of the "Ibbi-Sin catastrophe," so coined by Hanspeter Schaudig because of the term *šaḫluqti Ibbi-Sîn* ("Catastrophe of Ibbi-Sin") in some texts.[24] The Mesopotamian City Laments describe the end of the 3d Dynasty of Ur and the destructions of other cities (ca. 2004 B.C.), but they don't tell us as much about trauma as we might expect. Firstly, the disaster is dealt with in an open-minded manner, and there is no attempt to obscure or rationalize it. Secondly, and more importantly, it does not appear as though these disaster stories are relayed in order to heal wounds; instead, they are appealed to as part of an attempt to explain and to legitimize history. In the case of the lament over the destruction of Sumer and Ur, the disaster is remembered during the prosperous reign of the First Dynasty of Isin (ca. 2000–1800 B.C.). This ornate poetry describes how the capital, Ur, and other Mesopotamian cities were destroyed during the reign of King Ibbi-Sin, with Ibbi-Sin himself (among others) being deported to Elam, where he later died. We cannot refer to the disastrous events recalled here as "traumatic," because the city of Isin itself, as well as its governor, Išbi-Erra, played an intentional part in the fall of Ur. Furthermore, the laments over the destruction of Ur were written at a time when the dynasty of Isin enjoyed prosperity and was able to rebuild its temples and cities. The laments and dirges reveal themselves, not as expressions of actual traumatic feeling, but as highly sophisticated political tools. In the centuries that followed, this event was remembered as the "catastrophe of Ibbi-Sin." In this way, it did not pass on traumatic memory. Instead, it gave rise to a fixed, historical keyword to be used in artificial omina and chronicles. For example, in the Babylonian *Esagil-Chronicle* from the first half of the 1st millennium B.C., artificial legends were ascribed to various immoral kings, among them Ibbi-Sin, to explain history according to the sins of the kings against the Babylonian god, Marduk.[25] Obviously, the historical events were not remembered because of their traumatic impacts, but because of their usefulness for political and religious propaganda.

22 Cooper, *Curse of Agade*, 7.
23 Citation and Translation by Cooper, *Curse of Agade*, 9 and 63.
24 Cf. Schaudig, "Erklärungsmuster."
25 Ibid., 432–42.

We encounter a similar problem when looking at the Ancient Egyptian *high literary disaster-texts*. In the Admonitions, chapter 7 line 13 uses the *topos* of the world turned upside down:

Look, he who had no shade is the owner of shade;
(yet) the owners of shade are in the darkness(?) of storms.[26]

In former times, such Egyptian texts—for example, the Admonitions, the Man Tired of Life, or the Eloquent Peasant—were dated to the First Intermediate Period (2181–2055 B.C.) and said to portray the disastrous effects of a fallen monarchy and the loss of political unity; a time when local rulers were in power. However, nowadays, most scholars believe that the First Intermediate Period was not as disastrous as the texts describe, and they date many of the "First-Intermediate-texts" to the Middle Kingdom of the 12th Dynasty (1985–1773 B.C.), a time of military, political, economic and cultural prosperity. During this heyday, the *topos* of disaster was used to contrast the prosperous times of a united Egypt with the former period of local rule. So, in this case, the notion of disaster is employed by those who did not experience the catastrophe firsthand, but who describe it from a safe distance, and who elevate the events in an aesthetic way for aetiological and political reasons in an attempt to explain history, reject the past, and endorse the present.

The idiom *shipwreck with spectator*, which can be found in the poetry of Lucretius (*De rerum natura* 2.1–4) and was later developed by Hans Blumenberg, can help us to understand the above-mentioned use of disasters in literature.[27] With this idiom, Lucretius originally intended to describe the relationship between the philosopher and reality,[28] but the idiom can also be applied to the majority of storytellers of disasters. "Disasters with spectators" can even be found in iconography and does not necessarily point to trauma; for example, the Egyptian iconography of famine from the causeways of Sahure and Unas shows weak, hungry and very emaciated people.[29] However, these people are not Egyptians, but foreign Bedouins, representing "an exotic attraction for the ancient Egyptian dignitaries who once viewed them."[30]Although the fear of famine is depicted meticulously and realistically, the famine is projected onto the foreigners and, according to the king's ideology, is not part of the Egyptian culture (even if the king or his scribes should assist the foreigners). It belongs to the *aesthetics of disaster* that the

26 Translation by Enmarch, *World Upturned*, 38.
27 Cf. Dietrich, "Coping with Disasters."
28 Cf. Blumenberg, *Shipwreck*, 26.
29 For the famine scene from the causeway of Unas cf. Drioton, "famine," fig. 3,49; Hassan, "Causeway"; Schott, "Hungersnotrelief"; for the famine scene from the causeway of Sahure cf. Hawass and Verner, "Causeway of Sahure," fig. 2a and plate 55b.
30 Hawass and Verner, "Causeway of Sahure," 184.

depiction of the famine from the causeways is integrated into the scenes that praise the king. Therefore, the name of the pyramid of Unas was: "Beautiful are the sites of Unas" (*Nfr-swt-Wnjs*).

Three Case Studies of Cultural Trauma

It is not possible to locate examples of severe mental injuries in the high literary disaster-texts described above. Therefore, in our attempt to discover instances of cultural trauma in the cultural memories of the Ancient Near East, it is necessary to turn towards other sources.

We are trying to identify instances of haunting, cultural traumata; in other words, traumata that are not celebrated openly in high literature, but that display psychic mechanisms of haunting and perhaps even repression. Three examples may be given here: one from Anatolia, one from Mesopotamia, and one from Egypt:

- Anatolia: The Plague-Prayers of Muršili II
- Mesopotamia: The Death of Sargon II
- Egypt: Akhenaten's Revolution

The Plague-Prayers of Muršili II

Let us begin with the so-called Plague Prayers by Muršili II from the end of the 14th century B.C. Although the Plague Prayers themselves, being highly artificial products and ornate texts,[31] show signs of highly artificial collage, it could be argued that they also depict instances of trauma. There are three reasons for this. Firstly, in the Plague Prayers, the plague *(ḫenkan-)* is described as a disastrous event that continues to haunt the Hittite civilization for "20 years" (according to some texts) and at least two generations. It was the most devastating plague of the Ancient Near Eastern period. Here, the source of the trauma is not only a single event, but an ongoing process, by which disastrous experiences build up traumatically and etch themselves in the collective memory of the Hittite culture. Secondly, King Muršili II, whilst offering various reasons for the plague, searches desperately for answers from the gods about how to deal with it. The fact that every Plague Prayer offers another reason for the disaster, without mentioning the reasons given in the other respective Plague Prayers, could be an indication of the desperate nature of Muršili's search. Here, the haunting nature of the trauma reveals itself

31 Cf. Klinger, "Krankheit."

in the desperate attempt to find answers, without even looking for a coherent interpretation. Thirdly, it could be argued that the unusual and self-destructive reasons offered by King Muršili reveal a kind of traumatized desperation: in the first Plague Prayer, Muršili admits that his father, Šuppiluliuma, overthrew and murdered the legitimate king, Tutḫalija, thereby revealing Muršili's and his father's kingship as illegitimate.[32]

§2 (obv. 8-15) O gods, [my] lords! A plague broke out in Hatti, and Hatti has been severely damaged by the plague. And since for twenty years now in Hatti people have been dying, the affair of Tudhaliya the Younger, son of Tudhaliya, started to weigh on [me]. I inquired about it to the god through an oracle, and the affair of Tudhaliya was confirmed by the deity. Since Tudhaliya the Younger was their lord in Hatti, the princes, the noblemen, the commanders of the thousands, the officers, [the corporals(?)] of Hatti and all [the infantry] and chariotry of Hatti swore an oath to him. My father also swore an oath to him.

§3 (obv. 16-22) [But when my father] wronged Tudhaliya, all [the princes, the noblemen], the commanders of the thousands, and the officers of Hatti [went over] to my father. The deities by whom the oath was sworn [seized] Tudhaliya and they killed [Tudhaliya]. Furthermore, they killed those of his brothers [who stood by] him. (…)

§4 (obv. 23-40) (…) But now you, O gods, [my lords], have eventually taken vengeance on my father for this affair of Tudhaliya the Younger. My father [died(?)] because of the blood of Tudhaliya, and the princes, the noblemen, the commanders of the thousands, and the officers who went over [to my father], they also died because of [that] affair. This same affair also came upon the land of Hatti, and the population of the land of [Hatti] began to perish because of [this] affair. Until now Hatti […], but now the plague [has become] even [worse]. Hatti has been [severely] damaged by the plague, and it has been decimated. I, Mursili, [your servant], cannot [overcome] the worry [of my heart], I can no longer [overcome] the anguish of my soul.[33]

This differs so significantly from other confessions of guilt in the Ancient Near East that I would like to argue that Muršili is haunted by two events: firstly, the bloodshed of the murder on which his own kingship is built, and, secondly, the plague that continues to haunt him and his nations for generations. This accumulation of disastrous events appears to have a traumatic effect on Muršili.[34] Muršili seems to combine them, as though he seeks a cathartic effect by openly showing his and his country's wounds to the gods. This trauma was obviously something that was remembered in the culture of

32 Cf. Klinger, "Krankheit," 486-87, 491-94.
33 Translation by Singer, *Hittite Prayers*, 61-62.
34 "trauma is a prolonged process in which one experience follows another and where, really, you eventually have a summation, and more than a summation, a piling up of experiences" (Fromm, "Factors," 25.)

the Hittites, since we have other and even later texts that are similar to Muršili's Plague Prayers.[35]

The Death of Sargon

The second text to consider is the so-called Sin or Death of Sargon.[36] Sargon II ascended to the throne in Assyria in 721 B.C., during the time of Assyrian Hegemony over the Ancient Near Eastern lands. One of his main projects was to build himself a new capital city, Dūr-Šarrukēn ("Fortress of Sargon"; today's Khorsabad), which was to be more magnificent than any city ever built. Dūr-Šarrukēn was completed and dedicated in 706 B.C. However, only one year later, Sargon was killed in Anatolia during a campaign against the Luwian kingdom, Tabal. His body was lost and could not be buried at home (cf. Isa 14:19, 20aα), which meant that his spirit was left to wander, unburied; something dishonorable and disreputable that had never before happened to any of the Assyrian kings.[37] Interestingly, Sargon's son and successor to the throne, Sennacherib, tried to suppress the memory of Sargon. Sennacherib abandoned Dūr-Šarrukēn and declared Niniveh the new capital. Sennacherib, "contrary to the long-standing Assyrian royal custom of genealogical citation,"[38] never mentions the name of his father in his inscriptions. It could be that, already shortly after Sargon's death on the 27th of April 705 B.C., the Assyrian scribe from Nimrud (Kalḫu), Nabû-Zuqup-Kēnu, indirectly tried to come to terms with this disaster by copying the 12th tablet of the Gilgamesh-Epic on the death of Enkidu. Because of the similarity between the literary text and the historical event, Eckart Frahm suggests that Nabû-Zuqup-Kēnu copied it as a reaction to Sargon's death.[39] However, it is clear that Sargon and his fate are never mentioned by name during Sennacherib's reign, thereby disowning the traumatic events and repressing their effects. But traumatic experiences linger and lurk as unacknowledged experiences in the people's memories until they reveal themselves again. In the time of Sennacherib's follower, Esarhaddon, an inauthentic stele was erected in which Sennacherib tells of his father's sin and death:[40]

35 Cf. Klinger, "Krankheit," 486-87, 491-94.

36 Cf. Tadmor et al., "Sin of Sargon."

37 According to the Weidner Chronicle, the corpse of the Babylonian king Utu-hegal of Uruk was carried off by the river (cf. Grayson, *Chronicles*, 150 [= no. 19, line 62]; Finkel, "Fragments," 72-74; Hallo, "Death of Kings," 156-57). For the end of Aššūr-nādin-šumi cf. Parpola, "Letter," 22-23, 32-33.

38 Brinkman, *Prelude to Empire*, 54.

39 Cf. Frahm, "Nabû-Zuqup-Kēnu," 76-82.

40 This stele was also erected for political reasons concerning Babylonia: Cf. Tadmor et al., "Sin of Sargon," 45-51; Porter, *Images*, 144-45; Weaver, "Sin of Sargon."

(7) While thus [reverently] pondering [in my heart] over the deeds of the gods, the death of Sargon (*mi-tu-tu šá* ᴵLUGAL-GIN), [my father, who was killed in the enemy country (AD-*ia šá ina* KUR *na-ki-ri de-ku-ma*)] and who was not interred in his house (*ina* É-*šú la qeb-ru*), oc[curred] to my mind, [and I said to myself]:

(10) "[Let me examine] by means of extispicy the sin of Sargon, my father, let me then determine [the circumstances] and le[arn the ...... ; let me make] the sin he committed against the god an abom[ination to myself], and with the god's help let me save myself."

(13) I w[ent and collected the haruspices], who guard of the secret of god and king, the courtiers of my palace, divided them [into several (lit. three or four) groups] so that they could not ap[proach or speak to one another], and [investigated] the sins of Sargon, my father, by extispicy, [inquiring of Šamaš and Adad] as follows:

(17) "Was it because [he honored] the gods o[f Assyria too much, placing them] above the gods of Babylonia [...... , and was it because] he did not [keep] the treaty of the king of gods [that Sargon my father] was killed [in the enemy country and] was not b[uried] in his house?"

(21) [......] The haruspices whom [I had divided] into [several groups] unanimously [gave me a firm positive answer].[...... I opened the pal]ms of my hands and lifted [my hands, and prayed in supplication and humility on account of Sarg]on, [my] fat[her: (...)[41]

In contrast to the manner in which the shameful events of Sargon were repressed by his son and successor, Sennacherib, the new king, Esarhaddon, takes up the death of Sargon and even compares Sargon with the paradigmatic *Unheilsherrscher* Naram-Sin of the Cuthaean Legend.[42] Together, these acts show that the death of Sargon was not simply forgotten as a meaningless event, but as a "traumatic incident"[43], which was repressed and made into a taboo by Sennacherib. Only in the time of Sennacherib's successor, Esarhaddon, did the country dare to come to terms with this occurrence by atoning for it.[44]

41 K.4730 (+) Sm. 1876, Obverse lines 7-24. Translation according to Tadmor et al., "Sin of Sargon," 11; cf. Livingstone, *Court Poetry*, no. 33. For a slightly different reading of lines 17-20, see Weaver, "Sin of Sargon," 63. For a German translation, see Frahm, "Nabû-Zuqup-Kēnu," 75.

42 Cf. Tadmor et al., "Sin of Sargon," esp. 37-39, 46-48.

43 Wording according to Frahm, "Nabû-Zuqup-Kēnu," 74 ("traumatische[n] Begebenheit").

44 Cf. ibid., 86.

Akhenaten's Revolution

The last example of cultural trauma in the Ancient Near East is well known and frequently discussed because of Jan Assmann's theory on the "monotheistic trauma" or "trauma of theoclasm" ("trauma of deicide" in the English translations), which was forced upon the Egyptians under the rule of Pharaoh Akhenaten in the second half of the 14th century B.C. Although he rejected parts of Freud's theory on Moses and Akhenaten, Assmann was the first to apply psychoanalytic terms, most notably "trauma," but also terms such as "repression," "return of the repressed," "reaction formation," "psychic disturbance," etc., on the history of Akhenaten's monotheistic revolution. Therefore, I shall not discuss Assmann's interpretations of Moses, but I shall turn immediately to Assmann's "psychohistoric" interpretation of the history and impacts of the "collective psychic disturbance"[45] under Pharaoh Akhenaten.[46]

Traumatic events began when Pharaoh Amenophis IV changed his name to Akhenaten (also spelled Echnaton) ("living spirit of [the sun-god] Aten") and founded a new religious cult centered entirely on the sun-god, Aten. Akhenaten founded a new capital, which he called Akhetaten (Achet-Aten; "Horizon of Aten"), in a previously uncultivated area on the eastern side of the Nile in middle Egypt[47]—a "traumatic move."[48] The traditional gods were not mentioned anymore, and even the use of the plural *nṯrw* ("gods") was forbidden. This religious revolution was not only monotheistic, but also exclusive in terms of theoclasm, thereby enforcing the "most radical and violent eruption of a counter-religion in the history of humankind. The temples were closed, the images of the gods were destroyed, their names were erased, and their cults [including the public feasts; J. D.] were discontinued"[49]. This "true persecution, which generated a real and tangible fear among the Egyptian people,"[50] was not only conducted against the official monuments, but also against the normal people and their personal objects.[51] People had to change their names, if their names were originally compounded with "Amun,"[52] and

45 Assmann, "Monotheism," 61.
46 Cf. Assmann, *Moses*; idem, "Monotheism."
47 On nearly all aspects of life and architecture in Amarna cf. the omnibus volume edited by Tietze, *Amarna*.
48 Redford, "Hyksos Invasion," 48.
49 Assmann, *Moses*, 25.
50 Reeves, *Akhenaten*, 154.
51 On the other hand, one has to admit that, in the private households of Amarna, "old-fashioned" artifacts, representing traditional aspects of Egyptian religion, were also found (cf. Stevens, *Private religion*; Hornung, "Religion," 248f), next to artifacts that represented the new religion of Aten and the royal family (cf. Ikram, "Shrines"; Stevens, *Private religion*).
52 Cf. Redford, *Akhenaten*, 176.

even "small, personal items such as pots for eye make-up and commemorative scarabs were dealt with in the same relentless fashion."[53] It is likely that this traumatic event occurred together with another: the most terrible plague that haunted the Hittites, called "the Asiatic illness" by the Egyptians, and that probably haunted Egypt as well.[54] The so-called "Restauration-Stela" of Tutankhamun offers some glimpses of the traumatic experiences:

The temples of the gods and goddesses were desolated *(stp)*
from Elephantine as far as the marshes of the Delta,
their holy places were about to disintegrate *(wꜣ.w r mrḥ)*,
having become rubbish heaps (*jꜣꜣw*), overgrown with thistles.
Their sanctuaries were as if they had never been (*n ḫpr*),
their houses were trodden roads.
The land was in grave disease (*snj-mnt*).
The gods have forsaken this land.[55]

Assmann suggests that, "We have every reason to imagine the Amarna experience as traumatic."[56] Now, the questions still remain: why are the events mentioned here traumatic? Why is the Restoration Stela not simply ornate poetry, as in the case of other Ancient Near Eastern texts? Because, according to Assmann, the traumatic experiences were systematically repressed; and this relates to repression in its psychoanalytic meaning, applied not to individualistic, but to cultural memory, since "all the visible traces of the period were deleted."[57] A strong *damnatio memoriae* fell upon Akhenaten to forget his revolution. As Assmann writes, "Here, we do in fact find the Freudian model of latency and repression."[58] After Akhenaten's and Tutankhamun's death, the Egyptians converted back to their traditional religion. Akhenaten's name and those of his immediate successors—Smenkhare, Tutankhamun, and Ay—were banned from the list of kings and erased from most inscriptions. Akhenaten's city was abandoned (recall the abandonment of Sargon's Dūr-Šarrukēn) and his buildings dismantled or destructed. As far as possible, his inscriptions, portrayals and depictions were destroyed. This "cultural repression of the Amarna period"[59] led to "a 'crypt' in the cultural memory of Egypt."[60] However, dismantled buildings still persist, and the erasures of

53 Reeves, *Akhenaten*, 154. The emergence of the god Shed ("saviour") appears to be some kind of sublimation, because the earliest evidences stem from Akhetaten, cf. Schlögl, *Echnaton*, 70.

54 Cf. Assmann, *Moses*, 12 with reference to Goedicke, "Canaanite Illness." Critically judged e.g. by Weeks, "Medicine," 1791.

55 Translation by Assmann, *Moses*, 27. For the Egyptian text cf. Helck, *Inschriften*, 2027.

56 Assmann, *Moses*, 27.

57 Ibid.

58 Assmann, "Monotheism," 59.

59 Assmann, *Moses*, 29.

60 Ibid., 216.

names from stone inscriptions are themselves still visible. In some cases, the places where Akhetaten's and his follower's names were erased from the inscriptions were visible to the public, pointing not towards "complete oblivion"[61], but towards a "significant silence" and "disturbances in the past"[62]—especially if one realizes that "none of the erasures, however, had been carried through with consistency."[63] Though Assmann does not argue in this way, the erasures support, and do not contradict, his theory, since repression is never complete but always shows itself vaguely and indirectly, and the erasures clearly kept alive vague traumatic memories in cultural remembrance.[64] In the words of Cathy Caruth, "For history to be a history of trauma means that it is referential precisely to the extent that it is not fully perceived as it occurs; or to put it somewhat differently, that a history can be grasped only in the very inaccessibility of its occurrence."[65]

Let us now turn to the psychoanalytic concept of the return of the repressed. Repressed memories become placeless. In this case, they were no longer connected with Amarna, but reappeared repeatedly in later times with other kinds of associations. According to Assmann, the best example of this return of the repressed is to be found in Manetho's account.[66] Manetho was an Egyptian priest in Heliopolis during the first half of the third century, and parts of his lost work are cited in Josephus' *Contra Apionem*. Josephus believes that this account describes the time of the Hyksos. However, when referring to Amenophis Paapis (= Amenophis, son of Hapu) and a time of 13 years of suffering,[67] Manetho is, in fact, describing the coming events of Amarna (though he had no explicit knowledge of Akhenaten himself). According to Manetho, King Amenophis III, the father of Akhenaten, forced all the lepers in the land to be rounded up in the eastern desert quarries. The lepers erected a leper settlement in the old capital of the Hyksos, Avaris, and elected the Heliopolitan priest, Osarsiph, as their leader. The laws that Osarsiph enforced resemble Akhenaten's monotheistic revolution, but in displaced ways:

When the men in the stone-quarries had suffered hardships for a considerable time, they begged the king to assign to them as a dwelling-place and a refuge the deserted city of the Shepherds, Auaris, and he consented. According to religious tradition this city was from earliest times dedicated to Typhôn. Occupying this city and using the region as a base for revolt, they appointed as their leader one of the priests of Hêliop-

61 Next to Assmann, also Hornung, *Akhenaten*, 5, argues for "total oblivion."
62 Winthrop-Young, "Memories of the Nile," 344.
63 Redford, *Akhenaten*, 228.
64 Contra the otherwise conclusively argued and well-informed article on Assmann's theory by Winthrop-Young, "Memories of the Nile," 344–46.
65 Caruth, *Unclaimed Experience*, 18.
66 Cf. also Schlögl, *Echnaton*, 106: "Spuren der verdrängten Erinnerung," die besonders bei Manetho "ihren Niederschlag gefunden" haben.
67 Cf. Redford, "Hyksos Invasion," 39–50, esp. 49.

olis called Osarsêph, and took an oath of obedience to him in everything. First of all, he made it a law that they should neither worship the gods nor refrain from any of the animals prescribed as especially sacred in Egypt, but should sacrifice and consume all alike (μήτε προσκυνεῖν θεοὺς μήτε τῶν μάλιστα ἐν Αἰγύπτῳ θεμιστευομένων ἱερῶν ζῴων ἀπέχεσθαι μηδενός, πάντα δὲ θύειν καὶ ἀναλοῦν), and that they should have intercourse with none save those of their own confederacy. After framing a great number of laws like these, completely opposed to Egyptian custom (μάλιστα τοῖς Αἰγυπτίοις ἐθισμοῖς ἐναντιούμενα), he ordered them with their multitude of hands, to repair the walls of the city and make ready for war against King Amenôphis.[68]

This account of Manetho combines different "traumatic" experiences from various periods, such as the time of the Hyksos, the age of Amarna, and "especially the Assyrian and Persian conquests,"[69] but, most of all, according to Assmann, it reveals how "Akhenaten in the guise of 'Osarsiph' alias Moses reenters the literary tradition of Egypt."[70] A later gloss, either by Manetho himself, or by another scribe, perhaps even Josephus himself, says that Osarsiph adopted the name of Moses. However, the identification of events with the Jews in later texts is another story, and, from my point of view, is no longer a story of trauma and the return of the repressed, but, from then on, "simply" a story about the different, and sometimes deforming ways, cultural memory can develop.

Bibliography

Alexander, J. C. "Towards a Theory of Cultural Trauma." Pages 1-30 in *Cultural Trauma and Collective Identity*. Edited by J. C. Alexander. Berkeley: University of California Press, 2004.

Assmann, J. *Moses the Egyptian: The Memory of Egypt in Western Monotheism*. Cambridge: Harvard University Press, 1997.

—. "Monotheism, Memory, and Trauma: Reflections on Freud's Book on Moses." Pages 46-62 in *Religion and Cultural Memory: Ten Studies*. Stanford: Stanford University Press, 2006.

Berlejung, A., ed. *Disaster and Relief Management: Katastrophen und ihre Bewältigung*. Tübingen: Mohr (Siebeck), 2012.

Blumenberg, H. *Shipwreck with Spectator: Paradigm of a Metaphor for Existence*. Cambridge, Mass.: Massachusetts Institute of Technology, 1997.

Brinkman, J. A. *Prelude to Empire: Babylonian Society and Politics, 747-626 B.C.* Philadelphia: University Museum, 1984.

Burke, A. A. "Coping with the Effects of War: Refugees in the Levant during the Bronze and Iron Ages." Pages 263-87 in *Disaster and Relief Management. Katastrophen und ihre Bewältigung*. Edited by A. Berlejung. Tübingen: Mohr (Siebeck), 2012.

Caruth, C. *Unclaimed Experience: Trauma, Narrative, and History*. Baltimore: Johns Hopkins University Press, 1996.

Cooper, J. S. *The Curse of Agade*. Baltimore: Johns Hopkins University Press, 1983.

68 Josephus, *C. Ap.* 1.237-40. Translation by Waddel, *Manetho*, 125, 127.
69 Hornung, *Akhenaten*, 5.
70 Assmann, *Moses*, 33.

DIETRICH, J. "Religion und Gesellschafts-Charakter." Pages 187-202 in *Erich Fromm heute: Zur Aktualität seines Denkens*. Edited by R. Funk et al. München: Deutscher Taschenbuch Verlag, 2000.

—. "Coping with Disasters in Antiquity and the Bible: Practical and Mental Strategies." in *Past Vulnerability: Volcanic Eruptions and Human Vulnerability in Traditional Societies Past and Present*. Edited by F. Riede. Aarhus: Aarhus University Press, 2014 (in press).

DRIOTON, E. "Une représentation de la famine sur un bas-relief égyptien de la Ve dynastie." *Bulletin de l'Institut d'Égypte* 25 (1943): 45-54.

ENMARCH, R. *A World Upturned: Commentary on and Analysis of* The Dialogue of Ipuwer and the Lord of All. Oxford: Oxford University Press, 2008.

FINKEL, I. L. "Bilingual Chronicle Fragments." *Journal of Cuneiform Studies* 32 (1980): 65-80

FRAHM, E. "Nabû-Zuqup-Kēnu, das Gilgameš-Epos und der Tod Sargons II." *Journal of Cuneiform Studies* 51 (1999): 73-90.

FRISCH, M. *Man in the Holocene*. San Diego: Harcourt Brace Jovanovich, 1981.

FRISK, H. *Griechisches etymologisches Wörterbuch*. 3 vols. Heidelberg: Winter, 1954-1972.

FROMM, E. "Factors Leading to Patient's Change in Analytic Treatment." Pages 15-42 in *The Art of Listening*. Edited and with a Foreword by R. Funk. New York: Continuum, 1994.

—. "Therapeutic Aspects of Psychoanalysis." Pages 45-194 in *The Art of Listening*. Edited and with a Foreword by R. Funk. New York: Continuum, 1994.

GOEDICKE, H. "The Canaanite Illness." *Studien zur Altägyptischen Kultur* 11 (1984): 91-105.

—. "Seuche." Pages 918-19 in vol. 5 of *Lexikon der Ägyptologie*. Edited by W. Helck et al. 7. vols. Wiesbaden: Harrassowitz, 1984.

GRAYSON, A. K. "Assyrian and Babylonian Chronicles." Locust Valley, N.Y.: Augustin, 1975.

HALLO, W. W. "The Death of Kings: Traditional Histiograpgy in Contextual Perspective." Pages 148-65 in *Ah, Assyria ...: Studies in Assyrian History and Ancient Near Eastern Histiography presented to Hayim Tadmor*. Edited by M. Cogan and I. Eph'al. Jerusalem: Magnes, 1991.

HASSAN, S. "The Causeway of *Wnis* at Sakkara." *Zeitschrift für Ägyptische Sprache und Altertumskunde* 80 (1955): 136-39.

HAWASS, Z., and M. VERNER. "Newly Discovered Blocks from the Causeway of Sahure (Archaeological Report)." *Mitteilungen des Deutschen Archäologischen Instituts. Abteilung Kairo* 52 (1996): 177-86 with plates 53-56.

HELCK, W. *Inschriften der Könige von Amenophis III. bis Haremheb und ihrer Zeitgenossen*. Fascicle 22 of *Urkunden der 18. Dynastie*. Edited by W. Helck. Berlin: Akademie, 1958.

HORNUNG, E. *Akhenaten and the Religion of Light*. Translated by D. Lorton. Ithaca, N.Y.: Cornell University Press, 2001.

—. "Die neue Religion." Pages 236-55 in *Amarna: Lebensräume – Lebensbilder – Weltbilder*. Edited by C. Tietze. 2d ed. Weimar: Arcus, 2010.

IKRAM, S. "Domestic Shrines and the Cult of the Royal Family at el-'Amarna." *Journal of Egyptian Archaeology* 75 (1989): 89-101.

KRUGER, P. A. "Disaster and the *topos* of the World Upside Down: Selected Cases from the Ancient Near Eastern World." Pages 391-424 in *Disaster and Relief Management: Katastrophen und ihre Bewältigung*. Edited by A. Berlejung. Tübingen: Mohr (Siebeck), 2012.

LIVINGSTONE, A. *Court poetry and literary miscellanea*. Helsinki: University Press 1989.

MORENZ, S. "Die Bedeutungsentwicklung von *iyt* ‚Das, was kommt' zu ‚Unheil' und ‚Unrecht.'" Pages 343-59 in *Religion und Geschichte des alten Ägypten: Gesammelte Aufsätze*. Edited by E. Blumenthal and S. Herrmann. Weimar: Böhlau, 1975.

OPPENHEIM, A. L., et al., eds. *The Assyrian Dictionary of the Oriental Insititue of the University of Chicago*. 21 vols. Chicago: The Oriental Institute, 1956-2011.

PARPOLA, S. "A Letter from Šamaš-šumu-ukīn to Esarhaddon." *Iraq* 34 (1972): 21-34.

PORTER, B. N. *Images, Power, and Politics: Figurative Aspects of Esarhaddon's Babylonian Policy*. Philadelphia: American Philosophical Society, 1993.

REDFORD, D. B. "The Hyksos Invasion in History and Tradition." *Orientalia* 39 (1970): 1-51.

—. *Akhenaten: The Heretic King*. Princeton: Princeton University Press, 1984.

Reeves, N. *Akhenaten: Egypt's False Prophet*. London: Thames & Hudson, 2001.

Schaudig, H. "Erklärungsmuster von Katastrophen im Alten Orient." Pages 425-43 in *Disaster and Relief Management: Katastrophen und ihre Bewältigung*. Edited by A. Berlejung. Tübingen: Mohr (Siebeck), 2012.

Schlögl, H. A. *Echnaton*. München: Beck, 2008.

Schott, S. "Aufnahmen vom Hungersnotrelief aus dem Aufweg der Unaspyramide." *Revue d'Égyptologie* 17 (1965): 7-13.

Singer, I. *Hittite Prayers*. Atlanta: Society of Biblical Literature, 2002.

Stevens, A. *Private religion at Amarna: The material evidence*. Oxford: Archaeopress, 2006

Sztompka, P. "Cultural Trauma: The Other Face of Social Change." *European Journal of Social Theory* 3 (2000): 449-66.

Tadmor, H., B. Landsberger, and S. Parpola. "The Sin of Sargon and Sennacherib's Last Will." *State Archives of Assyria Bulletin* 3 (1989): 3-51.

Tietze, C., ed. *Amarna: Lebensräume - Lebensbilder - Weltbilder*. 2d ed. Weimar: Arcus, 2010.

Waddel, W. G. *Manetho*. Cambridge: Harvard University Press, 1980.

Weaver, A. N. "The 'Sin of Sargon' and Esarhaddon's Reconception of Sennacherib: A Study in Divine Will, Human Politics and Royal Ideology." *Iraq* 66 (2004): 61-66.

Weeks, K. R. "Medicine, Surgery, and Public Health in Ancient Egypt." *Civilizations of the Ancient Near East* 3 (1995): 1787-98.

Winthrop-Young, G. "Memories of the Nile: Egyptian Traumas and Communication Technologies in Jan Assmann's Theory of Cultural Memory." *Journal of Egyptian History* 1 (2008): 331-62.

Else K. Holt

Daughter Zion: Trauma, Cultural Memory and Gender in OT Poetics

Abstract

Discussing Kathleen M. O'Connor's understanding of the book of Jeremiah as a book by and for traumatized survivors of the collapse of Jerusalem (587 B.C.E.), this essay introduces the concepts of cultural memory (Jan Assmann) and cultural trauma (Jeffrey Alexander) as the methodological bases for a synchronic reading of the books of Jeremiah and Lamentations. It is suggested that the apparently chaotic shape of Jeremiah as well as the orderly style of Lamentations reflect the emphasis of the collective agents or carrier groups (Alexander) that stood behind the writing down of the books on the healing process of a society searching for meaning. This textual chaos is also reflected in the gendering of voices in Jer 2; 8–9, and Lam 1–2; 4 which constructs the audience as victims of their ancestors' transgressions.

Prologue

Last night I was transported from 1987 to earlier times: before the war and even back to the eighteenth and nineteenth centuries. In that way I have become part of Polish Hasidic life, and I also enter the world of my grandparents Dora and Josef.

Today we go to Auschwitz. By the time we enter, I have changed from being a "surviving grandson" to being equal, arriving at the gates from the past in the past. Only now can I finally die with Josef, Dora, and my father Hans. Later as I walk back through the camp entrance at Birkenau, I am reborn, in my present life. As witness, not as survivor.[1]

This testimony is quoted by Jack Kugelmass, Director of Jewish Studies at the University of Florida, in his article "Missions to the Past: Poland in Contemporary Jewish Thought and Deed." Kugelmass' article explores the significance and outcome of tours to Eastern Europe for groups of North American Jews. These tours are usually arranged by synagogues or by American high schools as part of the "March for the Living" project for Jewish youth. Kugel-

1 Kugelmass, "Missions," 202 (with reference to Dekro, "First Time Home").

mass describes these trips as a type of secular pilgrimage, aimed at strengthening Jewish identity for North American Jews who have experienced themselves as too assimilated, too secular, and thus lack an identity in a world challenged by "political and economic upheavals during the 1960s, (particularly in the United States in response to the Vietnam debacle)."[2] According to Kugelmass, this want of identity leads to a fear of assimilation into society's mainstream; Kugelmass quotes Jacob Neusner: "The central issue facing Judaism in our day is whether a long-beleaguered faith can endure the conclusion of its perilous age."[3] The trips to the old country are part of a striving for "symbolic ethnicity," Kugelmass claims, a striving which also leads to "heightened values placed on rites of passage in Jewish ritual."[4] Thus he asserts that "By evoking the Holocaust dramaturgically, that is, by going to the site of the event and reconstituting the reality of the time and place, North American Jews are not only invoking the spirits of the tribe, that is, wrestling claim to their martyrdom, they are also making past time present."[5]

"Making past time present" is an exact description of what goes on in the Old Testament—and in the Bible. Not only are we, as biblical scholars, trying to overcome Lessing's "garstigen, breiten Graben" (the ugly broad ditch) between the Biblical texts and our time and understanding, but the texts we encounter are themselves struggling to overcome "den garstigen, breiten Graben" between their defining past and their contemporary present in exilic/post-exilic times.

Jeremiah: Pain and Promise

My reflections in what follows are based methodologically on studies of cultural memory and cultural trauma. However, I will take my point of departure in Kathleen M. O'Connor's thought-provoking volume from 2011, *Jeremiah: Pain and Promise*. O'Connor presents the books of Jeremiah, Lamentations, Ezekiel, and Second Isaiah as testimonies of the historic catastrophe experienced by the people of Judah during the Babylonian Period. "Testimony is speech from the inside of the events," O'Connor contents; "it does not seek to prove something but to portray and interpret the experience from the inside."[6]

Most scholars, including O'Connor, describe the book of Jeremiah as a rather chaotic or at least disorderly and confusing book, made up of bits and

2 Ibid., 203.
3 Ibid., 204; no reference to Neusner indicated.
4 Ibid.
5 Ibid., 205.
6 O'Connor, *Pain and Promise*, 16.

pieces, poetry and prose, prayers, narratives and sermons. It is hard to find a coherent theology in it, even if Louis Stulman and others, including myself, have found the miscellaneous material ordered within a coherent, theological framework.[7] O'Connor follows Stulman's description of the composition of the book of Jeremiah as consisting of two parts: the first twenty-five chapters on anticipating and meeting disaster, and the final twenty-seven on life beyond the disaster.[8] She understands the underlying chaos as a manifestation of the "physical, spiritual, and psychological collapse that underlies the book of Jeremiah in the most visceral ways."[9]

The testimony which is found in the book of Jeremiah (as well as in other books of the Old Testament) is a testimony of collective trauma. O'Connor defines trauma as "the impact of violence upon individuals.... Traumatic violence comes as a shocking blow, a terrifying disruption of normal mental processes, distorting reality, even as it becomes the only reality."[10] Trauma is caused by disaster, defined—with Daniel Smith-Christopher—as events that exceed the ability of a group "to cope, to redefine and to reconstruct."[11] Disasters overwhelm, and the traumatic experiences cause a fragmentation of the memories of the violence, a breakdown of language, numbness, and a loss of faith.[12] This is the background for the book's "confusing shape." But the confusion is also the quality that makes the book into a therapy against trauma. The literary confusion of the book of Jeremiah contributes to the survivors' survival.[13]

O'Connor does not go into detail on the absolute or relative dating of the Jeremiah text. She abstains from redaction criticism or any other historical discussion, and she treats the texts synchronically in order to concentrate on the theological questions. In her own words, she is trying to "gain a glimpse of what the book might have meant for its early readers, survivors of the Babylonian disaster and their offspring, the ones who did not know if they would ever again be God's chosen people. Using trauma and disaster studies, I want to ask how the book helps them survive."[14] Thus, it is obvious that O'Connor's synchronic reading places the text of the book of Jeremiah within the Babylonian period and no later. I shall return to this dating shortly.

The dating of Jeremiah in the Babylonian, or templeless[15], age also corresponds to the normally supposed dating of the book of Lamentations, though

7 See e.g. Stulman, *Order*; Holt, "Meaning."
8 O'Connor, *Pain and Promise*, 31.
9 Ibid., 19.
10 Ibid., 3.
11 Smith-Christopher, *Biblical Theology*, 79; cf. O'Connor, *Pain and Promise*, 20.
12 Cf. the headlines in O'Connor, *Pain and Promise*, chapter 2.
13 Cf. ibid., 30.
14 Ibid.
15 Cf. Middlemas, *Templeless Judah*, 5.

it remains a point of discussion whether these poems belong to the early or late years of Babylonian hegemony.[16] However, the formation of Lamentations does not span as long a period as the formation of the book of Jeremiah, and thus the social, historical, and psychological Sitze-im-Leben of these laments do not pose the same question as the setting of the book of Jeremiah.[17] Therefore, it makes sense to treat Lamentations as survival literature, as Tod Linafelt does in his *Surviving Lamentations: Catastrophe, Lament, and Protest in the Afterlife of a Biblical Book.* The poems of Lamentations bear immediate witness to life in post-destruction Jerusalem, and call for trauma-oriented readings, as have recently been made by several scholars.

At first glance, the reading of the book of Jeremiah through the heuristic devices of trauma and disaster studies, as performed by O'Connor, also seems reasonable. Such a reading offers valid elucidations of the grotesque and outrageous poetry in Jeremiah with its semantics of despair,violence, sexism, nationalism, and xenophobia. O'Connor convincingly shows how the metaphors of the broken family, the weeping of the people and of God, Jeremiah's symbolic biography with all his suffering and social and religious marginalization, the diatribes in the Deuteronomistic sermons of guilt and breaking of the covenant, but also the hope in the little book of consolation, in short: all the diverse and chaotic messages—indeed the chaotic shape of the book itself—function within the framework of disaster and trauma and of coping with disaster and trauma through repeated interpretation.

However, upon further inspection, these readings call for refinement, since O'Connor's synchronic readings, regardless of how sympathetic I find them, leave at least one open question: how is it that even texts which cannot be substantiated as part of the exilic book of Jeremiah should be read through the lenses of trauma and disaster? Most scholars, including O'Connor herself, agree that the book of Jeremiah has experienced several substantial waves of redaction and elaboration spanning at least 300 years after the days of the catastrophe in the early sixth century B.C.E. up until (and even after) the Septuagint translation of the Hebrew *Vorlage*. Jeremiah scholars disagree widely on the relative dating of the voices of the book of Jeremiah, but this discussion simply points to the need for caution when it comes to claiming certain texts for specific historical periods with socio-psychological conditions such as trauma and its surmounting.

These considerations leave me in a tight spot between O'Connor's obviously fertile and rewarding reading strategy and my own historical reserva-

16 There is also an ongoing discussion as to whether the five chapters in Lamentations derive from one or more authors and periods; for the questions of dating and authorship, including "Jeremiah" as (implied) author of Lamentations, see Berlin, *Lamentations*, 30-36.

17 For a thorough discussion of the relation of Lamentations to the genre of Mesopotamian city laments, see Dobbs-Allsopp, *Daughter of Zion*; Berlin, *Lamentations*, 26-30.

tions. In what follows, I shall propose a way out of this dilemma. My proposal is to introduce the concepts of cultural memory and cultural trauma into the discussion as a means of overcoming the historical gap between the clearly traumatizing events of the fall of Jerusalem and its temple in 587 B.C.E. and the texts that embody and/or represent the disaster to later audiences, including the twenty-first century audience.[18]

Cultural Memory, Trauma, and Coping

The concept of cultural memory permeates large parts of the contemporary discourse in arts and theology. In what follows, I shall briefly present the ideas of the German Egyptologist Jan Assmann, who has in turn developed the thoughts of the French philosopher and sociologist Maurice Halbwachs. Halbwachs' basic comprehension is that all memory is embedded, understood and preserved in the social world; memory is a social phenomenon. Put simply, a person cannot remember anything without a social context to help structure and interpret his or her personal experiences or learning; in Assmann's words, her "episodic and semantic memory."[19] Therefore, "it is difficult, or even impossible, to distinguish between an 'individual' and a 'social' memory."[20] This leads Assmann to consider different modes of memory. Communicative memory is memory embedded in communication between persons. Such communication helps define and systematize individual memories, provide them with a horizon and make them relevant, so that they "imprint themselves on our minds," where they will be interpreted through our emotions, love, interest, sympathy, the wish to belong, but also hatred, enmity, etc.[21] However, communicative memory is practically limited to a three-generational time frame since, for obvious reasons, communicative memories must be communicated. Assmann labels communicative memory a synchronic memory space.[22]

Assmann—together with his wife, Aleida Assmann, who has influenced his writing immensely—opts for a broadening of the concept of communicative memory to *cultural memory*, i.e. communicative memory with a different temporal structure, a diachronic structure. With the help of tradition in-

18 O'Connor's goal is explicitly to make the book of Jeremiah useful in a religious, practical pastoral context. At the same time, she wishes to redeem the book—and the God portrayed in it—from its own semantics of despair, violence, sexism, nationalism and xenophobia, using trauma as her interpretative instrument; cf. O'Connor, *Pain and Promise*, ix–x, 135–37.

19 Assmann, *Religion and Cultural Memory*, 2.

20 Ibid., 3.

21 Ibid.

22 Ibid., 8.

formation, memory is transmitted through generations. Cultural memory is a diachronic axis which helps the individual understand and interpret his or her personal and cultural situation. Cultural memory, however, should not be seen as something mystical or as mere metaphor. Collective, cultural memory is not the mere "(illegitimate) transfer of a concept derived from individual psychology to social and cultural phenomena, but the interaction between the psyche, consciousness, society, and culture."[23]

Cultural memory, thus, needs vehicles to survive and remain effective; *aides-mémoires*, such as monuments, sites, landscapes and their roadmaps, rituals and narratives. The important word is "remember." Remember, do not forget—remember Amalek, remember Auschwitz, remember 1989. All these memories are preserved in the collective, cultural memory; not for the sake of archival interest, not just to preserve, but to preserve in order to understand.[24]

Part of cultural memory is cultural trauma, as defined by Jeffrey C. Alexander. According to Alexander:

> [C]ultural trauma occurs when members of a collectivity feel they have been subjected to a horrendous event that leaves indelible marks upon their group consciousness, marking their memories forever and changing their future identity in fundamental and irrevocable ways....
>
> It is by constructing cultural traumas that social groups, national societies, and sometimes even entire civilizations not only cognitively identify the existence and source of human suffering but "take on board" some significant responsibility for it.[25]

On this reading, collective, cultural trauma is a cultural construct. By adopting this reading, Alexander moves beyond the psychoanalytic insights of personal trauma (PTSD) as authoritatively described by the American Psychiatric Association. According to the definition in DSM-IV, "PTSD always follows a traumatic event which causes intense fear and/or helplessness in an individual. Typically the symptoms develop shortly after the event, but may take years. The duration for symptoms is at least one month for this diagnosis."[26] Alexander, of course, recognizes the psychoanalytic description on the personal level and, like O'Connor, he refers to Cathy Caruth's thor-

23 Ibid., 9.

24 Ibid., 7–9. Hans J. L. Jensen compares the affinity of modern thinking about memory to Augustine's concept of *memoria* in his *Confessiones*: "For Augustine a person's *memoria* includes not only what she or he may have witnessed and experienced in her or his life but also all that which this person may have recognized, acquired and learned, that is: everything this person knows.... What a person has experienced exists transformed into a synchronic state that tells more about the person remembering than about the experiences themselves." (Jensen, "Religion," 15, Jensen's unpublished translation).

25 Alexander, "Cultural Trauma," 1.

26 http://allpsych.com/disorders/anxiety/ptsd.html, consulted on December 18, 2012.

ough analyses in *Unclaimed Experience: Trauma, Narrative, and History.* Unlike O'Connor, however, Alexander goes beyond the psychoanalytical understanding of trauma. He contends that, from a sociological point of view, events do not *in and of themselves* create collective trauma:

> Events are not inherently traumatic. Trauma is a socially mediated attribution. The attribution may be made in real time, as an event unfolds; it may also be made before the event occurs, as an adumbration, or after the event has concluded, as a post-hoc reconstruction.[27]

For Alexander, the shaping of collective trauma is a social process which leads, or at least may lead, to the creation of a collective group identity. In other words, trauma is *imagined.* This is not to say that it is not real; Alexander refers to Durkheim's concept of "religious imagination" as intrinsic to any process of representation. "It is only through the imaginative process of representation that actors have the sense of experience.... What is at stake, ... is the collectivity's identity, its stability in terms of meaning, not action."[28] What is at stake is identity; the creation, or re-creation, of identity. This is also what a number of scholars in Biblical theology, including O'Connor, have acknowledged about Old Testament theology over the past two to three decades. I shall return to this below. At this point, I would just like to point to the well-known comprehension in disaster studies that an event does not cause catastrophe in and of itself; instead, disaster results from a society's lack of power to cope with the results of a given event.[29] This supports Alexander's understanding of collective trauma as something imagined in the Durkheimian understanding of imagination.

Collective trauma is a societal process, mediated through collective agents or carrier groups, who "broadcast symbolic representations—characterizations—of ongoing social events, past, present, and future." They present a "claim to some fundamental injury, an exclamation of some sacred value, a narrative about a horribly destructive social process, and a demand for emotional, institutional, and symbolic reparation and reconstruction." These car-

27 Alexander, "Cultural Trauma," 8. From the point of view of Old Testament historiography, Alexander's continuation is interesting: "Sometimes, in fact, events that are deeply traumatizing may not actually have occurred at all; such imagined events, however, can be as traumatizing as events that have actually occurred" (ibid.). Old Testament historiographers have discussed extensively whether the Babylonian exile should be considered a mainly historical or a mainly (perhaps solely) ideological event—or at least whether understanding the historical events can be based with necessary scholarly certainty on the accounts in the Biblical books; for an introduction to the discussion, see Grabbe, *Did Moses Speak Attic?*

28 Alexander, "Cultural Trauma," 9–10.

29 Smith-Christopher, *Biblical Theology*, 79 (with reference to Gilbert, "Studying Disaster," 17).

rier groups may be prestigious religious leaders, generational, national, or institutional leaders, "representing one particular social sector or organization against others in a fragmented and polarized social order."[30] They create trauma as a new master narrative, the contents of which is A) the nature of the pain, B) the nature of the victim, C) the relation of the trauma victim to a broader audience, and D) the attribution of responsibility.[31]

Such a created or re-created master narrative facilitates the creation or re-creation of societal structures, which enable individuals to achieve or re-achieve their identity as members of a threatened society. Ancient and contemporary examples are numerous, and the relevance of Alexander's descriptions for Old Testament exegesis is clearly apparent.

Jeffrey Alexander's concept of collective trauma as a strategy of imagination to create or re-create a society out of chaos helps overcome the problems of the chronological gap (alleged above) between the dramatic events in 597 and 587 B.C.E. and the Old Testament texts that revolve around the questions of guilt and just desert, pain and promise, and the wrath of God and reconciliation in the past, present and future. The carrier groups of collective trauma can be identified as the authors and editors who contributed to the shaping of the polyphonic poetic and prophetic books in the Old Testament. In light of this, it is indeed reasonable to describe the polyphony—or perhaps even cacophony—of some of these books as a result of and a strategy to overcome what became the collective trauma of the Babylonian conquest of Jerusalem, its temple, and population. In the last paragraph, I shall go more into detail with examples of chaos in the books of Jeremiah and Lamentations.[32]

Memory and Writing

The formative periods of Lamentations and the book of Jeremiah coincide with the general commencement of the writing down of the Old Testament

30 Alexander, "Cultural Trauma," 11.

31 Ibid., 12-15.

32 Trauma, of course, is not the only possible theological processing of the challenges of the templeless and Persian periods. In what has become a classic in Old Testament scholarship, *Exile and Restoration* (published 1968), Peter R. Ackroyd describes four main types of reaction to the events, 1) return to older cults, 2) acceptance of the religion of the conquerors, 3) the recognitions of divine judgment, and 4) as a variant of #3, the Day of Yahweh-theology (cf. Ackroyd, *Exile and Restoration*, 40-49). More recently, Bernhard Lang has pointed to the re-shaping of ancient Near Eastern fertility religion during the period (Lang, *Hebrew God*, 159-69). In an article in Danish, Hans J. L. Jensen argues for the existence in the Old Testament of a so-called "Merchant's religion." The figure of Abraham in Genesis is presented as "knight of politeness" (*høflighedens ridder*), a great negotiator; the Abraham narratives thus hold an indirect criticism of more militant and excluding religious movements in the Old Testament (see Jensen, "Abraham").

books in the so-called axial age. Writing is of ultimate importance to the development of what Robert Bellah labels "historic religion,"[33] and also of collective memory. Communication, and thus memory, can be extended over space and time with the aid of writing.[34] Of course, it is not writing *per se* that creates or constitutes memory—it is indeed "an ensemble of signs that … runs the risk of lapsing into a realm lying beyond lived and communicated meaning."[35] However, Assmann points to the circumstance that writing as a data-storage system needs "an appropriate memory-based culture that ensures the enduring readability of the texts."[36] The hermeneutical questions and problems posed to modern exegesis are just one attestation of this. Furthermore, the Old Testament texts themselves provide evidence to the ongoing discourse and discussion of what should be the essence of Judean collective memory, and thus points to the idea that writing is both memory-storage *and* communication, at least from the axial age and onwards. Moreover, as shown by Bellah, writing is the prerequisite of second-order thinking,[37] i.e. "thinking about thinking," which "attempts to understand how the rational exposition is possible and can be defended."[38]

The theological discussions we encounter in the books of Jeremiah and Lamentations are thus parts of the theoretical culture of the axial age, the period so labeled by Karl Jaspers,[39] indicating a period of cultural transformations in the first millennium B.C.E. of many antique societies, for example Greece, Israel, China, and India.[40] Indeed, the criticism of what Walter Brueggemann has labeled "common theology"[41] presupposes the theoretical culture of the axial age.[42]

33 Bellah, "Religious Evolution," 367.
34 Assmann, *Religion and Cultural Memory*, 86.
35 Ibid.
36 Ibid., 87.
37 "But graphic invention and the external memory it makes possible are only the essential prerequisites for the development of theoretic culture, which is the ability to think analytically rather than narratively, to construct theories that can be criticized logically and empirically." Bellah, "Axial Age," 79 (with reference to Donald, *Origins*, 23).
38 Bellah, "Axial Age," 80.
39 Jaspers, *Goal of History*.
40 Bellah, "Axial Age," 69–73, 88.
41 "Common theology" indicates a theology, common to all ancient Near Eastern communities that legitimizes political and religious structures; cf. Brueggemann, *Old Testament Theology*, 5–15.
42 "Once theoretic culture has come into existence, stories can be subjected to criticism—that is close to the heart of the axial breakthroughs…." Bellah, "Axial Age," 85. However, according to Bellah, theoretic, or second-order, thinking understood as "the capacity to examine critically the very foundations of cosmological, ethical and political order (ibid., 88), is not *per definition* communicated most effectively to a larger audience through theoretic discourse. He discusses the opinion of Eric Weil (cf. Weil, "Breakthrough") that the narrative approach to second-order thinking, characteristic of Israelite culture and reli-

The importance of writing is emphasized in the book of Jeremiah where writing is thematized in several instances. The most significant, of course, is the narrative of how Baruch the Scribe writes down Jeremiah's oracles from his dictation (Jeremiah 36) and how the king tries to nullify the power of the oracles by cutting the scroll into pieces and burning it—in vain, of course. God himself intervenes, hides the prophet and the scribe and dictates all the words again, even adding a few more oracles. This narrative authorizes, so to speak, the continued amplification and actualization of the divine word. Other important cases that focus on writing is Jeremiah's letter to the exiles in Babylon in ch. 29, and the narrative about Jeremiah's purchase of land in his hometown of Anatoth, where the writing of no less than two deeds—an open and a sealed—plays an important role. At Jeremiah's and God's command, Baruch the Scribe puts both deeds in an "earthenware jar, in order that they may last for a long time" as a witness to God's final mercy (Jer 32).

Writing is also important in Lamentations, though in a different way. Writing and literacy is the implied prerequisite for the very form of Lamentations, the alphabetic acrostic. It takes reading to acknowledge and recognize the form that is so important for conveying the message of Lamentations; that of assurance and "order amid chaos."

The importance of writing for our investigation of trauma in Lamentations and Jeremiah is obvious. Writing, of course, is an important *aide-mémoire*, and the redactional polyphony of the book of Jeremiah and the poetic form of Lamentations attest to their adherence to the axial age.

Chaos, Trauma and Gender in Lamentations and Jeremiah

At this point, let us return to O'Connor's understanding of the book of Jeremiah. I concur with many of her trauma-based readings, the same way as I have found immense inspiration in trauma-based readings on Lamentations. My question above—how is it that even texts which cannot be substantiated as part of the exilic book of Jeremiah should be read through the lenses of trauma and disaster?—was directed first and foremost to the implied dating of the texts.[43] My suggestion is that these texts be understood as representations or configurations of cultural trauma, used as an agent for the building

gion, such as it is continued in Judaism, Christianity and Islam, made biblical religion "able to contribute to ethical and political transformations of society that Greek philosophy and its Hellenistic and Roman successor traditions … never succeeded in doing." (Bellah, "Axial Age," 89).

43 In a private conversation, Prof. O'Connor acknowledged the problems and informed the present author that, in the monograph, she had deliberately circumvented the question in order to focus on the main methodology. My criticism, thus, mainly concerns the book.

or rebuilding of a national identity in the post-exilic centuries. That is what leads me to my last point: the function of the gendered language of Daughter Zion in Lamentations and Jeremiah.

One wonders why the main lamenter in Lamentations 1–2; 4 is a woman. What makes it so appropriate to hear a female voice expressing loss, pain, and despair? Is it due to female authorship (which I doubt)? Is it simply the traditional representation of the city as a woman, Daughter Zion? Or is there more to it? My proposal is to read intertextually the figure of *Daughter Zion* as we meet her in the woman of Jer 2, verbally abused by her own husband, Yahweh, and in the lamenting mother of Lam 1–2; 4, and the figure of *Yahweh* of Jer 8–9 who wants to cry over his daughter.

Jeremiah 2 is part of a larger poetic complex in which the grammatical and implied addressees alternate between the masculine and feminine, the root metaphor being that of a broken family.[44] The woman of Jer 2 is never directly named as Daughter Zion;[45] nevertheless, her role as Yahweh's (adulterous) wife makes an inclusion of the chapter within the framework of Daughter Zion natural. The text is abusive, both within the metaphor—the imagery is vulgar and explicitly sexist, also from an ancient Near Eastern perspective—and outside the metaphor as communication to a male audience who finds itself addressed as lustful, untamed females and thus emasculated. The accusations are those of a betrayed, frenetic husband:

Yet I planted you as a choice vine, from the purest stock.
How then did you turn degenerate and become a wild vine?
Though you wash yourself with lye and use much soap,
the stain of your guilt is still before me, says Yahweh God.
How can you say, "I am not defiled, I have not gone after the Baʿals"?
Look at your way in the valley; know what you have done
—a restive young camel interlacing her tracks,
a wild ass at home in the wilderness, in her heat sniffing the wind!
Who can restrain her lust?
None who seek her need weary themselves; in her month they will find her.
Keep your feet from going unshod and your throat from thirst.
But you said, "It is hopeless, for I have loved strangers, and after them I will go."
(Jer 2:21–25)[46]

44 O'Connor, *Pain and Promise*, 35–45.

45 From a text historical point of view, Jer 2 could very well be a *corpus mixtum*, and Christl Maier rightly considers the reference to Jerusalem in 2:2 a later addition (Maier, *Daughter Zion*, 103–6). This, however, is of minor importance for the intertextual reading of the passages in question.

46 All translations are according to the New Revised Standard Version (NRSV).

The accused wife never gets the opportunity to respond to the charges. Like her metaphorical brother, House of Jacob (2:4), she is muted by the divine wrath.[47]

The voice of Daughter Zion in Lamentations is first and foremost lamenting her loss, but she is also reflecting on her guilt. She admits her guilt but claims that Yahweh's punishment is unjust and disproportional; the second voice in Lam 1–2; 4, that of the implied narrator or commentator, complies with this view. Yahweh, on his part, is silent, absent, and Lamentations ends without any vestige of hope. However, the text remains orderly, using the firm form of the acrosticon to hold chaos in check.

This is not the case in Jer 8–9. Here, Yahweh laments:

My joy is gone, grief is upon me, my heart is sick.
Hark, the cry of my poor people from far and wide in the land:
"Is the LORD not in Zion? Is her King not in her?" (Jer 8:18–19)

He himself cannot do all the necessary crying (Jer 9:1):

O that my head were a spring of water, and my eyes a fountain of tears,
so that I might weep day and night for the slain of my poor people!

—and thus, Yahweh calls for the assistance of the wailing women:

Consider, and call for the mourning women to come;
send for the skilled women to come;
let them quickly raise a dirge over us,
so that our eyes may run down with tears,
and our eyelids flow with water.
For a sound of wailing is heard from Zion: "How we are ruined!" (Jer 9:17–19)

These quotations point to Yahweh's sought-for compassion with the woman Zion, so conspicuously absent in Jer 2. However, the same chapter also includes fierce diatribes, both poetic and in prose, particularly against the social deceit of the people and primarily addressed in the masculine.[48] The chaos, so prominent of traumatic contemplation, is obvious in this text. All parties in the conflict—Yahweh, Daughter Zion, and non-metaphorized male Judeans—are present, just as they are in Jer 2, where Yahweh scolds both his renegade son, House of Jacob/Judah, and his promiscuous wife.

Kathleen O'Connor understands the abusive language and thought world of Jer 2 as a rhetoric of responsibility and survival, and, in my opinion, this is a correct reading.[49] However, when read together with the confusing, self-

47 For an analysis of Jer 2, see Holt, "Stain."

48 There is some confusion in 9:6, where MT reads, 'People, my daughter" (בת־עמי), while LXX and Targum reads, 'their evil,' *BHS* b–b.

49 O'Connor, *Pain and Promise*, 43.

contradictory chapter 9, it becomes more than this. It also calls for delayed decision. It is an effective way of re-creating the feeling of victimization, of collective trauma, in a later period. The gendered language, which is so abusive to its primarily male audience, constructs the audience as a community of victims—victims of their ancestors' transgressions and their God's punishment. Every emotion, human and divine, becomes present; the audience comprehending themselves as villains and victims, their God as furious and compassionate. Mixing of genders adds to the confusion of these chaotic texts, thereby contributing to the healing traumatization.

The texts in Lamentations and the book of Jeremiah, though employing the same imagery and treating the same events, thus, appear to function differently. Could it be that the poems of Lamentations are texts that refer to experienced trauma from as late as circa 540 B.C.E.?[50] Later, these texts became part of liturgy,[51] and thus inspired or kept alive or even (re-)created the thoughts that fuel the collective traumatic texts of (among others) the book of Jeremiah. This would help explain why this prophetic book has such a long history of formation.

According to Jeffrey Alexander, cultural trauma is part of a necessary healing and society building process, driven by cultural memory. The need for such healing is aptly illustrated in the terrifying final chapters of Ezra-Nehemiah, which tell the story of the cleansing of templeless Judah by the returnees from Babylon during the Persian period. These chapters cope with the problems from quite another theological (and political) perspective than that of Jeremiah and Lamentations, yet they all aptly illustrate a society searching for meaning.

Epilogue

The force of cultural trauma is well illustrated in the creation of identity, as described in Kugelmass's article, which we referenced at the beginning of this essay. I will close with another citation from Kugelmass, which illustrates the power of collective trauma, conveyed by visits to designated places of memory, but also made possible through liturgy and liturgical texts, such as Lamentations, or emotional and disturbing texts, preserved in writing and claiming authority of old, such as the book of Jeremiah.

A participant on the international Jewish youth "March of the Living" writes of seeing the piles of shoes in Majdanek:

50 Cf. Berlin, *Lamentations*, 35; this late date can easily be understood as a result of post-traumatic numbness.

51 Ibid., 35–36.

'I glance at my own shoe, expecting it to be far different than those in this ocean of death, and my breath catches in my throat as I see my shoe, though lighter in color, is almost the same style as one, no, two, three of the shoes I see: it seems as though every shoe here is my shoe.

I wish I could throw my shoes into this pile, to grasp and feel each shoe, to jump into this sea, to become a part of it, to take it with me.'[52]

Bibliography

Alexander, J. C. "Toward a Theory of Cultural Trauma." Pages 1-30 in *Cultural Trauma and Collective Identity*. Edited by J. C. Alexander. Berkeley: University of California Press, 2004.

Assmann, J. *Religion and Cultural Memory*. Stanford: Stanford University Press, 2006.

Bellah, R. N. "Religious Evolution." *American Sociological Review* 29 (1964): 358-74.

—. "What is Axial about the Axial Age?" *Archives Européennes de Sociologie* XLVI, i (2005), 69-87.

Berlin, A. *Lamentations*. Louisville, Ky.: Westminster John Knox, 2002.

Brueggemann, W. *Old Testament Theology: Essays on Structure, Theme, and Text*. Edited by P. D. Miller. Minneapolis: Fortress, 1992.

Carroll, R. P. *Jeremiah: A Commentary*. London: SCM, 1986.

Caruth, C. *Unclaimed Experience: Trauma, Narrative, and History*. Baltimore: John Hopkins, 1996.

Dekro, J. "First Time Home: Poland Leaves Its Mark on a Visitor." *Reconstructionist* 54 (October/November 1988): 9-11, 14.

Dobbs-Allsopp, F. W. *Weep, O Daughter of Zion: A Study of the City-Lament Genre in the Hebrew Bible*. Rome: Editrice Pontificio Istituto Biblico, 1993.

Donald, M. *Origins of the Modern Mind: Three Stages in the Evolution of Culture and Cognition*. Cambridge: Harvard University Press, 1991.

Gilbert, C. "Studying Disaster: Changes in the Main Conceptual Tools." Pages 11-18 in *What is Disaster: Perspectives on the Question*. Edited by E. L. Quantarelli. London: Routledge, 1998.

Grabbe, L. L., ed. *Did Moses Speak Attic? Jewish Historiography and Scripture in the Hellenistic Period*. Sheffield: Sheffield Academic, 2001.

Holt, E. K. "The Meaning of an Inclusio: A Theological Interpretation of the Book of Jeremiah MT." *Scandinavian Journal of the Old Testament* 17 (2003): 183-205.

—. "'The Stain of Your Guilt is Still Before Me' (Jer 2:22): (Feminist) Approaches to Jeremiah 2 and the Problem of Normativity." Pages 101-16 in *Prophecy and Power: Jeremiah in Feminist and Postcolonial Perspective*. Edited by C. M. Maier and C. J. Sharp. London: T&T Clark, 2013.

Horn, D. "On Filling Shoes." *Hadassah Magazine* (November 1992): 16-22.

Jaspers, K. *The Origin and Goal of History*. London: Routledge, 1953.

Jensen, H. J. L. "Religion, hukommelse og viden: Jan Assmann, med udblik til Durkheim, Rappaport og Augustin." *Religionsvidenskabeligt Tidsskrift* 52 (2008): 3-17.

—. "Abraham, høflighedens ridder." *Dansk Teologisk Tidsskrift* 74 (2011): 3-21.

Kugelmass, J. "Missions to the Past: Poland in Contemporary Jewish Thought and Deed." Pages 199-214 in *Tense Past: Cultural Essays in Trauma and Memory*. Edited by P. Antze and M. Lambek. New York: Routledge, 1996.

52 Kugelmass, "Missions," 203 (with reference to Horn, "On Filling Shoes").

Lang, B. *The Hebrew God: Portrait of an Ancient Deity.* New Haven, Conn.: Yale University Press, 2002.
Linafelt, T. *Surviving Lamentations: Catastrophe, Lament, and Protest in the Afterlife of a Biblical Book.* Chicago: University of Chicago Press, 2000.
Maier, C. M. *Daughter Zion, Mother Zion: Gender, Space, and the Sacred in Ancient Israel.* Minneapolis: Fortress, 2008.
Middlemas, J. *The Troubles of Templeless Judah.* Oxford: Oxford University Press, 2005.
O'Connor, K. M. *Jeremiah: Pain and Promise.* Minneapolis: Fortress, 2011.
Smith-Christopher, D. L. *A Biblical Theology of Exile.* Minneapolis: Fortress, 2002.
Stulman, L. *Order amid Chaos: Jeremiah as Symbolic Tapestry.* Sheffield: Sheffield Academic, 1998.
—. *Jeremiah.* Nashville: Abingdon, 2005.
Weil, E. "What is a Breakthrough in History?" *Daedalus* (Spring 1975): 21-36.

Louis Stulman

Reading the Bible through the Lens of Trauma and Art

Abstract

Music, literature, poetry and other aesthetic expressions sustain us during the worst of times. Art and atrocity intersect and create a matrix for survival, whether the artistic expression takes the form of a poem by Garcia Lorca, a sermon by Oscar Romero, a sculpture by Julio González, or simple arts and crafts by thousands of Japanese Americans in "relocation camps" in the United States during the years 1942-1946 as a way to *gaman*, i.e., "to bear the seemingly unbearable with patience and dignity" (Delphine Hirasuna). This paper attempts to make the (methodological) case for reading the prophetic literature in the Hebrew Bible as "art of *gaman*," not art for art's sake but art (= poetry and *Kunstprosa*) for the sake of community survival. This ancient artistic expression refuses to deny the atrocities of war; it protests and dissents, it dares to place disaster in contexts of meaning, and most remarkably, it imagines a future for the historical losers. Put differently, biblical prophecy is disaster *and* survival literature for communities devastated by war, forced migration, and captivity—traumatic events in ancient as well as contemporary times.

In his groundbreaking work *The Structure of Scientific Revolutions* published fifty years ago, Thomas Kuhn argued that the development of science is defined by abrupt transformations rather than by linear and incremental accumulations of knowledge.[1] According to Kuhn, these abrupt transformations topple conceptual landscapes and erect in their place new theoretical frameworks. Kuhn maintained that the humanities and social sciences operate quite differently: they are not subject to paradigm shifts since they *trade in* competing methodologies and theoretical constructs.

Despite the force of this latter claim, significant shifts have certainly occurred in biblical studies since the 1960s, shifts that largely reflect the theoretical terrain across the humanities and social sciences. We have witnessed a metamorphosis in the way texts are read, perhaps most evident in the move from author-centered historical-criticism to postmodern scholarship. As important as historical-criticism is for doing exegetical work, it no longer mo-

1 Kuhn, *Scientific Revolutions*. For a critique of Kuhn's most noteworthy work on its 50th anniversary, see Weinberger, "Paradigm Shift." See also Shedinger, "Kuhnian Paradigms."

nopolizes the organizing categories of the field, at least in the USA. We have moved from author to text, text to reader, the universal to the particular, the center to the margins, and from so-called science to art and its rich *Nachleben*. While this characterization is somewhat overstated, John J. Collins is surely correct that the shift from modernity to the "postmodern situation" has resulted in "the collapse of paradigms."[2]

Another recent development across intellectual landscapes, a revolution of sorts, is evident in the emergent field of trauma studies—as this volume testifies.[3] The study of trauma in the second half of the 20th and early 21st centuries has taken center stage in fields as diverse as animal science and film, psychotherapy and education, aesthetics and international politics.[4] It is as if scholars and clinicians have put violence—the dialect of our time—under a microscope, examining the effects of domestic abuse, political terror, war, incest, rape, forced relocation, military occupation, captivity, torture, and other unspeakable acts of brutality. Researchers have employed quantitative and qualitative methods, including multi-informant, intergenerational, diagnostic, psychotherapeutic, and neurobiological, as well as various forms of criticism such as deconstructive, post-structural, feminist, and post-colonial—all to arrive at a greater understanding of the ravages of violence on the *psyche* and the *soma*, and on the individual and the community.

Biblical Studies is actually a latecomer on this scene. Few program units in the Society of Biblical Literature are devoted to traumatology and equally few articles published in the *Journal of Biblical Literature*.[5] Yet a number of works have begun to appear that explore the intersection of trauma and the Bible, including Daniel L. Smith-Christopher's *Biblical Theology of Exile*, Kathleen M. O'Connor's *Jeremiah: Pain and Promise*, Paul Kim and Louis Stulman's

2 Collins, *Bible after Babel*, 131. That much of biblical scholarship still pledges its allegiance to the old as well as the new—a hybridity of sorts—may actually support Kuhn's contention that the humanities and social sciences are resistant to abrupt and definitive transformations in organizing categories. See also Perdue, *Collapse*.

3 And as the earlier conference testifies: "Trauma and Traumatization: In and Beyond Biblical Literature," Aarhus University, Denmark, June 6-9, 2012. Specials thanks to the organizers of this important conference: Eve-Marie Becker, Jan Dochhorn, Else Kragelund Holt, and Erin J. Wright.

4 Not associated particularly with seminal figures who enact paradigm shifts in the world of knowledge (e.g., Einstein, Newton, Freud, Locke, Darwin, Wittgenstein), our current understanding of trauma is a composite of various voices, although Freud remains the dominant force. For recent works on trauma that have influenced this essay, see Caruth, *Unclaimed Experience*; Caruth, *Trauma*; Herman, *Trauma*; Kira, "Taxonomy;" Lemaire, "Humanitarian Interventions;" Gozdziak, *Refugee Women*. See also the incisive critique by Leys, *Trauma*.

5 Nonetheless, it is rare, it seems, to attend a session at the annual SBL meetings in which trauma is not mentioned, as if it is now part of a new wave, even if written formulations are still in their early stages.

You are My People: An Introduction to Prophetic Literature,[6] David M. Carr's *The Formation of the Hebrew Bible. A New Construction*, which considers the role of trauma in its treatment of the Babylonian exile,[7] and most recently Daniel Epp-Tiessen, *Concerning the Prophets: True and False Prophecy in Jeremiah 23:9–29:32*.

Although the integration of trauma and biblical studies is still in its infancy, Smith-Christopher could ask at the 2010 SBL Meeting in Atlanta whether the entirety of 20th century biblical scholarship should be reconsidered in light of what we now know about trauma,[8] a question that stretches the imagination. I could not agree more with the inference that recent trauma studies challenge the prevailing categories in the field. Indeed, the interdisciplinary field of traumatization might well reframe the interpretive landscape of biblical studies in the 21st century. This supposition is based on the far-reaching findings of trauma scholarship as well as what we now know about ancient Israel. To clarify this latter point, let me highlight two related observations, one made a number of years ago and the other more recently.

The first observation comes from Artur Weiser's dated-but-classic *Einleitung in das Alte Testament* which begins with the seemingly incidental note that "Palästinas Geschichte und Kultur ist weithin *bestimmt* [my italics] durch die Tatsache, daß das Land die Verbindungsbrücke zwischen Asien und Afrika bildet; Palästina und seine Bewohner waren hineingezogen in den politischen und kulturellen Kampf der Großmächte am Euphrat, in Kleinasien und am Nil."[9] I memorized those words for an exam in 1978 and recall the profound impression they made on me then: ancient Israel, whose God is still worshipped by millions today, *utterly vulnerable* to the great empires of the Near East. Of course any plausible historical reconstruction of ancient Israel must take into consideration the enormous toll exacted on this "little country" by colonizing forces on the Tigris and the Euphrates. In their 2011 work, *The Meaning of the Bible: What the Jewish Scriptures and Christian Old Testament Can Teach Us*, Douglas Knight and Amy-Jill Levine remind us anew that ancient Israel was "invaded and occupied repeatedly, each

6 See also Linafelt, *Surviving Lamentations*; Garber, "Trauma, History, and Survival." For the treatment of the broader categories of trauma and theological studies, see, e.g., Jones, *Trauma and Grace*; Kelle, *Interpreting Exile*, esp. 253–343.

7 Carr, *Formation*, 225–51.

8 Smith-Christopher, "Ruptured Self."

9 "The history and civilization of Palestine are largely *determined* [my italics] by the fact that the country forms the bridge connecting Asia and Africa; Palestine and its inhabitants were [thus] drawn into the political and cultural struggles of the great powers on the Euphrates, in Asia Minor and on the Nile." Weiser, *Einleitung*, 17 (Engl. transl. *The Old Testament*, 11).

time becoming *small provinces* [ital. mine] in vast empires extending from Egypt to Greece to the Indus River or beyond."[10]

The second and related observation has been made in the past few decades. Biblical scholars have come to pay increasing attention to exile and diaspora, and especially the Achaemenid Persian era (ca. 550–330 B.C.E.) as the *formative social location of ancient Israel and its literary corpus.*[11] Although some still argue for a historical Israel that largely coincides with the dominant biblical narrative, a significant interpretive perspective recognizes the importance of Persian hegemony, even the Hellenistic world, as decisive factors in the construction of Israel's meta-narrative.[12]

These interrelated points—ancient Israel's geographic liabilities as well as its protracted history of war, exile, diaspora, and captivity, all traumatic events in ancient and contemporary times—raise new lines of inquiry, especially when integrated with recent trauma studies.

How would reading the Hebrew Bible through the lens of trauma subvert ordinary interpretive strategies? What would the Tanakh look like, for instance, if it were broached as literature of disaster and survival? How might traumatic violence have informed theological or symbolic construction, i.e., dominant and competing images of the deity, the text's meta-narrative, its contested testimonies, and its myriad expressions of distress, pathos, dislocation, and hope? And how might the integration of trauma and biblical scholarship alter normative author/text-centered reading practices, such as source, form, redaction, and historical critical criticism? Such inquiries would demand enormous imagination, theoretical sophistication, and a full-fledged multidisciplinary effort.

For the purposes of this volume, I will consider one corollary of this massive venture which itself is rather unwieldy: reading the *Nevi'im*, the Prophets, as ancient Israel's trauma or disaster/survival literature.[13] Such an undertaking, it seems to me, reads along the grain of the text because the prophetic corpus is by and large a complex literary response to the massive collapse of social and symbolic structures. This collapse is largely the result of war, forced

10 Knight and Levine, *Meaning*, 27.

11 E.g., Albertz and Becking, *Yahwism*; Watts, *Persia and Torah*.

12 For an up-to-date discussion of Israelite history and the influence of Yehudite perspectives and experiences in the Persian and Hellenistic period on the formation of the Bible, see Knight and Levine, *Meaning*, 3–41.

13 Conference participants commented on the need to clarify the meaning of trauma, disaster, and survival terminology. While each comprises a distinct corpus of literature and carries distinct connotations, all are rooted in profound suffering, individual and communal, and are, it seems to me, rather porous in nature. I, therefore, do not make hard and fast distinctions in this context, while recognizing the need to do so as the interdisciplinary work evolves.

relocation, and captivity.[14] As Donald Gowen put it, the two focal points of the prophetic literature are the fall of Samaria in the eighth century B.C.E. (by the Assyrian military machine) and the collapse of Jerusalem in the sixth century (by the neo-Babylonian armies).[15] Along similar lines, Michael H. Floyd maintains that "[t]he prophetic books are concerned with developments that led to exile under the Babylonians and/or developments that followed from the reversal of exile under the Persians. Each book mines Israel's prophetic tradition to interpret theologically some aspect(s) of exile and restoration."[16] Building on these and other studies Paul Kim and I have suggested that written prophecy is "a meditation on the horror of war."[17] This corpus is "the disaster literature of those who survived the onslaught of the three great world powers—Assyria, Babylon, and Persia—and their imperialistic designs."[18] If there is a *Mitte* of this polyphonic literary tradition, it might be the trauma of war and the concerted attempt to survive it.

Even a superficial reading of so-called classical prophecy, or written prophecy, cannot obscure the central role played by war, empire, and violence, particularly in the formation of judgment oracles. Hosea opens the book of the Twelve with an ominous allusion to the violence of Jehu's house (Hos 1:4-5). Joel's metaphorical world is consumed by invading armies, imagined as "cutting locust," "swarming locust," "hopping locust," and "destroying locust" (Joel 1:4). The initial oracles against the nations in Amos are informed in large measure by abuses in warfare; the threat of military invasion is at the center of attention throughout the book. Obadiah is an expression of rage against Edom for "the slaughter and violence done to your brother Jacob" (Obad 10). Jonah, in contrast to Obadiah, elicits a more amenable response to life within the empire. Jeremiah, Isaiah, and Ezekiel bristle with images of divine violence and human cruelty, the vast majority of which can be subsumed under the heading of war. Even their configurations of hope are regularly set against the background of war.

It is significant that written prophecy "re-presents" or reenacts the community's unspeakable suffering in the form of poetry and *Kunstprosa*, or as

14 These forces spur competing *internal* power claims vying for survival and prominence—e.g., the pro-golah and Judah-based ideological platforms in the book of Jeremiah (see, e.g., Sharp, *Prophecy*).

15 Gowan, *Theology*, 9-16.

16 Floyd, "Production," 277.

17 Stulman and Kim, *My People*, 6.

18 Ibid. Ironically the sacred literature of millions is actually the literary legacy of the historical losers. Such a claim clearly subverts the dominant reading of the Bible by Christians in the world's richest countries who construe their sacred text as a story of the winners. Liberation theologians have challenged this assumption for decades and post-colonial readers continue to address the devastating power disparities inside and outside of the text. See the concluding comments of this essay.

Diamond and I have put it, as "textual art"[19]—not art for art's sake, but "savage art.[20] This layered and contested artistic expression refuses to deny the atrocities of war; it protests and dissents, throbs with pain, and dares to shatter structures of meaning. This "blood poetry" confronts cruel coercion and human brutality, all the while insisting that raw power is not ultimate power. Art for the sake of communal survival; art that defies, not denies, the wreckage of its times!

Communities under siege have long looked to art as witness, testimony, and as a way to cope with the unimaginable. Consider the drawings, poems, and diaries from the camps in Poland or the graffiti on the walls of prisons in El Salvador or the recycled glass work and embroidery by Palestinian women. I was confronted anew by the power of art as a form of survival, and resistance, when visiting an exhibition at the Renwick Gallery in Washington, DC entitled, "The Art of Gaman: Arts and Crafts from the Japanese American Internment Camps, 1942-1946." The exhibition, which was based on Delphine Hirasuna's 2005 book, *The Art of Gaman*, celebrated the resilience of the human spirit at the same time it raged against and mourned over a disheartening chapter of 20th century U.S. history.

Two months after the United States declared war against Japan, President Franklin D. Roosevelt signed an executive order to send all persons of Japanese ancestry to "relocation" camps, and nearly 120,000 Japanese Americans remained in those camps until the end of World War II.[21] To survive their harsh conditions and to endure the injustice and humiliation—and perhaps to cope with boredom and introduce beauty to their bleak surroundings—many interns made arts and crafts as a way to *gaman*, the Japanese term of Zen Buddhist origins for "bear[ing] the seemingly unbearable with patience and dignity."[22] Their work included the most intricately carved and painted birds, beautiful shelled pins, iron wood carving, teapots, ornaments, toys, purses, and furniture made in the camps in Poston, AZ; Tule Lake, CA; Topaz, UT; and elsewhere in the United States West—all incarnations of *gaman*—all attempts to "bear the seemingly unbearable with patience and dignity."

Music, literature, poetry, drama, story-telling and other artistic expressions sustain us in the worst of times. Art and atrocity, perhaps counter-intuitively, belong together and create a matrix for survival, whether the artistic expression takes the form of a poem by Garcia Lorca, a sermon by Oscar Romero, a sculpture by Julio González, a painting by Picasso, a lyric by Leonard Cohen, or arts and crafts by victims of xenophobia. Indeed, art steps for-

19 Diamond and Stulman, *Jeremiah*, 28.
20 Ibid.
21 See http://americanart.si.edu/exhibitions/archive/2010/gaman/
22 Ibid.

ward on behalf of victims of unspeakable violence. Art steps forward to imagine a world in and through and beyond the traumatic violence.

That is exactly what prophetic literature[23] attempts to do, it seems to me: help communities devastated by war and forced relocation survive the collapse of their worlds of meaning. The ancient sage Sirach put it more directly when alluding to the Twelve as comforting God's people and rescuing them with hopeful confidence.[24] *Written prophecy is ancient Israel's socially sanctioned survival literature, its art of gaman.* In the first place it breaks the silence that often debilitates victims of violence. It translates lived chaos into language, thereby creating a bearable distance between the traumatic event and its symbolic representation. It gives testimony, preserves memory, and imagines a future in the bleakest of times. Perhaps most importantly, this ancient literary art form makes victims of traumatic violence active meaning-makers; that is to say, it affords post-war survivors (and their children) the opportunity to act and create a future that was often denied the target audience of the spoken word. Prophetic poetry maps out meaning in radical suffering.

Written prophecy in the Hebrew Bible is thus not only art[25]; it is meaning-making art. In addition to its vast repertoire of cultural roles, it attempts to help suffering communities understand circumstances beyond their control.[26] Specifically, it functions as a complex theodicy (or anti-theodicy),

23 In contrast to oral prophecy, written prophecy enjoys its own distinctive anatomy. See Stulman and Kim, *My People*, 9–23, and the literature cited.

24 "May the bones of the twelve prophets sprout new life from their burial places, because they comforted Jacob and rescued them with hopeful confidence" (Sirach 49:10).

25 Ellen F. Davis and Richard B. Hays, along with other participants in the so-called "Scripture Project," have argued that "reading Scripture is an art, a creative discipline that requires engagement and imagination, in contrast to the Enlightenment's idea of detached objectivity." This reading strategy of engagement and subversion has long resonated with my own interpretive inclinations. But I would suggest that their case is all the more convincing because written prophecy *is* in fact art/poetry. See Davis and Hays, *Reading Scripture*.

26 Elzbieta Gozdziak suggests in her study on the psychological response of refugee women to forced migration that viable explanations of suffering are vital to individual and group survival. See Gozdziak, *Refugee Women*, 14. See also Kira, "Taxonomy." As Viktor Frankl noted in his classic work *Man's Search for Meaning*, after surviving the worst of circumstances, "to live is to suffer, to survive is to find meaning in this suffering" (11). In his introduction to poetry as survival, Gregory Orr says that "in the act of making [and reading] a poem at least two crucial things [take place] that are different from ordinary life. First, we have shifted the crisis [life's extremities] to a bearable distance from us; removed it to the symbolic but vivid world of language. Second, we have actively *made* and shaped this model of our situation rather than passively endured it as lived experience." See Orr, *Poetry as Survival*, 4–5. Orr came to an understanding of poetry's survival capacity early in his life. When he was 12, he killed his brother in a hunting accident, an event his family could never talk about. Two years after his brother's death, his mother died at the young age of 36 after a "routine" hospital procedure. At a very young age these experiences gave him "a

which is little more than a literary mechanism to make sense of the wreckage of war and forced relocation. *To speak of war as divine judgment, for instance, is to place the worst of human conditions within a context of meaning.* God's messengers garner an array of tropes to harness death and destruction: they employ accusations, disputations, indictments, covenant lawsuits, scathing sermons and vision reports, as well as terrifying sign-acts, all to create symbolic order out of otherwise inexplicable chaos. Amos sees a plumb line, Isaiah sings of a vineyard gone wild, Hosea calls Israel a whore, Zephaniah and others announce the terrible day of God, and Ezekiel outlines a morally exacting symbolic universe in which the horror of military defeat and forced migration does not impugn the divine character.

The prose sermons in Jeremiah attempt to make sense of disaster by drawing a clear correlation between Judah's supposed conduct and its condition. With the use of Deuteronomic categories, Jeremiah asserts that the wicked will be punished for their sins (e.g., Jer 11:1-13).

> Jeremiah received this word from Yhwh: Hear the terms of this covenant and announce them in the towns of Judah and on the streets of Jerusalem.... Obey the terms of this covenant and carry them out.... But they didn't listen or pay attention; they followed their own willful ambitions. So I brought upon them all the punishments I prescribed for defying this covenant—for refusing to obey. (Jer 11:1-2, 6, 8)

This kind of exacting speech clearly blames the victim rather than the perpetrators of violence,[27] but it also represents a sustained attempt to make suffering intelligible and manageable. As Orr notes, it is often less painful to live in a coherent moral universe that one can negotiate, *even with guilt*, than in a morally arbitrary world spiraling out of control.[28] Smith-Christopher notes that self-incrimination is a common survival strategy of traumatized people, employed seemingly to make sense of senseless acts of violence.[29] This ordering of chaos is part and parcel of the Jeremianic prose tradition.[30] To be sure, the attempt to create symbolic and social symmetry in the face of inexplicable human chaos may represent one of the enduring characteristics of the entire prophetic corpus in the Hebrew Bible (see, e.g., Ezek 1-11 which by and large contends that Judah's bad behavior led to the destruction of Jerusalem, its temple, and the exile).

terrifying sense of the frailty of life, how easily and quickly people can vanish" (Ibid., 6). In a high school honors English class, Orr testifies he found that he could survive these terrifying experiences through poetry—writing it and reading it.

27 Isaiah of Jerusalem follows suit in the sense that he condemns "the daughters of Zion" (Jerusalem) and details their afflictions, which in effect brings to light "the deprivations and even sexual violence of military defeat" (Is 3:16-17 and 3:24-4:1). See Tull, *Isaiah*, 105.

28 Orr focuses on "life's interplay of order and disorder" (4) in *Poetry as Survival*, 1-9.

29 Smith-Christopher, *Theology of Exile*, 54-64.

30 Cf. Stulman, *Order*.

It is worth noting here that scholars have long called attention to the surplus of blame in the prophetic literature as well as the resultant depiction of Israel as a people disposed towards idolatry and moral failings. Unfortunately a good number, both conservative and liberal, *believe it*, persuaded by the text's extraordinary rhetorical force. That is, they assume a direct correspondence between literary reality and social reality. As a case in point, notice how several recent commentators have described the people whom Jeremiah addresses in his first temple sermon (Jer 7:1–15):

1. "These 'Temple Oracles' address not the religiously indifferent, much less the transparently wicked who live and move about in Judah's largest city, rather the devout who have come to worship Yahweh ..."[31]
2. "Jrm was of course challenging the religious 'establishment' of his time...[32]
3. "Thus, in a perverse way, the citizens of Judah had twisted the very essence of their religion ..."[33]
4. "The people continue to trust in 'deceptive words' ... Theft, murder, adultery, perjury, and the worship of Baal flourished in the land ..."[34]
5. "The people had rejected the sole and complete sovereignty of Yahweh and had sought to share their allegiance with *other gods*."[35]
6. "If the wickedness of the people of Eli's days brought destruction to the sanctuary, what would happen to the people of Jeremiah's day who had *done all these things*?"[36]
7. Craigie, Kelley and Drinkard assert quite frankly, "Jeremiah's preaching is descriptive both of the social and religious conditions pertaining to his period ..."[37]

All accept at face value the text's rhetoric of blame. All accept the conceptual world of the text as realities on the ground. Reading the text as trauma literature challenges this assumption of correspondence and rejects the resulting caricature of Judah as an immoral nation. The Israel behind the text, as Knight and Levine have well argued, was more likely only "a tiny country buffeted by geopolitical forces it could scarcely repel."[38] The prophetic inclination to blame this "tiny country" for all its troubles and explain its political misfortunes by way of moral causality is a rigorous attempt to recreate symbolic coherence in times of social convulsion: the text places war, military

31 Lundbom, *Jeremiah*, 470.
32 Holladay, *Jeremiah*, 249.
33 Craigie et al., *Jeremiah*, 120.
34 Ibid., 121.
35 Thompson, *Jeremiah*, 279.
36 Ibid., 282
37 Craigie et al., *Jeremiah*, 127.
38 Knight and Levine, *Meaning*, 143.

occupation, exile, and captivity within a framework of meaning for the sake of community survival.

The prophetic literature, however, does more than construct coherent moral arrangements to "make sense" of senseless suffering. The so-called Confessions of Jeremiah, for instance, throw into question the orderly workings of the universe, albeit still for the sake of survival:

If I took you to court, Yhwh, you would win.
But I still have questions about your justice.
Why do the guilty prosper?
Why are evildoers content?
You plant them, and they take root;
they flourish and bear fruit.
You are ever on their lips
but far from their hearts. (Jer 12:1–2)

As a representative of a community that is suffering the ravages of traumatic violence, moreover, Jeremiah rants and rages against God's overwhelming power:

Yhwh, you enticed me, and I was duped.
You were too strong for me and prevailed.
Now I'm laughed at all the time;
everyone mocks me. (Jer 20:7)

Not unlike grief-stricken Job, the tortured prophet gives voice to those who languish for death:

Cursed be the day I was born.
May the day my mother
gave birth to me not be blessed.
Cursed be the one
who delivered the news to my father,
"It's a boy"—
filling him with happiness. (Jer 20:14–15)

Isaiah of the Exile complicates the orderly workings of the universe by envisioning suffering as innocent and redemptive, still another way of placing gratuitous suffering within context of meanings:

He was pierced because of our defiance,
crushed because of our crimes.
He bore the punishment that made us whole;
by his wounds we are healed. (Isa 53:5)

This well-known over-determined text assures *all* who suffer unjustly that their suffering is not futile.

In the face of terrible violence, Habakkuk expresses grave doubts about the moral sanity of deploying Babylon as an instrument of divine justice:

Yhwh, how long will I cry out for help
    and you not listen?
I cry out to you, "Violence!"
    but you won't deliver.
Why do you show me wrongdoing
    and look at anguish?
Why are devastation and violence before you
    and strife and conflict abound? (Hab 1:2-3; see also 1:5-14)

In addition to these isolated expressions of revolt against moral and symbolic symmetry, one could make the case that the prophetic corpus as a whole deconstructs its own coherent categories by transforming its heroes of judgment into heralds of salvation. When the tradition ends virtually every book with defiant hope *without cause*,[39] it undermines its own predictable moral structures. For instance, Amos imagines the restoration of the fallen booth of David despite the book's scathing announcements of divine retribution for social injustice and ritual misconduct (Amos 9:11-15), Joel speaks of a glorious future when mountains will "drip sweet wine [and] the hills will flow with milk" (Joel 3:17-21 [18]), Zephaniah envisions warrior Yhwh head over heels for daughter Zion (3:14-20), Micah celebrates the tenacity of God's forgiveness (7:18-20), and Ezekiel concludes his long scroll with the bold claim that "Yhwh is There" (48:35)—an assertion quite extraordinary in a refugee camp in Babylon.

Whether constructing coherent arrangements to tame the chaos or deconstructing symmetrical categories of meaning,[40] written prophecy addresses ancient Israel at its most inchoate moments and serves as a stunning expression of *gaman*, a corpus intended to help victims of traumatic violence survive the worst possible conditions.[41]

39 See Clements, "Patterns." These expressions of hope have often been dismissed as "inauthentic," "distortions," or as "mere accretions." While scholars, especially during the early part of the twentieth century, were likely correct in pointing out the late character of these pieces, their assumptions were unwarranted that utterances that do not derive from the prophet are insignificant. Such a view does not take into account the importance of the growth and development of the prophetic tradition, its dynamic literary character, and, in terms of trauma studies, the role of meaning-making in the life of the intergenerational community. The hopeful endings of the prophetic tradition may represent the meaningful construction of sufferers of secondary trauma, those who were temporally, spatially, and emotionally removed from ground zero, and thus were less inclined to be defined solely by the traumatic events.

40 See, e.g., Stulman and Kim, *My People*, 113-28.

41 See note 24. Moreover, the New Testament writers/readers most often allude to prophetic texts in salvific and messianic contexts.

I am therefore suggesting in this essay that written prophecy is disaster and survival art for communities living through the wreckage of war and captivity. This artifact of terror, this artifact of hope, dares to address the realities of traumatic violence. It refuses to banish memory and close down the senses, as W. G. Sebald suggests post-war nations are inclined to do.[42] It speaks of annihilated worlds and shattered communities, as well as the collapse of cherished institutions and understandings of life. And it will not flatten life into static and singular categories. Prophetic art provides at-risk communities a lens of hope, which survivors can see through and beyond their suffering. All told, this meaning-making literature is *a meditation on the horror of war and the audacity of hope*. The two—atrocity and hope—are inseparable.

As noted above, the prophetic literature is not the only textual art in the Hebrew Bible, nor is it the only body of trauma literature. Other sections of Hebrew canon can surely be read as artistic gaman for pariah communities eking out a life within the empire. Imagine, for example, liminal Torah voices as artistic expressions of the historical losers, as the legacy of the dispossessed. Consider Torah motifs of landless, fringe, and vulnerable people, whose worlds are placed in grave danger by infertility, famine, internal rivalries, and the empire itself.

Consider the focal concern for clear and precise internal boundaries in Leviticus and Deuteronomy—survival strategies employed by communities that feel themselves at risk and vulnerable to outsiders and/or dangerous insiders—as well as the stunning inversions of power arrangements in Exodus, most forcefully seen in the celebration of an unknown deity who rivals world historical powers. Yahweh not only emerges as *savior* in this literature, but as *survivor* who endures human encroachment, geo-political assault, cosmic violence, world-threatening chaos, and a people who are reluctant, even resistant, to enter covenant. All along the text revels in the routing of repressive power brokers, astonishingly with few weapons other than the art of gaman —textual/liturgical art that helps the wounded "bear the seemingly unbearable with patience and dignity."

One could move effortlessly beyond Torah and the Prophets to sections of the Writings as an expression of disaster and survival literature. Consider the focus on loss and liminality in the Psalter, and especially the imprint of lament on this corpus and the ubiquitous "enemy." The liturgical legacy of ancient Israel is a stunning display of worlds at risk to forces beyond human control, forces that place both individual and community in danger, as if Israel at worship lives in a perpetual state of complete and utter exposure. Furthermore, suffering and survival are center stage in the wisdom literature

42 Sebald, *Natural History*, see esp. 3-32, 41.

which seeks "to make sense of extreme adversity" and help people cope with life's vexing anomalies.[43]

What are the broader implications of reading the *Nevi'im* (as well as the Torah and Ketuvim) as trauma and disaster literature, as the art of gaman? Let me conclude with five preliminary suggestions. First, reading the prophetic corpus through the lens of trauma might broaden the conversation on the role and function of written prophecy in ancient Near East. Specifically it proposes that written prophecy, alongside other functions, serves as a mechanism to cope with communal disaster, re-order values, reconstruct meaning, and create new symbolic and social worlds in the aftermath of war and community dislocation.

Second, this contemporary reading strategy might shed light on ancient Israel as a culture suffering the intergenerational effects of traumatic violence (perhaps not unlike many Native American communities in the United States). Therefore, it would problematize moralistic characterizations of ancient Israel that are based on prophetic rhetoric. Whereas some interpreters, as suggested earlier, still view classical prophecy as a window into ancient Israel's battle with morality and idolatry, reading through the lens of trauma reveals a more primal concern for survival—*the survival of God, the survival of faith, the survival of the community.*

Third, a hermeneutic that broaches the text as disaster literature might well contribute to the lively conversation on violence in the Bible such as Eric Seibert's thought provoking books *Disturbing Divine Behavior* and *The Violence of Scripture.* A trauma reading finds textual violence no less repugnant than Seibert, but it refuses to banish it from the text. Instead it *reads* the violence as an integral part of a contested communal dialogue over the meaning of disaster. Moreover, it sees value in translating lived chaos into language, especially for victims of war.

Fourth, an interpretive perspective that is particularly alert to trauma, disjunction, and loss might more readily subvert our first world orientation to read our iconic classic text as the story of the winners. That is, it might challenge the time-worn assumption that the Bible is a canonical warrant for dominance, acquisition, and moral hegemony. No doubt reading one's sacred story as literature of the losers would demand a radical reorientation, indeed for some a scandalous shift in perspectives, but such a view reads along the grain of the text, both literarily and historically. For Christians this reading of the Old Testament coheres to and even prepares for the central place of the death of Jesus in the New Testament. For Jews this reading of the Hebrew Bible represents another painful way to engage Holocaust theology.

43 See Crenshaw, *Old Testament Wisdom*, 4.

Fifth, an interpretive perspective that is amenable to aesthetic sensibilities, such as reading the prophetic literature as survival art or the poetry of gaman, might pave the way for more sophisticated *affective* methodologies. And artistic expression, aesthetics, and the non-cognitive might appreciate the anguish of radical human suffering depicted in text traditions in ways not fully accessible to ordinary disciplines of modern criticism. I think it was Thomas Merton who said that the birds do not know they have names. There is beauty and pain that cannot be reduced to cognitive categories.

If nothing else, the present focus on trauma and the Bible might prompt us to reconsider Kuhn's claim that the social sciences and humanities are not subject to paradigm shifts.

Bibliography

Albertz, R., and B. Becking, eds. *Yahwism after the Exile: Perspectives on Israelite Religion in the Persian Era*. Assen: Van Gorcum, 2003.

Caruth, C., ed. *Trauma: Explorations of Memory*. Baltimore: Johns Hopkins Press, 1995.

—. *Unclaimed Experience: Trauma, Narrative and History*. Baltimore: Johns Hopkins Press, 1996.

Carr, D. M. *The Formation of the Hebrew Bible: A New Construction*. Oxford: Oxford University Press, 2011.

Clements, R. E. "Patterns in the Prophetic Canon," in *Old Testament Prophecy: From Oracles to Canon*. Louisville, Ky.: Westminster John Knox Press, 1996.

Collins, J. J. *The Bible after Babel: Historical Criticism in a Postmodern Age*. Grand Rapids: Eerdmans, 2005.

Craigie, P. C., P. H. Kelley, and J. F. Drinkard Jr. *Jeremiah 1–25*. Word Biblical Commentary 26. Dallas, Texas: Word Books, 1991.

Crenshaw, J. L. *Old Testament Wisdom: An Introduction*. Louisville, Ky.: Westminster John Knox, 2010.

Davis, E. F., and R. B. Hays, eds. *The Art of Reading Scripture*. Grand Rapids: Eerdmans, 2003.

Diamond, A. R. P., and L. Stulman, eds. *Jeremiah (Dis)Placed: New Directions in Writing/Reading Jeremiah*. London: T & T Clark, 2011.

Epp-Tiessen, D. *Concerning the Prophets: True and False Prophecy in Jeremiah 23:9–29:32*. Eugene, Oreg.: Pickwick Publications, 2012.

Floyd, M. H. "The Production of Prophetic Books." Pages 276–97 in *Prophets, Prophecy and Prophetic Texts in Second Temple Judaism*. Edited by M. H. Floyd and R. D. Haak. New York: T&T Clark, 2006.

Frankl, V. *Man's Search for Meaning*. New York: Washington Square, 1985.

Garber Jr., D. G. "Trauma, History, and Survival in Ezekiel 1-24." Ph.D. diss., Emory University, 2005.

Gowan, D. *Theology of Prophetic Books: The Death and Resurrection of Israel*. Louisville, Ky.: Westminster John Knox, 1998.

Gozdziak, E. M. *Refugee Women's Psychological Response to Forced Migration: Limitations of the Trauma Concept*, 2006. 26 pages. Cited 17 Febraury 2014. Online: http://issuu.com/georgetownsfs/docs/emg_2005_refugee_women.

Holladay, W. L. *A Commentary on the Book of the Prophet Jeremiah: Chapters 1–25*. Philadelphia: Fortress.

Herman, J. *Trauma and Recovery*. New York: Basic Books, 1992, 1997.

Hirasuna, D. *The Art of Gaman: Arts and Crafts from Japanese American Internment Camps 1942–1946*. New York: Random House, 2005.

Jones, S. *Trauma and Grace: Theology in a Ruptured World*. Louisville, Ky.: WJK, 2009.

Kelle, B. E., F. R. Ames, and J. L. Wright, eds., *Interpreting Exile: Displacement and Deportation in Biblical and Modern Contexts*. Atlanta: Society of Biblical Literature, 2011.

Kira, I. A. "Taxonomy of Trauma and Trauma Assessment." *Traumatology* 7, no. 2 (June 2001): 73–86.

Knight, D. A. and A.-J. Levine. *The Meaning of the Bible: What the Jewish Scriptures and Christian Old Testament Can Teach Us*. New York: HarperOne, 2011.

Kuhn, T. *The Structure of Scientific Revolutions*. Chicago: University of Chicago Press, 1962.

Lemaire, J.-M. "Disconcerting Humanitarian Interventions, and the Resources for Collective Healing." Pages 71–77 in *Psychosocial and Trauma Response in War-torn Societies: The Case of Kosovo*. Psychosocial Notebook, Vol. 1, November 2000. Under the direction of Natale Losi. Geneva: International Organization for Migration, 2000.

Leys, R. *Trauma: A Genealogy*. Chicago and London: University of Chicago, 2000.

Linafelt, T. *Surviving Lamentations: Catastrophe, Lament, and Protest in the Afterlife of A Biblical Book*. Chicago: University of Chicago Press, 2000.

Lundbom, J. R. *Jeremiah 1–20*. The Anchor Bible. New York: Doubleday, 1999.

O'Connor, K. M. *Jeremiah: Pain and Promise*. Minneapolis: Fortress, 2011.

Orr, G. *Poetry as Survival*. Athens, Ga.: University of Georgia Press, 2002.

Perdue, L. G. *The Collapse of History: Reconstructing Old Testament Theology*. Overtures to Biblical Theology. Minneapolis: Fortress, 1994.

Sebald, W. G. *The Natural History of Destruction*. New York: Random House, 2003.

Seibert, E. A. *Disturbing Divine Behavior: Troubling Old Testament Images of God*. Minneapolis: Fortress, 2009.

—. *Violence of Scripture: Overcoming the Old Testament's Troubling Legacy*. Minneapolis: Fortress Press, 2012.

Sharp, C. J. *Prophecy and Ideology in Jeremiah: Struggles for Authority in the Deutero-Jeremianic Prose*. Old Testament Studies, ed. D. J. Reimer. London and New York: T & T Clark, 2003.

Shedinger, R. F. "Kuhnian Paradigms and Biblical Scholarship: Is Biblical Studies a Science?" *Journal of Biblical Literature* 119 (2000): 453–71.

Smith-Christopher, D. L. *A Biblical Theology of Exile*. Minneapolis: Fortress Press, 2002.

—. "The Ruptured Self: War, Psychic Trauma, and the Promise of Narrative Repair." Paper given at the Annual Society of Biblical Literature Meeting, November 20, 2010, in Atlanta, Georgia.

Stulman, L. *Order Amid Chaos: Jeremiah as Symbolic Tapestry*. Sheffield: Sheffield Academic Press, 1998.

Stulman, L., and H. C. P. Kim. *You are My People: An Introduction to Prophetic Literature*. Nashville: Abingdon, 2010.

Thompson, J. A. *The Book of Jeremiah*. The New International Commentary on the Old Testament. Grand Rapids: Eerdmans; 1980.

Tull, P. K. *Isaiah 1–39*. Smyth & Helwys Bible Commentary. Macon, Ga.: Smyth & Helwys, 2010.

Watts, J. W., ed. *Persia and Torah: The Theory of Imperial Authorization of the Pentateuch*. Atlanta: Society of Biblical Literature, 2001.

Weinberger, D. "Paradigm Shift: Thomas Kuhn's Big Idea 50 Years Later," *The Chronicle Review* (27 April 2012): 6–9. Cited 17 February 2014. Online: http://chronicle.com/article/Shift-Happens/131580.

WEISER, A. *The Old Testament: Its Formation and Development*. Translated by D. M. Barton. 2nd English printing. New York: Association, 1963. Translation of *Einleitung in das Alte Testament*. 4th ed. Göttingen: Vandenhoeck & Ruprecht, 1957.

Elizabeth Boase

The Traumatized Body

Communal Trauma and Somatization in Lamentations

Abstract

The book of Lamentations arises out of a community which has experienced trauma. In order to explore how communal trauma is expressed, this paper considers the embodied language of Lamentations. A key feature of the book is the interplay of speaking voices—the personified city, the lamenter/narrator, and the man of Lamentations 3. All name pain and suffering, albeit using language within different experiential ranges. Each makes reference to the body, describing distress and trauma through bodily metaphors. These examples of somatization—somatic expressions of emotional distress—draw on culturally powerful and efficacious metaphors. Utilizing the typology of bodily suffering developed by Amy Cottrill, the somatic language of Lamentations is explored, arguing that the embodied language begins a process of re-membering (re-incorporation) within a community fractured by trauma. In evoking the body, individual bodily suffering is able to be expressed corporeally, thus providing a discursive space in which community can begin to be reformed.

Written in the wake of the destruction of Jerusalem by the Babylonians in 587 B.C.E., the book of Lamentations encodes in its poetry images of pain and suffering, hope and protest, and is, arguably, one of the clearest expressions of trauma literature in the Hebrew Bible. The poems provide a vehicle through which suffering is expressed, and, in its combination of theodic and anti-theodic statements, protests suffering and begins the difficult process of making meaning for a community which has seen the very fabric of its communal life destroyed. Given the wealth of writing in this field,[1] the aim of this paper is not to argue for Lamentations as trauma literature, but to consider, in particular, the use of embodied language in chs. 1–3 which describes distress through somatic expressions and metaphors. I will argue that the somatic language opens up a discursive space which allows the community to first

1 See, for example, Linafelt, *Surviving Lamentations*; Dobbs-Allsopp, *Lamentations*; Smith-Christopher, *Biblical Theology*; O'Connor, *Tears*; Boase, "Constructing Meaning."

identify and then name its trauma in a process that moves from third person gazing at the objectified body of a woman to first person voicing of communal lament. Through the use of somatic metaphors, the text embodies the trauma in a way that gives voice to the unutterable and allows the social body to come together in the first stages of re-membering[2] (reconstituting) the shattered community.

Drawing on Amy Cottrill's typology of the language of suffering in the individual lament psalms,[3] alongside insights from medical and cultural anthropology, I aim to privilege the body as a site of interpretation and resistance, and to explore the role of somatic language as a multilevel signifier.

Although the notion of communal trauma is contested,[4] for the purposes of this paper, Erikson's definition of collective trauma is fundamental;

> By collective trauma … I mean a blow to the basic tissues of social life that damages the bonds attaching people together and impairs the prevailing sense of community. The collective trauma works its way slowly and even insidiously into the awareness of those who suffer from it, so that it does not have the suddenness normally associated with "trauma." But it is a form of shock all the same, a gradual realisation that the community no longer exists as an effective from of support and that an important part of the self has disappeared … "I" continue to exist, though damaged and maybe even permanently changed. "You" continue to exist, though distant and hard to relate to. But "we" no longer exist as a connected pair or as linked cells in a larger communal body.[5]

Somatization

Arthur and Joan Kleinman define somatization as "the expression of personal and social distress in an idiom of bodily complaints."[6] Drawn from the fields of psychiatry and medical anthropology, the definition highlights a

2 The term re-membering points towards the commonly identified latency of memory experienced in trauma, and to the breakdown of community symptomatic of the isolating force of trauma.

3 Cottrill, "Articulate Body."

4 The notion of communal trauma is contested in the light of categories used in the medical profession for the diagnosis of PTSD and other conditions arising from trauma, which emphasize that it is individual and isolating. As is explored in other contributions in this volume, the definition of trauma itself is also contested. There is, however, some support for the notion of communal trauma. E.g., Erikson, "Notes on Trauma," and Alexander et al., *Cultural Trauma*.

5 Erikson, "Notes on Trauma," 187.

6 Kleinman and Kleinman, "Somatization," 430. The full definition includes an element of medical help seeking; however, this has not been included here due to its lack of relevance for the present study.

phenomenon in which individuals who experience serious personal and social problems "interpret and articulate them, through the medium of the body. Loss, injustice, failure, conflict—all are transformed into discourse about pain and disability that is a metaphor for discourse about the self and the social world. The body mediates the individual's perception, experience, and interpretation of problems in social life."[7]

Somatization is both cross-cultural and culturally bound.[8] Setha Low identifies that while the embodiment of distress may be universal, specific metaphors are culturally particular.[9] Low argues that embodiment is "constructed by local discourse and institutions, then expressed and acted upon as a metaphor of social, psychological, political, and economic distress."[10] The metaphors used in this process of embodiment convey lived experience in a culturally meaningful way, providing a means to express the inexpressible nature of suffering. The bodily metaphors allow "one to move from the abstract and inchoate of lived experience to the concrete and easily graspable … metaphor allows for the communication of otherwise senseless and unspeakable suffering."[11]

Somatic expressions have communicative power. The body acts as a "mediating symbolic device."[12] Kleinman argues that embodied language forms a bridge between the personal and the transpersonal, the bodily and the cultural. He suggests that metaphors of physical distress contribute towards the formation or re-formation of the corporeal body, stating that

> moral somatic interconnections indicate … that the flow of experience is thoroughly dialectical. In that flow, cultural representation, transpersonal relations, and embodied subjectivity interact so as to transform experience. The idea of the spread of experience, like the shifting biphasic wave-particle, from social metaphor to corporeal sensibility (and vice versa) can convey a notion of lived connection (or vital disconnection) among otherwise seemingly distinctive phenomenological domains.[13]

The recourse to bodily metaphors in times of distress has the function of grounding both the individual and the community in common experience and language. In *The Body in Pain*, Elaine Scarry suggests that during times

7 Kleinman, *Social Origins*, 51. A somatic element has been identified in relation to clinical definitions of PTSD: see, for example, van der Kolk, "Body." It is not my intention to argue specifically from PTSD symptomology to the text (contra Birnbaum, "Collective Trauma"), but rather to explore the function of somatic metaphors in the literary world of Lamentations.

8 Mumford, "Somatization".

9 Low, "Embodied Metaphors," 141.

10 Ibid., 142.

11 Ibid., 142.

12 Ibid., 143.

13 Kleinman, "Everything," 326.

of societal crisis, when there is a breakdown of cultural ideology, belief, and identity, "the sheer material factualness of the human body will be borrowed to lend that cultural construct the aura of 'realness' and 'certainty.'"[14]

In Lam 1-3, three personas use or have somatic language attributed to them.[15] In chs. 1-2 the personified city is both described and speaks herself. The lamenter describes his own somatic response, as does the man of Lam 3. The analysis which follows explores the use of embodied language in order to argue that the metaphors help to reform (re-member) connections in a traumatized community, a significant function given the sense of isolation that is so often wrought by trauma.[16]

Articulating the Body: Cottrill's Typology of Body Language

In her work on the language of suffering in the individual lament psalms, Cottrill identifies four main categories of body language.[17]

1. *The language of the diminished and overwhelmed body*: which describes the body as weakened, languishing, losing strength, suggesting physical powerlessness and lack of agency.
2. *The language of bodily creation and disintegration*: which "juxtaposes images of the making and unmaking of the body," accentuating the body's "vulnerability and precariousness."[18]
3. *The language of wounds and weapons,* which speaks of visible, public wounding.
4. *The language of inarticulateness,* in which pain and suffering are represented through audible, but nonverbal language.

Alongside this typology, it is helpful to draw on the work of David Mumford, who notes that within the Hebrew Bible, somatic expressions are frequently paired with psychological expressions.[19]

14 Scarry, *Body in Pain,* 14.
15 Persona refers to the different speaking voices. They are: the lamenter (I adopt this term for the voice usually referred to as the narrator [Lam 1:1-10; 2:1-19; 3:49-66; 4:1-16], from Bier, "Perhaps There is Hope"), the city-woman Zion, and the man of Lam 3. The Lamenter is as much a persona as Zion and the man, and it is not assumed that it is the voices of the actual or implied author.
16 Erickson, "Notes on Trauma," 198.
17 Cottrill, "Articulate Body," 104-7.
18 Ibid., 104.
19 Care must be taken in not separating out somatic and psychological into dualistic categories when dealing with ancient texts. Kleinman argues, that it is only in recent Western

The Traumatized Body in Lamentations

Somatic language occurs in the first person speech of the female and male personas in Lam 1-3 (1:11-22; 2:20-22; 3:1-18 [19-39]), and is also attributed to the personified city-woman by the lamenter in 1:1-11. The somatization will be discussed from the perspective of the female body as object, the female body as subject, the lamenter's body as subject and the male body as subject respectively.[20]

Lamentations 1:1-11: The Female Body as Object

In Lam 1:1-11, the lamenter introduces the embodied persona of the city, portrayed as an object to be observed.[21] Three of Cottrill's categories of body language occur, alongside the use of more abstract psychological language.

Diminished and Overwhelmed Body	Widowed, alone, emptied (1:1-2) Rape and violation (1:8-10)
Inarticulate Body	איכה (1:1; 2:1; 4:1) Weeping (1:2) Groaning (1:8)
Wounded Body	Rape and violation (1:8-10)
Abstract Psychological Language	Distress (1:3) Bitterness (1:4) Suffering (1:5)

The opening wail—איכה—gives way to an image of the personified city, sitting alone (1:1). Immediately our attention is drawn to the materiality of the body as a means of naming and expressing suffering. This woman is presented as an inarticulate and diminished body, once full, now emptied of life.

culture that a clear distinction and/or preference for psychological idiom as opposed to somatic idiom has emerged (*Social Origins*, 51-58).

20 Although I read the lamenter a male, the somatic response of the lamenter and the man of Lam 3 are treated separately because they are different personas.

21 The third person description of the metaphorical city in Lam 1 could be seen to function in a similar way to O'Connor's notion of the poetry in Jeremiah identifying trauma "at a slant" (*Jeremiah*, 33). She says of Jeremiah "rather than confronting matters head on, Jeremiah tells and retells the catastrophe indirectly, metaphorically, in unforgettable poetic ways." In being poetic the trauma is placed "in other dimensions, in symbolic realms of art. Because the book is a work of art, it can provide language to enable Judean victims to speak of the disaster, and because it is art, it can reach through the ages to touch people who have known many kinds of suffering."

This woman is identified as a widow, who, in the world of ancient Israel, represents those without means of support.[22] An interesting perspective on widowhood can be brought to bear on this portrayal of the city/community through the writings of Mamphela Ramphele on political widowhood in South Africa during the Apartheid period. Ramphele argues that "widowhood sweeps women into a liminal phase." Her spouse has gone, yet she is still considered married. "The widow becomes the embodiment of loss and pain occasioned by the sting of death, and her body is turned into a focus of attention, both as subject and object of mourning rituals. The individual suffering of a widow is made social, and her body becomes a metaphor for suffering."[23]

The lamenter's speech metaphorically represents the city as an embodied woman in order to portray the devastation of the destruction, including the loss of the religious and political status of Jerusalem. The metaphor is able to represent the loss of the city and all for which it stood.[24] In this, the metaphorical widow can be seen as a type of political widow. Through the use of embodied language, the loss is encoded into an object able to be visualized. Her body becomes the locus of suffering. Her diminishment represents the diminishment of the social body. In attending to the woman's body, the bodies of those who gaze at her body are also evoked.

In the course of Lam 1:1-11 the woman is described in the language of inarticulateness (vv. 1, 2, 8), and more abstract emotions are also attributed to her: she is in distress (מצר v. 3), her lot is bitter (מרר v. 4), she has been made to suffer (יגה v. 5). Different roles of the woman are named—mother, princess, lover—and each of these roles are emptied in the course of the chapter. Her children have gone (v. 5), she has not been able to protect them (v. 16); she has become a vassal (v. 1), and does hard service (v. 2); her lovers are absent, have become enemies (v. 2), deceived her (v. 19).

Verses 8-10 introduce the language of exposure, rape and violation, suggesting both the overwhelmed and the wounded body.[25] This wounding is an internal wounding, different to the wounding seen of the male body in Lam 3.

22 O'Connor, *Tears*, 20.

23 Ramphele, "Political Widowhood," 99. In discussing the symbolic function of the woman's body, Ramphele refers to "a woman's body, as an embodiment of the generative and reproductive power that knits generations together." (115). This aspect is highlighted in the personification of the city in 1:1-11, in that Zion is referred to in the roles widow, princess, vassal, mourner and mother.

24 For a detailed discussion of the spatial representation of the Daughter Zion metaphor see Maier, *Daughter Zion*.

25 For a discussion of rape imagery in Lam 1:10 see Dobbs-Allsopp and Linafelt, "Rape of Zion." Maier (*Daughter Zion*,145) notes that שׁממה (desolate) used in vv. 4, 13 and 16 is also used of Tamar after her rape in 2 Sam 13:20. שׁממה "intertwines the violation of a woman's body with that of the city."

The violated woman elicits both horror and empathy.[26] In gazing at the objectified body of the woman, the community is able to name its violation and exposure.

This initial embodiment does not include the breadth of somatic language to come in the first person speeches, but does prepare the way for what follows. The body of this objectified woman evokes the communal body, thus beginning to bridge the isolation of trauma. The woman's body is "turned into a focus of attention," opening the way for other bodies to be given voice. She is both subject and object. Her individual suffering "is made social" and her body "becomes a metaphor for suffering."[27]

The Female Body as Subject

Somatic language increases in the woman's speech in 1:11–22. The woman shifts from the position of an object to be observed to a speaking subject crying out to be acknowledged.[28] The lamenter also addresses the woman as subject in 2:18–19. The language of embodiment becomes stronger, and the portrayal of suffering more immediate and personal.

The woman's voice is first heard in the context of the language of violation and rape. In 1:9c she petitions God to see her affliction, with her extended speech commencing in v. 11. Significantly, this speech occurs in response to the lamenter's report of the inarticulate groaning of the people (v. 11a). In speaking, the woman resists the silence of trauma.

The language of the diminished and overwhelmed body dominates the somatic language, which occurs alongside language of the inarticulate body and (possibly) the language of disintegration. Abstract, psychological language also occurs.

26 Given that the personified city is widely recognized as being representative of the inhabitants of the city, the embodiment of trauma in the language of rape is a bold move, at least inasmuch as it relates to the male bodies in the community. In her discussion of rape language in Jeremiah, O'Connor (*Jeremiah,* 55) states "Rape makes apt language for invasion because it 'reproduce(s) the difficulty of the world itself.' War is rape on a national scale. Rape conveys life-threatening violence, intrusive and painful physical penetration, traumatic powerlessness, and shameful humiliation of women, husbands, brothers, and sons. God's rape of Jerusalem expresses the horrors Judah experienced as a society. It reveals aspects of the nation's destruction, now reduced to an attack on one vulnerable figure who embraces the whole. Rape is what happened to them. It is their collective history rendered symbolically, their fractured memories drawn into a narrative, into new speech for a speech-destroying disaster."

27 Mamphele, "Political Widowhood," 99.

28 Discussing the body of Zion as both site and sign, Maier ("Body Space," 135) similarly identifies that "female Jerusalem forces the readers and the interpreters to attribute agency and subjectivity to the victims of war and violence …"

	Examples	Significance
Diminished and Overwhelmed Body	Fire in bones (1:13)	Represents whole person; seat of vigor and/or disease.
	Desolate (שׁממה) and faint (דוה) (1:13)	Can be associated with rape (2 Sam 13:20)
	Yoke on neck (1:14)	Evokes warfare, however guilt is yoked here
	Stomach/bowels churning (1:20)	Seat of fear or distress (Jer 4:19; Job 30:27; Lam 2:11)*
	Heart faints (דוי 1:22)	דוה (faint) is used exclusively with heart, in contexts of grief and despair (Isa 1:5; Jer 8:18)
Creation and Disintegration	Heart wrung out (1:20)	Can be associated with loss of coherence
Inarticulate	Weeping (1:16) Groaning (1:21-22) Tears (2:18) Petition to not grow numb (פוגת 2:18)	
Abstract Psychological Language	Incomparable sorrow (1:12)	

* Maier, *Daughter Zion*, notes that the bowels in Hebrew thought are the seat of the emotions and the heart the seat of thought (151). See also Mumford, "Somatization," 232-33.

Initially the woman describes her diminishment and sorrow (1:12). Somatic images in vv. 13-22 ground the suffering in physical sensation, drawing on culturally powerful metaphors used elsewhere in the Hebrew Bible to express emotional distress.

Verse 13 includes aspects of the diminished body and the wounded body. The first somatic reference is to fire going deep into the bones, with God as the sender of the fire.[29] Bones can be synecdochic for the whole person or

29 Maier, emphasizes here the downward movement of the body, noting that God assaults her from on high (*Daughter Zion*, 148).

body, and can refer to the seat of bodily vigor (e.g., Job 20:11) but also disease and pain, as here.[30] In contexts of lament, reference to bones is frequently associated with physical and psychological collapse.[31] Association of bones with fire and/or extreme heat within lament occurs in Job 30:30, which refers to bones charred by heat, and Ps 102:4 to bones burning like a furnace. Jer 20:9 refers to God's word being like fire shut up in Jeremiah's bones.[32]

The language then turns to that of wounding, with reference to a net being set for the city-woman's feet—a possible reference to war practices—and in the continued language of rape. Desolate (שׁממה) can be associated with rape, with faint (דוה) often used of ritually unclean, menstruating women.[33] These words form a double function, reflecting both the outcome of war on women's actual bodies, and the emotional anguish wrought by war.

The reference to the yoke in v. 14 is again suggestive of practices of war. That it is transgressions that are yoked introduces the language of guilt, an emotion often associated with trauma.[34]

The inarticulate body returns in v. 16 (weeping, בכה), associated with the language of the overwhelmed body, as Zion refers to the absence of someone to revive her courage (v. 16b). The woman's children are now described as desolate (שׁממה).

In v. 20, Zion cries out for God to see her distress (צר), then describes two bodily sensations; her stomach churns (חמר) and her heart is wrung out. Stomach (מעה) can be associated with fear or distress (Jer 4:19; Job 30:27; Lam 2:11). According to Maier, the reference to the heart indicates the loss of formerly held beliefs, or the inability to evaluate the situation. She states that "the bodily pain inside mirrors the situation in the house—a feeling of bitterness, despair, and unwillingness to live has taken over."[35] Collapse of meaning is a common outcome of trauma, so its occurrence alongside the naming of physical distress comes as no surprise.

The chapter closes with the language of the inarticulate body, although paradoxically, the groaning (vv. 21 and 22) is named, again resisting inarticulateness. The final somatic reference is to the faint heart, an idiom used elsewhere in contexts of grief and despair (e.g., Isa 1:5; Jer 8:18).[36]

Within this speech, the perspective on the woman shifts from her being an object to be gazed at to her taking on a subjective position. This embodied

30 BDB 782.

31 TDOT 9:305.

32 More common references to bones occur in metaphors of shaking and trembling (Job 4:14; 33:19; Pss 6:2; Jer 23:9), shattering/crushing (Ps 42:11; 51:10; Lam 3:4; 4:7–8) or sticking out, (Job 33:19; Pss 32:3; 102:6).

33 Maier, *Daughter Zion*, 149.

34 Yokes are associated with sin elsewhere: Deut 28:48; Jer 27–28.

35 Maier, *Daughter Zion*, 151.

36 Williamson, *Isaiah*, 62.

woman invites participation in her suffering, offering the possibility for communal reincorporation—re-membering. For male members of the community, however, the association with the figure may only be partial.[37] While the embodied woman might echo the experiences of those women who were raped, for men the use of a female body allows a certain distance. The invitation to become incorporated into this body is present, but not assumed.

The lamenter again uses somatic language in 2:18–19 when he addresses the city-woman. In v. 18, he implores her to cry out to God, which assumes a degree of inarticulateness. She is called to let tears stream down, and to give herself no rest (NRSV) / relief (NAS). An alternate rendering of "relief" (פוגת) is "to grow numb."[38] This is evocative. Is the lamenter calling on the woman to resist the numbing and isolating impact of trauma—to continue to voice her suffering?

In v. 19 the metaphor "pour your heart out like water" is used. This is the same verb (שׁפך) used in 2:11–12, when the lamenter embodies his own pain (v. 11 in reference to the lamenter's liver/bile) and in relation to the death of children (v. 12). Zion is called to embody the diminishment and death of the community within herself. The final somatic idiom is a call for Zion to lift up her hands to God for the life of her children, again echoing 2:12. This is a gesture of supplication, suggesting the diminished and desperate body of a mother.

The Lamenter's Body as Subject

Much of the speech in Lam 2 focuses on the physical destruction of the city, even though the personification of the city is still present. Although parts of the city and its environs are given emotions, little somatic language of the city itself occurs. In 2:11, however, the lamenter uses somatic language similar to that of the city-woman (1:16, 20) to name his own grief (eyes weeping, bowels churning, liver poured out). The language is that of the overwhelmed and inarticulate body. This somatization draws the audience further into the naming of trauma. Now it is a (presumably) male voice who reports embodied suffering, providing a different possibility for incorporation into the communal body.

37 Maier (*Daughter Zion*, 149–52) notes that these body parts are not gender specific (bones, heart, bowels). The language is, however, feminine, and the subject is clearly a woman.

38 BDB and DCH.

	Examples	Significance
Diminished and Overwhelmed	Stomach/bowels (מעה) churning (2:11)	Fear/distress
	Liver (כבד) poured out (שׁפך) (2:11)	Seat of emotion and life
Inarticulate	Weeping (2:11)	

The Male Body as Subject

Lam 3 introduces a third voice, a man (גבר), who specifically sets his identity apart from that of the embodied woman in chs. 1-2 and of the lamenter. Although much has been written as to the identity of the man, historical or otherwise, the man's body is as much a subjective site of embodiment as is the woman's in the previous chapters. As with the other voices, the man uses somatic metaphors, now dominated by the language of wounding and weapons, a more external, visible wounding suggesting physical violence, torture, and imprisonment.[39] The language of the diminished and the inarticulate body are also present, as is more abstract psychological language.

	Examples	Significance
Diminished and Overwhelmed	Wasted flesh (v. 4)	Consequence of imprisonment/ deprivation
	Arrow in kidneys (v. 13)	Emotion/consciousness*
	Grinding teeth on gravel (v. 16)	Ps 20:17—lamenter's mouth filled with gravel
	Cower in ashes (v. 16)	Worthlessness; ashes usually mourning
Inarticulate	Tears (vv. 49-51)	

* Job 16:13 makes reference to kidneys pierced by arrows in the context of complaint.

39 So also Maier, "Body Space," 132-34.

Wounds and weapons	Broken bones (v. 4) Targeting with bow and arrow (v. 12) Arrows into kidney (v. 13) Oppression (vv. 7–9) Sitting in darkness Walled up Ways blocked Chained
Abstract psychological language	Bitterness and tribulation (v. 5) Desolation (v. 11)

The language used in the man's speech in vv. 1–18 draws on imagery of warfare, in particular imprisonment and physical violence against the body. The language is suggestive of torture.[40] The abuser in the speech is initially nameless, although many translations insert God's name into v. 1 under the influence of both the wider literary context and the naming of God in v. 18. The distinction between report and metaphor is blurred in the speech of the man. The man reports his oppression and his sense of victimization using seemingly concrete language of external forces acting against him. Images suggesting warfare are present, as are metaphors of hunting. The body of the man is implicitly present throughout the text, but not always explicitly evoked. Despite this seemingly "concrete" representation, metaphoric language depicting the man's distress and suffering is still present.

Specific body parts are mentioned. Language of wounding includes references to broken bones (v. 4), being targeted with bow and arrow (v. 12), being shot into the kidneys (v. 13), teeth being made to grind on gravel. Diminishment is seen in references to the wasting of flesh and skin (v. 4). Language of physical oppression occurs in the many references to imprisonment (sitting in darkness, being walled up, heavy chains vv. 7–9). Equally, many of the metaphors can suggest the diminishment of trauma. For example, kidneys (which are shot into) are associated with human consciousness and emotions. The metaphors can evoke multiple meanings. More abstract language such as desolation, bitterness and tribulation also occurs.

A shift in the man's speech occurs in vv. 20–21, as he moves from lament to more wisdom-like speech, expressing a sense of hope and trust in God. Somatic references also occur in the hope-filled vv. 28–30, with suffering de-

40 So also Maier, "Body Space," 132–34; Berlin, *Lamentations*, 84.

picted in terms of bearing a yoke imposed by God, putting the mouth to the dust and turning the cheek. The sufferer sits alone (echoing Lam 1). Although this is language of diminishment, it is transformed here in the service of a hopeful theodicy—the suffering is educative.[41]

Finally, in Lam 3:49–51 the speaker refers to eyes flowing with tears, echoing the woman and the lamenter in Lam 1–2.

This is trauma from a different perspective. Bodily experiences of physical violence and the somatic responses to suffering are again encoded, but the wounds are more external and visible than those of the woman, although an interior disintegration is also evoked.

Male and Female embodiment

Somatization in Lamentations is neither accidental or irrelevant, nor to be dismissed as simply hyperbolic or stereotypical. When viewed from the perspective of trauma, somatic language plays an important role in symbolizing and negotiating experiences of distress and trauma in ways that are socially defined and culturally powerful. The language reflects culturally acceptable rhetoric, which serves an important role in helping the community to reconstitute—re-member—itself in the wake of disaster.

The somatic expressions represent and name the types of physical experiences which bodies may have suffered (rape, being shot at, imprisoned) but also include more metaphoric expressions which express distress.

The language of the overwhelmed and diminished body dominates, alongside the language of weapons and wounds. Although severe physical duress and wounding were real, there is an emphasis on the traumatic aftermath, embodied through the somatic language, which occurs alongside what Mumford refers to as "abstract psychological language."[42] There is also strong reference to the inarticulate body. References to groaning, wailing, and tears all suggest the loss of language, however, this loss is constantly resisted by the very process of putting the distress into words.[43] The language of creation and disintegration is largely absent.

The distribution of the types of body language reinforces the function of this text in the context of communal trauma. Although severe physical duress and wounding are not to be denied in the experiences of the community, the physical wounding itself is in the past. We see in this poetry the language of a community overwhelmed and diminished by the ongoing impact of the disaster.

41 Boase, "Constructing Meaning," 462.

42 Mumford, "Somatization," 232.

43 Dobbs-Allsopp, *Lamentations*, 33–38; O'Connor, *Tears*, 128.

There is both similarity and difference between the representations of male and female bodies. The actual bodily parts named—inner organs and bones—are similar, and both male and female bodies weep and groan. The language which surrounds these somatic references, do, however, evoke different types of experience. The language of rape and violation is present in the description of the woman's body, evoking a more internal, invisible wounding.[44] By contrast the descriptions surrounding the bodily harm of the male figure are more external, using the language of physical violence, weapons, and torture. Trauma emerges from both internal and external forces, and these two figures evoke different realms of experience.[45]

Somatization and Re-membering

In order to draw together the discussion of the somatic language in Lamentations, I want to turn more specifically to the issue of how trauma is lived out in community, to the role of literature in trauma, and the importance of the somatic language in relation to re-membering within community.

One of the defining features of trauma is its tendency to cause a sense of isolation. Erickson speaks of trauma as having both centripetal and centrifugal forces within communities. It isolates, in that it draws the sufferer away from the centre of a group. At the same time, however, trauma can form different types of community centered on shared suffering.[46]

The use of embodied language in Lamentations can be understood as a means of facilitating communal identity. Naming suffering through the use of culturally familiar, embodied metaphors helps to bridge isolation

Embodied language names experience in a form that is both individual and communal.[47] We experience the world in our bodies. Evoking bodies connects us to other bodies. The language and metaphors help re-member the body, to bring back together the communal body by the naming of shared experience. Specific metaphors, which medical anthropology would suggest have cultural significance, are used because they were familiar, meaningful, and culturally efficacious.

44 Although reference is made to stains on the woman's clothes in Lam 1:9.

45 The differences noted here coincides with Paula Cooey's statement that "even though human rights are abused irrespective of gender, gender is not incidental to the form the abuse will take." (*Religious Imagination,* 11)

46 Erikson, "Notes on Trauma," 186.

47 Cooey (*Religious Imagination,* 63) states that "Verbal and visual images teach us to 'see,' to imagine; they do so in part by providing concrete, particular bodies that cue us to attribute subjectivity to the self or another, or to withhold it. In short, the body locates a human being as object of interpretation by the self and others."

The sequence of voices naming the trauma is, I believe, significant. The movement from the third person description of the objectified body of a metaphorical widow, to her first person claiming of her subjective voice begins the process of reincorporating the community. The use of the female body is at one level culturally familiar as cities were frequently personified as female in the ancient world. The attribution of bodily sensation to the city aligns her experience of loss and violation with that of the audience. As argued by Maier, "This representation helps the initial audience … to embed their individual suffering into the fate of the community. Their personal story becomes part of a larger story and thus gets national significance."[48] The body of the woman represents the body of those who suffer.

That this is a woman's body, however, means that the alignment is, at least for male hearers, only partial. A woman's body is not a man's body, and so the invitation to enter into the pain of this body is present, but not assumed.

In the return to the lamenter's (male) voice in Lam 2, third person gaze is again evoked, however, the lamenter now voices his own bodily response to the trauma. For male hearers, the potential for incorporation into the body becomes more overt.

In ch. 3, male embodiment takes over. This speaker names trauma and distress inflicted on a male body, decreasing the distance between male hearers and the speaker. It is significant that a communal voice is not heard in Lamentations until after these other, individual voices have spoken. The accounts of suffering, grounded in language which names and evokes bodily experiences of distress, make possible the re-membering of the community which together voices its distress, partially in Lam 3 and 4, but fully in Lam 5. The final communal lament suggests that a form of re-membering has occurred. The community has been reconstituted, able to name together its distress.

This understanding of Lamentations as a text which helps to re-member the community in the ancient world, giving voice to that which cannot be articulated, expressing distress and suffering in culturally efficacious metaphors, accounts for the ongoing power of Lamentations to function in liturgical contexts of grief, and speak into contemporary contexts of trauma and disaster. Although the somatic language of the text may not use the same metaphors that are powerful in the many and varied contemporary communities of suffering, the very act of naming suffering in language which evokes the physical materiality of the human body links us with this ancient community. Lamentations provides one model for the power of language to help reform—re-member—a community in the wake of disaster, forming a bridge

48 Maier, "Lost Space," 194.

between the personal and the transpersonal, opening up new possibilities for being again in community.

Bibliography

Alexander, J. C., R. Eyerman, B. Giesen, N. J. Smelser and P. Sztompka. *Cultural Trauma and Collective Identity.* Berkeley: University of California Press, 2004.

Berlin, A. *Lamentations.* Louisville, Ky.: Westminster John Knox, 2002.

Bier, M. "Perhaps There is Hope: Reading Lamentations as a Polyphony of Pain, Penitence, and Protest." Ph.D. Diss. University of Otago, 2012.

Birnbaum, A. "Collective Trauma and Post-Traumatic Symptoms in the Biblical Narrative of Ancient Israel." *Mental Health, Religion & Culture* 11 (2008): 533-46.

Boase, E. "Constructing Meaning in the Face of Suffering: Theodicy in Lamentations." *Vetus Testamentum* 58 (2008): 449-68.

Cooey, P. *Religious Imagination and the Body.* New York: Oxford University Press, 1994.

Cottrill, A. C. "The Articulate Body: The Language of Suffering in the Laments of the Individual." Pages 103-12 in *Lamentations in Ancient and Contemporary Cultural Contexts.* Edited by N. C. Lee and C. Mandolfo. Atlanta: Society of Biblical Literature, 2008.

Dobbs-Allsopp, F. W. *Lamentations.* Louisville, Ky.: Westminster John Knox, 2000.

Dobbs-Allsopp, F. W., and T. Linafelt. "The Rape of Zion in Thr 1,10." *Zeitschrift für die alttestamentliche Wissenschaft* 113 (2001): 77-81

Erikson, K., "Notes on Trauma and Community," Pages 183-99 in *Trauma: Explorations in Memory.* Edited by C. Caruth. Baltimore: Johns Hopkins University Press, 1995.

Kleinman, A. *Social Origins of Distress and Disease: Depression, Neurasthenia, and Pain in Modern China.* New Haven: Yale University Press, 1986.

—. "'Everything that Really Matters': Social Suffering, Subjectivity, and the Remaking of Human Experience in a Disordering World." *Harvard Theological Review* 90 (1997): 315-35.

Kleinman, A., and J. Kleinman. "Somatization: The Interconnections in Chinese Society among Culture, Depressive Expereinces, and the Meanings of Pain." Pages 331-68 in *Culture and Depression: Studies in the Anthropology and Cross-Cultural Psychiatry of Affect and Disorder.* Edited by A. Kleinman and B. Good. Berkely: University of California Press, 1985

Linafelt, T. *Surviving Lamentations: Catastrophe, Lament and Protest in the Afterlife of a Biblical Book.* Chicago: University of Chicago Press, 2000.

Low, S. "Embodied Metaphors: Nerves as Lived Experience." Pages 139-62 in *Embodiment and Experience: The Existential Ground of Culture and Self.* Edited by T. J. Csordas. Cambridge: Cambridge University Press, 1994.

Maier, C. *Daughter Zion, Mother Zion: Gender, Space, and the Sacred in Ancient Israel.* Minneapolis: Fortress, 2008.

—. "Body Space as Public Space: Jerusalem's Wounded Body in Lamentations." Pages 119-38 in *Constructions of Space II: The Biblical City and Other Imagined Spaces.* Edited by J. L. Berquist and C. V. Camp. New York: T & T Clark, 2008.

—. "Lost Space and Revived Memory: From Jerusalem in 586 B.C.E. to New Orleans in 2009." Pages 189-201 in *Interpreting Exile: Displacement and Deportation in Biblical and Modern Contexts.* Edited by B. E. Kelle, F. R. Ames and J. L. Wright. Atlanta: Society of Biblical Literature, 2011.

Mumford, D. B. "Somatization: A Transcultural Perspective." *International Review of Psychiatry* 5 (1993): 231-42.

O'Connor, K. *Lamentations and the Tears of the World.* New York: Orbis, 2002.

—. *Jeremiah: Pain and Promise.* Minneapolis: Fortress, 2011.

Ramphele, M. "Political Widowhood in South Africa: The Embodiment of Ambiguity." Pages 99–117 in *Social Suffering*. Edited by A. Kleinman, V. Das and M. Lock, Berkeley: University of California Press, 1997.
Scarry, E. *The Body in Pain: The Making and Unmaking of the World*. New York: Oxford University Press, 1985.
Smith-Christopher, D. L. *A Biblical Theology of Exile*. Minneapolis: Fortress, 2002
Van der Kolk, B. A. "The Body Keeps the Score: Memory and Evolving Psychobiology of Posttraumatic Stress." *Harvard Review of Psychiatry* 1 (1994): 253–65.
Williamson, H. G. W. *Isaiah 1–5*. International Critical Commentary. London: T & T Clark, 2006.

Kathleen M. O'Connor

How Trauma Studies Can Contribute to Old Testament Studies

Abstract

This essay argues that, while there are dangers when biblical scholars borrow from other disciplines, trauma and disaster studies can illuminate both content and function of some biblical texts. Key interpretive issues in Jeremiah studies—the book's literary confusions, mixture of genre, voices, viewpoints, lack of chronology, deep misogyny, and violent portraits of a punishing God—emerge as literary art in a complex process of symbol-making. This process, evident in Jeremiah, Ezekiel, and Lamentations, contributes to the survival of the Judean people in the aftermath of the Babylonian invasions and its massive disruption of life, government, economy, and theological meaning. One of the harshest books of the Bible turns out to be a kind of survival manual.

1. Methodological Challenges in Two Directions[1]

Trauma theories claimed my interest when I first encountered the work on the prophet Ezekiel by Daniel Smith-Christopher in his important book on the exile,[2] and several papers given at Annual Meetings of the Society of Biblical Literature. His use of trauma and refugee studies pointed me in new directions and reignited my passion for biblical studies. I have been using trauma theories in the study of the book of Jeremiah and that effort has also prompted methodological questions about the relationship of trauma theories to the investigation of biblical texts and their functions in the ancient world.

When biblical scholars use theories of trauma and disaster, displacement and catastrophe, it seems unlikely that our appropriations will satisfy our social science colleagues. This is because biblical interpreters often borrow theories of other disciplines in a hit or miss fashion. We choose concepts solely

1 I begin by expressing gratitude to Professors Eve-Marie Becker and Else K. Holt for organizing this international conference on the interdisciplinary study of trauma at Aarhus University in Denmark, June 2011. I believe that this conversation is a sacred one, not only because it deals with texts that Christian and Jews name as sacred but because it plunges into grave pain and asks about survival.

2 Smith-Christopher, *Biblical Theology*, esp. 27–104.

for their benefit to the study of ancient texts. We seek less to advance knowledge about trauma than to use trauma theories to gain knowledge of our documents and the contexts that produced them.

At the same time, the difficulty of borrowing across disciplines is not one-directional. Smith-Christopher reminds biblical interpreters to be wary of adopting these theories uncritically. Trauma theories often focus on the individual and usually study effects of violence as mental disorders and other dysfunctions such as PTSD (Post-traumatic stress disorder). Interventions, in turn, frequently center on medical treatments or counseling therapies appropriate to modern western societies but not easily transferable to the ancient world or to many communities in the modern world. Biblical texts arise in community-oriented cultures rather than individually-oriented ones. To the extent that biblical texts address wounds of traumatic violence, they do so in non-medical ways, through artistic and intuitive literary approaches, using resources already available in the culture. Differences in purpose among our disciplines in the conversation remain important. This conference has helped us explore further how our exchanges advance knowledge in both biblical studies and social sciences.

To remind myself of these problems, I refer to my amalgamation of trauma theories as "trauma and disaster studies." I use the term "disaster" to refer to the impact of traumatic violence upon whole communities for which they have little or no capacity to cope, where institutions and traditions collapse, daily life breaks down, and survival of the society itself remains in grave doubt. Trauma and disaster do not refer to ordinary human suffering that afflicts most human beings, but catastrophic and overwhelming disaster. Overwhelming is the key term to express disaster's impact. Disaster overwhelms nearly everything.

Whether biblical interprets borrow trauma theories appropriately or not, insights from a variety of trauma and disaster studies greatly benefit biblical interpretation. I think they change Jeremiah studies in significant ways. They help us to see deeper dimensions of human suffering in the complex historical settings that gave rise to biblical texts. They change the focus of attention from the history of the text's production to ways the texts functioned for traumatized readers, and they illuminate content that perplexes and disturbs modern western readers.[3]

In return, I wonder if biblical scholarship has something to offer trauma theorists, namely, to show how literature and biblical literature specifically aids survival after traumatic experiences. My examples in this essay come from my study of the Babylonian Period in general and the book of Jeremiah

3 See essays in Kelle et al., *Interpreting Exile*, particularly, Smith-Christopher, "Reading War and Trauma"; Morrow, "Deuteronomy 7"; Gerber, "Vocabulary of Trauma"; Rumfelt, "Reversing Fortune"; and Balentine, "Prose and Poetry of Exile."

in particular.[4] I prefer the term "Babylonian Period" to the more typical "Exilic Period" because the latter is not expansive enough. I think that both Jeremiah and Lamentations attend to the people who remain in Judah and not simply to those exiled.

Jeremiah is a famously vexing text due to its literary confusions, mixes of genre, voices, and viewpoints, lack of chronology, deep misogyny, and violent portraits of a punishing God. Yet trauma and disaster theories show these troublesome features of the book to be literary survival strategies for a destroyed society. The book aids survival by generating potent symbolic speech in response to catastrophe.

2. Contributions of Trauma and Disaster Theories to OT Studies

Trauma and Disaster Theories Expand Historical Imagination

Trauma and disaster theories broaden what we can know about life in ancient Judah during and after the Babylonian Period. Shoshanna Felman observes that the writing of history often obscures human suffering.[5] It condenses massive pain into abstract cause and effect frameworks. Because trauma and disaster theories can pierce through the "objective" veneer of history to the human suffering beneath the surface, they assist historical investigations into ancient contexts they produce the texts.

Even while historical details of the Babylonian Period remain disputed among biblical scholars, a growing number recognize that military invasions, famine, deportations, internal migrations, and the collapse of government undermined Judah's economic and social life and left its capital city left in ruins.[6]

Trauma and disaster theories also expand our historical imagination by pointing to typical lingering effects of disaster upon victims even after physical safety has been restored. Here are some long-term consequences of traumatic violence:

(1) Because victims are unable to absorb violent events as they happen, the events imprint themselves upon the mind[7] and take up residence in the brain in recurring memories as if they were still happening in mental space.[8]

4 O'Connor, *Jeremiah*.
5 Felman, "Education and Crisis"; idem, *Juridical Unconscious*; Felman and Laub, *Testimony*.
6 See recently, Faust, *Judah*; and idem, "Deportation and Demography."
7 Fivush and Seelig, *Interdisciplinary Responses*.
8 Caruth, "Introduction II"; and idem, *Unclaimed Experience*.

(2) Victims can rarely speak adequately about traumatic violence because memories of violence keep overwhelming them. Language fractures and breaks down so people are unable to express their experiences, leaving them bereft and isolated.

(3) Victims emotions shutdown automatically as a protection from overload. They can become emotionally dead and cannot access grief at overwhelming losses.

(4) Of most importance for biblical interpretation, victims lose faith and trust in institutions, traditions, and in God. After disaster beliefs that once supported life breakdown in a vacuum devoid of meaning.

To summarize these consequences of trauma, I borrow from the late psychoanalytic researcher and clinician, Norbert Freedman, who spoke of a mental condition he called "desymbolization."[9] Desymbolization is a defensive mental state in which "psychic space can be said to be frozen,"[10] experience cannot be accessed, and mental connections are destroyed, so that people lack meaning and a sense of control. I have only recently discovered Freedman's concepts of desymbolization and symbolization and find in them a helpful way to speak about survival processes in Jeremiah.

The Text as Symbol-Maker

The purpose of the book of Jeremiah is to re-symbolize reality for the decimated nation. Perhaps we can join the alphabetic academic craze and call the biblical text a "post-traumatic literary intervention" (PTLI). Freedman's theory of symbolization provides a three-part schema to name ways the literature helps readers cope with disaster: Incipient or Beginning Symbol-Making, Discursive Symbol-Making, and Dynamic Symbol-Making.[11] I think the book of Jeremiah shows evidence of all three levels. First, the book of Jeremiah finds symbolic language to talk about the disaster; second, it employs multiple symbolic languages to explain the disaster; and third, it creates further symbolic language to point to life beyond the disaster. Within Jeremiah these symbol-making processes overlap inseparably, but I separate them to understand coping mechanisms of the literature. Of course, Freedman's symbolic processes concern psychoanalytic health of individuals, so I wonder if it is legitimate to apply this model to study the ancient community-centered text, a question that still lingers many months after the Aarhus Conference.

9 Silverman, "Refractoriness"; and Lasky, "Introduction," 19-20.
10 Ibid., 19.
11 Ibid., 20-23; Schimek, "Symbolization and Transference."

Incipient Symbol-Making

To manage life even minimally in a de-symbolized world, victims of disaster need language to express the violence of their collective experiences and begin to face it or they may not survive. They have to find ways to speak of the unspeakable. Incipient or beginning symbol-making involves speech that begins to bridge the emotional and mental splitting that follows trauma.

This early process of symbol-making is a delicate one because literal retellings of traumatic events can call forth recurring memories of the original violence and re-traumatize victims, who then remain stuck in the recurring memories of the violence. To protect victims from being overwhelmed again by memories and to expose them gently, slowly, and partially to the violence they have endured, language has to be flexible, allusive, and evocative. Jeremiah brings violent experience to speech in symbolic, poetic worlds. Every chapter of the book expresses violence in one form or another, in poetry about God's broken family, about warfare, in stories about the prophet's life, in prophetic sign acts of ruined loincloths, broken jugs, of a celibate prophet, in sermons, prayers, and in the book's very few history-like accounts of destruction.

The overarching purpose of the book from the vantage point of trauma and disaster theories is to symbolize the disaster. The book is a quest for meaningful speech about the multiple catastrophes that afflicted Judah in the Babylonian Period into subsequent generations. Rather than recording violent historical events in literal fashion, the text transposes them into mythic scenes, into poetry, drama, and story.

Jeremiah's war poems (Jer 4:5–6:30; 8:16–17; 10:17–22; 13:20–27) and poems about God's Broken Family (2:1–4:4; 6:1–30; 13:20–27), for example, illustrate incipient or beginning symbol-making. These collections of poems encode collapse in both military and domestic arenas. In them, the Babylonian invasions take place on a mythic plane where the combatants are not the nations of Judah and Babylon but a mysterious "foe from the north," an alien invading force—superhuman, unstoppable, beyond resistance, and an agent of God. The foe attacks a woman, the Daughter of Zion, who personifies Judah and Jerusalem. Marriage scenes, or as I prefer, "broken family" scenes, narrow the battle to a domestic rupture in which a betrayed Husband/God shames and ultimately rapes his beloved wife, the Daughter of Zion (13:20–27). Poetic events jump episodically from military battle to family battle, and back again. In doing so, they mirror the circumstances and fragmented memories of the book's audience. They reenact the Babylonian invasions in a literary world, so the victims can see the violence at a distance, as if it were happening on a stage to someone else, even as it brings to the fore the violence of the nation's fall. Readers can see the destruction in a world outside themselves and slowly begin to face it. This is one way the books functions as medium of survival.

Another symbolic way to name the violence is Jeremiah's confused chronology. The book skips around from decade to decade with little heed to creating an accurate time line of events. "Traumatic memory," according to Judith Herman, "is wordless and static, and initial accounts of events may be pre-narrative and never progress in time."[12] Time markers in Jeremiah lack order. Pete Diamond aptly called Jeremiah's relation to time "dischronologization."[13] It portrays a temporal disruption that conveys how the violent past invades the present when "events … appear in mental space without order."[14] Past, present, and future coexist in the literary world of Jeremiah because they coexist in the lives of trauma victims, in their fractured memories and among haunting ghosts.

Another way Jeremiah symbolizes the circumstance of survivors of trauma is that it creates speech to bridge feelings and thinking in poems I call "the weeping poems." Found largely in chapters 8-9, these poems work to overcome the emotional death that often automatically follows trauma. They express how impossible it is to grieve, to feel anything, even locating inability to grieve in God's own being. "O that my head were waters and my eyes a fountain of tears that I might weep day and night for the virgin daughter of my people" (8:22). God's language here is in the optative voice, wishful—"Oh if only …!" God is the one who awakens grief by calling for the mourning women to come and kick-start the tears of the people and of the divine Self. These poems both articulate emotional and mental splitting that follows trauma and begin to address it.

Discursive Symbol-Making

Freedman called the second phase of symbol-making after disaster, "discursive" symbol- making. By this he means that survivors begin to create coherent narratives, interpretive words to "explain" why disaster has occurred, to arrive at understandings of cause and effect, and to identify responsible parties. Once disaster victims begin to perceive the violence of their situation and absorb reality, they must interpret it. Interpretation seems to me to be inevitable. Why did it happen? How did it happen? Who failed? Think of Newtown, of the floods from Sandy and Katrina, and of 9/11. As much as Jeremiah is a quest for language to speak of violence, the book is also a relent-

12 Herman, *Trauma and Recovery*, 132, n. 16.
13 Diamond, *Jeremiah*, 545-46.
14 Langer, *Holocaust Testimonies*, 133.

less search for explanation, for order in a world that appears to be completely without order.

To survive, victims need interpretations, even bad ones, even false ones, even partial ones, even self-blaming ones. Explanations assert that chaos does not rule the cosmos, that structure and stability underlie incomprehensible, chaotic events. Studying rape victims and cancer sufferers, Romie Janoff-Bulman insists that partial, inadequate, or wrong explanations are better for long-term survival and healthy functioning than no explanation at all.[15] People have to have reasons for disasters and "know" why it happened. Explanations provide stability and trustworthiness to the world again and create a sense of safety, even when they are false.

Jeremiah is packed with such discursive symbol-making, that is, with interpretations of the Judean disaster. Who caused it? Why did it happen? Whose fault was it? War poems, for example, place responsibility on the city of Jerusalem, the Daughter of Zion, her children, and all the people. Prose verses single out community leaders: "Courage shall fail the kings, and officials and priests" (4:9). Jeremiah blames God (4:10; 20:7–8). God blames the community; the disaster is judgment against Judah for its turning to other gods (2:1–4:4). In a complex distribution of blame, texts report that leaders failed, God failed; everybody failed. Holding someone accountable is a stab at finding justice and order when all signs of justice and order have vanished. Looking for responsible parties is a strategy of survival.

One major dimension of discursive symbol-making is Jeremiah's portrait of God as divine Punisher, the one who sends disaster upon the sinful people for their sins. This portrait of the divine is one of the main reasons Jeremiah is not a popular book. Yet this harsh fire-and-brim-stone picture of God helps survivors in Jeremiah's time. Its depiction of God the Punisher makes claims: Judah's God is powerful, active, and present, lord of the world, and not a defeated lesser being. God has not lost the war to Babylonian deities but, instead, commanded it; God has more power than Bel and Marduk and is fully in charge. Such a narrative line functions to restore trust in God by insisting that Judah's God is still there. God the Punisher is a way to defend God; it offers a theodicy without which Judah would likely have disappeared after the Babylonian assaults upon the land and the people.

In Jeremiah, the assertion that God punishes is not an ontological claim about the divine. It is, rather, an explanation after disaster, a work of theological creativity that provides cause and effect so that the people may survive (across history, religious communities have cemented this *ad hoc* theology into place as a fixed truth about the Holy One).

15 Janoff-Bulman, *Shattered Assumptions*, 95–104.

The corollary of God the Punisher is the claim that people brought the punishment upon themselves by their sin of idolatry and harlotry. Such a viewpoint is a largely a self-blaming process wherein the victims are seen to be the cause of their own sufferings. But self-blaming is also a survival strategy, a form of discursive symbol-making, or in the words of the American poet Robert Frost about poetry it is "a momentary stay against confusion."[16] The interpretation that *we caused* it helps survivors because it brings the cataclysm down to a palatable size even as a partial or bad explanation of the nation's fall. If we caused it, perhaps we can undo it, or at least, by turning from sin, prevent it from happening again. We can manage the world a bit, move forward and act.

Jeremiah's predictions of future disaster provide another example of discursive symbol-making. Against a long tradition of biblical scholarship, I do not think predictions of catastrophe in Jeremiah function as literal predictions of coming destruction no matter when Jeremiah may or may not have said them. For the book's readers, disaster is already history, their past that has already happened to them when the book comes to its final form (Jer 1:1–3). When God announces to Jeremiah in chapter one, "Out of the north disaster shall break out upon all the inhabitants of the land … and I will utter my judgments against you," the disaster has happened and the prediction is now after the fact. According to anthropologist Kai Erickson, victims of disaster often feel they have lost control of their circumstances making them very vulnerable.[17] They exist in an unregulated universe with "terrors all around" (Jer 20:4, 10). But if the disaster was predicted, capable of prediction, traumatic experience becomes "intelligible, readable, set in a framework of normalcy."[18] When God announces traumatic events in advance of their coming, such as the kings will fail, Jerusalem will fall, the prophet will suffer as the book says repeatedly, then this serves as evidence of order in the world, cause and effect, a reliable canopy of meaning upon which the community may rest securely. And the One who orders it is Judah's God, not Babylonian deities, not fate, not luck, not chaos.

Dynamic Symbol-Making

Freedman's called his last symbol-making phase, "dynamic symbolization."[19] This refers to a transformative process where victims begin to imagine a different future. In increasing self-awareness "Language and emotion converge"

16 Benfey, "Robert Frost," 49.
17 Erikson, "Notes."
18 Schwartz, *Imagining the Holocaust*, 134.
19 Lasky, "Introduction," 22.

to create symbols that point beyond mere survival.[20] Although re-symbolizing is far from a linear process, victims cannot begin to imagine a different future without the first two phases of finding language to express and interpret the disaster. Even if they can see over the horizon to a possible new reality, they usually fall back into the previous phases in an unsteady back and forth between collapse and hope. Jeremiah encodes this too when it sets the hopeful "book of consolation" (chs. 30–33), not at the end but just after the middle of the book, to be followed by more accounts of violence and turmoil.

Simply reasserting old truths does not usually revive faith and trust after traumatic violence. But neither can a society abandon its past traditions and remain who they are. They need to transform beliefs of the past. Jeremiah' new covenant (Jer 31:31–34) offers one such example. The old covenant with Moses on Mt. Sinai has clearly failed. How could the people of Judah believe they are still God's chosen, protected people after these many horrors?

To solve the problem of the failed covenant, Jeremiah takes the old covenant tradition and makes it new, or more precisely, tinkers and fiddles with it to reinstate it under a new guise. The new covenant will be different from the old one, but it really is not very different at all. It is the old one reasserted, reaffirmed, and re-inaugurated. It is the old one internalized, made more democratic, written in their hearts, no longer requiring of instruction of one to another. It is a promise of God's recommitment to the people. The new covenant is a highly conservative theological act that transforms the old tradition into a new dynamic symbol. It points beyond the catastrophe to life beyond mere survival.

Biographical narratives of Jeremiah's captivities scattered across the book's second half are another example of dynamic symbol-making. Captivity stories (20:1–6; 26; 32; 37:11–38:13; 40–43) follow an identical pattern. Enemies capture Jeremiah, beat him, and attack him; they humiliate him, threaten his life, deport him, and every single time he escapes with his life under mysterious circumstances, as if miraculously. The prophet's captivities embody the fate of the community. Like them, he sinks into the pit of suffering and he survives. These stories illustrate a motif in the book's second half to the effect that various characters will "escape with your life as booty for war" (Jer 38:2; 21:9; 39:18; 45:5). That is, after this war you win nothing but survival; you live. Like the new covenant text, these stories are promises; they function to encourage victims, give them energy to endure, and show them a way forward through their own captivity.

For these and other reasons, I call the book of Jeremiah a "survival manual." It names, interprets, and explains; it reframes the suffering and discovers meanings that both order and provide continuity in a world turned to chaos.

20 Lasky, "Introduction," 22.

It revives faith in God by defending God in the midst of free-floating chaos. In short, it re-symbolizes life for a destroyed nation.

Applied to Jeremiah, trauma theories show that disaster and trauma can be approached and told in many ways, as mythic poetry, as story, as the life of the prophet, as prayers of lament, sermons, letters. And yet the catastrophe can never be told because traumatic violence, like the person of God, is beyond telling. It can only be glimpsed indirectly, struggled toward, and reframed. It remains "unsayable" as does the Holy One.

Survival and recovery in this biblical book are works of literary artistry, of poets, story tellers, and theological thinkers able to invent and re-invent language that both echoes and evokes the audience's experiences of violence and simultaneously stands outside them. The literature mirrors back traumatic wounds; it invents language to tell of the disaster and then offers multiple interpretations and discursive narratives to explain it. That the book of Jeremiah arrives at no dominant interpretation also functions as a survival mechanism. The multiplicity of explanations forces readers to become interpreters themselves, to see their interpretations set next to other interpretations, to move out of passive victimhood to become agents of meaning, symbol-makers who invent meaning from the ashes. Even in its most brutal theological claims, Jeremiah is a work of resilience and of repair of the world.

3. Several Conclusions

Trauma and disaster theories can inform many aspects of biblical interpretation.

- They enhance historical imagination by illuminating the suffering that underlies violent historical contexts and the needs that arise from them.
- They realign scholarly attention away from the history of the text's composition and its sources towards the study of the literature's interactions with the lives of its readers, deepening reader- response analysis.
- They ask how the text's content functions rather than attending merely to what the text says, as if it arose in a vacuum or as served up universal truths about God.
- They magnify the symbolic nature of the text and reject genre decisions that hold the texts to be literal reports of events or simple recountings of spoken words.
- They see the text as symbol-generating literary artistry, artistic therapy, post-traumatic literary intervention.

- Ironically, trauma and disaster theories also seem to reinforce traditional dating of literary strands of the book of Jeremiah but on different grounds from the source-critics. Freedman's 3 phases of recovery accord roughly with traditional layers of Jeremiah's composition. As survivors emerge from initial trauma, survivors move toward simplified cause and effect narratives. Interpretations grow smoother, clearer, more standardized, like Jeremiah's sermons. Trauma and disaster studies may help to confirm matters of dating of sources within texts like Jeremiah and across biblical books that reflect the period. One aspect of narrative creation after disaster is that the further and further groups get from the traumatic events, the more simplified become interpretive explanations. Causal links provide a sense of control over what has happened and eventually reduce events to "a standard set of narratives."[21] Jeremiah scholars have long seen Jeremiah's sermons as part of a late layer of redaction, and these sermons provide the most simplified interpretations of Judah's predicament.[22]
- For modern readers, trauma and disaster theories turn this prophetic book filled with fire and brimstone, sin and punishment, into a book of pastoral care. They expose processes of recovery in the literature and reveal the ways psychological and spiritual recovery is the work of poets, story tellers, painter, and, by implication, musicians, preachers—symbolizers who take death and loss to and reframe it, explain it, beautify it and, in the words of Claude Lanzman, help to "make the unbearable bearable."[23]
- Theologically, trauma and disaster theories help redeem Jeremiah's depiction of the punishing God from the charges that Jeremiah's portrait of God who punishes and blames victims must be rejected as unpalatable. When treated as universal or ontological claims about the character of the divine, these texts are unpalatable. But for the victims of violence, the harsh rhetoric provides cosmic support to go forward, to keep God alive, and to restore a canopy of meaning for the community. Trauma theories point to the temporary nature of all theological language as a stammering to say the unsayable.

Once one works with trauma and disaster theories, one begins to see evidence of traumatic violence and its effects everywhere. My work has been narrowly focused on one book, but other Old Testament scholars are using these theories to examine other biblical books: Ezekiel and Daniel, Deuter-

21 Fivush and Seelig, "Interdisciplinary Responses," 5.

22 See Stulman, *Order amid Chaos*.

23 "Lanzmann said, 'I believe very deeply that art and morality are identical. I didn't try to make a document but a real movie, and I wanted it to be beautiful,' in order to 'make the unbearable bearable.' The result was a resounding response to Adorno's assertion that 'to write poetry after Auschwitz is barbaric.'" (Brody, "Witness," 4).

onomy, Job, Lamentations, and Psalms. Others are studying Jerusalem, Daughter of Zion and other passages, themes, and motifs. Historians are revising the history of the Babylonian Period. I think the whole of the Deuteronomistic History's account of Israel's rise and fall awaits further attention, as well as Second and Third Isaiah as later responses to disaster. New Testament scholars might turn to the Gospel accounts of Jesus' passion, death, and resurrection.

Recently, I have moved away from Jeremiah research to write a commentary on the book of Genesis, a book that is, not surprisingly, is beginning to resemble a Post-Traumatic Literary Intervention. Genesis tells of creation for the sake of recreation; it contains story upon story of mythic and human catastrophes from which only a few, but always a few, escape; it presents future promises for Abraham's family that are utterly impossible of realization from a human viewpoint, as Judah's own survival and revival may have seemed in the post-exilic period. Survival is Genesis' overarching concern in the face of external and internal calamities. The *Akedah* itself (Gen 22), wherein the future of the family is at stake in the life of one child who sits on the brink of extermination at divine command and who survive when God rescinds his sacrifice, encapsulates in structure, if not in content, the challenge facing the people of Judah in post Babylonian period. We will see if these arguments can be sustained by closer work on the text.[24] To be continued.

Bibliography

Balentine, E. E. "The Prose and Poetry of Exile." Pages 345-64 in *Interpreting Exile: Displacement and Deportation in Biblical and Modern Contexts*. Edited by B. E. Kelle, F. R. Ames and J. L. Wright. Atlanta: Society of Biblical Literature, 2011.

Benfey, C. "The Storm over Robert Frost." *New York Review of Books* (4 December 2008): 48-50.

Brody, R. "Witness: Claude Lanzmann and the Making of 'Shoah.'" (review of Claude Lanzmann, The Patagonian Hare). 5 Pages. Cited 28 February 2012. Online: http://www.newyorker.com/arts/critics/books/2012/03/19/120319crbo_books_brody.

Carr, D. M. "Reading into the Gap: Refractions of Trauma in Israelite Prophecy." Pages 295-308 in *Interpreting Exile: Displacement and Deportation in Biblical and Modern Contexts*. Edited by B. E. Kelle, F. R. Ames and J. L. Wright. Atlanta: Society of Biblical Literature, 2011.

Caruth, C. "Introduction II: Recapturing the Past." Pages 151-57 in *Trauma: Explorations in Memory*. Edited by C. Caruth. Baltimore: Johns Hopkins University Press, 1995.

—. *Unclaimed Experience: Trauma, Narrative, and History*. Baltimore: Johns Hopkins University Press, 1996.

Diamond, A. R. Pete. "Jeremiah." Pages 543-616 in *Eerdman's Commentary on the Bible*. Edited by J. G. D. Dunn and J.W. Rogerson. Grand Rapids: Eerdmans, 2003.

24 David M. Carr ["Reading into the Gap"] talks about "unrepresentable horror" in Gen 2-3.

Erikson, K. "Notes on Trauma and Community." Pages 183-99 in *Trauma: Explorations in Memory*. Edited by C. Caruth. Baltimore: Johns Hopkins University Press, 1995.

Faust, A. "Deportation and Demography in Sixth-Century B.C.E. Judah." Pages 41-169 in *Interpreting Exile: Displacement and Deportation in Biblical and Modern Contexts*. Edited by B. E. Kelle, F. R. Ames and J. L. Wright. Atlanta: Society of Biblical Literature, 2011.

—. *Judah in the Neo-Babylonian Period: The Archeology of Desolation* (Atlanta, Georgia: Society of Biblical Literature, 2012),

Felman, S. "Education and Crisis or the Vicissitudes of Teaching." Pages 13-60 in *Trauma: Explorations in Memory*. Edited by C. Caruth. Baltimore: Johns Hopkins University Press, 1995.

—. *The Juridical Unconscious: Trials and Traumas in the Twentieth Century*. Cambridge: Harvard University Press, 2002.

Felman, S., and D. Laub. *Testimony: Crises of Witnessing in Literature, Psychoanalysis, and History*. New York: Routledge, 1992.

Fivush, R., and B. Seelig, eds. *Interdisciplinary Responses to Trauma: Memory, Meaning, and Narrative*. Atlanta: Academic Exchange of Emory University, 2005.

Gerber, Jr., D. G. "A Vocabulary of Trauma in the Exilic Writings." Pages 309-22 in *Interpreting Exile: Displacement and Deportation in Biblical and Modern Contexts*. Edited by B. E. Kelle, F. R. Ames and J. L. Wright. Atlanta: Society of Biblical Literature, 2011.

Herman, J. L. *Trauma and Recovery*. New York: Basic Books, 1992.

Janoff-Bulman, R. *Shattered Assumptions: Toward a New Psychology of Trauma*. New York: Free Press, 1992.

Kelle, B. E., F. R. Ames and J. L. Wright, eds. *Interpreting Exile: Displacement and Deportation in Biblical and Modern Contexts*. Atlanta: Society of Biblical Literature, 2011.

Langer, L. L. *Holocaust Testimonies: The Ruins of Memory*. New Haven: Yale University Press, 1991.

Lasky, R. "Introduction." Pages 19-20 in *Symbolization and Resymbolization: Essays in Honor of Norbert Freedman*. Edited by Richard Lasky. New York: Karnac, 2002.

Morrow, W. "Deuteronomy 7 in Postcolonial Perspective: Cultural Fragmentation and Renewal." Pages 275-294 in *Interpreting Exile: Displacement and Deportation in Biblical and Modern Contexts*. Edited by B. E. Kelle, F. R. Ames and J. L. Wright. Atlanta: Society of Biblical Literature, 2011.

O'Connor, K. M. *Jeremiah: Pain and Promise*. Minneapolis, Fortress, 2011.

Rumfelt, J. L. "Reversing Fortune: War, Psychic Trauma, and the Promise of Narrative Repair." Pages 323-43 in *Interpreting Exile: Displacement and Deportation in Biblical and Modern Contexts*. Edited by B. E. Kelle, F. R. Ames and J. L. Wright. Atlanta: Society of Biblical Literature, 2011.

Schimek, J. "Some Thoughts on Symbolization and Transference." Pages 252-60 in *Symbolization and Resymbolization: Essays in Honor of Norbert Freedman*. Edited by R. Lasky. New York: Karnac, 2002.

Schwartz, D. R. *Imagining the Holocaust*. New York: St. Martin's, 1999.

Silverman, D. K. "The Refractoriness of the Desymbolizing Function." Pages 230-51 in *Symbolization and Resymbolization: Essays in Honor of Norbert Freedman*. Edited by R. Lasky. New York: Karnac, 2002.

Smith-Christopher, D. "Reading War and Trauma: Suggestions Toward a Social-Psychological Exegesis of Exile and War in Biblical Texts." Pages 253-274 in *Interpreting Exile: Displacement and Deportation in Biblical and Modern Contexts*. Edited by B. E. Kelle, F. R. Ames and J. L. Wright. Atlanta: Society of Biblical Literature, 2011.

—. *A Biblical Theology of Exile*. Overtures to Biblical Theology. Minneapolis: Fortress, 2002.

Stulman, L. *Order amid Chaos: Jeremiah as Symbolic Tapestry*. Biblical Seminar 7. Sheffield: Sheffield Academic, 1998.

Daniel L. Smith-Christopher

Trauma and the Old Testament: Some Problems and Prospects

Abstract

Recent work on biblical literature that draws on trauma studies has resulted in suggestive, even provocative, new ways of reading and understanding biblical literature. It is important to note that trauma studies as a growing discipline is engaged in several different discussions, some of which can be important for biblical scholars to consider. For example, Vamik Volkan's concept of "Chosen Traumas" proposes that specific traumas can become part of a cultural/ethnic identity over several generations. This concept calls into question a common assumption in biblical studies that different authors within a book are not likely to be addressing the same historical issues. Caruth's notion of "latent" trauma that is not directly expressed can raise other difficulties for textual analysis. Finally, are there inherent problems in working on religious texts by drawing on (some) psychological theories that define religiosity itself as a symptom of difficulties to be ameliorated?

Introduction

Among the opening sentences in the preface to his book on using psychological categories to further understand historical events and personalities (e.g. "Psychohistory"), Peter Loewenberg issues the following challenge:

> All investigators have feelings and predispositions toward the subject of their research. The problem is whether these feelings are in awareness and how they are dealt with. Is the researcher's model conscious or unconscious? Is it the richest and most complex model available which can subsume disparate and apparently incoherent types of behavior?[1]

For some years I have argued in almost precisely the same manner with regard to using social science comparisons in biblical studies. It would seem obvious that there is clear significance to studying social science literature on group behavior in particular circumstances[2], assumptions about class rela-

1 Loewenberg, *Decoding the Past*, xix.
2 E.g. forced removal and relocation, see now Ahn, *Exile*.

tions and group loyalties,[3] attitudes to mixed marriage,[4] etc. Despite this, it is unfortunately still common to hear the criticism of ancient historians and biblical scholars who try to apply social science to the analysis of ancient texts, especially the Bible. The common phrase goes something like this: "We just don't have enough information," and "Application of modern psychological or sociological categories of analysis is always anachronistic and reads into the data…." However, it isn't difficult to illustrate how reading contemporary models can helpfully illuminate a reading of historical texts. Two examples should suffice.

In his recent analysis of Assyriology as a discipline, written as a preliminary to his own analysis of specific questions of Neo-Assyrian imperial practices, Holloway trenchantly points out the influences of the typically unacknowledged social or political "models" often implied in early academic analysis of the Neo-Assyrian Empire, especially by British scholars who were influential at the time when the major cuneiform discoveries were coming to light. One prominent "model," for example, was precisely British attitudes about the "sick man," the Ottoman Empire. Holloway also cited the impact of World War I, and also especially the revelations of Belgian King Leopold II's horrific massacres and tortures of native peoples of the Congo Free State in Africa. These events, argues Holloway, had clear impact on the work of A. Olmstead and his views of Neo-Assyrian 'terrorism,' which is to say, Olmstead was arguably "sensitized" to his reading of Neo-Assyrian policies by contemporary events.[5]

Such sensitizing can continue. Gorst-Unsworth and Turner, who work on treatment of terror and torture victims, define the phrase "State-Sponsored Terrorism" as follows:

> [E]ssentially the act of a state against an individual or group, with the aim of achieving specific psychological changes (directly) in their victims and often (indirectly) in their communities … the survivor of torture has not merely been the accidental victim of physical injury or threat of death such as might occur, for example in a natural disaster or accident…. He or she has received the focused attention of an adversary determined to case the maximal psychological change…. Neither is it the individual who suffers. For every person tortured there are mothers and fathers, wives, husbands and children, friends and relatives who wait in uncertainty and fear…. Torture has effects on communities and on whole societies …[6]

When we read Ezekiel, or Lamentations, or Baruch, or the Gospel of Mark, or Revelation—do we have any substantive reason to excuse ancient regimes

3 Houston, *Contending for Justice.*
4 Southwood, *Mixed Marriage Crisis.*
5 Holloway, *Assur is King,* 49.
6 Turner and Gorst-Unsworth, "Sequelae of Torture," 475–76.

from the accusation of state-sponsored terrorism merely because it is ancient history we speak of rather than 20th and 21st century? In reference to the Neo-Assyrian Empire, Kuhrt writes of reliefs depicting its kings reclining near the severed heads of enemies, as well as Assyrian inscriptions boasting of the dead rebels draped on their city walls, or rebellious rulers entrapped in cages with wild animals that are then suspended at the entrance to cities. The king, she writes:

> was awe-inspiring; the fear that filled his enemies was the terror of those knowing that they will be ruthlessly … punished. The royal power to inspire fear was visualizes as a shining radiance … a kind of halo, that flashed forth from the royal face … it made him fearsome to behold and it could strike his enemies down, so that they fell to their knees before him, dazzled by the fearful glow …"[7]

Jonker writes that:

> In the first part of the first millennium the surrounding lands, including Babylonia, were terrorized by the Assyrians. Their diplomatic policy of "peace" involved deportation and demolition … deportations totally disrupted life in the inhabited world in the first millennium. It was not enough for the conquerors to raze every sign of human habitation to the ground, not enough to cut down the trees and burn the crops in what today would be described as a scorched-earth policy; they disinterred the dead and denuded the earth by removing the fertile topsoil.… We know of 157 mass deportations undertaken by Assyrian dictators, by means of which they intended to do their utmost to eradicate any traces of the memory of their opponents; they were not content "until nothing remained" …[8]

In reading these descriptions from otherwise sober historical analysis, are we really so far from the military parades of Moscow, the killing fields from American drones, or the incessant third-world proxy wars of the last 100 years?

In my own continuing interest in the Babylonian Exile and the Persian Period (ca. 600–333 B.C.E.), I continue to be enlightened by reading contemporary analysis in the (sadly growing) field of "Refugee Studies." A good example of this literature is Milica Bookman's 2002 work: *After Involuntary Migration: The Political Economy of Refugee Encampments*. Bookman begins by stating the shocking statistics: over 90 countries have refugee camps with over 1000 members in them. Most of these are long term, and her analysis includes the United States—counting removed Native groups, as well as in the developing countries, many of which have long-term refugee encampments such as in Africa and the Middle East.

7 Kuhrt, *Ancient Near East*, 517.
8 Jonker, *Topography of Remembrance*, 47–48.

Bookman's analysis of encampment economics raises especially important questions. She asks, for example, about questions of economic self-sufficiency and what this means for long-term encampments. If self-sufficiency means that encampment populations can survive without outside assistance, it does *not* mean that it does not interact with local populations.[9] This raised interesting questions for me about the exilic communities in their economic contexts in southern Mesopotamia. Of course they were not "self-sufficient," but historians continue to insist on hard evidence for Jewish interaction with Babylonian culture before we can safely talk of the influence of, for example, Enuma Elish on Genesis.[10] Perhaps one piece of unheralded evidence is precisely their economic survival in the decades before we finally have textual evidence in the famous Murashu Archive of business documents of the Persian Period that explicitly list Israelite/Judean names.

Even more interesting was Bookman's notes on what people *did* purchase when food and shelter were stabilized. Vietnamese refugees in Hong Kong bought suit-cases, which not only provided short to medium term storage, they also had important symbolic value: "We aren't staying long." After this, she notes, is the popularity of fish-tanks and televisions. Bookman points out an aspect of refugee culture that I admit that I simply would not have thought of before—namely sheer boredom! Bookman writes that boredom in the camps is a huge problem:

> The enforced idleness of unemployed camp residents is further reinforced by the nature of encampment life that entails wasted time and a lot of waiting time … one waits for food distribution, one waits for the water truck, one waits at the clinic …[11]

Bookman's observation raises an obvious question to biblical scholars who may not have reflected much on the social realities of refugee experiences: how much biblical literature—song and story—is the product of leisure time in diaspora? Proverbs ch. 1 suggests idle time leading to gang violence among young Hebrews, and Ezekiel's street theatre[12] suggests weeks if not months of time in the demonstration of his little plays. Jeremiah's letter of peace in ch. 29 suggests planting gardens and building homes, something I had previously thought was only a reference to Deuteronomy 20[13]—but may be more practical than I had considered! After all, references to huge increases in knitting, gardening, and artwork in the Japanese Internment Camps during World War II in the Western United States are ubiquitous in the literature discussing these events. Here again, it isn't until we find a serious discussion

9 Bookman, *Involuntary Migration*, 89.
10 But cf. Middleton, *Liberating Image*.
11 Bookman, *Involuntary Migration*, 99.
12 Lang, "Street Theatre."
13 Smith-Christopher, "Jeremiah."

of the significance of these facts of refugee existence that it occurs to us that these may be exegetically meaningful models for textual analysis.

Do models bias an otherwise objective reading? I agree with Loewenberg that the choice is never between some proposed "pure and objective history" on the one hand, and then some kind of "history that is tainted by the introduction of social science models." Rather, the choice is between the application of consciously and critically reflective models of human behavior, and unreflective or unconscious use of models based on untested notions of common sense. The fact is that we think by analogy to what we already understand—or think we understand. Arguably, trauma studies is another powerful model we must now consider for the reading of biblical texts, and recent studies of Ezekiel now routinely raise issues associated with trauma and PTSD.[14] Ever since my first exposure to trauma studies, refugee studies, and other social science literatures of human tragedy, I confess that my study of the Bible has been haunted. In my view, those of us who work in biblical studies cannot escape these ghosts— not only the ghosts of ancient disaster and trauma, but the ghosts of 20th and 21st century trauma that inevitably—*inevitably*—impact on our thinking about ancient history and ancient texts. Let me illustrate my most recent encounters with these ghosts of trauma.

Micah and Violence: Encountering the Realities of Warfare in Biblical History

Because my most recent major project in biblical studies is a new commentary on the book of Micah, I have enjoyed a careful review of the significant literature on this book, and reviewing the historical literature on the 8th century context of the prophet himself. I would have been very pleased if my review of work on Micah had only to consist of re-reading many of the standard historical recitations of what we can know about the Neo-Assyrian involvements in Israelite territories in the 8th century B.C.E.—and the constant claims that much of Micah is from the Neo-Babylonian period or even later. However, when I laid out a reference list of specifically mentioned military events from Assyrian and biblical historical sources of the 8th century, and focused only in Judean vicinities, and then aligned this list with the language of the book of Micah itself, I found the result frankly startling. I should note that I have tried to limit this to events that could reasonably be construed to have impacted on the territories around the traditional home of Micah the prophet, the Shephelah village of Moreshet, arguably modern Tell Judeidah/Goded. Here is my result.

14 Cf. Kelle, *Ezekiel.*

Violence in the Lowlands

Ca. 790	Amaziah's wars with Edom, and challenging Israel
Ca. 786/5	Jehoash defeats Amaziah at Beth Shemesh (10 miles from Moreshet)
Ca. 785	Jerusalem sacked
Ca. 785-759	Massive military build-up under Uzziah, including state building projects in the Shephelah, state-run farms, and mustering of soldiers.
Ca. 785-759	Uzziah initiates battles in Philistia, mentioning Gath (5 miles from Moreshet)
Ca. 759-745	Jotham fights Ammon, fortifies towns (in "highlands"), and is noted for his many "wars."
Ca. 735	Pekah engages in "great slaughter" in Judah, and tries to take massive numbers of hostages among Judeans.
Ca. 735	Philistines raid Judean Shephelah territories (many villages near Moresheth are captured).
Ca. 734	Pekah and Rezin lay siege to Ahaz in Jerusalem.
Ca. 734	Tiglath-Pileser III against Philistia
Ca. 734-725	Ahaz taxes his people heavily to pay Assyrian tribute payments.
Ca. 722	Conquest of North sends large numbers of refugees south.
Ca. 716	Likely campaign in West by Sargon II against Philistia[15]
Ca. 713-712	Likely campaign in West by Sargon II against Philistia; fall of Ashdod[16]
Ca. 705-70	Hezekiah fortifies his line against Assyria, including Shephelah (probable time of a large number of the hundreds of "LMLK" jars at Lachish and nearby towns often thought to be royal preparations for the Assyrian invasion)[17]
Ca. 702/1	Sennacherib conquers Lachish, and quarters Assyrian armies in Shephelah

I quickly point out that I have not included the possibility of further impact from the famous earthquake noted in Amos 1:1, ca. 759, the impact of which may well have had traumatic implications for decades, depending on how serious it was, even in a later work like Micah. Furthermore, we can no longer confidently presume that the only trauma we can reasonably speak of is the result only of the invasions and policies of supposed enemies:

3:1 And I said: Listen, you heads of Jacob and rulers of the house of Israel! Should you not know justice?—2 you who hate the good and love the evil, who tear the skin off my people, and the flesh off their bones; 3 who eat the flesh of my people, flay their

15 Younger, "Deportations."

16 Ibid.

17 Ussishkin, "Destruction of Lachish," but now see Lipshits, "Archaeological Facts."

skin off them, break their bones in pieces, and chop them up like meat in a kettle, like flesh in a caldron. (Micah 3:1–3, cf. Micah 6:9–16)

An important point is this: Charts like the brief list I drew up could be prepared for virtually any biblical book, from books like Obadiah with one chapter, to Isaiah with 66. We have fine studies already moving in these directions. O'Connor's important analysis of the trauma in Lamentations[18] (2002) is an important landmark, and Janzen's new work *The Violent Gift,* goes even further, and represents a significant step not only because of his helpful brief review of trauma literature, but also his application to ways of thinking about the editorial work of the entire Deuteronomic Historical work.[19]

What should our reaction to be to this kind of historical analysis that turns up these levels of violent events and violent images? Of course, we could simply examine a list like this and shrug our historical-critical, objective scholarly shoulders and discuss the textual and archaeological evidence behind such a list. Do I have my dates right, am I reading the texts reasonably well, etc.

Or we can pause—and deal with our human temptation to reach across the centuries to the writer of a work like this and put our hand on their shoulder and simply ask, "Are you OK?...." I don't think that it is bad historical analysis to think like this as part of our biblical analysis. *The basis for this discussion is that I suspect, and continue to suspect, that many of the writers of the Bible are not "ok," and part of our task is to think together about what this might mean.*

So, my initial point is the recognition, with Loewenberg, that we are quite simply not being very good historians if we don't raise questions about the human impact of all these military and economic activities. For the Prophets, this involves not merely a review of events noted in the literature of Mesopotamian or biblical texts from the 8th and 6th centuries, but a question about what this means for our notions of "normal" and "traumatized" in the writing and reading of this material. Trauma has already proven itself, it seems to me, to be a powerful model for thinking about exegesis.

Having said that, I heartily endorse the conscious application of social science models for biblical texts. However, in this study I wish to raise some notes of caution in relation to the specific dialogue between certain aspects of trauma studies and our reading of Scripture. While it is true that trauma studies have haunted my work on Old Testament texts ever since I started thinking about this some years ago,[20] I would like to raise four concerns that

18 O'Connor, *Lamentations.*
19 Janzen, *Violent Gift.*
20 Smith-Christopher, "Ezekiel."

keep coming back to in one form or another, especially in regard to thinking about the use of trauma literature in the analysis of the Old Testament.

Trauma Studies and Biblical Studies: Converging Disciplines and Problematic Definitions?

It is interesting to reflect on the timing of this convergence of biblical studies and trauma studies. I don't think it is only a reflection on the fact that the 20th and 21st centuries have featured catastrophic traumas that have received unprecedented publicity because of the rise of rapid, world-wide, and easily accessible media. The interesting fact is—extensive social-science related analysis of the Bible, and trauma studies itself, have both emerged at roughly the same time, and therefore psychological, anthropological, and sociological readings of biblical Texts are arguably only possible toward the end of the 20th century, and now into the 21st century. I think it is interesting, therefore, to review recent scholarship on the issue of trauma studies in the 20th century, and how the questions have started to emerge.

My first concern arises from some recent reflections on the development of the field of trauma studies in the 20th century. Consider, for example, the recent work by Didier Fassin and Richard Rechtman, whose excellent analysis of the development of trauma in the 20th century works from just before World War I, and moving to the development when PTSD was finally listed in the 1980 Diagnostic and Statistical Manual. Fassin and Rechtman state that for most of the 20th century, a human being:

> [S]uffering from trauma was seen as different from others: weak, dishonest, perhaps a phoney or a profiteer. Then a few decades ago she or he became the very embodiment of our common humanity. It is this shift from one truth to another, from a realm in which trauma was regarded with suspicion to a realm in which it carries the stamp of authenticity, that we seek to analyze.[21]

Provocatively, Fassin and Rechtman suggest that the refusal of foot soldiers to continue to accept their designated role as cannon fodder was directly related to the refusal of the workforce to accept their role as mindless automatons.[22]

Thus, military psychiatry at the early stages was only willing to consider trauma in warfare with the same contempt with which they treated workplace accidents—hysteria, malingering, laziness (39–47). But circumstances began to change, and Fassin and Rechtman suggest that it was from the late 1920s onwards that "hysteria and shell shock" were indeed no longer dishon-

21 Fassin and Rechtman, *Empire of Trauma*, 23.
22 Ibid., 39.

orable conditions that brought shame on anyone suffering from them. It was, in fact, World War II and especially the Holocaust that dramatically forced the most notable changes:

> The notions of malingering, cowardice, selfishness, overdeveloped narcissism, secondary gains, class interest—all the stigmas attached to traumatic neurosis, could not be applied to these people in striped pajamas who were emerging directly from hell. An entirely different paradigm was called for …"[23]

However (and here we confront my main concern in this first point), listen to the note of caution suggested in Fassin and Rechtman's words: "This development both establishes and reinforces a new figure, one that is central to an understanding of contemporary society—the figure of the victim."[24]

The rise of the victim. The important question is this: is this a *Western* social phenomenon? Fassin and Rechtman place the development of PTSD squarely in the context of European social developments, and they clearly allude to the role of struggles in French attitudes toward working classes and colonized subjects in contributing to this development of the victim—the traumatized.

In refugee studies, Derek Summerfield has raised very similar concerns about the *Western* context of conceptions of trauma. After noting the dramatic rise in the numbers of counselors who accompany the physical relief workers around the world, Summerfield notes seven assumptions of Westernized mental health workers in disaster circumstances:

(1) Experience of war and atrocity are so extreme and distinctive that they do not just cause suffering, they cause trauma,

(2) There is basically a universal human response to highly stressful events, captured by Western psychological frameworks of PTSD,

(3) Large numbers of victims traumatized by war need professional help,

(4) Western psychological approaches are relevant to violent conflict worldwide—victims do better if they vent or "work through' their experiences,

(5) There are vulnerable groups and individuals who need to be specifically targeted for help,

(6) Wars represent a mental health emergency; and rapid intervention can prevent serious mental problems as well as subsequent violence, and

(7) Local workers are overwhelmed and may themselves be traumatized.[25]

23 Ibid., 71.
24 Ibid., 278.
25 Summerfield, "Seven Assumptions," 1449-62.

Referring to the "medicalization" of distress, Summerfield notes a globalization of Western assumptions, especially Western assumptions about the relation of the individual to the group, and the tendencies to identify the biological instead of the social, and the assumption that the prevention of wars is a mental health issue and require that "brutalization be nipped in the bud." Silove, Steele and Bauman, for example, also wonder whether some PTSD symptoms consist of genetic responses to conflict that trace to the savannahs of Africa, such as rapid heartbeat, and heightened awareness. Similarly, are recurring dreams at attempt to learn from mistakes and prepare for the future? Does going over the trauma cause more problems than it relieves, especially in non-Western societies?[26] Even though everyone seems to agree that trauma has symptoms, they may be different in different cultures.

Here, then, is the significant challenge for Old Testament scholarship: Is the disturbing level of violent imagery of war, violence, and destruction in scripture a "coping mechanism" of some kind that is culturally relevant to ancient Hebrews?

The point is—in different cultural contexts—some actions that are pathologized in Western assumptions could rather be coping strategies and not behaviors or responses that need to be treated, relieved, or removed.

It seems that there are two serious issues here. First, the concern that Westernized notions are being universalized uncritically (on the role of the individual in relation to the social, especially) but just as important is the postcolonial accusation that medicalization of trauma can effectively avoid the colonial context of the development of many of these psychological categories in the first place! In other words—not only are we depending on Westernized notions of trauma, but these are not innocent notions, but rather themselves deeply influenced by the colonial experience of the 17th–21st centuries.

In their introduction to their very provocative 2011 collection of essays entitled: *Unconscious Dominions: Psychoanalysis, Colonial Trauma, and Global Sovereignties*, the editors note the dependence of Freud on highly contentious imagery driven by colonial power relations, e.g. references to the female body as the "dark continent," the conceptualization of primitive societies in Totem and Taboo. Keller writes that: "many Europeans were beginning to suspect that destabilizing colonial tropics were lodged deep within their own mentality"[27]. Irrational desire and passionate violence relied on imperial imagination to structure colonial space as starkly opposing terms to Western enlightenment and order. Similar to recent analysis of the language of Marduk and Tiamat, order vs. chaos, as clearly functioning as an ideological prop

26 Silove et al., "Trauma and PTSD."

27 Keller, "Introduction," in Anderson et al., *Unconscious Dominions*, 3.

of Mesopotamian violence,[28] colonial literature of the 17th–20th centuries especially, provided grist for the psychological portrait of "primitive mentalities" and "primitive internal forces." The challenge is to consider Westernized bias in the very act of applying what seems an enlightened perspective on the human reactions to violence.

The point is *not* that we are incorrect in thinking about the traumatic impact of ancient events. It is not that we Westerners are simply weak minded and psychologically troubled, but ancient people simply exhibited stiff upper lips and carried on. The ideological motivations of such ideas are now patently clear. It is simply that the *way* we approach trauma and refugee studies is the concern, especially in cross-cultural circumstances.

To summarize my first concern—I have always thought that a post-colonial approach to biblical analysis should draw on refugee and trauma studies as precisely a *corrective* to falsely objectified historical analysis that denies reading the social and emotional and psychological impact of historical events. It would be ironic indeed to simply replace one overly Westernized historical methodology with a questionable and overly-Westernized analysis of trauma and disaster.[29] Attention to the internal debates on cross-cultural applications of trauma concepts are important here.

Before leaving this concern, there is a good illustration of the difficulties of using social science concepts that are themselves in the midst of serious debate. For example, there is an interesting problem of defining "refugee" in "Refugee Studies"—even in contemporary applications, much less historical applications.

In her summary of refugee studies in the 1995 *Annual Review of Anthropology*, Liisa Malkki noted that there are considerable difficulties simply defining the term "refugee,"[30] especially given the context of the rise of refugee studies in the immediate post-war years of the twentieth century. Where this becomes interesting for biblical analysis is in the way that refugee studies have been separated from a wider study of social and political contexts:

> If nothing else, the development of the discourse on refugees has sometimes facilitated the continued de-politicization of refugee movements; for instead of foregrounding the political, historical processes that generated a given group of refugees, and that reach far beyond the country of asylum and the refugee camp, development projects tend to see a whole world in a refugee camp.[31]

Malkki, notably, refers in her work to a "sedentarist bias" that now defines the refugee as a "problem" precisely because the refugee is *stateless*. Thus, this

28 So Middleton, *Liberating Image*.
29 Cf. Robbins and Suarez-Orozco, *Cultures under Siege*.
30 Malkki, "Refugees and Exile," 496.
31 Ibid., 507.

bias suggests the necessity of territory and sealed borders, and therefore invites xenophobic reactions to the presence of such refugee groups.[32] Malkki herself has called for an approach to the study of the phenomenon of refugees that also incorporates a study of what "being home" is! In the light of the rise of a group of scholars around Steven Grosby's recent work on nationalism in Ancient Israel,[33] such a call to question the presumed normative contrasts between "home" with "diaspora" or "refugee" in the kind of "bipolar analysis" well known to postcolonial methodologies, was downright prophetic in 1995. But what is particularly suggestive in Malkki's analysis is her questioning of the territorial, nationalist bias of present refugee research:

> [A] denaturalizing, questioning stance toward the national order of things, presents itself as a promising site from which to identify new research directions in the study of refugees, exile, displacement, and diaspora—*as well as for imagining new forms of political engagement* (my emphasis).[34]

Malkki's interest in refugees being defined by a certain assumption about the "naturalness" of statehood reminds us of the problem always faced by nomadic peoples, or historically the Roma populations of Europe, and the 19th century American desperation to turn Plains Indians into European-styled farmers, etc. But what I find interesting is that she calls for an analysis of the wider ideological foundations for even defining "refugee," in precisely the same way that many psychologists are questioning the roots of the concepts of PTSD and Westernized notions of victimhood that depoliticize the contexts and backgrounds.

In short, it is difficult to be attentive to the politics of even defining terms in the use of our models borrowed from the social sciences. These are treacherous waters for us innocent biblical scholars, especially any who still believe in the safe harbor of "ancient history" as dependent only on simply reading and translating texts—as if it is methodologically safe to stick to dictionaries and leave the diagnostic manuals to the social scientists. But what we are finding is that dictionaries *are* diagnostic manuals. Definitions have contexts.

Transgenerational Trauma and Redaction Criticism

My second concern has to do with the work on trans-generational trauma. In a number of recent works, Vamik Volkan has developed his interest in an expansion of the analytical tools and language of psychoanalysis to become a more useful theoretical basis for understanding group behavior, and specifi-

32 Ibid., 511.
33 Grosby, *Biblical Ideas*.
34 Malkki, "Refugees and Exile," 517.

cally violent group behavior in 20th century political and especially ethnic conflict. But his work on trauma, and especially trans-generational trauma, is of particular relevance here. In his 1997 work entitled *Blood Lines*, he outlines a few aspects of group identity that are quite interesting:

(1) The importance of shared symbols associated with positive emotions (e.g. Finns and their saunas).

(2) The absorption of what others think are bad qualities—"self-hating" (a classic example being African-American desire to straighten their hair in the mid-20th century),

(3) The social absorption of leader's qualities (Volkan speaks of Turkish obsession with Ataturk's fashion sense),

(4) Chosen glories (the focus on historic events of the past, often distant past, as social markers of identity), and

(5) Chosen traumas (the focus on historic tragedies as particularly potent symbols of contemporary social identity).

What is especially interesting about Volkan's ideas, however, is his notion that many of these aspects of group identity can be transferred across many generations. His concept of "chosen traumas" is especially suggestive for biblical studies. For example, he quite powerfully notes that:

> As unlikely as it may seem, for example, the chosen trauma critical for understanding the tragedies in Bosnia in 1992 and in Kosovo in 1999 is the Serbian people's defeat at the Battle of Kosovo in 1389.[35]

This idea of trans-generational transmission is, I think, especially challenging for biblical studies. How does this work? The late Palestinian-American theorist Edward Said observes in a famous essay on exile that:

> exile is fundamentally a discontinuous state of being. Exiles are cut off from their roots, their land, their past. They generally do not have enemies, or states, though they are often in search of these institutions. This search can lead exiles to reconstitute their broken lives in narrative form, usually by choosing to see themselves as part of a triumphant ideology or a restored people. Such a story is designed to reassemble an exile's broken history into a new whole.[36]

This process can lead to a search into history to find those narratives, and thus we are describing what Volkan called "chosen traumas." Volkan even

35 Volkan, *Blood Lines*, 50.
36 Said, "Mind of Winter," 51.

suggests the mechanics of how these chosen traumas can then be passed on for generations:

Transgenerational transmission is when an older person unconsciously externalizes his traumatized self onto a developing child's personality. A child then becomes a reservoir for the unwanted, troublesome parts of an older generation. Because the elders have influence on a child, the child absorbs their wishes and expectations and is driven to act on them. It becomes the child's task to mourn, to reverse the humiliation and feelings of helplessness pertaining to the trauma of his forebears.... Because the traumatized self-images passed down by members of the group all refer to the same calamity, they become part of the group identity, an ethnic marker on the canvas of the ethnic tent.[37]

Finally, the trauma can travel across many generations:

[T]he memory of the past trauma remains dormant for several generations, kept within the psychological DNA of the members of the group and silently acknowledged within the culture—in literature and art, for example—but it reemerges powerfully only under certain conditions. For instance, a political leader may reignite a dormant group memory that affects collective thinking, perceptions, and actions. When such a shared mental representation of the original injury is reactivated, it may distort a large group's perceptions. New enemies involved in current conflicts may be perceived as extensions of an old enemy from a historical event.[38]

If trans-generational transmission of trauma is a real and viable social phenomenon among all human groups, then *some* of the assumptions that drive standard historical-critical decisions about the editing of biblical books are rendered highly questionable at best. Let me give an example from Micah that I have struggled with.

There is a famous problem that is taken up by virtually all commentaries on Micah, and that is the relation of the judgment passages in chs. 1–3, especially 3:12, and the famous "Swords into Plowshares" passage in 4:1–5.

9 Hear this, you rulers of the house of Jacob and chiefs of the house of Israel, who abhor justice and pervert all equity, 10 who build Zion with blood and Jerusalem with wrong! 11 Its rulers give judgment for a bribe, its priests teach for a price, its prophets give oracles for money; yet they lean upon the LORD and say, "Surely the LORD is with us! No harm shall come upon us." 12 *Therefore because of you Zion shall be plowed as a field; Jerusalem shall become a heap of ruins, and the mountain of the house a wooded height.*

4:1 In days to come the mountain of the LORD's house shall be established as the highest of the mountains, and shall be raised up above the hills. Peoples shall stream to it, 2 and many nations shall come and say: "Come, let us go up to the mountain of

37 Volkan, *Blood Lines*, 43, 45.
38 Ibid., 46.

the LORD, to the house of the God of Jacob; that he may teach us his ways and that we may walk in his paths." For out of Zion shall go forth instruction, and the word of the LORD from Jerusalem. 3 He shall judge between many peoples, and shall arbitrate between strong nations far away; they shall beat their swords into plowshares, and their spears into pruning hooks; nation shall not lift up sword against nation, neither shall they learn war any more; 4 but they shall all sit under their own vines and under their own fig trees, and no one shall make them afraid; for the mouth of the LORD of hosts has spoken. 5 For all the peoples walk, each in the name of its god, but we will walk in the name of the LORD our God forever and ever. (Micah 3:9–4:5 NRSV)

Of course, there is a prevailing assumption about the radical break between 3:12 and 4:1–5. Wolff writes that this passage "… stands in antithesis to the fearsome judgment prophesied in 3:12,"[39] and McKane, for example, repeated the famous observation of Wellhausen that 4:1–5 was a plaster (a "band-aid") on the wound of 3:12.[40] Jeppesen observes:

Even if one takes a long pause for breath between Mic 3:12 and 4:1, the change in outlook for the future is surprising; it is like moving suddenly from night to day—and that is, of course, one of the reasons why scholars declined to read the two texts together …[41]

I am aware of the weight of opinion that I am challenging by suggesting that this "break" between the notions of 3:12 and 4:1 has been far too starkly drawn in the literature. For one thing, the prevailing opinion that 4:1 starts a section written at least 100 years later is a central pillar in the argument that these are two radically different thoughts. Therefore, the trauma that gave rise judgment in 3:12 is long forgotten, and this allows the "utopia" of 4:1–5.

But what if a similar trauma is defining both passages—even if they are separated by a number of generations!? What if 4:1–5 is being driven by the same emotion, the same anger, the same "chosen trauma" as chs. 1–3 with their angry judgment? Then, 4:1–5 would *follow the plowing of Jerusalem!* Jerusalem then becomes a center of world arbitration of disputes precisely *because* the old, violent Jerusalem has been plowed under! The old Jerusalem, with its preparations for war —preparations that arguably brought Sennacherib down on Micah's home town is ended, and therefore *now* the era of peace can begin. In short, we simply cannot assume that different times mean different issues, and old tragedies are long in the past. A "chosen trauma" can inform ancient writers generation after generation, and our standard approach to historical-critical assignment of texts has rarely considered this, in my view. We have often talked about the inability to be confident about the historical details after so much time, but perhaps we have neglected the social

39 Wolff, *Micah*, 117.
40 McKane, *Book of Micah*, 117.
41 Jeppesen, "Because of You!" 209.

power of these events, however they are perhaps inaccurately described, for identity over many centuries. Different times do not always mean different issues.

Reading Ancient Narratives: What if Trauma is not Obvious?

One of the most important scholars working on the implications of trauma for the study of comparative literature is Cathy Caruth, whose 1996 work, *Unclaimed Experience: Trauma, Narrative and History*, has become an important example of one kind of argument about trauma. I am only interested in pointing to one aspect of Caruth's arguments, namely the interesting suggestion that many experiences of trauma are not often explicitly or even rationally discussed— they can only be analyzed by decoding/exegeting latent effects—and these traumatized responses can sometimes only be seen in artistic expression, poetry, or images. Volkan, too, spoke of artistic expressions of trauma:

> Regression is not an all-or-nothing experience and is typically accompanied by attempts to adapt; sometimes these efforts to cope with the trauma will take the shape of artistic creativity.[42]

So, the impact of trauma might not be expressed in explicit and detailed, even clinical, discussions of the events themselves. Sometimes they are dealt with in creative, abstract, or other expressive means, and Volkan even considers some of these artistic expressions to be adaptive and healing.

So here is an interesting dilemma. Caruth and Volkan's work suggests latent impacts that can be expressed in artistic or non-rational constructions and writings, and this raises important questions for the interpretation of the non-historical narratives or literature of the Bible (esp. tales and visions, e.g. in the book of Daniel). We simply cannot dismiss the stories of Daniel or Esther or Judith as not expressing historically significant experiences of the writers and early readers of these works *simply because they are fictional stories*. We must ask: What traumas, angers, or creative testimonies are latent in these tales? And are the tales themselves an attempt to heal and adapt?

The literature on the Truth and Reconciliation Commissions adds to this, it seems to me. Here, however, there is an emphasis on the importance of *telling* the stories or *expressing* the artistic works. In her 2004 book, *Shattered Voices: Language, Violence, and the Work of Truth Commissions*, Teresa Godwin Phelps suggests a number of reasons why she believes that telling stories in the Truth Commissions, even apart from trials (which are criticized for *not*

42 Volkan, *Blood Lines*, 59.

allowing expressions of stories and ideas) can be healing and freeing. It is worth citing Phelps at length here:

While it is well documented in psychological literature and elsewhere that telling the story of a traumatic experience can be therapeutic for victims, the value of shaping one's experience into story form extends far beyond the therapeutic. Storytelling is an essentially human act that enables all of us to make sense of our lives and to feel integrated as members of a community. Through the recovery of language, a victim can constitute the story of his or her identity, tell a personal history that locates him or her in time and space

Second, the appropriation and manipulation of language and of people's ability to speak words for themselves in their own voices are major weapons in an oppressive regime's arsenal. The retrieving of language and the restoration of the ability to speak in one's own voice can therefore go a significant way in balancing the harm done … the retrieval of language puts the world back into some kind of order …

Third … the truth enables people to be vindicated, in that the false stories told about them or their loved ones can be corrected …

… stories can communicate the experience of pain and suffering between people who normally cannot understand each other … the enactment of storytelling, in a display akin to Bakhtin's sense of carnival that overturns and disrupts an oppressive social order, can restore victim's dignity …

Finally … the stories collected and the larger narrative that contains them (the report) can actualize a radically new kind of constitutive history for an emerging democracy …[43]

Needless to say, such insights, Caruth and Volkan's ideas about latent trauma in artistic expressions, and Phelps analysis of the power of expressing those ideas, all have serious implications for the way in which trauma studies can guide contemporary exegesis of biblical texts.

Problems with Psychological Assumptions about Religion Itself?

My final concern can be stated briefly. There seems an inevitable problem in the application of any trauma theory that is deeply informed by, for example, the orthodox canons of psychoanalysis. The Bible is a religious text. As Vamik Volkan himself states—religious belief itself is a form of regression in Freudian analysis. The frankly absurd historical suggestions about two different people named Moses in Freud's "Moses and Monotheism" and his depen-

43 Phelps, *Shattered Voices*, 55.

dence on very old speculation about Akhenaten's Egyptian religion only serve to emphasize the point. He is clearly not all that concerned with even basic historical-critical analysis of the Torah because in the end it is all a regressive retreat that can be decoded into displaced father figures in an authoritarian monotheistic god and guilty desires to kill the father—in this case also father Moses.

We cannot be so cavalier with religious categories in biblical analysis. We work with clearly more sophisticated historical notions of religion and religiosity if we are identifying conceptual differences in Priestly and Temple-centered religiosity as compared to divination-based concepts, as compared to concepts of miracle and magic, as compared to nuances between Jeremiah and Ezekiel, or even Isaiah and Deutero-Isaiah, Wisdom and cosmology vs. Apocalyptic and the bizarre, etc. I don't think it will do to simply go along with psychologically based observations that wave away the entire lot as merely insignificant variations on regressive irrationality. But to be fair: Volkan is not so simplistic either.

Among the signs of a regressive religious social movement, according to Volkan, is religiously driven attempts to radically differentiate between "them" and "us"; an increase in magical thinking and reality-blurring; language of infection and purification. Yet, even Volkan as a Muslim born scholar suggests that it is possible to marshal the symbolism and ideology of the Quran for progressive social movements that: Encourage compromise without calling that a betrayal of identity; raising families to be places of trust and stability rather than questioning familial loyalties; halting the devaluation of women; valuing freedom of speech; and maintaining the ability to question moral and aesthetic categories.[44]

But how can we identify the positive movements toward healing that may be attempted already in Scriptural writing, if healing is defined by many psychological disciplines as a form of atheism (rather than, at the very least, consisting of a healthy avoidance of dependency issues and misplaced father issues, ideals which many theists may well agree with!). These are issues of some historical-critical importance, but they are especially significant issues for those of us whose interest in Bible is also its potential for normative ethics and social progress! The use of social sciences can raise quite interesting issues for those of us interested in constructing viable and contemporary biblical Theologies.

So, my last concern is simply this: in challenging the borders of our own discipline we must also challenge the borders of the disciplines we are learning from. If we are suspicious of all "totalizing disciplinary canons" in biblical studies, I think we should apply the same critical eye to the canons of the

44 Volkan, *Blind Trust*, 86–87.

other disciplines we are talking to. I don't think I need to point out, however, that for psychology, and especially psychoanalysis itself, we don't need to worry too much about this as they are clearly as divided into rival theories as we are!

Concluding Thoughts

Reading trauma and refugee studies clearly raises some provocative challenges for our contemporary textual and theological analysis of the Bible. Doing better historical analysis is not, however, the only moral challenge that arises from working with these concepts of trauma in literature and theory. My closing point derives from a reading of Catherine Cole's 2010 work on the Truth and Reconciliation Commissions entitled *Performing South Africa's Truth Commission*. She writes that one of the most important aspects of the Truth and Reconciliation Commissions was precisely its' public context:

> We must consider that the TRCs public hearings required the presence of an audience and thereby implicated that audience as both participant and witnesses. South Africa's truth commission conveyed its findings through a voluminous text, but it conveyed its process through embodiment, the grain of the voice, the cadence of spoken language, the potency of emotional expressiveness. Performance provided a necessary corrective to the often-narrow epistomologies that governed the TRCs statement-taking protocols, investigative and collaborative processes, and fundings …[45]

It is an interesting point and reminds us of our interest in Scripture as oral event or at least a social event—literature with readers and eventually a canonical context. But what really arrested my attention was her concluding observation the burst through the anonymity of being a reader of a scholarly text. She writes:

> this experience of national witnessing implicated everyone who experienced it, and it may even implicate you, the reader, for this text is part of the ongoing … interpretation process that the commission began. This book has made you a secondary witness![46]

Even if we are not primarily concerned with the construction of a normative theology based on a Bible that quite likely contains the writings of traumatized writers (who may not be entirely in control of their rational faculties or emotional responses to that trauma) we cannot thereby simply evade the fact that reading about trauma—ancient trauma and the models from modern trauma—has made us all "secondary witnesses" to the suffering of others in

45 Cole, *Truth Commission*, 162.
46 Ibid.

both the ancient and modern world. Initially in this essay, I spoke of being haunted by trauma studies. For me, that is the final ghost I cannot ignore. Perhaps it's the Holy Ghost.

Bibliography

AHN, J. *Exile as Forced Migrations: A Sociological, Literary, and Theological Approach on the Displacement and Resettlement of the Southern Kingdom of Judah*. Berlin: De Gruyter, 2010.

ANDERSON, W., D. JENSON and R. KELLER, eds. *Unconscious Dominions: Psychoanalysis, Colonial Trauma, and Global Sovereignties*. Durham, N.C.: Duke University Press, 2011.

BOOKMAN, M. *After Involuntary Migration*. Lanham, Md.: Lexington Books, 2002.

CARUTH, C. *Unclaimed Experience: Trauma, Narrative and History*. Baltimore: Johns Hopkins University Press, 1996.

COLE, C. *Performing South Africa's Truth Commission*. Bloomington: Indiana University Press, 2010.

HOLLOWAY, S. *Assur is King! Assur is King! Religion in the Exercise of Power in the Neo-Assyrian Empire*. Leiden: Brill, 2001.

FASSIN, D. and R. RECHTMAN. *The Empire of Trauma: An Inquiry into the Condition of Victimhood*. Princeton: Princeton University Press, 2009.

GROSBY, S. *Biblical Ideas of Nationality*. Winona Lake, Ind.: Eisenbrauns, 2002.

HOUSTON, W. *Contending for Justice: Ideologies and Theologies of Social Justice in the Old Testament*. London: T & T Clark, 2006.

JANZEN, D. *The Violent Gift: Trauma's Subversion of the Deuteronomic History's Narrative*. London: T & T Clark, 2012.

JEPPESEN, K. "'Because of You!': An essay about the Centre of the Book of the Twelve." Pages 196–210 in *In Search of True Wisdom*. Sheffield: Sheffield Academic, 1999.

JONKER, G., *The Topography of Remembrance: The Dead, Tradition, and Collective Memory in Mesopotamia*, Leiden: Brill, 1995.

KELLE, B. E. *Ezekiel*. NBBC. Kansas City: Beacon Hill, 2013.

KUHRT, A. *The Ancient Near East c. 3,000–330 BC*. 2d ed. London: Routledge, 1995.

LANG, B. "Street Theatre, Raising the Dead, and the Zoroastrian Connection in Ezekiel's Prophecy." Pages 802–5 in *Ezekiel and his Book. Textual and Literary Criticism and their Interrelation*. Edited by J. Lust. Leuven: Peeters, 1986.

LIPSCHITS, O. "Archaeological Facts, Historical Speculations and the Date of the *LMLK* Storage Jars." *Journal of Hebrew Scriptures* 12.4 (2012). 15 pages. Cited 17 February 2014. Online: http://www.jhsonline.org/Articles/article_166.pdf.

LOEWENBERG, P. *Decoding the Past: The Psychohistorical Approach*. New Brunswick, N.J.: Transaction, 1996.

MALKKI, L. "Refugees and Exile: From 'Refugee Studies' to the National Order of Things," *Annual Review of Anthropology* 24 (1995): 495–523.

MARRS, R. "Micah and a Theological Critique of Worship," Pages 184–203 in *Worship in the Hebrew Bible*. Edited by M. P. Graham and S. L. McKenzie. Sheffield: Sheffield Academic, 1999.

MCKANE, W. *The Book of Micah: Introduction and Commentary*. Edinburgh: T & T Clark, 1998.

MIDDLETON, J. R. *The Liberating Image: The Imago Dei in Genesis 1*. Grand Rapids: Brazos, 2005.

O'CONNOR, K. M. *Lamentations and the Tears of the World*. Maryknoll, N.Y.: Orbis, 2002.

PHELPS, T. G., *Shattered Voices: Language, Violence, and the Work of Truth Commissions*. Philadelphia: University of Pennsylvania Press, 2004.

ROBBINS, A. C. G. and M. M. SUAREZ-OROZCO, eds. *Cultures under Siege: Collective Violence and Trauma.* Cambridge: Cambridge University Press, 2000.

RUNIONS, E. *Changing Subjects: Gender, Nation and Future in Micah.* Sheffield: Sheffield Academic, 2001.

SAID, E. "The Mind of Winter," *Harpers* (September 1983): 49–55.

SILOVE, D., Z. STEELE and A. BAUMAN. "Mass Psychological Trauma and PTSD: Epidemic or Cultural Illusion?" Pages 319–36 in *Cross Cultural Assessment of Psychological Trauma and PTSD.* Edited by J. Wilson and C. C. So-Kum Tang. New York: Springer, 2007.

SMITH-CHRISTOPHER, D. "Jeremiah as Prophet of Nonviolent Resistance." *JSOT* 43 (1989): 95–107.

—. "Ezekiel on Fanon's Couch: A Postcolonist Critique in Dialogue with David Halperin's Seeking Ezekiel." Pages 108–44 in *Peace and Justice Shall Embrace.* Edited by T. Grumsrud and L. Johns. Telford, Pa.: Pandora, 1999.

SOUTHWOOD, K. *Ethnicity and the Mixed Marriage Crisis in Ezra 9–10: An Anthropological Approach.* New York: Oxford University Press, 2012.

SUMMERFIELD, D. "A Critique of Seven Assumptions Behind Psychological Trauma Programmes in War-Affected Areas." *Social Science and Medicine* 48 (1999): 1449–62.

TURNER, S., and C. GORST-UNSWORTH. "Psychological Sequelae of Torture: A Descriptive Model." *British Journal of Psychiatry* 157 (1990): 475–80.

USSISHKIN, D. "The Destruction of Lachish by Sennacherib and the Dating of the Royal Judean Storage Jars." *Tel Aviv* 4 (1977): 28–60.

VOLKAN, V. *Blood Lines: From Ethnic Pride to Ethnic Terrorism.* New York: Farrar, Straus & Giroux, 1997.

WOLFF, H. *Micah: A Commentary.* Minneapolis: Augsburg Fortress, 1990.

YOUNGER, K. L. "The Deportations of the Israelites." *Journal of Biblical Literature* 117 (1998): 201–27.

Andreas Mehl

Individual and Collective Psychiatric Traumas in Ancient Historiographical Literature*

Abstract

The essay assesses criteria for identifying traumas in ancient historical narratives. First it defines, explains and discusses individual and collective psychiatric trauma following today's psychologists and psychiatrists, and their associations. Then it deals with ancient historiography (including historical biography). On the one hand this genre may remind its readers of traumas from a more remote past, and on the other hand since contemporary history is a large and perhaps the most important part of Greek and Roman historiography, it may give fresh impressions of actual traumas. As a prominent example, a discussion is presented of Tacitus and his co-senators' attitude and feeling as victims, but eventually also as culprits during the Roman principate. A few further instances of ancient collective traumas, and additionally of situations that might seem to be, but do not qualify as traumas, are added from other works of ancient Greek and Roman historiography and related genres.

1. Introduction

In his first literary work, the biography of his father-in-law Gnaeus Iulius Agricola, a Roman senator and for a few years the governor of Roman Britain, (Publius) Cornelius Tacitus—himself a Roman senator, too, and in the year before he wrote this biography even a consul—discusses and complains bitterly about the conditions under which the members of the traditional Roman ruling class live during the reign of the emperors. As Tacitus demon-

* The paper (and in particular its second section) could not have been written without the help of Prof. Dr. Ursula Gast, a psychiatrist specializing in research on psychiatric trauma, and its language would be clumsy without the help of my colleague and friend G. H. R. Horsley (University of New England at Armidale, NSW, Australia). – The author became aware of Toner, *Roman Disasters*, only after the manuscript had been written. Toner's definition of 'disaster' (1-16) is of course much wider than the definition of psychiatric trauma or post-traumatic stress disorder, but indeed Toner deals also with "The Psychological Impact" (ninth chapter: 153-70), post-traumatic stress disorder included, and he stresses the fundamental difference between modern and ancient patterns of how to interpret human behaviour.

strates by giving some examples, Roman senators are at threat of being killed by the emperor or compelled to kill themselves, if they have made achievements in policy and warfare which could eclipse the fame of the emperor. Even those senators who praise the achievements of another senator are threatened by violent or enforced death. This is the background of Agricola's life under the tyranny of the emperor Domitian (A.D. 79–96), as Tacitus portrays it. It is the background, too, of Tacitus himself who began his career under Vespasian and continued it under Titus and Domitian and who, as a member of the Roman ruling class, has witnessed his father's-in-law fate but been silent about it, describing it only after Domitian has been murdered and the elderly new emperor Nerva (96–98) and his successor Trajan (98–117) grant or seem to grant more liberty, in particular freedom of speech.[1]

Does Tacitus describe a situation of trauma here? Are there further descriptions of traumas in ancient historical narratives? The essay will deal first with individual and collective psychiatric trauma, or more precisely with post-traumatic stress disorder as it is defined, explained, and discussed by today's psychologists and psychiatrists and may be used by historians in their interpretations of historical persons, events and situations. Then the paper will return to Tacitus and his co-senators' attitudes and feelings both as victims and eventually also as culprits within the Roman imperial system, the principate. A few further instances of traumas, including situations that might seem to be, but actually are not traumas, will be added from works of ancient Greek and Roman historiography and from biographies of statesmen.[2] The author has chosen ancient historiography and political biography for his argument, because on the one hand both these literary genres may remind their readers of traumas of a more remote past, and on the other hand the writing of contemporary history may give direct and vivid impressions of actual traumas at the time of writing. Contemporary history is a justifiable focus here because it is a large and perhaps the most important part of Greek

1 Tacitus, *Agr.* 1–3 and 39–45. Cf. Ogilvie and Richmond, *Vita Agricolae* and Mehl, *Historiography*, 136–37, 141–44 and 150; and for the date of the composition of the "Agricola" Flach, *Geschichtsschreibung*, 192–93: during Nerva's reign (A.D. 96–98), but the first and last chapters at the very beginning of Trajan's reign (98).

2 Greek and Roman literary authors separated biography from historiography because of the different interest of historians and biographers in using the historical material. Cf. Mehl, *Historiography*, 83 and 185. But as the historical material is for both very often the same, it seems sound to combine here historiography and biography. For the time of the early Roman emperors cf. Mehl, *Historiography*, 149 and 165. Regarding Tacitus, one should not forget that his "Agricola" is more than a mere biography, and that Tacitus only a few years later began to write historiographical works. Cf. Flach, *Geschichtsschreibung*, 190ff. and Mehl, *Historiography*, 136ff.

and Roman historiography, as far as we can judge from the works which have come down to us.[3]

2. Psychiatric Trauma / Traumatizing Events / Post-traumatic Stress Disorder: Psychologists / Psychiatrists, and Modern and Ancient Historians

In a widely-used German textbook a psychiatric trauma is defined as "the experience of a vital discrepancy between threatening factors of situations and the individual chances of coping with them. This experience is combined with the feeling of being helpless and of lacking any defence; and so it shakes severely and continuously the way the person sees him- or herself and the world."[4] The German "Guideline for the therapy of post-traumatic stress disorder (PTSD)," drawn up by a committee appointed by the leading German psychological and psychiatric societies and based on the "International classification of psychiatric diseases (ICD)" of the World Health Organization (WHO), is much more detailed in its definition of the burden of post-traumatic disorder.[5] It makes distinctions between many types of traumatic events and of post-traumatic disorders and it adds the remark that a person hit by a traumatic event may be traumatized as well as a person that has wit-

3 For another trauma to be found in ancient literature cf. the contribution of F. Ursin in this volume.

4 Fischer and Riedesser, *Lehrbuch*, 82: "… vitales Diskrepanzerlebnis zwischen bedrohlichen Situationsfaktoren und den individuellen Bewältigungsmöglichkeiten, das mit Gefühlen von Hilflosigkeit und schutzloser Preisgabe einhergeht und so eine dauerhafte Erschütterung von Selbst- und Weltverständnis bewirkt."

5 Flatten et al., "Leitlinie," 202 (cf. Deutsches Institut für Medizinische Dokumentation und Information, *ICD-10-GM* [GM = German Modification]): "Die Posttraumatische Belastungsstörung ist eine mögliche Folgereaktion eines oder mehrerer traumatischer Ereignisse (wie z.B. Erleben von körperlicher und sexualisierter Gewalt, auch in der Kindheit (sogenannter sexueller Missbrauch), Vergewaltigung, gewalttätige Angriffe auf die eigene Person, Entführung, Geiselnahme, Terroranschlag, Krieg, Kriegsgefangenschaft, politische Haft, Folterung, Gefangenschaft in einem Konzentrationslager, Natur- oder durch Menschen verursachte Katastrophen, Unfälle oder die Diagnose einer lebensbedrohlichen Krankheit), die an der eigenen Person, aber auch an fremden Personen erlebt werden können. In vielen Fällen kommt es zum Gefühl von Hilflosigkeit und durch das traumatische Erleben zu einer Erschütterung des Selbst- und Weltverständnisses.
Das syndromale Störungsbild ist geprägt durch:
- sich aufdrängende, belastende Gedanken und Erinnerungen an das Trauma (Intrusionen) oder Erinnerungslücken (Bilder, Alpträume, Flashbacks, partielle Amnesie),
- Übererregungssymptome (Schlafstörungen, Schreckhaftigkeit, vermehrte Reizbarkeit, Affektintoleranz, Konzentrationsstörungen)
- Vermeidungsverhalten (Vermeidung traumaassoziierter Stimuli) und
- emotionale Taubheit (allgemeiner Rückzug, Interessenverlust, innere Teilnahmslosigkeit)

nessed another person (who does not need to be a relative or a friend of the witness) being hit by a traumatic event and that symptoms of disorder may become manifest immediately after the traumatic event, but also after a delay of several years.

Today's historians may be still interested in individuals, especially in those 'big men' and now also in 'big women' who are said to make history, but much more they are interested in what groups of people do or suffer: social groups and classes and ethnic groups as tribes and nations as well. So a historian's central question is whether only individuals can be traumatized or also groups of people so that one can speak of a *collective* trauma. The short definition quoted and translated above seems to exclude the possibility of collective traumas, because it speaks of "*individual* chances of coping with" the traumatizing events or situations. However, the more detailed definition given in the "Guideline" widens the range of people who may be traumatized in such a way that the same event or situation may traumatize two and more persons: not only the individual who is hit by an event or situation, but also another who is affected by witnessing someone else being hit. But in regard to collective trauma this must be qualified. We may postulate that the same event or situation can traumatize a group of people insofar as all individuals in the group are impacted by the same event or situation or by witnessing it, and as each of them reacts to the traumatic event or situation in his or her feelings and behaviour in the same or a comparable way as the others. Consequently, a collective trauma would be the sum of equal or similar individual psychological dispositions and affections of the same traumatizing event or situation.

Indeed, not only non-specialists (these very frequently), but also psychologists and psychiatrists speak of "collective trauma."[6] However, the latter are aware that this concept is really problematic, because you cannot make a simple projection from individual trauma to collective trauma.[7] We may allow

- im Kindesalter teilweise veränderte Symptomausprägungen (z.B. Wiederholtes Durchspielen des traumatischen Erlebens, Verhaltensauffälligkeiten, z.T. Aggressive Verhaltensmuster)

Die Symptomatik kann unmittelbar oder auch mit (z.T. mehrjähriger) Verzögerung nach dem traumatischen Geschehen auftreten (verzögerte PTBS)."

6 One will find plenty of publications in research on antiquity in which the notion of trauma, both individual and collective, is used. However, this is done in different ways regarding modern psychological and psychiatric trauma-research, and very often 'trauma' is a very imprecise concept. The general bibliography in research of antiquity, the "Année Philologique," the electronic version of which was looked at on April 16, 2013 under http://www.annee-philologique.com (subscription access), enumerates 27 titles published between 1976 and 2010, but there will be more publications in which the use of 'trauma' is less obvious.

7 Cf. the slightly differing positions of A. Kühner, D. Becker, and H. Joas in Westhoff and Westhoff, *Wunden*, 2-4; and with very very detailed argument Kühner, "Traumata," 10-19.

that a group itself cannot be traumatized; but as hypothesized in the paragraph above, all or many members of a group can be struck by the same traumatizing event or situation and react in the same or similar way. In the informative radio discussion and commentary "Wunden der Völker" ("Wounds of Nations") H. Joas emphasizes that the concept of collective traumas is adequate "because some traumas are suffered not by an individual on his own, but by an individual in company with with other men." This is the case "especially when the whole social cohesion has been upset or even destroyed by the event."[8] Academics, historians included, will be convinced by this explanation and they will even say that Joas describes what for them is the central symptom of collective trauma. The following shorter definition of collective traumas as "events of violence which for a long time leave marks in the collective memory and so influence the behaviour of the society"[9] will also satisfy historians, especially because it combines collective trauma with collective memory, the latter being a central issue for any historical research.[10] For the therapy of collective post-traumatic stress disorder it is not sufficient to treat the traumatized individuals; collective measures have to be taken, because collective trauma is always in tension between individual trauma and collective memory.[11] One may sum up that "altogether, the concept of collective trauma is good for making us understand better social and political courses of events and in this way for explaining the behaviour of groups, nations or

8 H. Joas in Westhoff and Westhoff, *Wunden*, 3: "weil es doch so ist, dass manche Traumata eben nicht von einem vereinsamten Individuum erlitten werden, sondern von diesem Individuum zusammen mit anderen Menschen. Vor allem wenn ihr ganzer sozialer Zusammenhalt durch das Ereignis erschüttert worden ist oder vernichtet worden ist."

9 Westhoff and Westhoff, *Wunden*, 4: "Gewaltereignisse, die langfristig tiefe Spuren im kollektiven Gedächtnis hinterlassen und dadurch das Verhalten der betroffenen Gemeinschaft beeinflussen." In the Humanities the concept of "collective memory," established by Halbwachs, *Gedächtnis*, seems now to have been replaced by the concept of "cultural memory," which at least in Germany has been promoted by J. Assmann, *Gedächtnis* and in other of his publications, also those written together with his wife Aleida Assmann, or those written by her alone (cf. the contribution of F. Ursin in this volume). This development may have been influenced by the effect of Assmann's publications in a wider German speaking public. However, Joas in Westhoff and Westhoff, *Wunden*, 14–15 criticizes "cultural memory" as being undifferentiated and prefers "collective memory" ("kollektives Gedächtnis"). Kühner, "Traumata," 20 (who refers to Halbwachs, *Gedächtnis*), does the same, though on page 66 she refers to Assmann, *Gedächtnis*, esp. 50–52 and explains his differentiation between "communicative memory" (up to three or four generations) and "cultural memory" (long-time symbolic remembrance with a tendency to mythification of the remembered objects).

10 The topic has been dealt with in many publications of the last decade. For antiquity cf. only Walter, *Memoria*, who cites a lot of relevant literature, and Mehl, "How the Romans Recorded."

11 Kühner, "Traumata," 20ff.

states."[12] There are a lot of examples of collective traumas in modern times, and one will begin with the Shoah that has shaped the identity of today's Jews and the state of Israel, and one may add, e.g., post-Apartheid South Africa.[13] Reactions of post-Shoah Jews and Israelis show that such an experience and suffering can be transmitted to the next generation and perhaps to further generations. As a result, collective traumas can be 'inherited'.[14] Nonetheless there are two dangers in using the concept of collective trauma. As has been mentioned, non-specialists and general parlance have the tendency to broaden the concept of trauma so much that every misfortune can be called an individual or collective trauma. The other danger is political misuse: September 11, 2001 was a trauma for a large number of people, but it was not a collective trauma of the American nation, it only was styled in such a way by the Bush-administration especially for carrying through the war in Afghanistan (and then that in Iraq).[15] Consequently, to call September 11, 2001 "a traumatizing event of unique dimension in American history," as the historian K. Krakau does, is the result of being caught in the trap of the Bush-administration—a trap of a type that a psychiatrist or psychologist will in general better avoid than a historian relying on his documents. What the American government did with September 11, 2001, has not been the only political misuse of the concept of collective trauma. This is an additional reason why claims about societal trauma must be analyzed with extreme care by historians.

The concept of psychiatric trauma as it is defined in the literature quoted above might induce us to think that there is a clear distinction between those who suffer from a post-traumatic stress disorder that others, individuals as well as groups, have caused by their actions, and those others who cause trau-

12 Westhoff and Westhoff, *Wunden*, 5: "Der Begriff 'kollektives Trauma' ist also durchaus geeignet, gesellschaftliche und politische Vorgänge besser verständlich zu machen, und so das Verhalten von Gruppen, Völker oder Staaten zu erklären."

13 Also for the following text Westhoff and Westhoff, *Wunden*, 6ff. with more examples from our times and about the risk that events and situations are misused for political aims by defining them as collective traumas. In Westhoff and Westhoff, *Wunden*, 11–14 examples are discussed of 'therapies' for collective traumas, after the traumatizing situation—e.g., a dictatorial or totalitarian regime—has been removed. Cf. Kühner, "Traumata," 85ff.

14 Kühner, "Traumata," 45 calls this conveniently "a bridge between collective and individual trauma" ("Brücke zwischen kollektivem und individuellem Trauma").

15 Kühner, "Traumata," 131–36 for those traumatized by September 11, 2001 and above note 13. For the following text see Westhoff and Westhoff, *Wunden*, 9–11 with quotations of D. Becker and K. Krakau (quotation Krakau: "ein traumatisierendes Ereignis von einmaliger Dimension in der amerikanischen Geschichte"). For Kühner, "Traumata," 120 September 11, 2001 is "between traumatizing and exploiting it as a political instrument" ("zwischen Traumatisierung und politischer Instrumentalisierung"). Only a little bit more than one year after the event, in December 2002, Kühner, "Traumata," 121–22 differentiated groups of Americans traumatized by September 11, 2001 and symptoms of post-traumatic stress disorder; and she followed D. Becker, quoted in an interview given on another occasion, in assuming the political construction of a pan-US-trauma (ibid., 135–36).

mas in other persons but themselves do not suffer from a post-traumatic stress disorder. But this clear distinction between victims (the traumatized) and culprits (the traumatizing) is not expressed in the two definitions given above. Indeed, the wars mentioned here show a different scheme: the simple distinction between civilians as the traumatized and soldiers as the traumatizing, or between soldiers of one side as the traumatized and those of the other side as the traumatizing, does not work. Soldiers can be 'Opfer und Täter zugleich' ('victim and culprit at the same time'), and so both traumatized and traumatizing, and they can be both even in the same event and situation. One may deduce from this realization that there can be situations in which men suffer so severely from their own actions that they succumb to post-traumatic stress disorder. For a classicist the question arises if such situations have been perceived and described by ancient historians.

The history of the concept of trauma, both individual and collective, is quite short and it is connected with two wars:[16] the First World War and the American-Vietnamese War have shaped the idea that men belonging to certain groups have been (or, at least, may have been) affected severely by the same situation in the same way. Of course, one will not forget the impact of September 11, 2001 on the concept of collective trauma and its misuse, as mentioned above. Other modern—or perhaps more realistically—all modern wars may be added, the war-like present situation in Afghanistan included. However, becoming and being aware of psychiatric problems of soldiers and veterans did not mean that the cause for being traumatized was sought in external events and situations: the evidently pejorative German word "war-neurosis" ("Kriegsneurose") suggests what was widely thought in Germany about traumatized German World War I soldiers and veterans: that the cause for suffering from mental problems was at least partially internal, within the personalities of those soldiers and veterans. In the USA psychiatric trauma was generally accepted as a diagnosis only in 1980. The connection between the 'discovery' of trauma and war may obscure other factors that can produce traumas. Nonetheless, being aware of the fact that a significant aspect of history—in our own times no less than in others—is war, the historian will search for traumas especially in wars. In doing so, he will take into consideration two peculiarities. Before these will be dealt with, it is essential to be aware of a general difficulty in looking for psychiatric traumas in past times. It is difficult and sometimes even impossible to get a an idea about what a *physical* disease reported by an author of a past era is in terms of modern medicine. Thus, many theories have been developed about the so-called plague that struck Greece and especially Athens about 430 B.C. in the first years of the Peloponnesian War as reported by the Athenian Thucydides,

16 Westhoff and Westhoff, *Wunden*, 3, also for the following text.

who described not only what he became aware of in watching his ill compatriots and his own disease, but had also his own ideas in composing his portrayal of the Peloponnesian War and of Athens' fate in this war and besides, followed rhetorical conventions.[17] To define *psychiatric* symptoms, diseases and abnormalities is in any case even more difficult than to define somatic symptoms, diseases and abnormalities. So today's historian can do nothing but present and discuss those issues where he supposes that a traumatic event and a post-traumatic stress disorder was reported by an author who lived and wrote many centuries ago.

War can be both external and internal. Some of the most cruel and also long-lasting wars in history have been armed civil strifes. In antiquity one will remember the war between the citizens of Kerkyra (Korfu), reported by the first author of pure political history, Thucydides, and the hundred years of civil wars that put an end to the Roman republic and created the quasi-monarchy of the principate of Augustus and his successors, witnessed by several authors.[18] To distinguish between external and internal wars is of extreme importance, because this distinction was and may still be made today in several cultures in a very simple scheme: external wars are good *per se* or at least may be good, whereas civil wars are bad and disastrous *per se*. If this distinction is internalized, civil strife may be traumatic for those exposed to it, whereas external war cannot become traumatic for all its participants, but only for those for whom it ends in a military and political disaster, and perhaps only as long as the negative results of the defeat do exist. Ancient Greeks and even more Romans—one might say: all Romans—thought about external and internal war in precisely this way.

In ancient historical thought there are peculiarities that have to be considered in dealing with trauma. A common motif in ancient—but not only ancient—historiography is to praise individuals or groups for deeds which the author considers honest (in the moral sense) and useful (in the practical sense), and to criticize individuals or groups for deeds which the author thinks to be bad and useless or even damaging. Among ancient historians the

17 Thucydides, *Hist.* 2.48-54. In the rich literature on the plague as described by Thucydides cf. Bellemore and Plant, "Thucydides" and Morgan, "Plague."

18 Thucydides, *Hist.* 3.70-85. For some decades of the fourth century B.C. there was a tendency among the Greeks in the Aegean region to regard wars between Greek states as internal, i.e. civil wars, and attempts were made to put an end to them for all time by a general peace (*koiné eiréne*). Cf. Ryder, *Koine Eirene*, and Jehne, *Koine eirene*. For the Roman civil wars many sources tell about disastrous situations and events and their psychiatric impact on people. They cannot be enumerated here, but they can be found in any detailed narrative account of Roman history between 133 and about 30 B.C. as well as in histories of Roman literature. Especially in the works of some poets of the last decades of the Roman civil wars and of the early Augustan time, Horace, Virgil, and Propertius, one will find obvious echoes of those wars.

Roman Tacitus provides a clear statement of the moral task of the historian; nonetheless, he is only one among several examples:[19] "I think that the main task of historiography is that virtues should not be concealed, and that resulting from bad reputation in posterity there should be fear for wicked deeds and words." Patterns of moral historical judgement like that of Tacitus, or of more practical judgement as is to be found in the Greek Polybius (middle and second half of the 2d century B.C.), presuppose that any human action results from a practical intention and/or a moral position. On this condition alone an action and its effect can be ascribed to an individual or a defined number of individuals. But when we look again to the more detailed definition of post-traumatic stress disorder quoted above, we will find among the traumatizing events listed there not only intended actions of individuals or groups, but also events that happen among men by chance and even those that are caused not by men, but by nature: "disasters … caused by nature, accidents or the diagnosis of a life-threatening disease."[20] So a trauma does not necessarily result from intended deeds or from human actions at all; and consequently the traumatized person has not in each situation the chance of blaming an individual or a group for being traumatized, but in certain situations has to be content with the banal explanation that an accident or a coincidence of events has caused the trauma. Indeed, in spite of their pattern of moral praise and censure ancient historians included in their writings reports of natural disasters as plagues (in a wider sense), earthquakes and volcanic eruptions, the latter two common events in the Mediterranean. As is shown by Thucydides' report on the 'plague' and the younger Pliny's report on the eruption of the Vesuvius in A.D. 79 (written to his friend the historian Tacitus to be included in the latter's so-called "Histories"), ancient historians and their readers were intensely interested in psychological reactions of those deeply affected by natural disasters.[21]

From the point of view of modern historians, ancient historiography may seem all the same. Nonetheless, in the writings of ancient historians there is considerable variety in time, place, topic, philosophy of life, temperament, and style. This is relevant also for the question, to what extent ancient historians restrict themselves to the 'objective' level of events (devoted in most cases to power politics, but often also to social relations) or analyse the internal motivations of the individuals and groups they discuss. Indeed, a psychological interest by a historian is absolutely necessary for there to be any

19 Tacitus, *Ann.* 3.65: "… praecipuum munus annalium reor, ne virtutes sileantur utque pravis dictis factisque ex posteritate et infamia metus sit." Cf. Mehl, *Historiography*, 150; idem, "How the Romans Recorded," chapter "Examples, persons, and learning from the past."

20 Cf. above note 5: "Natur- … Katastrophen, Unfälle oder die Diagnose einer lebensbedrohlichen Krankheit."

21 For Thucydides cf. above with notes 17 and 18. Pliny the younger, *Ep.* 6.16 and 20.

chance of finding in his portrayals something that might be interpreted as a trauma. Here is not the place to discuss this question in detail; only a few hints can be given. Thucydides, known for his sober reports on events of power politics, actually includes views and judgements which reach down into deeply non-rational levels of human motivation. He does so not only when he narrates events outside politics like the famous plague mentioned above, but also when he deals with political situations like the civil war in Corcyra also mentioned above, or the Athenians' debate about the question how to treat the Mytileneans who had deserted from Athens but then had been reconquered, or the Athenians' expectations regarding their project of a war against Syracuse. Yet Thucydides deals with all these topics in an extremely intellectual, rational, and cool manner.[22] On the other hand, Tacitus is known for his psychological interpretations of the behaviour and the actions and reactions of Roman emperors, their wives and their opponents; and he has been both admired and criticized for this by modern historians and philologists.[23] A few historians of the 4th to 3d century B.C., inspired to some extent by Aristotle's theory of tragedy, have been labelled in modern research as the "tragic historians" and their works as "tragic historiography."[24] Phylarchus (3d century) notably sought to affect the soul of his readers in order to move the reader with devices he had adopted from tragedy, devices which he used wherever he believed that this was appropriate. In this way he portrayed the people (individuals as well as groups) with all manner of pathos, like the characters of a tragedy who do extraordinary deeds, suffer extreme fates and show their feelings openly. In consequence, one might hope to explore the extent to which the reactions and psychological dispositions of Phylarchus' historical persons are near to what modern men will subsume under the concept of psychiatric trauma. However, his way of dealing with the behaviour

22 Mytilene resp. Syracuse: Thucydides, *Hist.* 3.36–49 resp. 6.8–32.

23 Of course, psychology in ancient authors is far from the modern scientific discipline. For Tacitus cf. Cousin, "Rhetorik." Another author who has to be mentioned for his psychological interpretations of history, is Posidonius. Cf. Bringmann, "Geschichte." One has to be aware that in antiquity (and perhaps not only in that epoch) psychology was near on the one hand to ethics and on the other to rhetoric. Cf. Cousin, "Rhetorik" and Bringmann, "Geschichte." We might expect that psychology alone and in its relations to both morals and rhetoric is a topic which cannot be omitted in modern discussions of ancient historiography. Nonetheless, it is astonishing that—apart from the role of *psychagogia* (an ancient term and concept) as a means applied in writing history: Lendle, *Einführung*, 197–202 and 227; Scott Ryberg, "Innuendo"—nothing of it, or only cursory hints, appears in some new publications as, e.g., Feldherr, *Companion;* Marincola, *Historiography;* and Näf, *Geschichtsschreibung*. Psychology might be expected particularly in Näf's chapter, "Gestaltung von Geschichtswerken," p. 111–30, where he deals *inter alia* with rhetoric; but it contains no mention of psychology or *psychagogia*.

24 For the following discussion note also Ullman, "History"; Walbank, "Tragic History" and "History"; Flach, *Geschichtsschreibung*, vii and 42–52; Meister, *Geschichtsschreibung*, 95–102; Näf, *Geschichtsschreibung*, 122–23.

and the feelings of persons in extreme events as battles or conquests of towns seems to have become very quickly a literary *topos*. Unfortunately, only a tiny number of fragments of these "tragic historians'" is extant. We learn about their presentation of history mainly by the harsh criticisms written by Polybius, one of the 'rational' historians.[25] As a result, what we know about Phylarchus tells us something about his mental world, his predilection for trauma-like events included; but details of what he portrayed in his special way and their historical worth remain doubtful.

Thus, we may hope to find in ancient historiography situations which we may interpret as portrayals of traumatic events and situations and as post-traumatic stress disorder. Nonetheless, we have to be cautious: in looking for traumas in ancient historiography we have to be aware of the simple fact that the concept of trauma is modern and that in consequence we are looking for traumas before 'trauma'. On the other hand this may be even an advantage: we can be sure that no ancient historian has modelled the persons described by himself according to the modern definition of post-traumatic stress disorder, and thereby against historical truth. So from this point of view we may trust those writers. But there might be another problem with the trustworthiness of psychological, eventually trauma-like portrayals in ancient historiography. In the last paragraph the question has been put if ancient historians have been interested in the psychological dispositions of the characters of their reports. To the extent that this question can be answered in a positive way, we have to continue with another question: was interest in psyche and pathos the only reason why an ancient historian made his characters suffer more or less like the heroes of a tragedy? If it were, it would be dangerous for the veracity of psychological, historical reports, because such a historian might have been tempted to characterize his 'heroes' according to tragedy, but not conforming to what he found in documents and other sources and, as it were, to write in a very special sense 'virtual history'. This was indeed central to Polybius' criticisms of Phylarchus. So we should look for another motivation of ancient historians to describe psychological reactions and especially suffering of persons in their reports: A historian may have felt obliged to include in his report what he found in the works of earlier historians. This so-called 'Chronistenpflicht' ('duty of the chronicler') is occasionally mentioned in the writings of ancient historians; sometimes it includes informing the reader about diverging versions of the same event with or without a judgement of those versions and their authors.[26] Of course, this practice helps the reader to get trustworthy information about a more remote past only on the assumption that those earlier historians whose works are used by

25 Polybius, *Hist.* 2.56–63.

26 The first author known to have followed this principle was Herodotus, e.g., *Hist.* 7.152. Cf. Meister, *Geschichtsschreibung* 34 and 36.

the current writer have included in their works psychological portrayals, and that they have reported correctly what they themselves knew or had learned. Here another peculiarity of ancient historiography helps. As has been said above in §1, a large part of the ancient reports of 'grand' history, the history of empires, emperors, kings, and other important men of politics, was written as the history of contemporary events. The authors were members of the ruling classes and often hold high positions in their state. So they were part of the events both as objects and subjects of what happened. It follows that this may have induced an author of contemporary history to defend himself and to embellish his actions and positions against truth. In any case, those authors were affected themselves by the events and situations they described in their works. Indeed, one will not be astonished to find descriptions and diagnosis of all sorts of feelings and psychological reactions in portrayals of ancient contemporary history.

3. A Few Examples of Traumas and Alleged Traumas in Ancient Historiography; and Conclusions

We return now to the ancient text presented in the introduction. For Tacitus Agricola, other senators mentioned by him, and he himself are victims of the emperors as well as of a system, the Roman quasi-monarchy established more than hundred years earlier by Augustus, with all its deficiencies. According to Tacitus, a senator can do nothing to avoid the emperor's envy and hatred. Even the prudent Agricola becomes Domitian's victim: he does not receive the renown he deserves for his achievement in Britain, has to decline further administrative positions, and is perhaps murdered by the emperor. It is precisely the senators' feeling of helplessness that causes Tacitus' and, as one has to conclude from his words, also his co-senators' heavy pain, even after Domitian's tyranny has come to an end.[27] Indeed, it is typical for traumatized persons that their post-traumatic disorder does not end at all: when the traumatizing situation stops, its effects continue. Insofar as Tacitus and the other senators are silent witnesses to the emperor's misdeeds and do not oppose the emperor as the culprit, they all are a part of the system of suppression from which they suffer; and so they themselves are not only victims and witnesses but also culprits. In this way, the psychological disposition characterized by Tacitus shows several symptoms typical for people who have been trauma-

27 Tacitus' use of the plural in *Agr.* 2–3 is not a *pluralis auctoris* ('we' instead of 'I'), but as the context of these chapters and again of chapter 45 at the end of the work shows, Tacitus refers both to himself and his co-senators. The indecisiveness of Ogilvie and Richmond, *Vita Agricolae*, 131 (comment on "legimus" in *Agr.* 2.1) is not necessary. For the date of the composition of the *Agricola*, cf. above note 1.

tized. We may conclude that Tacitus describes both an individual trauma (his own) and, what is essentially identical with it, a collective trauma (that of the class of which he is a member).

Against this interpretation it may be suggested that Tacitus, in describing Domitian's and—in his later works—other emperors' behaviour and its impact on himself as well as on other senators, was not influenced so much by his own experience with Domitian as by works of historiography about earlier Roman emperors like Tiberius or Nero written by authors living one or more generations earlier which he may have read prior to writing the "Agricola."[28] Indeed, ancient authors, and especially historians, used older writers of their genre. Very often they did so silently; but by no means all of them depended slavishly on their predecessors. So a third possibility is possible to account for Tacitus' attitude. He may have felt personally what he wrote about Domitian, though he knew that roughly the same condition was described by earlier authors regarding the reigns and personalities of earlier emperors and used those descriptions in some way in his *Agricola* and, of course, later on in his portrayals of the Julio-Claudian (in his *Annals*) and the Flavian periods (in his *Histories*).[29] So the description Tacitus presented of his and of other senators' condition in his *Agricola*, needs not to be a literary *topos*. And as far as it is not a *topos*, it is indeed the description of a trauma and a post-traumatic stress disorder. For Tacitus it was also a long-lasting trauma: About twenty years after he wrote his *Agricola* he still thought about the specific risks faced by the members of Rome's ruling class under the reign of the emperors, and found no general solution for how a senator could behave without compromising himself by flattering the emperor and his family, and at the same time make his way as a senator and an officeholder in the service of the emperor. So he wonders why Marcus Lepidus, a Roman senator in the time of the emperor Tiberius, opposed Tiberius' flatterers yet nonetheless was held in high esteem by the emperor and enjoyed his sympathy and support. The case of Lepidus "makes me doubt if like anything else the emperors' affection for certain persons and their aversion to other persons is destined by fate and chance of birth or if there is something in our own decisions and it is possible to make one's way between harsh stubbornness and shameful submissiveness free from ambition and dangers."[30] So even in his

28 Some decades ago there was a discussion about this topic in German classical research between Urban, *Untersuchungen* and Flach, *Tacitus*. Cf. Mehl, *Historiography*, 141–42.

29 Besides the short Roman History written by Velleius Paterculus in the time of the emperor Tiberius, only sketchy fragments of the Roman historians of the time between Augustus and Tacitus, and little information about them and their works, have come down to us. Cf. Mehl, Historiography, 123 and 133ff.

30 Tacitus, *Ann.* 4.20.3: "unde dubitare cogor, fato et sorte nascendi ut cetera ita principum inclinatio in hos, offensio in illos, an sit aliquid in nostris consiliis liceatque inter abruptam contumaciam et deforme obsequium pergere iter ambitione et periculis vacuum."

older age Tacitus was preoccupied with a question of vital significance for himself personally, the answer to which would solve his central problem; but he had no answer, and so he—and, one may add, also his co-senators—remained in their traumatic condition.

Two other historical situations described by ancient historians and other authors with historical interest are more ambiguous and even quite doubtful in regard to the question whether they were traumatic or not. The Roman defeat against the invading Gauls near the small river Allia in the early 4th century B.C. gave the victorious warriors the chance of conquering, sacking, and burning the city of Rome. Consequently, even centuries later the anniversary of that battle was retained in the Roman mind as a "day of misfortune" ("dies ater"). However, we have to be cautious: as our sources were written centuries after the event, we do it know if it had already become such a portentous day for the Romans immediately or at least within a short time of their defeat.[31] The fact that the battle on the banks of the river Allia—together with its consequence for Rome—was not forgotten and was regarded as an extremely bad and sad day may have been caused by later disasters or at least dangerous events, all of which were connected with Gauls (or peoples believed by the Romans to be Gauls) invading Italy and more or less threatening Rome itself.[32] In the early 3d century the Romans fought against a coalition of the Italian tribes of the Samnites and Lucanians, Etruscan cities, and Gauls from North Italy. In the course of those events in 285 B.C. Gauls and Etruscans were defeated near the Lacus Vadimonicus (today Lago di Bassano) only about 100 kilometers north of Rome. Precisely 60 years later another invasion of Gauls defeated a Roman army near Clusium (modern Chiusi) about 160 kilometers north of Rome; their advance was stopped near Telamon (modern Talamone, on the Tyrrhenian coast between Grosseto and Orbetello) about 160 kilometers northwest of Rome. When only a few years later Hannibal between 218 and 216 defeated and even crushed large Roman armies in northern and central Italy in several battles, (including Cannae, another "dies ater" in Roman memory), and occupied a large part of Italy, many Gauls living in the valley of the river Po served in his army. Many Gauls were also in other Carthaginian armies coming to Italy in the later years of the second Punic War.[33] Finally, at the end of the 2d century B.C., within a few

31 Livy (time of Augustus), *Hist.* (*Ab urbe condita*) 5.36-39.1 and 6.1; Gellius (about A.D. 125/130), *Noct. att.* 5.17.2-5. The notion of "dies Alliensis" as such or as a "dies ater" was common: besides the two sources quoted here (in Livy see 6.1.28) cf. Varro, On the Latin Language, 6.32; Cicero, *Att.* 9.5; Virgil, *Aen.* 7.717; Lucanus, *Bell. civ.* (*Pharsalia*) 7.408-9; Tacitus, *Hist.* 2.91.

32 Bellen, "Metus Gallicus"; idem, *Grundzüge*, passim as well as other modern histories of Rome or the Roman republic.

33 For Gauls fighting on the side of Carthage in the second Punic War cf. Stark, "Kybele," 94-105: "Der metus Gallicus und die Bedeutung der Gallier im 2. Punischen Krieg" ("The

years the Germanic tribes of the Cimbri, Teutones, and Ambrones who were all considered by the contemporary Romans to be Gauls, defeated three Roman armies in the Eastern Alps and in the lower Rhone valley, before they were defeated by the Romans after the latter had made enormous preparations. One of these Roman defeats, fought near Arausio (modern Orange), in 105 with huge losses of Roman soldiers, was called a "dies ater" too. Thus, a "fear of the Gauls" ("metus Gallicus") could indeed arise among the Romans; and if it was not a trauma from the beginning, it must have become a trauma throughout the years given the continuing extremely bad experience the Romans had with the Gauls. As the "dies ater" of the battle on the river Allia was remembered by educated writers even in Roman imperial times, the question may be raised whether this constituted an, as it were, 'perpetual trauma'. However, at that time all the Gauls' territory on the continent had been conquered by the Romans and was since long split up into provinces of the Roman Empire, and so the Gauls were subjects to the Romans or even Roman citizens. So one we should interpret this later remembrance not as an expression of a traumatic stress disorder, but as the memory of something that long time before had been a trauma and was handed down by late Roman authors, simply because it was Roman history.

However, much earlier, in the year 200 B.C. the leading Roman politicians used—or misused—the fresh experience with Hannibal and the "metus Gallicus" to demonstrate that another enemy might invade Italy, trouble the Romans severely and even conquer the city of Rome. In this way they were successful in convincing the Roman citizens, who had just refused to make war against Philip V, to change their minds and declare war on the Macedonian king.[34] This special use of a trauma or trauma-like experience may be compared with the evident misuse of September 11, 2001 by George Bush junior.[35] Manipulations like those two may raise the question, not only whether traumas and trauma-like conditions were used or misused but also if such situations were invented for the sake of political goals. There is an obvious example in Greek history, if one compares historiography with works of other genres: In the late 5th century B.C., during the Peloponnesian War waged by Athens, Sparta and other Greek states, the famous orator Gorgias suggested in a public speech that the Greeks should not make war on each other, but unite and make war together against Persia.[36] Some decades later in the 4th century this became the program of Isocrates, the orator, teacher of rhetoric

metus Gallicus and the importance of the Gauls in the second Punic War"); Bellen, "Metus Gallicus."

34 Livy, *Hist.* (*Ab urbe condita*) 31.1ff., especially 6–8.

35 For the latter cf. above § 2.

36 Diels and Kranz, *Vorsokratiker*, Gorgias A 1 = Schirren and Zinsmaier, *Sophisten*, Gorgias Fr. 1 = Philostratos, *Vit. soph.* 1.9.1ff.

and author of political addresses. In several works stretching over four decades, he summoned the Greeks to unite against the Persians to avenge their attack on Greece (the mainland and the Aegean islands) and the destruction of cities like Athens in the early 5th century.[37] As he became aware very soon that the Greeks did not want to follow his idea, he turned to some princes outside the Greek democratic or oligarchic city states: to Euagoras the king of the Cypriot city-state of Salamis and the Macedonian king Philip II. The fact that the Greeks failed to react, and that in consequence Isocrates had to look to people in other regions of the Greek world, should have shown him that his proposal to avenge the misdeeds of the Persians over a century earlier did not move the Greeks at all—in modern terms, that the Greeks of his own days did not suffer from a post-traumatic stress disorder caused by the Persians. Indeed, what might have become a trauma was prevented from occurring because after only one year of Persian occupation of North and Central Greece the Greeks defeated the Persians in two famous battles, drove them from Greece, and even made counterattacks. Isocrates must have known that the two most important Greek authors to describe the so-called 'Persian' Wars did not show any sign of resentment against the Persians or hint at Greeks being traumatized by the Persians. These writers were Aeschylus (who himself had fought against the Persians) in his play "The Persians," written and performed only a few years after the events; and a few decades later the historian Herodotus in his "Histories." Consequently, Isocrates should—or even must—have been aware that he was fabricating a Greek resentment against the Persians and a Greek 'trauma' caused by them, which did not exist both in his time and had never existed previously.

To conclude briefly: on the one hand, ancient historians knew and portrayed situations and conditions which modern men will interpret as traumas and post-traumatic stress disorders. On the other hand, ancient historians described situations in which conditions that were or may have been traumatic were used or even misused by individual politicians or the ruling class for their own political ends. Other authors who were quite close to, or even active in politics, even fabricated historical or contemporary situations as traumatizing. The modern historian of antiquity doing research on the topic of trauma has to be aware of these diverging realities.

37 Isocrates, *Panegyricus* (380 B.C.), *Evagoras* (374/3), *Philippus* (346), Letter to Philip (344), and *Panathenaicus* (339). Cf. Bringmann, *Studien*. Much modern literature on this subject is listed at the end of the article Weibenberger, M. "Isokrates," 1142. See also the English version of this entry in Brill's *New Pauly*, and Markle, "Support."

Bibliography

Assmann, J. *Das kulturelle Gedächtnis: Schrift, Erinnerung und politische Identität in frühen Hochkulturen*. München: Beck, 1992.

Bellemore, J., and I. Plant. "Thucydides, Rhetoric, and the Plague in Athens." *Athenaeum* 82 (1994): 385–401.

Bellen, H. "Metus Gallicus – metus Punicus: Zum Furchtmotiv in der römischen Republik." *Akademie der Wissenschaften und der Literatur Mainz, Abhandlungen der geistes- und sozialwissenschaftlichen Klasse* 3. Stuttgart: Steiner, 1985.

—. *Von der Königszeit bis zum Übergang der Republik in den Prinzipat*. Vol. 1 of *Grundzüge der römischen Geschichte*. 2d ed. Darmstadt: Wiss. Buchgesellschaft, 1995.

Bringmann, K. *Studien zu den politischen Ideen des Isokrates*. Göttingen: Vandenhoeck & Ruprecht, 1965.

—. "Geschichte und Psychologie bei Poseidonios." Pages 29–66 in *Aspects de la philosophie hellénistique*. Edited by H. Flashar and H.Vandoeuvres. Geneva: Fondation Hardt, 1986.

Cousin, J. "Rhetorik und Psychologie bei Tacitus." Pages 104–29 in *Tacitus*. Edited by V. Pöschl. 2d ed. Darmstadt: Wiss. Buchgesellschaft, 1986. Translation of "Rhétorique et psychologie chez Tacite." *Revue des Études Latines* 29 (1951): 228–47.

Deutsches Institut für Medizinische Dokumentation und Information, *ICD-10-GM Version 2010*. Cited 17 February 2014. Online: http://www.dimdi.de/dynamic/de/klassi/downloadcenter/icd-10-gm/vorgaenger/version2010/.

Diels, H., and W. Kranz. *Die Fragmente der Vorsokratiker*. 2 vols. 6d ed. Berlin: Weidmann, 1952.

Feldherr, A., ed. *The Cambridge Companion to the Roman Historians*. Cambridge: University Press, 2009.

Fischer, G., and P. Riedesser. *Lehrbuch der Psychotraumatologie*. 3d ed. Munich: Reinhardt, 2003.

Flach, D. *Tacitus in der Tradition der antiken Geschichtsschreibung*. Göttingen: Vandenhoeck & Ruprecht, 1971.

—. *Römische Geschichtsschreibung*. 3d revised ed. Darmstadt: Wiss. Buchgesellschaft, 1998.

Flatten, G. et al. "S3-Leitlinie Posttraumatische Belastungsstörung." *Trauma & Gewalt* 3 (2011): 202–10.

Halbwachs, M. *Das kollektive Gedächtnis*. Stuttgart: Enke, 1967 (reprinted in later years: Frankfurt/Main: Fischer).

Jehne, M. *Koine eirene: Untersuchungen zu den Befriedungs- und Stabilisierungsbemühungen in der griechischen Poliswelt des 4. Jahrhunderts v. Chr.* Stuttgart: Steiner, 1994.

Kühner, A. "Kollektive Traumata: Annahmen, Argumente, Konzepte; Eine Bestandsaufnahme nach dem 11. September." *Berghof Report* 9 (December 2002). 152 pages. Cited 17 February 2014. Online. http://www.berghof-conflictresearch.org/documents/publications/br9d.pdf.

Lendle, O. *Einführung in die griechische Geschichtsschreibung: Von Hekataios bis Zosimos*. Darmstadt: Wiss. Buchgesellschaft, 1992.

Marincola, J., ed. *Greek and Roman Historiography*. Oxford: University Press, 2011.

Markle III, M. M. "Support of Athenian Intellectuals for Philip: A Study of Isocrates' *Philippus* and Speusippus' *Letter to Philip*." *Journal of Hellenic Studies* 96 (1976): 80–99.

Mehl, A. *Roman Historiography: An Introduction to its Basic Aspects and Development*. Translated by H.-F. Mueller. Malden, Mass.: Wiley-Blackwell, 2011. Translation of *Römische Geschichtsschreibung*. Stuttgart: Kohlhammer, 2001.

—. "How the Romans Recorded, Remembered, Thought About, and Used Their Past." Pages 256–75 in *Thinking, Recording, and Writing History in the Ancient* World. Edited by K. Raaflaub. Malden, Mass.: Wiley-Blackwell, 2013.

Meister, K. *Die griechische Geschichtsschreibung: Von den Anfängen bis zum Hellenismus*. Stuttgart: Kohlhammer, 1990.

Morgan, T. "Plague or Poetry? Thucydides on the Epidemic at Athens." *Transactions and Proceedings of the American Philological Association* 124 (1994): 197-209.

Näf, B. *Antike Geschichtsschreibung: Form - Leistung - Wirkung*. Stuttgart: Kohlhammer, 2010.

Ogilvie, R., and I. Richmond. *Cornelii Taciti de vita Agricolae*. Oxford: Clarendon, 1967.

Ryder, T. T. B. *Koine Eirene*. Oxford: Oxford University Press, 1965.

Schirren, T., and T. Zinsmaier. *Die Sophisten: Ausgewählte Texte; Griechisch/Deutsch*. Stuttgart: Reclam, 2003.

Scott Ryberg, I. "Tacitus' Art of Innuendo." *Transactions and Proceedings of the American Philological Association* 73 (1942): 383-404.

Stark, I. "Kybele als keltische Göttin: Zur Aufnahme der Kybele von Pessinus als Mater Magna unter die römischen Staatsgötter 205/204 v. Chr." *Klio* 89 (2007): 67-117.

Toner, J. *Roman Disasters*. Malden: Polity Press, 2013.

Ullman, B. L. "History and Tragedy." *Transactions and Proceedings of the American Philological Association* 73 (1942): 25-53.

Urban, R. "Historische Untersuchungen zum Domitianbild des Tacitus." PhD. Diss., Munich, 1971.

Walbank, F. W. "Tragic History: A Reconsideration." *Bulletin of the Institute of Classical Studies of the University of London* 2 (1955): 4-14.

—. "History and Tragedy." *Historia* 9 (1960): 216-34.

Walter, U. *Memoria und res publica: Zur Geschichtskultur im republikanischen Rom*. Frankfurt/Main: Verlag Antike, 2004.

Weibenberger, M. "Isokrates." Pages 1138-43 in vol. 5 of *Der Neue Pauly: Enzyklopädie der Antike*. Edited by H. Canciz et al. Stuttgart: Metzler, 1998.

Westhoff, A., and J. Westhoff. "Wunden der Völker: Das Phänomen 'kollektives Trauma.'" *Deutschlandradio Kultur. Forschung und Gesellschaft* (11 October 2007). 15 Pages. Cited 17 February 2014. Online: http://www.deutschlandradiokultur.de/wunden-der-voelker.1088.de.html?dram:article_id=176525.

Alexandra Eckert

Remembering Cultural Trauma

Sulla's Proscriptions, Roman Responses, and Christian Perspectives

Abstract

This paper explores the traumatic nature of Sulla's proscriptions as the first legalized massacre in Roman history directed at the members of the Roman elite and the profound repercussions the proscriptions of 82/81 B.C.E. produced in antiquity. I will first focus on theoretical aspects by introducing Jeffrey C. Alexander's sociological concept of cultural trauma and relating it to the theory of cultural memory developed by Aleida and Jan Assmann. The second part of my paper will discuss the memory of Sulla's proscriptions in the context of cultural trauma and elaborate on how incorporating the proscriptions into Roman cultural memory was governed by 'the principle of normative inversion' (Jan Assmann). I will conclude by examining the way Christian authors utilized the cruelty of Sulla's proscriptions to prove the superiority of a clement Christian society.

1. Sulla's Proscriptions and Their Historical Context

On November 1st 82 B.C.E., Lucius Cornelius Sulla defeated his enemies in the battle at the Colline Gate and thus remained victorious in the civil war.[1] Shortly thereafter, he established a device hitherto unheard of in Roman history. In order to eliminate his political enemies in Rome and Italy, he introduced the proscriptions.[2] The names of proscribed persons were inscribed on public lists in the forum in Rome. Anyone whose name appeared on these lists was outlawed, condemned to death, and his property was confiscated. Wives of proscribed men were deprived of their endowment, their children lost their inheritance and their political rights. Sulla granted immunity to

1 Velleius, *Hist.* 2.27.1.

2 For a detailed study on Sulla's proscriptions cf. Hinard, *Proscriptions*. For the beginning of the proscriptions see: Heftner, "Sullas Proskriptionen," 33–52 who refutes Hinard's position that the proscriptions began immediately after Sulla's victory at the Colline Gate on November 1st, 82 B.C.E. and argues for a beginning later in November or early December 82 B.C.E.

anyone killing a proscribed person, rewarded an extraordinary amount of money for the cruel deed and proclaimed the death penalty for anyone supporting a proscribed man. The property of proscribed Romans was sold in public auctions in the forum far below its true value. Soon, Sulla did not confine himself to proscribing political enemies, but proscribed many Romans purely to please his followers or to confiscate their property. The majority of the Romans lived in an atmosphere of constant fear.[3] Even the official end of the proscriptions on June 1st 81 B.C.E., as defined in Sulla's law on the proscriptions,[4] did not end the terror. Cicero's famous speech *Pro Sex. Roscio Amerino* shows that even after June 1st 81 B.C.E., the names of Roman citizens were added to the proscription lists so that Sulla's supporters could seize their property for a fraction of its true value.[5] At the end of these months of terror the death toll of Sulla's proscriptions, as recorded in Rome's public archives, amounted to 4,700 Romans.[6]

In this paper, my chief goal is to examine the traumatic nature of this legalized form of mass murder and its long-term consequences on Roman society.

First, I will introduce Jeffrey C. Alexander's concept of cultural trauma as a theoretical foundation for further analysis. Alexander's key observation is that events that inevitably induce trauma in many individuals do not necessarily traumatize societies at large. According to Alexander, a socially mediated process is an essential prerequisite for cultural trauma.[7]

Detailing the close relation between Alexander's concept of cultural trauma and Aleida and Jan Assmann's theory of cultural memory forms the basis for the second part of my paper. Here I investigate how Sulla's proscriptions were established as cultural trauma in Roman society and finally became incorporated into Roman cultural memory. I will demonstrate that the concept of "normative inversion," first described by Jan Assmann, governed the memory of Sulla's proscriptions for many centuries.[8] I will conclude by examining

3 Plutarch, *Sull.* 31.4.

4 Cicero, *Rosc. Amer.* 126; 128. Cf. Kunkel, *Staatsordnung*, 707. Vervaet, "Lex Valeria," 21.

5 Cicero, *Rosc. Amer.* 6; 80–81; 93.

6 Valerius Maximus 9.2.1.

7 Alexander, "Toward Cultural Trauma," 1–30. This paper was republished in a slightly revised version in 2011: Alexander, "Cultural Trauma," 6–30. For case studies of Alexander's theory of cultural trauma see the individual papers in Alexander, *Cultural Trauma and Collective Identity* as well as the papers in Eyerman, *Narrating Trauma*, a collection of essays discussing the concept of cultural trauma for a wide range of horrendous events in modern societies.

8 For a more detailed discussion of the close relationship between cultural trauma, cultural memory, and normative inversion see my PhD thesis: Eckert, "Kulturelles Gedächtnis und die antike Erinnerung an Lucius Cornelius Sulla." My PhD thesis examines the memory of Sulla from the 1st century B.C.E. to the 3d century C.E. from the perspective of Aleida and Jan Assmann's theory of cultural memory.

how "normative inversion" illuminates Christian reinterpretations of Sulla's proscriptions in the 5th century C.E.

2. Jeffrey C. Alexander's Concept of Cultural Trauma

In his innovative essay "Toward a Theory of Cultural Trauma" Jeffrey C. Alexander, Professor of Sociology at Yale University, describes cultural trauma as follows:

> Cultural trauma occurs when members of a collectivity feel they have been subjected to a horrendous event that leaves indelible marks upon their group consciousness, marking their memories forever and changing their future identity in fundamental and irrevocable ways.[9]

> This identity revision means that there will be a searching re-remembering of the collective past, for memory is not only social and fluid, but deeply connected to the contemporary sense of the self.[10]

Alexander accentuates the fundamental distinction between individual trauma affecting many members of a society and cultural trauma affecting a society at large. Whenever human beings are exposed to a horrendous event, they may experience individual trauma. Thus, trauma on an individual level is a consequence of the event itself. However, a horrendous event, even if it has individually traumatized many members of a society, is not inherently traumatic on a collective level. At the collective level, a socially mediated process must occur for a horrendous event to cause cultural trauma. Once the social process of cultural trauma has concluded, those who were not personally exposed to the horrendous event will acknowledge the traumatic nature of the event and its relevance for the society at large, and will feel personally involved in—and accept responsibility for—overcoming its consequences.

In emphasizing the difference between individual and collective trauma, Alexander explicitly rejects the notion that a traumatic event induces dissociation and latency on a collective level.[11] These phenomena are observed in traumatized individuals, and describe mechanisms protecting the individual's psyche from the devastating consequences of consciously remembering a traumatic event. Dissociation and latency encompass the process of separat-

9 Alexander, "Toward Cultural Trauma," 1.

10 Ibid., 22.

11 In particular, Alexander criticizes Cathy Caruth's psychoanalytical approach, who utilizes Freud's work on individual trauma when applying concepts of individual trauma on a collective level. See Alexander, "Toward Cultural Trauma," 6f. on Cathy Caruth's work. Alexander calls these approaches "psychoanalytic thinking." See Alexander, "Toward Cultural Trauma," 5–8.

ing a traumatic event from the conscious self of the traumatized individual and repressing the memory to the subconscious. It is widely acknowledged in psychiatry and psychotherapy that individual trauma and latency-induced suffering can be overcome by remembering the traumatic event in a safe environment. However, as Alexander states, dissociation, latency, and the effect of healing trauma through remembering cannot be transferred from an individual to a collective level. On the contrary, he emphasizes that a society at large cannot *be* traumatized, but can only *feel* traumatized after experiencing different stages of a social process of cultural trauma.

Whenever a horrendous event leaves members of a society individually traumatized, the initial stage of a corresponding "process of cultural trauma" involves so called "carrier groups," i.e. individuals who recognize the importance of the traumatic event for the society at large. Members of carrier groups may have experienced individual trauma themselves by being exposed to the horrendous event in question. Individuals who have not been directly traumatized, yet recognize the social, economic, legal, or moral significance of the horrendous event, may also form carrier groups. The overarching objective of carrier groups is to raise public awareness of the significance of the traumatic event to such an extent that the vast majority of a society accepts that coping with the horrendous event is not merely an individual, but a collective responsibility.

As Alexander points out, a key factor for raising awareness for the existence of a traumatic event on the collective level is what he calls the "creation of a master narrative," i.e. a convincing and compelling description of the traumatic event and its effects on the individual as well as on the collective level. As such, a "master narrative" must clearly depict the nature of the traumatic event, the effects it had on the persons directly exposed to it, the victims, and how it affected the society as a whole. In addition to the key elements of the "master narrative" just outlined, Alexander emphasizes the relevance of clearly attributing responsibility for a traumatic event, or in other words, to openly name the perpetrators.

Once the master narrative has been established, the next stage of the social process of cultural trauma is to start a "working through" of the traumatic event in "institutional arenas." Alexander names religious, aesthetic, legal, political, and scientific arenas and emphasizes that mass media and state bureaucracy represent particularly important arenas for modern societies. Experiencing trauma on a collective level can be understood "as a sociological process that defines a painful injury to the collectivity, establishes the victim, attributes responsibility and distributes the ideal and material consequences."[12]

12 Alexander, "Toward Cultural Trauma," 22.

Continually re-remembering a traumatic event, thus integrating it into collective identity, constitutes the final stage of Alexander's social process of cultural trauma. Hence, cultural trauma revises cultural identity.

3. Cultural Trauma and Cultural Memory

Recollecting the past and cultural identity are not only integral to Alexander's social theory of cultural trauma, they are also cornerstones in Aleida and Jan Assmann's theory of cultural memory. In their pioneering essay "Collective memory and cultural identity," published in 1988, Aleida and Jan Assmann define cultural memory as follows:

> Cultural memory encompasses the body of permanently re-enacted texts, images and rites specific to each society and epoch that is maintained to stabilize and reflect the self-perception of a society. This body of permanently re-enacted texts, images and rites represents a society's collective knowledge, primarily (but not exclusively) of the past, conveying a society's common understanding of unity and originality.[13]

First, it is important to observe the close correspondence between Alexander's "searching re-remembering of a collective past" and Aleida and Jan Assmanns' "set of permanently re-enacted texts, images and rites specific to each society" representing "a society's collective knowledge … of the past." Based on this analogy, it may be concluded that Alexander's integration of a cultural trauma into the cultural identity of a society by "searching re-remembering of the collective past" can also be understood as integration of a cultural trauma into a society's cultural memory.

Because of this close relation, combining Alexander's theory of cultural trauma and Aleida and Jan Assmann's theory of cultural memory provides a

13 Translation by Alexandra Eckert; for the German text see Assmann, "Kollektives Gedächtnis," 15: "Unter dem Begriff des kulturellen Gedächtnisses fassen wir den jeder Gesellschaft und jeder Epoche eigentümlichen Bestand an Wiedergebrauchs-Texten, -Bildern und -Riten zusammen, in deren Pflege sie ihr Selbstbild stabilisiert und vermittelt, ein kollektiv geteiltes Wissen, vorzugsweise (aber nicht ausschließlich) über die Vergangenheit, auf das eine Gruppe ihr Bewusstsein von Einheit und Eigenart stützt." Jan Assmann's essay was published in English in 1995: Assmann, "Collective Memory," 125–33 (trans. John Czaplicka). John Czaplicka's translation of Aleida and Jan Assmann's definition of cultural memory reads as follows (see p. 132): "The concept of cultural memory comprises that body of reusable texts, images, and rituals specific to each society in each epoch, whose ‚cultivation' serves to stabilize and convey that society's self-image. Upon such collective knowledge, for the most part (but not exclusively) of the past, each group bases its awareness of unity and particularity." For a broader discussion of the concept of cultural memory see: Assmann, A. *Cultural Memory and Western Civilization*; Assmann, J. *Cultural Memory and Early Civilization*. Erll, *Memory in Culture*, provides a comprehensive overview in English on Aleida and Jan Assmann's work on cultural memory.

solid foundation for my analysis on how Sulla's proscriptions were established as cultural trauma in Roman society and finally incorporated into Roman cultural memory.

4. Sulla's Proscriptions as a Cultural Trauma for the Romans

Several factors contribute to classifying Sulla's proscriptions as a horrendous and traumatic event for Roman society under Alexander's criteria. The high death toll among the members of the Roman elite—4,700 proscribed Roman citizens—as well as the circumstances of their deaths—namely: publication of their names in the forum, public homicide, and public auctions of their confiscated property—created enormous visibility for Sulla's proscriptions. Moreover, the legalized murder of proscribed Roman citizens did not just individually traumatize many family members and friends; it also affected countless other Romans, irrespective of their social status, who were eyewitnesses to the cruelty of the assassinations. In addition, the atmosphere of terror in Rome and Italy, provoked by the horrors of the homicides and the arbitrary extension of the proscription lists, contributed significantly to the traumatic nature of Sulla's proscriptions.

Though the horrifying atmosphere did not necessarily induce individual trauma for all Romans, it definitely promoted awareness for Sulla's proscriptions in Roman society and stimulated the formation of carrier groups that initiated the "social process of cultural trauma." Those carrier groups aimed for general acceptance of the grave consequences of Sulla's proscriptions for Roman society at large. Hence, they also lobbied for a collective effort by a vast majority of the Romans to cope with them. A notable carrier group consisted of the children of the proscribed, who had not only lost their inheritance, but also their political rights, in particular the right to run for public office. Even though they remained influential as members of renowned Roman families, more than 30 years had to pass until Caesar restored their rights in 49 B.C.E.[14]

Various other activities in political and legal arenas proved successful much earlier, indicating a high degree of public awareness and the efficiency of the carrier groups' lobbying. Cicero openly addressed the injustice and cruelty of arbitrary proscriptions and public auctions of confiscated property far below its true value in his famous speech for Sextus Roscius of Ameria as early as 80 B.C.E., when Sulla still held office as dictator. Sextus' father had been proscribed after the official terminal date, June 1st 81 B.C.E., by Chrysogonus, one of Sulla's most influential partisans. And indeed, Cicero pre-

14 Plutarch, *Caes.* 37.1; Cassius Dio, *Hist.* 44.47.4.

vailed in court.[15] Just two years later, while Sulla was still alive, the consul Lepidus openly declared that he would repeal Sullan measures and restore the confiscated estates to their lawful owners, but could not realize his plans.[16]

A decade later, in 70 and 69 B.C.E., the successful trial against Sulla's supporter Verres[17] and the expulsion of many Sullan partisans from the Roman senate indicated substantial progress in rescinding the effects of Sulla's proscriptions.[18] The following years between 68 and 60 B.C.E. saw key decisions in the legal arena. In several exceptional court judgments, former supporters of Sulla were sentenced to return the money they had been rewarded for killing proscribed Roman citizens. Even more spectacular were subsequent court decisions to convict the very same persons of homicide, irrespective of the immunity Sulla's law on the proscriptions had granted them. Plutarch illustrates the importance of these court decisions by pointing out that prosecuting Sulla's partisans and sentencing them to death signified far more for many Romans—namely: prosecuting and sentencing to death Sulla himself, the man responsible for the proscriptions.[19]

Without doubt, the rapid and determined legal action during these years benefitted from the Roman state archives having recorded the names of both assassins and proscribed Romans.[20] Openly naming perpetrators and victims, the state archives thus provided an official "master narrative" of Sulla's proscriptions.

The understanding of Sulla's proscriptions as cultural trauma, and their integration into Roman cultural identity, is illustrated by the testimony of Valerius Maximus, who flourished in the reign of emperor Tiberius in the first half of the 1st century C.E. In his *Memorable Deeds and Sayings*, a collection of educational *exempla* characterizing various forms of acceptable and despicable human behavior, Valerius Maximus unequivocally condemns Sulla's proscriptions as violating essential values of Roman society.[21] Valerius Maximus concisely summarizes the cruelty of Sulla's crimes, providing a succinct master narrative of Sulla's proscriptions.

15 See Cicero's speech for S. Roscius of Ameria.
16 Granius Licinianus 36.35–36 (Criniti); Florus 2.11.3.
17 See Cicero's speeches against Verres.
18 Asconius 84C (Clark); Cassius Dio, *Hist.* 37.30.4.
19 Plutarch, *Cat. Min.* 17.5.
20 Appian, *Bell. civ.* 4.11; Cassius Dio, *Hist.* 47.6.4.
21 Valerius Maximus 9.2.1.

5. The Proscriptions and Jan Assmann's Concept of "Normative Inversion"

Drawing on the aforementioned analogy between incorporating cultural trauma into a society's cultural identity (Alexander) and integrating a horrendous event into a society's cultural memory (A. and J. Assmann), Valerius Maximus' account of the cultural trauma of Sulla's proscriptions as part of Roman cultural memory illustrates another important purpose of remembering the past. Valerius Maximus does not merely describe the cruelty of Sulla's proscriptions, but also compares Sulla's cruelty with that of Rome's archenemy Hannibal. It is tempting to interpret the integration of the cruelty of Sulla's proscriptions into Roman cultural memory and the comparison with a foreign enemy as an example of "normative inversion."

The term "normative inversion" was coined by Jan Assmann in his book *Moses the Egyptian*,[22] in which the author discusses the formation, transmission and transformation of the memory of the Exodus from Jewish and non-Jewish perspectives.[23] Assmann argues that normative inversion can be observed whenever a society distinguishes its own cultural identity by continually remembering a severe violation of its fundamental values committed by members of a foreign society. In Assmann's words, continually remembering such a violation of values serves the purpose of "contra-distinctive self-definition."[24] Contra-distinctive self-definition can be understood as accentuating a society's own cultural identity by inter-cultural distinction, i.e. distinction with respect to a foreign society. Here, remembering an alien and abominable violation of a society's values attributed to members of a foreign society serves as a counter-example for cultural identity and elucidates what

22 Assmann, *Moses*. For the significance of normative inversion see 23–54 and 216f. For a discussion of Assmann's book see Schraten, *Jan Assmann*, 104–6.

23 It is important to note that Jan Assman explicitly applies Sigmund Freud's concepts of latency and repression for individual trauma to explain collective phenomena. Assmann tries to demonstrate how the 17 years of monotheistic religion in Egypt during the rule of pharaoh Akhnaton in the 14th century B.C.E. caused traumatic effects for Egyptian society. In particular, Assmann argues for latency and repression in the Egyptian society at large as a consequence of the 17-year interlude of monotheistic religion and discusses how collective latency and repression played an important role in the formation of the memory of the Jewish Exodus. Cf. esp. Jan Assmann's concluding remarks in Assmann, *Moses*, 215-18. For a similar use of latency and repression on a collective level cf. Asssmann, "Monotheismus," 227-44 and Assmann, *Religion und kulturelles Gedächtnis*, 62-80. While I follow Jan Assmann's arguments regarding his concepts of cultural memory and normative inversion, I would suggest that not Sigmund Freud's concepts of latency and repression, but Jeffrey C. Alexander's concept of cultural trauma should be considered when investigating traumatic effects for societies at large. In his paper "Toward Cultural Trauma" Alexander has convincingly demonstrated that latency and repression cannot be applied on a collective level. Cf. section 2 of this paper.

24 Assmann, *Moses*, 216.

shall never be accepted as part of said society's own cultural identity. Assmann convincingly demonstrates the key role of inter-cultural normative inversion in the recollection of the Exodus and the formation of Jewish cultural identity. Egyptian polytheism, depicted as alien and abominable in the Old Testament's narrative of Moses, the ten plagues and the Exodus, served as counter-example for Jewish monotheism.

Extending Assmann's normative inversion beyond inter-cultural distinction to describe a society trying to distinguish itself from a severe violation of its fundamental values *committed by members of that very same society*, we arrive at a new intra-cultural interpretation of normative inversion. Here, accentuating a violation of values as alien and abominable serves to prevent such a violation from ever occurring again. Intra-cultural normative inversion is a promising concept when investigating cultural trauma provoked by human acts of cruelty as it helps to understand how a society copes with the corresponding violation of its fundamental values.

Returning to the cruelty of Sulla's proscriptions as depicted by the Roman Valerius Maximus, it becomes evident that this example of Roman cruelty was regarded as irreconcilable with Roman values, foreign to Roman behavior and a counter-example for Roman cultural identity. Thus, Valerius Maximus' account of Sulla's proscriptions represents intra-cultural normative inversion. To accentuate the alien and abominable character of Sulla's proscriptions, Valerius introduces a comparison to the non-Roman Hannibal. Comparing the cruelty of the Roman Sulla with the cruelty of the non-Roman Hannibal underlines the extreme transgression of Roman values by Sulla. It also highlights the horrendous character of Sulla's proscriptions and the ensuing strong desire to never experience such cruelty again.

Cicero's speeches against Sulla's partisan Verres, dating to 70 B.C.E., further elucidate that Sulla's proscriptions had not only been incorporated into Roman cultural memory as cultural trauma, but also served the purpose of intra-cultural normative inversion. A mere eight years after Sulla's death in 78 B.C.E., Cicero recalled Sulla's violent transgressions of Roman values—murder, expropriation, and deprivation of civil and political rights as a consequence of the proscriptions—and concluded with an entreating exclamation: "May the immortal gods grant that there may never be another Sulla."[25]

25 Cicero, *Verr.* 2.3.81.

6. Recollecting Cultural Trauma: Sulla's Proscriptions from a Christian Perspective

The grave and long-lasting effects of Sulla's proscriptions become evident once more when taking a closer look at Christian perspectives. Almost 500 years after Cicero's appeal to the gods, Christian authors of late antiquity still referred to Sulla's proscriptions as a horrendous event in Roman history.[26]

Of particular interest for our discussion are two passages in Augustine's *The City of God*. In the first passage, at the end of book three,[27] Augustine depicts in great detail Sulla's revenge after his victory in the civil war. In the second passage, in book five,[28] he refers to Sulla when describing the reign of the Christian emperor Theodosius I.

In book three Augustine describes how Sulla's vengeance in the aftermath of the civil war culminated in an organized massacre among members of the Roman elite, the proscriptions. He emphasizes that Sulla had not stopped bloodshed with the official end of the civil war, but decreed the murder of Roman citizens in what was supposed to be a time of peace. Augustine continues by comparing the death toll of Sulla's proscriptions among Roman senators with the death tolls of the sack of Rome by the Gauls in 387 B.C.E. and the conquest of the city by the Goths in 410 C.E. According to Augustine, Sulla's proscriptions proved even more disastrous for Roman society than these two horrendous defeats by foreign enemies.

Augustine's comparison between the terrible consequences of Sulla's proscriptions and Roman defeats by the Gauls and the Goths closely resembles Valerius Maximus' comparison between Sulla and Hannibal. However, by depicting Sulla's proscriptions as even worse than the horrendous defeats of the Romans by the Gauls and the Goths, Augustine's account expresses a much higher degree of alienation.

When taking a closer look at Augustine's portrayal of the Christian Roman emperor Theodosius I in book five it becomes evident that alienating Sulla's proscriptions to such a degree served to prepare the reader for Augustine's key conclusion.

Augustine highlights the clement attitude of emperor Theodosius, who, after his victory in the civil war of 394 C.E., refrained from any form of re-

26 For a general discussion of the perspective of Latin authors of late antiquity on the Roman Republic and in particular the civil war between Marius and Sulla see: Felmy, *Geschichtsbild der Spätantike*, 231–64.

27 Augustine, *Civ.* 3.27–29.

28 Augustine, *Civ.* 5.26. Further references to Sulla in Augustine's City of God describe omens foretelling Sulla's victory in the civil war (*Civ.* 2.23–24) and compare Sulla to Fimbria in the context of the destruction of Ilium by Fimbria during the first Mithridatic War (*Civ.* 3.7).

venge against the followers of the Roman usurper Eugenius.[29] Augustine accentuates Theodosius' clemency by contrasting it with the cruelty of Sulla's proscriptions, hence making a clear distinction between Rome's cruel pagan past, represented by Sulla's proscriptions, and clement Christian rule exemplified by the Roman emperor Theodosius. As opposed to Cicero and Valerius Maximus, Augustine's description of Sulla's proscriptions is not intended to illustrate the desire that Romans never repeat the proscriptions, but to prove the utter impossibility of proscriptions ever reoccurring in a Christian society. Hereby Augustine rebuts pagan allegations of the Christians being responsible for the decay of the Roman Empire, which circulated after the conquest of Rome by the Goths in 410 C.E.[30] Having emphasized the merits of the inherent clemency of Christian rule by contrasting the mercy of Theodosius to the cruelty of Sulla, Augustine, in the final section of book five, explicitly returns to these allegations, outlined in the foreword as his main motivation for writing the *The City of God*.[31]

Augustine's depiction of the cruelty of Sulla's proscription represents another example of normative inversion, more specifically intra-cultural normative inversion. Augustine perceives himself as Roman and refers to Sulla as Roman. However, in contrast to both Cicero and Valerius Maximus, Augustine's point of view reflects a radical change in Roman society, namely the official recognition of Christianity as the state religion. Thus, the Christian author Augustine is naturally aware of the distinction between the pagan society of the Roman past and the Christian society of the late 4th and early 5th century C.E. This distinction allows Augustine to place the cultural trauma of Sulla's proscriptions in an inherently cruel pagan Roman society, whereas the clement attitude of Theodosius after the civil war in 394 C.E. exemplifies a merciful Christian society and, according to Augustine, proves the superiority of Christianity.

Orosius, a Christian historian of the early 5th century C.E. who dedicated his *History against the Pagans* to his mentor Augustine, countered pagan allegations of Christian responsibility for the decay of Rome in a manner similar to that of Augustine.[32] He describes the striking contrast between the vicious civil wars of the pre-Christian era in Rome, which lasted for many years and had an extremely high death toll, and the "mild and merciful"[33] civil wars of his own times. In this context, Sulla's proscriptions are a counter-image for a clement Christian society, as Orosius continues by pointing out that pro-

29 Augustine, *Civ.* 5.26.
30 Demandt, *Fall Roms*, 49f.
31 Augustine, *Civ.* 1 praef.; 5.26.
32 Orosius, *Hist.* 5.22.11-13.
33 Orosius, *Hist.* 5.22.11.

scriptions as a means of revenge after a civil war seem inconceivable in a Christian society.

7. Conclusion: Sulla's Proscriptions, Cultural Trauma, Cultural Memory, and Normative Inversion

Sulla's proscriptions had long-lasting consequences for Roman society at large. They were incorporated into Roman cultural identity soon after Sulla's death in 78 B.C.E. and remembered as cultural trauma for many centuries to come.

Jeffrey C. Alexander's concept of cultural trauma has substantially increased our awareness that applying the terms trauma and traumatization to societies at large requires caution and careful consideration. Alexander criticizes the transfer of well-known phenomena from psychiatry and psychotherapy to scholarly discussion of collective trauma—in particular dissociation, latency, and repression. He argues that horrendous events will induce trauma on a collective level, i.e. cultural trauma, only after a society has initiated and experienced a socially mediated process of cultural trauma.

Because of the grave consequences of the proscriptions for individuals and the high death toll, the social process of cultural trauma was initiated as early as 80 B.C.E. and completed about two decades later when Sullan partisans, who had killed proscribed Roman citizens, were sentenced to death for murder.

Combining Alexander's concept of cultural trauma and Aleida and Jan Assmann's concept of cultural memory explains how horrendous events are established in a society's cultural memory by continuous recollection as cultural trauma. Normative inversion, as first described by Jan Assmann, proved a valuable concept for enhancing the understanding of horrendous events provoked by human acts of cruelty. Yet, whenever perpetrators and victims belong to the same society, the concept of normative inversion, confined to inter-cultural normative inversion by Jan Assmann, needs to be extended to encompass intra-cultural normative inversion as well. In the case of intra-cultural normative inversion, a society distinguishes itself from its own past by continually remembering a horrendous event to prevent such an extreme transgression of its values from ever occurring again.

The recollection of Sulla's proscriptions in Roman society was governed by intra-cultural normative inversion from the 1st century B.C.E. to the 5th century C.E. However, the advent of Christianity caused a striking change in the way the memory of Sulla's proscriptions was utilized. The writings of the Christian authors Augustine and Orosius demonstrate that Sulla's proscriptions, due to their association with cruel pre-Christian behavior, now served as a counter-image for a clement, Christian society and were thus suited to prove the superiority of Christianity.

Bibliography

ALEXANDER, J. C. "Toward a Theory of Cultural Trauma." Pages 1-30 in *Cultural Trauma and Collective Identity.* Edited by J. C. Alexander et al. Berkeley: University of California Press, 2004.

—. "Cultural Trauma. A Social Theory." Pages 6-30 in *Trauma: A Social Theory.* Edited by J. C. Alexander. Cambridge: Polity Press, 2012.

ASSMANN, A. *Cultural Memory and Western Civilization: Functions, Media, Archives.* Cambridge: Cambridge University Press, 2011.

ASSMANN, J. "Kollektives Gedächtnis und kulturelle Identität." Pages 9-16 in *Kultur und Gedächtnis.* Edited by J. Assmann et al. Frankfurt: Suhrkamp, 1988.

—. "Collective Memory and Cultural Identity." Translated by John Czaplicka. *New German Critique* 65 (1995): 125-33.

—. *Moses the Egyptian.* Cambridge: Harvard University Press, 1997.

—. "Monotheismus, Gedächtnis und Trauma: Sigmund Freuds archäologische Lektüre der Bibel." *Internationale Zeitschrift für Philosophie* 2 (1999): 227-44.

—. *Religion und kulturelles Gedächtnis: Zehn Studien.* 3d Ed. München: Beck Verlag, 2007.

—. *Cultural Memory and Early Civilization: Writing, Remembrance and Political Imagination.* Cambridge: Cambridge University Press, 2011.

DEMANDT, A. *Der Fall Roms: Die Auflösung des römischen Reiches im Urteil der Nachwelt.* München: Beck Verlag, 1984.

ECKERT, A. "Das kulturelle Gedächtnis von Römern und Griechen und die antike Erinnerung an Lucius Cornelius Sulla." PhD diss., University of Halle-Wittenberg, 2012 (publication forthcoming).

ERLL, A. *Memory in Culture.* Translated by S. B. Young. Basingstoke: Palgrave McMillan, 2011.

EYERMAN, R., J. ALEXANDER and E. BREESE, eds. *Narrating Trauma: On the Impact of Collective Suffering.* Boulder: Paradigm Publishers, 2011.

FELMY, A. *Die Römische Republik im Geschichtsbild der Spätantike: Zum Umgang lateinischer Autoren des 4. und 5. Jahrhunderts n. Chr. mit den exempla maiorum.* Berlin: dissertation.de Verlag im Internet, 1999.

HEFTNER, H. "Der Beginn von Sullas Proskriptionen." *Tyche* 21 (2006): 33-52.

HINARD, F. *Les proscriptions de la Rome républicaine.* Rome: Publications de l'École française de Rome, 1985.

KUNKEL, W. et al. *Staatsordnung und Staatspraxis der römischen Republik.* München: Beck Verlag, 1995.

SCHRATEN, J. *Zur Aktualität von Jan Assmann: Einleitung in sein Werk.* Wiesbaden: VS Verlag für Sozialwissenschaften, 2011.

VERVAET, F. J. "The lex Valeria and Sulla's Empowerment as Dictator." *Cahiers du Centre Gustave Glotz* 15 (2004): 37-84.

Adele Reinhartz

The Destruction of the Jerusalem Temple as a Trauma for Nascent Christianity

Abstract

The destruction of the Second Temple in 70 C.E. is considered to be one of the most traumatic events in Jewish history, having an impact on Jewish groups across the entire spectrum of Second Temple Judaism. Yet scholarly opinions are divided as to whether 70 constituted a trauma for communities of Jewish Christ-believers. Some suggest that the event had relatively little impact on nascent Christian communities, while others view the event as both traumatic and formative in the development of Christianity. Scholars on both sides of this debate use the language and concept of trauma to describe the impact of 70 in the development of Christianity. Missing from the discussion, however, is a consideration of what exactly constitutes a trauma. On the basis of Jeffrey Alexander's theories about communal trauma, this paper will argue that the destruction was experienced as a trauma by at least some Jewish followers of Christ. This response was, however, negated or denied by church leaders who argued that the event had been foretold and indeed was the deserved punishment for the Jewish role in Jesus' crucifixion, and therefore should not be traumatic for Christ-believers, even those of Jewish origin.

In the year 70 C.E., after several years of conflict with Jewish rebel forces, the Roman army besieged, conquered, and sacked the city of Jerusalem, and destroyed the Jerusalem temple. Almost two thousand years later, this event still resonates in Jewish liturgy, literature and practice. The daily and weekly prayer services, as well as the traditional grace after meals, express hope for the restoration of the temple and its sacrificial cult. On the ninth day of the Hebrew month of Av, many Jews observe a day of fasting; they gather in synagogues, where they sit on the floor, read the biblical book of Lamentations by candlelight, and mourn the loss of the temple, as one of the most important of many national tragedies.[1]

1 The destruction of the temple stands alongside the Holocaust as one of the most traumatic events in Jewish history and the impact of and responses to this event have been studied from many different perspectives. See, for example, Stein, "Collapsing Structures"; Akenson, *Surpassing Wonder*; Wimpfheimer, *Narrating the Law*.

The trauma of 70 is palpable at the most revered site in the Jewish world: the Western Wall—sometimes called the Wailing Wall—which stands at the western side of the temple mount in the Old City of Jerusalem. There one can still see the huge Herodian stones strewn on the plaza in front of the wall. Jews from all over the world come there to pray, to slip petitions to God into the cracks between its stones, to imagine the majesty of the temple in the days of Herod and thereby to place themselves at the center of this quintessentially Jewish sorrow. Many tourists go on to visit another site, a short distance away from the Western Wall, known as the Burnt House. At this site, they can watch a dramatic sound and light show that dramatizes the events of 70 as experienced by the priestly family that apparently occupied this house: armed conflict, confusion, noise, fire, armed conflict, injury, exile, and death. Nor was the trauma confined to Judea, for the temple's destruction horrified Diaspora Jews who, despite their geographical distance from Jerusalem, nevertheless "presumed the central importance of the Temple in Jewish worship."[2]

But what about those Jewish groups whose identification with the temple and temple cult was more ambivalent? In the case of the Dead Sea Community, which left Jerusalem in part due to its opposition to the current temple establishment, we will never know;[3] this group apparently ceased to exist after the Jewish Revolt, or, to be more precise, no evidence for their post-70 existence has yet been discovered. In the case of nascent Christian community, however, we are more fortunate.[4] Not only are there references to and interpretations of the temple's destruction in patristic writings from the second century onwards, but there is also evidence within the New Testament itself that can be dated to the period of the revolt and its aftermath. The question before us is therefore as follows: was the destruction of the temple a traumatic event for those who believed Jesus to be the Messiah and Son of God?[5]

Scholarly opinions are divided as to whether 70 constituted a trauma for communities of Christ-believers. Richard Bauckham, for example, suggests that for this non-militant messianic movement, "the loss of the temple was no kind of problem."[6] Others, however, view 70 as both traumatic and formative in the development of Christianity. S. G. F. Brandon insisted that: "It would … not be an exaggeration to say that Christianity was in a certain sense reborn as a result of the Jewish catastrophe of A.D. 70."[7] More recently, Jonathan

2 Goodman, "Diaspora Reactions," 27. Other scholars, however, minimize the impact of the war on Diaspora Jews. See Aberbach, *Roman-Jewish War*, 8; Collins, *Between Athens and Jerusalem*, 117. For further detailed discussion, see Marshall, *Parables of War*, 98-120.

3 E.g., Gärtner, *Temple and the Community*; Haber, *They Shall Purify Themselves*, 106-24.

4 For a measured exposition of the problems in using the term "Christian" with regard to first-century believers in Christ, see Lieu, *Neither Jew nor Greek?*, 192-209.

5 See Marshall, *Parables of War*, 5-6.

6 Bauckham, *Jewish World*, 188.

7 Brandon, *Fall of Jerusalem*, 249.

Draper has argued that "the destruction of the temple in 70 C.E. must rightly be seen as the major turning point in the development of the Jesus movement from a movement for the physical restoration of Israel into something else."[8] In his study of the Gospel of Mark, Philip Cunningham comments that "Mark's Christians must have shared in the trauma of Jerusalem's conquest and the destruction of the temple.... They would have been among the vast throng that lined the streets of the city to witness the triumphant return of the victorious Titus as he marched through the capital city."[9] Andreas Köstenberger argues that the destruction of the temple—not the putative expulsion of the Christ-confessors from the synagogue—constitutes the historical matrix for the Gospel of John.[10]

As the above quotations show, scholars on both sides of this debate use the language and concept of trauma to describe the impact of 70 in the development of Christianity. Missing from the discussion, however, is a consideration of what exactly constitutes a trauma. On one level, of course, the word is common parlance, the concept is well-understood, and the experience is universal. In ordinary language, trauma is a label that objectively identifies certain experiences—car accidents, terminal illnesses, genocides, tsunamis, wars—that happen to people, communities, or nations. Certainly the destruction of the temple qualifies as one such event.

But this common sense understanding may not be a precise enough foundation for addressing the question. Indeed, in the view of cultural sociologist Philip Alexander, events as such are not inherently traumatic. [11] Rather, "trauma is a socially mediated attribution. The attribution may be made in real time, as an event unfolds; it may also be made before the event occurs, as an adumbration, or after the event has concluded, as a post-hoc reconstruction. Sometimes, in fact, events that are deeply traumatizing may not actually have happened at all; such imagined events, however, can be as traumatizing as events that have actually occurred."[12] He continues: "Traumatic status is attributed to real or imagined phenomena, not because of harmfulness or abruptness per se, but because they are believed to have abruptly, and harmfully, affected collective identity." In other words, traumas are socially constructed; what is at stake is identity. Only events that are perceived as threats to group identity—which Alexander defines as a group's "sense of who they are, where they came from, and where they want to go"—are described as

8 Draper, "Mystical Experience," 264.

9 Cunningham, *Mark*, 66.

10 Köstenberger, "Second Temple." See also Kerr, *Jesus' body*.

11 This view is contrary to the usage of the term in numerous studies, which conceive of trauma as an objectively identifiable event. For one example among many, see Kaplan, *Trauma Culture*, 1-2.

12 Alexander, "Cultural Trauma," 8.

traumas.[13] According to Alexander, "cultural construction of trauma begins with a claim to some fundamental injury, exclamation of the terrifying profanation of some sacred value, a narrative of some horribly destructive social process and a demand for emotional, institutional, and symbolic reparation and reconstitution."[14] Alexander argues that the process that results in such a construction is initiated by agents who interpret and respond to the event at hand.[15]

Alexander's work suggests that the destruction of the temple will be seen as traumatic for nascent Christianity if reliable agents declare that the event violated a fundamental value of the community and therefore required restitution and reparation; and that it disrupted group identity, requiring a change in a group's sense of their raison d'être, origins and direction.

The most explicit ancient Christian responses to the destruction of the temple are to be found in the writings of the Church Fathers beginning in the second century. Justin Martyr, a second century father, made several references to 70 in his *Dialogue with Trypho*.[16] In *Dial.* 16.4, for example, he argued that the destruction and suffering were foretold by the Hebrew scriptures: "For the circumcision according to the flesh, which is from Abraham, was given for a sign; that you may be separated from other nations, and from us; and that you alone may suffer that which you now justly suffer; and that your land may be desolate, and your cities burned with fire; and that strangers may eat your fruit in your presence, and not one of you may go up to Jerusalem." Justin further asserts that the tragedies that the Jews have experienced "have happened to you in fairness and justice, for you have slain the Just One, and His prophets before Him; and now you reject those who hope in Him, and in Him who sent Him—God the Almighty and Maker of all things—cursing in your synagogues those that believe on Christ." Dialogue 51-52 similarly associates 70 with the Jews' role in Jesus' death, after which "you ceased to exist under your own king, your land was laid waste, and forsaken like a lodge in a vineyard."

The point that the Jews brought the destruction upon themselves, by their treatment of Jesus, is made most forcefully in Origen's treatise *Contra Celsum* 4.22: "Any one who likes may convict this statement of *falsehood*, if it be not the case that the whole *Jewish* nation was overthrown within one single generation after Jesus had undergone these sufferings at their hands. For forty and two years, I think, after the date of the crucifixion of *Jesus*, did the destruction of Jerusalem take place."

13 Ibid., 10.
14 Ibid., 11.
15 Ibid., 12.
16 All patristic quotations are taken from http://www.earlychristianwritings.com/.

According to Origen, the fact that the expulsion has continued for so many years demonstrates Jesus' divinity, which is the very point that the Jews refuse to acknowledge. He points out that prior to the destruction of the temple, the Jews had never been expelled from their land for such a long period of time, "for if at any time they appeared to be abandoned because of their sins, they were notwithstanding visited (by God), and returned to their own country, and recovered their possessions, and performed unhindered the observances of their law." For this reason, the length of this expulsion stands out: "One fact, then, which proves that Jesus was something divine and sacred, is this, that Jews should have suffered on His account now for a lengthened time calamities of such severity." Furthermore, this expulsion will last forever, "for they committed a crime of the most unhallowed kind, in conspiring against the Saviour of the human race in that city where they offered up to God a worship containing the symbols of mighty mysteries." The destruction of Jerusalem was a fitting punishment for these terrible acts that took place in the holy city: "It accordingly behooved that city where Jesus underwent these sufferings to perish utterly, and the Jewish nation to be overthrown, and the invitation to happiness offered them by God to pass to others—the Christians, I mean" (4.22).

Other church fathers, perhaps implicitly acknowledging the chronological difficulty inherent in viewing the destruction in 70 as divine punishment for an event that occurred some forty years prior, point instead to the stoning of James, the brother of Jesus, on the basis of Josephus' account in *Antiquitates Judaicae* 20.200-201, which states that James was stoned by the order of Ananus ben Ananus, a Herodian-era High Priest—and the youngest brother-in-law of Caiaphas—who died c. 68 C.E. This view is expressed in graphic detail by Eusebius (263-339) in his *Church History* 2.23.16-20:

So they went up and threw down the just man, and said to each other, 'Let us stone James the Just.' And they began to stone him, for he was not killed by the fall; but he turned and knelt down and said, 'I entreat you, Lord God our Father, forgive them, for they know not what they do' (Luke 23:34). And while they were thus stoning him one of the priests of the sons of Rechab, the son of the Rechabites, who are mentioned by Jeremiah the prophet, cried out, saying, 'Stop. What are you doing? The just one prays for you.' And one of them, who was a fuller, took the club with which he beat out clothes and struck the just man on the head. And thus he suffered martyrdom. And they buried him on the spot, by the temple, and his monument still remains by the temple. He became a true witness, both to Jews and Greeks, that Jesus is the Christ. And immediately Vespasian besieged them. These things are related at length by Hegesippus, who is in agreement with Clement. James was so admirable a man and so celebrated among all for his justice, that the more sensible even of the Jews were of the opinion that this was the cause of the siege of Jerusalem, which happened to them immediately after his martyrdom for no other reason than their daring act against him. Josephus, at least, has not hesitated to testify this in his writings, where he says, These things happened to the Jews to avenge James the Just, who was a brother of Jesus, that is called the Christ. For the Jews slew him, although he was a most just man."

The connection between the death of James and the destruction of the temple is made also in apocryphal texts attributed to James. In the *First Apocalypse of James* (36:16–18) God tell James that after his death "immediately war will be made with this land."[17] The point is reiterated in *2 Apocalypse of James* 10, 12–22, in which James prophecies on God's behalf: "Behold, I gave you your house, which you say that God has made—that (house) in which he promised to give you an inheritance through it. This (house) I shall doom to destruction and derision of those who are in ignorance. For behold, those who judge deliberate [...]."[18]

Origen, however, disputes this interpretation, which he attributes, with some admiration, to Josephus. In Origen's words, Josephus "ought to have said that the conspiracy against Jesus was the cause of these calamities befalling the people, since they put to death Christ, who was a prophet" but at least Josephus was on the right track in attributing the disasters to the Jewish rejection of the Christian faith (*Contra Celsum* 1.47). Even Eusebius ultimately connects the destruction to the Jews' treatment of Jesus: "For it was right that in the very days in which they had inflicted suffering upon the Saviour and the Benefactor of all, the Christ of God, that in those days, shut up as in a prison, they should meet with destruction at the hands of divine justice" (*Church History* 3.6).

Finally, the Pella legend, according to which Jewish believers in Christ managed to escape Jerusalem before the destruction, provides a compelling reason for the lack of trauma: they simply were not there, and therefore were not personally affected. In book three of his Church History, Eusebius tells the following story:

After Nero had held the power thirteen years, and Galba and Otho had ruled a year and six months, Vespasian ... was proclaimed sovereign in Judea and received the title of Emperor from the armies there. Setting out immediately, therefore, for Rome, he entrusted the conduct of the war against the Jews to his son Titus. 2. For the Jews after the ascension of our Saviour, in addition to their crime against him, had been devising as many plots as they could against his apostles. First Stephen was stoned to death by them, and after him James, the son of Zebedee and the brother of John, was beheaded, and finally James, the first that had obtained the episcopal seat in Jerusalem after the ascension of our Saviour, died in the manner already described ... 3. But the people of the church in Jerusalem had been commanded by a revelation, vouch-

17 Schoedel, "Gnostic Interpretation," 174–75.
18 http://www.gnosis.org/naghamm/2ja.html; translation by Charles Hedrick.

safed to approved men there before the war, to leave the city and to dwell in a certain town of Perea called Pella. And when those that believed in Christ had come there from Jerusalem, then, as if the royal city of the Jews and the whole land of Judea were entirely destitute of holy men, the judgment of God at length overtook those who had committed such outrages against Christ and his apostles, and totally destroyed that generation of impious men" (*Hist. eccl.* 3.5).

This story provides yet another explanation as to why the Jewish believers in Jesus were not—or should not be—traumatized by the temple's destruction: thanks to a prophetic revelation, they left Jerusalem before the worst of the fighting took place.[19]

In Philip Alexander's terms, Justin, Origen and Eusebius act as agents who interpret the events of 70 to their audiences. These agents agree that the destruction of the temple was not a trauma for Christians, for it did not alter the identity of Christians in any way; on the contrary, it served to vindicate their belief that God was on their side, for it was God who had visited punishment upon the Jews on account of their persecution of Jesus and James. Furthermore, these agents insist, while the destruction may have been traumatic for Jews, it should not have been unexpected, for it was prophesied both by Jesus and by their own scriptures. Indeed, it was entirely in keeping with the well-established biblically-based worldview that political and military failures, as well as disasters natural and otherwise were consequences of sinful behavior, in this case, the Jews' behavior towards Jesus, the leaders of the Church, and rank-and-file Christians themselves.

These writers, however, lived a century or more after the events they are interpreting. What about those communities of Christ-believers who lived at the time of the destruction or in the decades that immediately followed? Whether they experienced the destruction as a trauma is much more difficult to assess, but nevertheless there are some New Testament materials that provide at least some hints as to how 70 was perceived in, and interpreted by, Jews who believed Jesus to be the Messiah.

Perhaps the earliest relevant passage is found in Mark's Gospel. The Gospel of Mark, thought by most New Testament scholars to have been a source for the Gospels of Matthew and Luke, is usually dated to around 70.[20] Chapter 13, known as the Little Apocalypse,[21] includes a prophecy of the temple's

19 The historicity of this account is uncertain; see Lüdemann, "Pre-70 Christianity," 172. See also Bourgel, "Jewish-Christians' Move," 129, 135.

20 The literary relationships among the Gospels of Matthew, Mark and Luke constitute the so-called "Synoptic Problem." For a good introduction, see Goodacre, *Synoptic Problem*.

21 Mark 13 is often referred to as the "Little Apocalypse" due to its use of motifs held in common with other examples of apocalyptic literature such as the book of Daniel in the Hebrew Bible and the book of Revelation in the New Testament. For an account of the debate, see Hogeterp, *Expectations of the End*, 143–52.

destruction: "As [Jesus] came out of the temple, one of his disciples said to him, "Look, Teacher, what large stones and what large buildings!" 2 Then Jesus asked him, 'Do you see these great buildings? Not one stone will be left here upon another; all will be thrown down.'" (13:1–2) The continuation of the passage describes the terrifying signs that will herald the end times: "When you hear of wars and rumors of wars, do not be alarmed; this must take place, but the end is still to come. For nation will rise against nation, and kingdom against kingdom; there will be earthquakes in various places; there will be famines. This is but the beginning of the birth pangs" (13:7–8). The overall structure of the passage suggests that the destruction itself is the beginning of the end, a time of suffering that will herald God's final intervention into history on behalf of the faithful.

Ullucci comments that "through an ingenious interweaving of apocalyptic prophecies from the book of Daniel the author of Mark suggests that the temple's destruction is (1) a clear sign of the imminent end of the world, and (2) vindication of Jesus' true identity as the Messiah and the son of man in Daniel's prophecy."[22] Matthew adopts Mark's view that the temple's destruction is a sign the end of the world is coming soon[23] but Luke tones down these apocalyptic forebodings. For Luke, "the temple's destruction cannot indicate the imminent end of the world both because Luke, writing much later, knows that the world did not end soon after 70 and because Luke does not believe Jesus was preaching an impending apocalypse. Luke does not draw any implications from the temple's destruction … they [Luke and his audience] did not have a clear explanation for why God had allowed the temple to be destroyed … [because they] were far removed from the context of Judea; the war in 70 and the temple's destruction were far away in space and time … it took other forces to get such Christians thinking about the temple again."[24]

Allusions to the destruction are also found in the Fourth Gospel. Like Luke, the Gospel of John dates from close to the end of the first century, that is a generation or more after 70. Even more than the Synoptics, John reflects quite directly on the temple and its significance in relationship to Jesus. The theme is introduced in the Prologue, which identifies Jesus as God's dwelling place on earth: "And the Word became flesh and lived among us, and we have seen his glory, the glory as of a father's only son, full of grace and truth" (1:14). Jesus is the new tabernacle, the locus of God's presence, and therefore the focus of worship.

That Jesus replaces or supersedes the temple is made clear in John's version of the temple cleansing, in which Jesus objects to those who would make the temple—his father's house—a marketplace. After he has thrown out all

22 Ullucci, *Christian Rejection*, 79.
23 Ibid., 84.
24 Ibid., 88.

the merchants, the Jews challenge him: "What sign can you show us for doing this?" Jesus answered them, "Destroy this temple, and in three days I will raise it up." The Jews then said, "This temple has been under construction for forty-six years, and will you raise it up in three days?"[21] But he was speaking of the temple of his body" (John 2:18-22). Whether or not this passage is based on a historical event, the fourth evangelist interprets this scene in light of his conviction that Jesus, or his body, is the new, improved divine temple. Whereas the historical temple destroyed in 70 was not rebuilt, Jesus was resurrected, an act which confirms the Gospel's Christology and therefore the notion that faith in Jesus as the messiah is now essential in order to remain in covenantal relationship with God.

This theme continues in John 4:19-23, in which a Samaritan woman tells Jesus: "Sir, I see that you are a prophet. Our ancestors worshiped on this mountain, but you say that the place where people must worship is in Jerusalem." Jesus said to her, "Woman, believe me, the hour is coming when you will worship the Father neither on this mountain nor in Jerusalem.... But the hour is coming, and is now here, when the true worshipers will worship the Father in spirit and truth, for the Father seeks such as these to worship him." Here, the Johannine Jesus prophesies that soon both the Jerusalem temple and the Samaritan temple on Mount Gerizim will be irrelevant for true worship of God; because Jesus will replace them both, worship will henceforth not be tied to a specific geographical and cultic location.

The final, and most important, passage for our theme is John 11:47-52. In the aftermath of Jesus' dramatic resurrection of his dead friend Lazarus, "the chief priests and the Pharisees called a meeting of the council, and said, 'What are we to do? This man is performing many signs. If we let him go on like this, everyone will believe in him, and the Romans will come and destroy both our holy place and our nation.' But one of them, Caiaphas, who was high priest that year, said to them, 'You know nothing at all! You do not understand that it is better for you to have one man die for the people than to have the whole nation destroyed'" (11:47-50). The narrator then explains that Caiaphas "did not say this on his own, but being high priest that year he prophesied that Jesus was about to die for the nation, and not for the nation only, but to gather into one the dispersed children of God. So from that day on they planned to put him to death" (John 11:50-53).

The "holy place" is the temple;[25] but why the leadership (or John) believes that Jesus' behavior would lead the Romans to destroy the temple is not at all clear. One possibility is that (as John portrays it), the Jews are convinced that wide scale belief in Jesus would signify a loss of attachment to God, which in turn would lead God to use Roman might to inflict punishment on the na-

25 Brown, *Gospel according to John*, 1:439.

tion, just as in earlier days God sent the Assyrians and Babylonians to punish the Jews for turning away from the covenant.[26] In the Maccabean era, a similar explanation was used for the ability of Antiochus IV to desecrate the temple (2 Maccabees 5:15–20). A second possibility is that widespread belief in Jesus might make Rome fear rebellion or civil war, and therefore prompt Rome to move quickly by moving against the temple. The Romans were indeed often motivated by fear of rebellion and turmoil, as indicated in Acts 21:38, in which a Roman tribune asks Paul whether he is "the Egyptian who recently stirred up a revolt and led the four thousand assassins out into the wilderness," and in the writings of Josephus (*A.J.* 20.97–99; 20.169–72; 20.188; *B.J.* 2.258–63).[27]

These passages in John imply some sort of response to the events of the destruction, although the Gospel itself is thought to have reached its final form in Ephesus, far from Judea.[28] The worries of the Jewish leaders ring ironically in the aftermath of the destruction, which could then be interpreted as a consequence of the Jews' action against Jesus—though not for the reasons that the Jews themselves might have proposed.

That faith is concentrated now in Jesus is a theme developed in greatest detail in the Letter to the Hebrews, which portrays Jesus as the high priest par excellence. As stated in Hebrews 10, "This is the covenant that I will make with them after those days, says the Lord: I will put my laws in their hearts, and I will write them on their minds.... [S]ince we have confidence to enter the sanctuary by the blood of Jesus, by the new and living way that he opened for us through the curtain (that is, through his flesh), and since we have a great priest over the house of God, let us approach with a true heart in full assurance of faith, with our hearts sprinkled clean from an evil conscience and our bodies washed with pure water" (Heb 10:16–22).

This brief overview hints at a perspective similar to that of the Church Fathers who wrote one or more centuries later. New Testament and patristic authors emphasize that the destruction itself was foreseen by Jesus and it was part of the divine plane communicated by prophets including Jesus. The destruction itself is not to be seen as a negative event, for since Jesus came as a God's tabernacle in the world, worship must be focused on him rather than

26 See, for example, 2 Kings 21:14–15, in which God responds to Judea's idolatry under King Manasseh by prophesying its destruction, and John 12:10–11, in which belief in Jesus is seen as desertion of Judaism.

27 See Schwartz, *Jewish Background*, 31–34; Gray, *Prophetic Figures*, 112–44; David M. Miller, "Whom Do You Follow?"173–83. For more detailed discussion, see Reinhartz, *Caiaphas*, 40–44.

28 Although there is no "hard evidence" for the Gospel's provenance, the ancient witnesses are unanimous in situating the Gospel in Ephesus, a conclusion that is supported, though not conclusively, by internal evidence. For detailed discussion and bibliography see Brown and Moloney, *Introduction*, 199–206.

on a cult that can take place in only one geographical location. In other words, the evangelists as well as the author of Hebrews, like the church fathers, acted as agents to interpret the destruction of the temple as an event that was not traumatic for Jewish believers in Christ because their focus had already shifted—or needed to shift—away from the temple and towards Christ.

Does the fact that the New Testament writers find a benign explanation for 70 mean that they are arguing against others who did view 70 as a trauma? The canonical evidence does not provide a basis for answering this question in one direction or another, with one possible exception: the book of Revelation. Revelation is a work of apocalyptic literature usually dated to the era of Domitian, in the last decade of the first century. Yet at least one scholar, John Marshall, has argued that Revelation is in fact war-time literature written during the revolt but before the actual destruction of the temple. If so, the air of destruction, dread, and chaos that emerges from some sections of the book may reflect the anxieties of Jewish believers in Christ who fear for their own lives, and for the divine judgment that was generally associated with disasters whether natural or humanly made.[29] Marshall looks at four text-complexes: synagogue of Satan (Rev 2:9; 3:9); those who keep the commandments of God (12:17; 14:12); the 144,000 people drawn from Israel or gather on Zion (7:4ff.; 14:1ff.), and the vision of the trial of holy city and the destruction of the great city (11:1–14). For example, with respect to Rev 11:1–2, Marshall notes that "the temple and the city were surrounded by a substantial Roman force, and there was little reason for confidence in a Jewish victory by military means. Within the context of the period of the cessation of hostilities, from late 68 to early 70 C.E., Rev 11:1–2 communicates the expectations that although the city and the outer courts of the temple may fall [sic], such a defeat would only be temporary." In the view of John of Patmos, it was not Israel that would be punished, but Rome that will face the consequences of rejecting the emissaries of God.[30]

Conclusion

It seems possible, perhaps even likely, that the destruction of the Temple in 70 C.E. was experienced and understood as traumas by at least some Jewish followers of Christ, especially if, as many scholars now argue, such Jews did not yet position themselves outside of and over-against other Jews. Yet from a very early point, it would seem that the leaders of the church—the agents

29 Marshall, *Parables of War*. See also Pagels, *Revelations*.
30 Marshall, *Parables of War*, 167–68.

whose activities, including the writing and transmission of scriptures, shaped Christian identity as it came into being—carefully constructed an interpretation that not only avoided but actively counteracted the potential interpretation of 70 as a traumatic event. The destruction was domesticated through arguments that it was foretold by scripture and by Christ himself; that it was an inevitable punishment for Jewish transgressions such as the killing of Christ, Stephen and James, and that it had no impact at all on the beliefs and practices of Christ-confessors, whose focus had already turned from the sacrificial cult localized in a temple towards Christ as the universal savior.

Jeffrey Alexander's insights into trauma as a "socially mediated attribution" draws attention to the role of agents, or community leaders, in interpreting events to their followers, and thereby in defining whether events are to be seen as traumatic, or not. This approach allows for clarity and precision in the debate concerning the significance of 70 for those communities who eventually defined themselves as Christian.

The attempts of New Testament and patristic writers to steer their audiences away from viewing the temple's destruction as traumatic has important implications for one of the most vexed issues in the study of early Christianity: the "parting of the ways" between Christianity and Judaism. In recent years, the consensus view that Christianity began to define itself as distinct from Judaism in the period after 70 has been questioned, with many scholars pushing the date into the fourth century C.E. or even later.[31] The claim that Christ-confessors do not, or perhaps better, should not, view the destruction as a trauma already implies the development of an identity quite distinct from the Jews who did. While the arguments that have been marshaled against a first-dating for the separation of the Christ-confessors from the Jewish community have much to commend them, the distancing of nascent Christianity from this central Jewish trauma suggests that some process of differentiation was already underway.

Bibliography

ABERBACH, M. *The Roman-Jewish War (66–70 A.D.), its Origin and Consequences*. London: Jewish Quarterly/R. Golub, 1966.

AKENSON, D. H. *Surpassing Wonder: The Invention of the Bible and the Talmuds*. Chicago: University of Chicago Press, 2001.

ALEXANDER, J. C. "Toward a Theory of Cultural Trauma." Pages 1–30 in *Cultural Trauma and Collective Identity*. Edited by Philip S. Alexander et al. Berkeley: University of California Press, 2004.

31 For discussion of the controversy on the dating and process of the "parting of the ways," see for example, Becker and Reed, *Ways that Never Parted*; Boyarin, *Border Lines*; Reinhartz, "Fork in the Road."

Bauckham, R. *The Jewish World around the New Testament*. Grand Rapids: Baker Academic, 2010.

Becker, A. H., and A. Y. Reed. *The Ways That Never Parted: Jews and Christians in Late Antiquity and the Early Middle Ages*. Minneapolis: Fortress Press, 2007.

Bourgel, J. "The Jewish-Christians' Move from Jerusalem as a Pragmatic Choice." Pages 107-38 in *Studies in Rabbinic Judaism and Early Christianity.* Edited by D. Jaffe. Boston: Brill, 2010.

Boyarin, D. *Border Lines: The Partition of Judaeo-Christianity*. Philadelphia: University of Pennsylvania Press, 2004.

Brandon, S. G. F. *The Fall of Jerusalem and the Christian Church; A Study of the Effects of the Jewish Overthrow of A.D. 70 on Christianity.* London: S.P.C.K., 1951.

Brown, R. E. *The Gospel according to John*. 2 vols. Anchor Bible 29-29A. Garden City, N.Y.: Doubleday, 1966-70.

Brown, R. E., and F. J. Moloney. *An Introduction to the Gospel of John*. New York: Doubleday, 2003.

Collins, J. J. *Between Athens and Jerusalem: Jewish identity in the Hellenistic Diaspora*. New York: Crossroad, 1983.

Cunningham, P. J. *Mark: The Good News Preached to the Romans*. New York; Mahwah, New Jersey: Paulist Press, 1995.

Draper, J. A. "Temple, Tabernacle and Mystical Experience in John." *Neotestamentica* 31, 2 (1997): 263-288.

Gärtner, B. E. *The Temple and the Community in Qumran and the New Testament: A Comparative Study in the Temple Symbolism of the Qumran Texts and the New Testament.* Cambridge: Cambridge University Press, 1965.

Goodacre, M. S. *The Synoptic Problem: A Way through the Maze*. London: Sheffield Academic, 2001.

Goodman, M. "Diaspora Reactions to the Destruction of the Temple." Pages 27-38 in *Jews and Christians: the Parting of the Ways A.D. 70 to 135.* Edited by James D. G. Dunn. Tübingen: Mohr (Siebeck), 1992.

Gray, R. *Prophetic Figures in Late Second Temple Jewish Palestine the Evidence from Josephus.* New York: Oxford University Press, 1993.

Haber, S. *"They shall purify themselves": Essays on Purity in Early Judaism*. Edited by Adele Reinhartz. Atlanta: Society of Biblical Literature, 2008.

Hogeterp, A. L. A. *Expectations of the End: A Comparative Traditio-Historical Study of Eschatological, Apocalyptic, and Messianic Ideas in the Dead Sea Scrolls and the New Testament*. Leiden: Brill, 2009.

Kaplan, E. A. *Trauma Culture: The Politics of Terror and Loss in Media and Literature*. New Brunswick, N.J.: Rutgers University Press, 2005.

Kerr, Alan Richard. *The Temple of Jesus' Body: the Temple Theme in the Gospel of John*. Sheffield: Sheffield Academic, 2002.

Köstenberger, A. J. "The Destruction of the Second Temple and the Composition of the Fourth Gospel." *Trinity Journal* 26, 2 (Fall 2005): 205-242.

Lieu, J. *Neither Jew nor Greek? Constructing early Christianity*. Edinburgh: T & T Clark, 2002.

Lüdemann, G. "The Successors of Pre-70 Christianity: A Critical Evaluation of the Pella Tradition." Pages 161-73 in vol. 1 of *Jewish and Christian Self-Definition*. Edited by E. P Sanders. Philadelphia: Fortress, 1980.

Marshall, J. W. *Parables of War: Reading John's Jewish Apocalypse*. Waterloo, Ont.: Wilfrid Laurier University Press, 2001.

Pagels, E. H. *Revelations: Visions, Prophecy, and Politics in the Book of Revelation*. New York: Viking, 2012.

Reinhartz, A. *Caiaphas the High Priest*. Columbia, S.C.: University of South Carolina Press, 2011.

—. "A Fork in the Road or a Multi-Lane Highway? New Perspectives on the 'Parting of the Ways' between Judaism and Christianity." Pages 280–95 in *The Changing Face of Judaism, Christianity, and Other Greco-Roman Religions in Antiquity*. Edited by I. H. Henderson et al. Gütersloh: Gütersloher, 2006.

Schoedel, W. R. "A Gnostic Interpretation of the Fall of Jerusalem: The First Apocalypse of James." *Novum Testamentum* 33, 2 (1991): 153–78.

Schwartz, D. R. *Studies in the Jewish Background of Christianity*. Tübingen: Mohr, 1992.

Stein, D. "Collapsing Structures: Discourse and the Destruction of the Temple in the Babylonian Talmud." *The Jewish Quarterly Review* 98, 1 (2008): 1–28.

Ullucci, D. C. *The Christian Rejection of Animal Sacrifice*. New York: Oxford University Press, 2012.

Wimpfheimer, B. S. *Narrating the Law: A Poetics of Talmudic Legal Stories*. Philadelphia: University of Pennsylvania Press, 2011.

Frank Ursin

Handling Traumatic Events in Greek Past

Plutarch's 'Political Precepts' as a Struggle between Memory and Omission

Abstract

The trauma of the imperial Greeks consisted in giving up their struggle for freedom, which up to then had been an integral part of their identity. As a consequence of this Plutarch recommends other politics of memory: the Greeks should omit the reference points of the struggle for freedom in the political space and recall peaceful cultural techniques that have been practiced by the Greeks after traumatic experiences.

Introduction

In this paper[1] I shall focus on the interrelation between the handling of cultural traumata in Greek history and the functions of memory and omission with regard to Plutarch's 'Political Precepts.'[2] This work is a kind of letter-essay addressed to a certain Menemachus from Sardis,[3] written between 96 and 114 A.D.[4] The addressee asked for a discussion enriched with many examples about how to become and to be a politician in a Greek *polis* in the Roman Empire. The restrictions of a politician on the level of a city facing the Roman

1 I have to thank Prof. Dr. Angela Pabst for her helpful suggestions and comments at different stages of conception of this paper. And also thanks to Thomas Köntges, André Bünte and Stefanie Däne who helped with proofreading.

2 The *praecepta gerendae rei publicae* are very famous in scholarship and have been treated e.g. by several papers in Nikolaides, *Unity*; De Blois, *Statesman*; esp. Cook, "Imitable Events"; see also Spawforth, "Symbol of Unity?"; Desideri, "Greek Poleis"; Swain, *Hellenism*, 166–68 is very good for my subject. See also Halfmann, "Selbstverwaltung," 83 n. 1 with a good bibliography.

3 On Menemachus see e.g. Renoirte, *Conseils politiques*, 69–79 or Puech, "Prosopographie," *ANRW* 33.6:4859.

4 Cf. Jones, "Chronology," 72 and also Bowersock, "Persons," 270 supposes as latest date 114 A.D. For more detailed but uncertain dates see Aalders and de Blois, "Politische Philosophie," *ANRW* 36.5:3386 n. 9.

power, regarded as a foreign one, are obvious.[5] When dealing with examples a politician could make while speaking to the masses in Athens, Plutarch advises to banish the mentioning of the Greek victories of the Persian Wars into the apolitical space of the sophistry schools.[6] Instead of presenting the glorious past in front of the *plêthos* the masses should be reminded of examples which create (*êthopoiein*) common values like *sôphrosyne*. This is remarkable in the context of the omnipresent references to the past made by the sophists in this period.[7]

Plutarch recommends examples of the handling of disastrous experiences in Athenian history, of which the *plêthos* can be proud. A distinction has to be made between (1) the disastrous experience, (2) the handling of a disastrous experience and (3) the function of recalling them in Plutarch's own time. Thereby, he does not understand the function of this recollection in his own time as a therapeutic action of coping with individual traumata of people that experienced the disasters. I think one aspect of the text is to manipulate the masses by means of politics of memory, which would help them coping with another persisting cultural trauma, i.e. the Roman domination over Greece and the relinquishment of the struggle for freedom. This 'politics of memory' consists of which past exactly should be mentioned to the masses by the Athenian archons or other politicians of the city. The omission of the glorious Greek struggle for freedom is the key element. Plutarch's examples are intended not to make the masses rebellious like the memory of the Persian wars does, but make them prudent. The masses should still remain controllable.[8] The relation of the political leader to the people is like "the relation of the doctor with his patients, a captain to his ship, of a charioteer to his

5 The greatest blessings states can enjoy are peace, liberty, plenty, abundance of men and concord—but "of liberty the peoples have as great a share as our rulers grant them, and perhaps more would not be better for them" (Plutarch, *Praec. ger. rei publ.* 824c, [Fowler, LCL]). Plutarch goes on: concerning peace the people have no need of statesmanship and all war is gone between Greeks and Barbarians (824c, cf. 784f). One can serve on embassies to the emperors (815d) or deliver speeches at the lawcourts (805a–b). Preserving concord and friendship are the only tasks of a politician left (824d).

6 The sophistry schools are the apolitical space: "But Iphicrates was jeered at when he did exercises in speaking at his home in the presence of many hearers; for even if he had been a good speaker, and not, as he was, a poor one, he ought to have been contented with glory in arms and to have left the school to the sophists" (Plutarch, *Praec. ger. rei publ.* 813a [Fowler, LCL]).

7 Philostratus' 'Lives of the Sophists' is full of historical themes regarding the classical period, especially the Persian wars, cf. Bowie, "Geography," 82-83; Bowie, "Greeks and Their Past," 3-41.

8 Cf. Plutarch, *Praec. ger. rei publ.*, cap. 3, especially 799c: the statesman has to take care of what brings pleasure to the dêmos and what the dêmos dislikes. On the one hand the Athenians become angry very quickly and on the other hand they show their pity. Who praises them brings them most pleasure. Cf. Saïd, "Plutarch and the People," about Plutarch's attitudes to the masses, esp. p. 16 about manipulating the masses: "According to

horses, even of a gardener to his plants."[9] The people are lazy, ignorant, uneducated, and prone to overconfidence, insolence and violence, associated with disorder, uproar, meddling and sedition.[10]

Plutarch wants to avoid senseless revolts against the Romans by the *plêthos* and moreover interventions by the Romans into politics of Greek cities by showing how to be a Greek politician and simultaneously a subject in the Roman Empire.[11] Being a patriot, he is aware of the Greek norm of struggling for freedom[12] which was no longer appropriate due to the weakness of his contemporary Greece.[13] That means precisely to omit the former struggle for freedom in the political space to the end that the *plêthos* will not imitate it vainly today.

Trauma, Traumatization and Disaster

This paper will not treat Plutarch, his contemporaries or the protagonists of his examples as PTSD patients.[14] It works, however, with the idea of cultural trauma as a category of analysis. This is a possible key for understanding Plutarch's 'Political Precepts,' esp. 813d–814c. Beside the contemporary political interpretation of this text the idea of cultural trauma could be applied fruitfully to the Greeks in times of the Roman Empire in general and in particular to their handling and conceptualization of the Roman power considering the former freedom and glorious past.

Plutarch, the good statesman has not only to oppose the impulses of the masses. He has also to manipulate them, given that the mob is inaccessible to rational arguments."

9 Bremer, "Liberation of Greece," 267. Cf. also n. 29.

10 Cf. Saïd, "Plutarch and the People," 10.

11 Cf. Plutarch, *Praec. ger. rei publ.* 813e: "You who rule are a subject, ruling a State controlled by proconsuls, the agents of Caesar" (Fowler, LCL). It is significant that Plutarch, who hardly mentions the emperors in the 'Political Precepts,' is confined to local Greek politics: he ignores the ambitions of the Greek elite to go into imperial service (cf. Swain, Hellenism, 182f.) because then these politicians were perceived as Romans (cf. Pabst, "Mobilität und Stabilität," n. 49).

12 Cf. Plutarch, *Flam.* 11.2-3 as Plutarch's own thoughts: the Greeks had waged many wars for the sake of freedom (cf. Bremer, "Liberation of Greece," 263 n. 25; Swain, *Hellenism*, 127 n. 5; Jones, *Plutarch and Rome*, 98).

13 Cf. Plutarch, *Praec. ger. rei publ.* 824e–f; Arrian, *Diss. Epict.* 3.7.3; Dio Chrysostom, *Rhod.* 157-60. Cf. also for language and sentiment of Greek weakness in the past Pausanias, *Descr.* 1.4.1; 7.17.1; 10.19.8; Plutarch, *Phil.* 8.3.

14 It has become common to state psychological retrospective diagnostics in historical pasts, especially in ancient history. A representative bibliography in Melchior, "Caesar in Vietnam," 210 n. 5. Aislinn Melchior is very critical concerning the assumption that the Romans (I may add the Greeks), must have suffered psychological trauma, because they were exposed to combat so often. She concludes: "definitive evidence for the existence of PTSD in the ancient world does not exist" (ibid., 212).

We have to be aware that we cannot transfer the idea of an individual trauma of one body into a collective trauma of one big social body consisting of several individual bodies. In both cases, however, we find an underlying (constructed) disaster. This disaster has to be an existential experience of contingency which is so overwhelming that one cannot cope with this trauma: "Cultural trauma occurs when members of collective feel they have been subjected to a horrendous event that leaves indelible marks upon their group consciousness, marking their memories forever and changing their future identity in fundamental and irrevocable ways."[15] In this way a cultural trauma could become a fundamental part of group identity and it is also possible to share a trauma by empathy and sympathy over generations, as we will see the Athenians did when they were still recollecting Sulla's sack of their city in Plutarch's time.[16] The other perspective on the past, Plutarch wants to create with his examples, therefore creates another identity of the *plêthos* than the memory of the Persian Wars would do. In the case of the Greeks, it was not a single event which was traumatizing them. It was the circumstance that despite having inherited the struggle for freedom since the Persian Wars they are now ruled by the Romans.

Alexander states that for collectives there is no repression, denial and working through and "[c]ollective traumas are reflections of neither individual suffering nor actual events, but symbolic renderings that reconstruct and imagine them."[17] Different from Alexander I will show that the evidence for the Greeks show a tendency of either repression as omission (in the case of Phrynichos and the Amnesty) or working through a collective trauma (in the case of Thebes, Argos and the Harpalos Affair).

The disaster is not automatically a trauma and Alexander is right when he pays attention to the naturalistic fallacy 'events cause traumas': "… I maintain that events do not, in and of themselves, create collective trauma. Events are not inherently traumatic. Trauma is a socially mediated attribution."[18] Still Philostratus discusses the destruction of Thebes by Alexander the Great and the fear it had caused among the Greeks.[19] Destroying a whole *polis* was not

15 Alexander, *Trauma*, 6.

16 For a discussion of Sulla's conquest of Athens see Eckert, *Sulla* (forthcoming).

17 Ibid., 4. But he also speaks of a phase of "calming down," ibid. 26.

18 Alexander, *Trauma*, 13. Cf. Meier, *Justinian*, 33 for parallels, where he states concerning coping experience of contingency that the underlying event does not have to be horrendous, cf. ibid., 27 n. 9 for earthquakes which caused no damage. There are also other disasters like solar eclipses, comets or prodigia which caused no material or physical consequences but were perceived as disasters and evoked coping strategies or patterns of explanation.

19 Philostratus, *Vit. soph.* 2.15 p. 596 about the favorite theme that the Thebans accuses the Messenians of ingratitude because they refused to receive the Theban refugees when Thebes was taken by Alexander. Cf. Civiletti, *Filostrato*, 599 n. 6.

common in Ancient Greece. Thus the destruction by Alexander the Great was traumatic to them, because it injured their cultural norms.[20] Another case for the long range over time of cultural traumata are the battles between the Greeks which were traumatic for Plutarch[21] as the *symphora* of Roman rule was for Pausanias.[22] In these two cases I would identify the perception of a collective disaster with the perception of a cultural trauma.

Past and Present

First I present the text and after treating Plutarch's analysis of his present against the backdrop of the Greek past I will discuss the examples and their function in Plutarch's own time.

> Furthermore when we see little children trying playfully to bind their fathers' shoes on their feet or fit their crowns upon their heads, we only laugh, but the officials in the cities, when they foolishly urge the people to imitate the deeds, ideals, and actions of their ancestors, however unsuitable they may be to the present times and conditions, stir up the common folk and, though what they do is laughable, what is done to them is no laughing matter, unless they are merely treated with utter contempt. Indeed there are many acts of the Greeks of former times by recounting which the statesman can mould and correct the characters of our contemporaries, for example, at Athens by calling to mind, not deeds in war, but such things as the decree of amnesty after the downfall of the Thirty Tyrants, the fining of Phrynichus for presenting in a tragedy the capture of Miletus, their decking their heads with garlands when Cassander refounded Thebes; how, when they heard of the clubbing at Argos, in which the Argives killed fifteen hundred of their own citizens, they decreed that an expiatory sacrifice be carried about in the assembly; and how, when they were searching the houses at the time of Harpalus's frauds, they passed by only one, that of a newly married man. By emulating acts like these it is even now possible to resemble our ancestors, but Marathon, the Eurymedon, Plataea, and all the other examples which make the common folk vainly to swell with pride and kick up their heels, should be left to the schools of the sophists. (Plutarch, *Praec. ger. rei publ.* 814a–c [Fowler, LCL])

20 Cf. Xenophon, *Hell.* 2.2.19-20: Corinth and Thebes claimed the destruction of Athens after the Peloponnesian War, but the Lacedaemonians rejected it due to the former merits of the Athenians in the Persian Wars. But Alexander has not destroyed Thebes due to the city's role in the Persian Wars.

21 Plutarch, *Flam.* 11.3-4: If one excepts Marathon, Salamis, Plataeae, Thermopylae and Cimon's achievements at Erymedon and Cyprus (all battles against a foreign threat), "Greece has fought all her battles to bring servitude upon herself, and every one of her trophies stands as a memorial of her own calamity (symphora) and disgrace …" (Perrin, LCL).

22 Cf. Hutton, "Disaster of Roman Rule," about Pausanias, *Descr.* 8.27.1. It is highly discussed in scholarship whether Pausanias means "a disaster incident at times of Roman rule" or "disaster [consisting] of Roman rule." I follow Hutton who favors the latter translation.

Whereas Brad Cook discussed these examples and saw self-control and moderation as the common thread for Greek politics, I would like to draw attention to the handling of disastrous events in Greek history and in Plutarch's own time. In opposition to Cook, who searched for the examples in the extant work of Plutarch, I maintain that we have to look at the recent rhetoric to understand the role of the examples and how they were perceived by the *plêthos*.[23] In addition, Cook neglected *what* Plutarch recalls or omits in *which* context.

Cook supposed that the examples are carefully chosen by Plutarch, but that they "are not so great or famous—one might call them obscure."[24] However, they are not obscure because these examples are part of well-known examples belonging to the recent rhetoric of the Second Sophistic. They have to be famous because otherwise Menemachos and the *plêthos* would not understand them. Plutarch gives five historical examples which the politician should mention to the masses in Athens. They could be seen, in contradiction to Cook's approach, as specific Greek cultural practices of coping with disasters so they will not become cultural traumata. All of them are dealing with the reaction to an external power (oligarchic state, Persians, Thebes, Argos and Alexander) and this external power in Plutarch's own time, i.e. the object of comparison, is Rome. Therefore two layers can be observed: first the layer of the disastrous experience in historical past and its handling; second the layer of the handling of the cultural trauma in Plutarch's own time.

Although Plutarch states "political oratory admits more generalization, more history, myth, and metaphor than you find in the courtroom" (803a [Fowler, LCL]), the politician should omit the battles of Marathon, Eurymedon and Plataeae in Athens. Plutarch emphasizes the Athenian role in these battles and not the panhellenic frame because the reference to these battles in other *poleis* could have other consequences than stirring up the masses, since the Athenians still identified[25] themselves with their classical glorious ances-

23 It is senseless to search e.g. for the use of *amnêstia* in the extant work of Plutarch, if one is interested in how Menemachos could understand and imitate the examples. In that case one has to look for the common sources of Plutarch, Menemachos and the *plêthos* in order to be able understand the examples in the same way as Plutarch does.

24 Cook, "Imitable events," 201. He also supposed that Plutarch has chosen them "in explicit opposition to the standard, famous, well-known episodes from the glory days of Hellas ..." But if you consider these examples as part of far better known examples, the strong judgement by Cook will solve itself. It is only correct to claim that the examples do not belong to war, but take place after war or civil strife.

25 Greek identity consists not exclusively of cultural choice but also of local identities (as a countermovement to 'Roman globalization') and that's why Plutarch had to choose one polis as a test case. Cf. Whitmarsh, *Microidentities* and Jones, "Multiple Identities." However, the Greeks had never been romanized like the people in the western provinces and had not established a province-identity. Cf. Woolf, "Becoming Roman," and Pabst, "Identitätssuche."

tors. If stirring up the masses was not a real outcome, in fact Plutarch would not have been cautious about this particular impact.

Initially Plutarch constructs several opposites. The appeal to imitate the deeds (*erga*), thoughts (*phronêmata*) and actions (*praxeis*) of the ancestors makes the Archons appear like fools. But the result of an agitated mass is not ridiculous. On the one hand Plutarch fears the mob[26] and on the other hand the Roman intervention.[27] In the 'Political Precepts' the *dêmos* is criticized because of its stubbornness and violence.[28] In another context the people are a "suspect and unstable wild animal."[29]

There were recent Roman interventions: in Pergamum under Nero, in Rhodes under Domitian and in Thessaly under Augustus.[30] The past deeds of war are unequal (*asymmetros,* compared to the present) and it is impossible to imitate them in the present.[31] The memories of the great victories of Athens are reserved for the private space of the sophistry schools (where one can be proud of them) and should not be mentioned to the masses,[32] because they are inviting to struggle for the lost freedom.

In his life of Arat Plutarch interprets the political role of the Achaean League and of Aratus as evidence of the Greek strength (*hellenikê alkê*): they "showed the world that Greek prowess was invincible, whenever it enjoyed good order, harmonious discipline, and a sensible leader" (Plutarch, *Arat.* 9.5 [Perrin, LCL]).[33]

26 Cf. Saïd, "Plutarch and the People," 7–25: Plutarch's sentiments towards the masses are negative in general.

27 Cf. Swain, *Hellenism*, 166. On several occasions the Romans intervene in the Greek poleis and Plutarch is aware of it, cf. Plutarch, *Praec. ger. rei publ.* 815a. Cf. Dio Chrysostom, *Tumult.* 14 warning a rioting crowd of the risk of proconsular intervention. But if you show the Romans that you live in concord in a Greek polis, they have no need to limit your freedom.

28 Plutarch, *Praec. ger. rei publ.* 801e.

29 Plutarch, *Praec. ger. rei publ.* 800c. Cf. Saïd, "Plutarch and the People," 18–24 about Plutarchean similes.

30 Plutarch, *Praec. ger. rei publ.* 815d; Tacitus, *Ann.* 16.23; Cassius Dio, *Hist.* 60.24.4. Cf. Bowersock, "Römisches Thessalien," 50–52. Cf. about these events and much more Pekáry, "Seditio," 141.

31 Cf. Plutarch, *An seni* 784f; *Praec. ger. rei publ.* 805a, 824c: all war is gone between Greeks and Barbarians and there is no need of statesmen for this, so to speak: peace is unpolitical in this understanding.

32 Cf. Plutarch, *Praec. ger. rei publ.* 813e, where Iphicrates is exercising a speech at home. But he is advised that he should take his weapons and relinquish the schools to the sophists. On another occasion Plutarch speaks of Marathon, Salamis and Plataeae as *ta kallista kai lamprotata kai prôta tôn Hellenikôn ergôn* (Plutarch, *Comp. Arist. Cat.* 5.1). Cf. Plutarch, *Glor. Ath.* 350b: "And when at Salamis and Mycalê and Plataeae they had firmly established, as in adamant, the liberty of Greece, they handed it down to all mankind" (Babbitt, LCL). Here the three battles represent the freedom of the Greeks. Therefore the omission of the battles to the masses is like repression of the former Greek freedom.

33 Cf. also Polybius, *Hist.* 2.39.11.

Greece always struggled for its freedom, as Plutarch states in his 'Flamininus.'[34] In his speech 'To Rome' Aelius Aristides emphasizes the struggle for freedom as a Greek achievement and Appian stresses the Greek skill to be *adoulôton* (unenslaved) till the Macedonian rule.[35] I may cite Appian's own sentiments:

Their wars were waged not so much for the sake of acquisition of empire, as out of mutual rivalry, and the most glorious of them were fought in defense of Greek freedom against the aggression of foreign powers.... [T]heir history since the time of Philipp ... and Alexander ... is in my opinion most inglorious and unworthy of them. (Appian, *Praef.* 8 = 29–31 [White, LCL])

Plutarch shows a similar picture of the Greek past by comparing Flamininus and Philopoemen: "Titus, in his quest of fame, availed himself of the culminating power of Rome; whereas Philopoemen flourished when Greece was already in decline." (Plutarch, *Comp. Philop. Flam.* 2 [Perrin, LCL]). The last Hellenic achievement was, however, the liberation of Corinth, Acrocorinth and Lechaeon from the Macedonian domination in 243 B.C.[36] Now, however, the Greek strength is gone and Plutarch advises the contemporary politician to point to the present weakness of Greece:

Then he will instruct his people both individually and collectively and will call attention to the weak condition of Greek affairs, in which it is best for wise men to accept one advantage — a life of harmony and quiet — since fortune has left us no prize open for competition. For what dominion, what glory is there for those who are victorious? What sort of power is it which a small edict of a proconsul may annul or transfer to another man and which, even if it last, has nothing in it seriously worthwhile? (Plutarch, *Praec. ger. rei publ.* 824e–f [Fowler, LCL])

Vespasian cancelled the freedom granted to Greece by Nero in 66/7 A.D.,[37] making Achaea once again a senatorial province. According to Pausanias, the reason for this act was that the Greeks were fighting among themselves and had forgotten how to be free.[38] In its glorious past the Greeks were free but the price was permanent war. In Plutarch's own time the Greeks enjoyed the benefits of peace but the price was the loss of freedom.[39] Therefore Plutarch

34 Cf. n. 12.

35 Aristides, *Or.* 26.51; Appian, *Praef.* 8 = 31 and cf. Pabst, "Mobilität und Stabilität," n. 37–38.

36 Plutarch, *Arat.* 24. Cf. also ibid., 16 where Arat participated in the conquest of Acrocorinth not to help the Sikyonians or Achaeans but to expel the Macedonians from Greece.

37 SEG 3II 814 (= Supplementum Epigraphicum Graecum).

38 Pausanias, *Descr.* 7.17.4. On the other hand Plutarch, *Glor. Ath.* is a treatise of recollecting the former Greek freedom in classical times and in Plutarch, *Sera*, cap. 32 = p. 568a Nero appears in a positive way because he gave freedom to the Greeks.

39 Ángeles Durán López, "Plutarco," 41: "... en los Preceptos Políticos Paz y Libertad como terminus antitéticos: en su glorioso pasado Grecia gozaba de esta última, pero las guerras

writes that the only wise thing a statesman can do is to further concord and friendship among his relatives and fellow citizens and to remove strife, discord, and all enmity.[40] Plutarch, Dio Chrysostom and Aelius Aristides point to the importance of *homonoia* and the avoidance of internal quarrels.[41] Otherwise the Romans could intervene in the *polis*. If someone enters an office, you should "keep your eyes upon the orators' platform, and not have great pride or confidence in your crown, since you see the boots[42] of Roman proconsuls just above your head" (Plutarch, *Praec. ger. rei publ.* 813e [Fowler, LCL]). Plutarch also writes,

> you must not only call to mind those considerations of which Pericles reminded himself when he assumed the cloak of a general 'Take care, Pericles; you are ruling free men, you are ruling Greeks, Athenian citizens,' but you must also say to yourself: 'You who rule are a subject, ruling a State controlled by proconsuls, the agents of Caesar.' (ibid.)

Plutarch himself was a Greek patriot and never suppressed the glorious past in his other writings.[43] Here we have the other side of the politics of memory: Menemachos as a future *archon* should recall Pericles' words while the *plêthos* should not imitate the struggle for freedom.

eran constantes; actualmente disfruta de los beneficios de la paz, pero es al precio de su libertad."

40 Plutarch, *Praec. ger. rei publ.* 824d.

41 "... [A] whole ideological industry was established around this word." (Swain, *Hellenism*, 181). Cf. the *homonoia* speeches of Dio Chrysostom, *2 Tars.* 38 (Nicomedaea and Nicaea), 41-42 (Prusa and Apamaea) and also Plutarch, *Praec. ger. rei publ.* 824c–e, 808c; Aristides, *Or.* 23-24 (Keil). Cf. also Theriault, *Culte d'Homonoia* for further evidence on *homonoia*.

42 Apelt translates "Patrizierschuhe" and for Swain, *Hellenism*, 166 n. 93, 387 n. 40, Jones, *Plutarch and Rome*, 133 and Fowler they are the boots of the proconsuls. Whereas de Blois, "Classical and contemporary Statesmen," 59 translates the *kaltious* as boots of roman soldiers (like Bowie, "Greeks and Their Past," 18 n. 49 "legionaries' boots"). His whole argumentation is based on this failure and leads to a wrong conclusion by emphasizing the role of the Roman military concerning Plutarch's knowledge of the real power structures. Cf. Plutarch, *Aem.* 5, where *kaltion* (lat. *calceus*) are the boots of a patrician and not of a simple soldier.

43 Note his Cimon which commemorates the battle of Eurymedon or Aristides at Plataea (Plutarch, *Comp. Arist. Cat.* 5.1). The motif of 'On the Glory of the Athenians' (the men of action are superior to the men of art) can be found everywhere in the 'Parallel Lives.' But he is not alone: Aristides stresses the Athenian military power massively in his 'Panathenaicus' and is simultaneously able to deliver a 'Panegyricus' to Rome. Cf. Swain, *Hellenism*, 168.

Phrynichos and Amnesty

In an survey covering the time from ancient Greek history to the reunified Germany Christian Meier comes to the conclusion that, contrary to the current imperative of remembering traumatic events, in history there has always been an imperative of oblivion.[44] The Greeks in particular and especially the Athenians were dominated by the idea of *mê mnêsikakein*, i.e. not to recall something bad after civil strife and wars.[45] For Meier the amnesty and the punishment of Phrynichos are also examples of this phenomenon. On the contrary, the historian's profession is to remind of wars and defeats to learn from history.[46] The Athenians continued completely different with the fining of Phrynichus or the Amnesty after the Tyranny of the Thirty. There is no imperative of oblivion at the historians being individuals but at the collective of the citizens. Their strategy seems to be drawing a line, i.e. politics of memory which focus on oblivion to save the peace and suppress vengeance. That is why the *mê mnêsikakein* can be found in inscriptional contracts between *poleis* or inside a *polis* after *staseis* or wars.[47]

On the one hand one has to be well aware of the particular events which Plutarch has chosen for his examples and of the particular actions he has chosen to imitate on the other. Concerning the Phrynichos example it is the punishment for recalling the devastation of Miletus in a tragedy. Herodotus is our earliest source for the event and he writes that the destruction of Miletus was the beginning of disasters for Greeks and Barbarians.[48] The audience broke out in tears, Phrynichus had to accept a monetary fining[49] of 1000 Drachmae and the revival of the play was banned because it recalled 'domestic bad' (*anamnêsanta oikêia kaka*).[50] Herodotus speaks of *kaka* (bad thing, disaster) which is the underlying event of trauma caused by the memory of it.[51] There is a scientific controversy about what *oikêia* meant: either it was

44 Meier, *Gebot zu vergessen*, 9–10.

45 The earliest evidence is Herodotus, *Hist.* 8.29.8. The Phocians should pay 50 talents of silver for freedom with the Thessalians (that they forget the bad things done to them by the Phocians). The events took place in 480 B.C. but Herodot wrote his Histories in the thirties or early twenties of the 5th century B.C.

46 Cf. Thucydides, *Hist.* 1.22; Polybius, *Hist.* 6.1.

47 E.g. Werner and Bengtson, *Staatsverträge*, no. 187. More examples are no. 204 (emended), 215 (= Xenophon, *Hell.* 2.4.43) and 289, line 82.

48 Herodotus, *Hist.* 5.97.3.

49 Ryan, "Phrynichos kommt vor Gericht," about the question who had imposed the penalty which should not be discussed here.

50 Herodotus, *Hist.* 6.21.2. Cf. Meier, *Gebot zu vergessen*, 16.

51 Cf. Meier, *Justinian*, 31 states that the Greeks denoted a bad event often by a concrete term but did not use the term katastrophê very often for disasters (which are rapid and radical incidents). But one has to be careful in using this disaster definition because you have to take a normal case for granted. Cf. also Melchior, "Caesar in Vietnam," 220–21. about the

the shared grief of the Milesians by the Athenians (earlier dating of the play: 493/2)[52] or it was the grief of the Athenians because their own city was destroyed by the Persians (later dating: 480/79 B.C.). I favor the earlier dating of the tragedy and the thesis that it deals with the shared grief.[53] The context of the passage in Herodotus is that he blames the Sybarites, who did not fall in grief for the Milesians, although the Milesians did so for the destruction of Sybaris in 510 B.C. Therefore Herodot praises the Athenians for grieving about the Milesians[54] whereas Plutarch's focus is on the punishment of Phrynichos and therefore on the oblivion.

However, the cause for breaking out into tears was the *anamnêsanta* (remembrance) of the destruction of Miletus and therefore the remembrance was banned. And indeed, there is no surviving fragment of the tragedy. It seems that the prohibition of performance was like a prohibition of remembrance. This oblivion as repression shows one way of coping with cultural trauma by the Greeks. To conclude and apply the result to Plutarch's own time, we have to suppose, that the Greeks should imitate the punishment of one who recalls e.g. the destruction of Corinth by Mummius[55] or the sack of Athens by Sulla.[56] These two incidents could also be seen as traumatic events for the Greeks caused by the foreign Roman power like the power of the Persians in the Phrynichos example. Plutarch is familiar with Sulla's sack of Athens and the Piraeus. He shows, what happened to the Athenians as they were too proud of their glorious past:

But after a long time, at last, with much ado, he (Aristion) sent out two or three of his fellow-revellers to treat for peace, to whom Sulla, when they made no demands which could save the city, but talked in lofty strains about Theseus and Eumolpus and the

question whether there was a desensitization of ancient people caused by omnipresent disasters.

52 Normally the play is dated to the archonship of Themistocles in 493/2 B.C., because he was *chorêgos* for another play of Phrynichos in 476 B.C. (Plutarch, *Them.* 5). Athenians and the Milesians saw themselves as Hellenes and Ionians, therefore the destruction of Miletus was a common trauma for them. Cook, "Imitable events," 205 sees the Athenians and Milesians as a "socio-political entity" with a common identity. Because the Athenians supported Miletus in the Ionian Revolt the destruction of Miletus was also their own suffering.

53 Contra Roisman, "Phrynichos," 17–19, who assumed *oikêia* as the grief of the Athenians about the destruction of their own city and therefore the play must be dated to 480/79 B.C.

54 Herodotus, *Hist.* 6.21.1. Still Pausanias reports that only the Athenians had an altar of compassion (*Eleou bômos*, Pausanias, *Descr.* 1.17.1).

55 Strabo, *Geogr.* 8.6.23 p. 381–82 (= Polybius, *Hist.* 39.2) states that Polybius described the destruction pitifully. Cf. also Diodorus 32.26–27 (= *Exc. sent.* 379–80) and Plutarch, *Phil.* 21: disastrous days of Greece following the fall of Corinth.

56 Plutarch, *Sull.* 13–14 (about Sulla's cruelty); Pausanias, *Descr.* 1.20.4–7 (not until Hadrian Athens flourished again), 9.33.6. Appian, *Mithr.* 38–39 reports in a hostile way Sulla's inglorious conquest of Athens (the inhabitants were weak because of suffering from hunger; therefore, the reader has to conclude, that it was not Sulla's merit). Also the Piraeus had been destroyed and never reached its former function, cf. Habicht, *Athen*, 306–10.

Persian wars, said: 'Be off, my dear Sirs, and take these speeches with you; for I was not sent to Athens by the Romans to learn its history, but to subdue its rebels.' (Plutarch, *Sull.* 13.4 [Perrin, LCL])

One cause, Plutarch states for Sulla's passion for capturing Athens, was "a sort of ardour against the shadow of the city's former glory" (Plutarch, *Sull.* 13.1 Perrin, LCL]). The memory of Sulla's conquest was still alive in Plutarch's own time. He states that the oldest Athenians still know the place where Sulla had taken the wall[57] and that up to his day the number of the slain "is determined only by the space that was covered with blood" (Plutarch, *Sull.* 14.3 [Perrin, LCL]). These two memories indicate that in daily life the horrendous events still took a greater part than in literature. Furthermore Diodorus states that the wasted Corinth still causes the recalling of the city's destruction:

This was the city that, to the dismay of later ages, was now wiped out by her conquerors. Nor was it only at the time of her downfall that Corinth evoked great compassion from those that saw her; even in later times, when they saw the city levelled to the ground, all who looked upon her were moved to pity. (Diodorus 32.26.1 [Walton, LCL])

As in the life of Cicero, Plutarch uses the amnesty of 403 B.C. in the sense of oblivion.[58] The function of the amnesty was in his eyes the refoundation of peace and the avoidance of vengeance. So, what was the function as a reference point of remembrance in Plutarch's own time? In the rhetoric, e.g. in Aelius Aristides' *Panathenaïkos*, the amnesty belongs to the glory of Athens in the same way like the Persian Wars do.

It (Athens) not only bore more gracefully its defeats in war than others their successes, but it also settled its troubles at home in such a way that all mankind had a definition of moderation and no one later could discover a better arrangement than theirs. No traveller passing by but wept, though he beheld but a few scant relics of her past prosperity and glory.[59] (Aristides, *Or.* 1,253 [Behr])

As an Athenian in times of the Roman Empire one can still be proud of all achievements of the past in private or rhetorical space but the glory of Athens should be reduced to its nonmilitary achievements in the political space.

57 Plutarch, *Sull.* 14.2.

58 Plutarch, *Cic.* 42.3: Cicero persuaded the senate to imitate the Athenians and decree an amnesty for the attack upon Caesar and to assign provinces to Cassius and Brutus. Cook, "Imitable events," 203 supports the identification of *amnêstia* with *oblivio*. Other occurrences of amnesty in Plutarch are *Ant.* 14.3, *Brut.* 19.1 and *Caes.* 67.8.

59 Cf. also Aristides, *Or.* 23,43–52 (Keil) where the Persian Wars and the amnesty are treated together and show the benefit of concord.

Cook interprets the fining of Phrynichos by the Athenians as a manifestation of their self-control.[60] On the one hand there is the deep grief for the Milesians and on the other hand there is the suppression of any uncontrolled reaction to the grief.[61] This might be conceded for the year of performance 493/2 B.C., but what about Plutarch's present? According to Cook the Phrynichos example stands in a logical line with the amnesty. While the amnesty should suppress internal strife and therefore not provoke Rome's intervention, the Phrynichos example shows how you don't cross the limits of your political opportunities. Although the problem of *stasis* is a theme in the 'Political Precepts,'[62] here it is not. In order to conduct Cook's interpretation of the Phrynichos example into another direction I have to add Plutarch's remarks about Pardalas.[63] Pardalas and his fellows forgot (*eklanthanein*) their limits and in consequence were put to death by the Romans.[64] Plutarch recalled Menemachos of Pardalas because his addressee has an "excellent example at home in the enmity of Pardalas and Tyrrhenus,[65] which came near to destroying Sardis by involving the state in rebellion and war (*apostasis kai polemos*) as the result of petty private matters"[66] (Plutarch, *Praec. ger. rei publ.* 825d [Fowler, LCL]). This remark shows how internal policy becomes for-

60 Cook, "Imitable events," 205.

61 But it is not quite clear what this uncontrolled reaction could be. Cook, "Imitable events," 205 says "uncontrolled reaction (as the Athenians' initial aid to the Milesians brought about two invasions!)." Does he have in mind that the Athenians declared war to the Persians in the 5th century B.C. and now in the 2nd century A.D. the Athenians declare war to the Romans? Plutarch is far away from considering war with Rome, cf. nn. 5 and 36 ('all war is gone between Greeks and Barbarians').

62 Cf. Plutarch, *Praec. ger. rei publ.* 824b, 805e and also Plutarch, *Sol.* 21.1 on Solon's law. Plutarch's position is that the politician should involve in civil strife in the role of a mediator to restore harmony.

63 He and his family cf. IvSardeis (= Inschriften von Sardeis) 121, 127; OGIS (= Orientis Graeci Inscriptiones Selectae) 470, line 10 and Habicht, *Inschriften*, no. 140. There is a C. Iulius Pardalas as a priest of Augustus and Roma in IvE (= Inschriften von Ephesos) 7.2 n. 3825 and a Ti. Iulius Pardalas at ILS (= Inscriptiones Latinea Selectae) 1988.

64 Plutarch, *Praec. ger. rei publ.* 813f.

65 Tyrrhenus is completely unknown. Maybe Plutarch translates a 'Tuscus' into attic Greek but this means it was a Roman/Etruscan. There is a link between Lydia and Etruria made by Herodotus, *Hist.* 1.94 and still known in Imperial times by Tacitus, *Ann.* 4.55 (inhabitants of Sardis competed for a temple of Tiberius and pointed to the connection between Lydia and Etruria) and Strabo, *Geogr.* 5.2.2 p. 219. Plutarch did also know this link, cf. Plutarch, *Quaest. rom.* 53 p. 277c.

66 Cf. also Plutarch, *Praec. ger. rei publ.*, cap. 14, esp. 809d where he claims to end personal enmity in favor of the patris. What does apostasis mean? Probably the same incident like in the episode of Sthennon and Pompey, who said to him that he was responsible for the revolt of the Marmertineans, cf. Plutarch, *Praec. ger. rei publ.* 815e and also 203d and Plutarch, *Pomp.* 10. The crisis of Sardis takes place on an unknown date at the end of the first century A.D., cf. Meyer-Zwiffelhofer, *Politikôs archein*, 306.

eign policy and where Plutarch's focus lies. He opposes drawing in the Romans into affairs of the polis:

... [T]he statesman, while making his native State readily obedient to its sovereigns, must not further humble it; ... some who do, by referring everything, great or small, to the sovereigns, bring the reproach of slavery upon their country, or rather wholly destroy its constitutional government, making it dazed, timid, and powerless in everything.... [T]hose who invite the sovereign's decision on every decree, meeting of a council, granting of a privilege, or administrative measure, force their sovereign to be their master more than he desires.... [A]nd as a result senate, popular assembly, courts, and the entire local government lose their authority. (Plutarch, *Praec. ger. rei publ.* 814f–815a [Fowler, LCL])

A Greek politician makes foreign policy when he struggles with the Romans and the focus is on the relation to an outer political entity. Therefore, the sympathy is limited: if the Athenians would show their sympathy with Sardis in the case of Pardalas it would be equal to a declaration of war against the Romans (because the relation between Sardis and Rome was nearly *apostasis* and *polemos*). Therefore Plutarch insists on fining one who is recalling the grief of another Greek polis, otherwise the *plêthos* could sympathize with the Sardians and the Romans would also be forced to intervene in Athens.

Thebes and Argos

Thebes had been destroyed by Alexander in 336 B.C. and according to Pausanias the Athenians had taken a big part in the refoundation by Cassander in 316 B.C.[67] According to Plutarch's own words in his 'Life of Alexander,' they have shown grief about the destruction and the misfortune of the Thebans.[68] If the Athenians were crowning themselves[69] with a wreath, it would mean that they like to show their pleasure about the refoundation. Rather than being hereditary enemies the Athenians displayed their sympathy with the Thebans.

The refoundation of Corinth could also stand in the background of this example. The Greeks could not fail to notice that Corinth was an entirely Ro-

67 Pausanias, *Descr.* 9.7.1. But on occasion of the list of cities which fought against Philipp II. Pausanias states that the Boeotians were allies of the Macedonians because they feared that Thebes would be resettled by the Athenians (Pausanias, *Descr.* 1.25.4).

68 Plutarch, *Alex.* 13.1. The destruction caused the vengeance of Dionysos (Plutarch, *Alex.* 13.4).

69 All examples are from the perspective of the Athenians, but Apelt, *Moralische Schriften*,103 translates "... daß sich die Thebaner bekränzten, als Kassander Theben ...," whereas the Athenians showed their pleasure on occasion of the refoundation of Thebes. Cf. Pausanias, *Descr.* 9.7.1-2 where he states explicitly Athens support for the refoundation.

man city, which has been refounded by Caesar.[70] Although there was a tendency of becoming more Greek due to the Greek environment of the city[71] Corinth was a (re)foundation of the former enemy. Plutarch wants to say: as Athenians in the Roman Empire show your pleasure about the refoundation of Corinth, even though you have quarreled with this *polis* and the Romans in the past. This ability of reconciliation is something glorious the contemporary Athenian should be proud of instead of the glorious Persian Wars.

The case of Argos is similar. There was a horrendous civil strife in Argos between the democratic and the oligarchic party in 370 B.C. of an incomparable magnitude as Diodorus writes.[72] It was common to start the assembly in Athens with a *katharsion*.[73] But the democratic Athenians, sitting in the assembly, made again an expiatory sacrifice after they heard of the victory of the democrats in Argos.[74] Instead of being happy about the defeat of the oligarchs, they purified themselves in sympathy with the Argivic oligarchs from the bloodguilt of the democrats.[75] Cook, however, follows Dionysius of Halicarnassus[76] and thinks that the Athenians would protect themselves from falling into civil strife with this apotropaic act. "With this fourth exemplum, then, Plutarch stresses the governmental means whereby the benefits of the first three exempla can be maintained and protected."[77] It is right that Plutarch is generally against civil strife and that Isocrates, Diodorus and Dionysius had treated the Argivic exemplum regarding civil strife. But the *katharsion* and the relation to another *polis* are in the focus of this example. I suggest that this example like the former example deals with empathy for the former enemy which were the Romans in Plutarch's time.

Harpalos

Athenian politicians had been bribed by Harpalus with money of Alexander the Great, among them maybe Demosthenes. This exemplum was extensively

70 Cf. Pausanias, *Descr.* 2.1.2: No one of the old Corinthians are still living in Corinth, but Roman colonists.
71 Cf. Dio Chrysostom, [Cor.] 26 (Favorinus).
72 Diodorus 15.57.3–58.4. Isocrates wants Philipp to save the Greeks and cites the example of the Argives whose killed the notable and rich citizens (Isocrates, *Phil.* 52). At Aristides, *Or.* 24.27 (Keil) an Athenian embassy advises the Argives to offer an amnesty on occasion of internal strife.
73 Cf. Aeschines, *Tim.* 23 and Harpocration, *Lex.* s.v. *katharsion*.
74 Cf. Parker, *Miasma*, 21: it was a "vivid symbolic action."
75 Purifying from blood like in Herodotus, *Hist.* 1.44 (*kathairô*, *Zeus katharsios*). Cf. also Parker, *Miasma*, 104–43.
76 Dionysius of Halicarnassos wants to save the Romans from civil war with the Argivic example (Dionysius of Halicarnassus, *Ant. rom.* 7.66.5).
77 Cook, "Imitable events," 208.

discussed in the time of the Second Sophistic.[78] The Athenians feared Alexander and therefore searched for the betrayers. Nevertheless, they did not surrender their own sacred laws by disturbing the wedding night. If the house of the newly married couple was passed,[79] it should show the prudence of the Athenians. Against a foreign threat the Athenians upheld their cultural norms and insofar Cook is right by stating that the line of the preceding four examples is crowned by this one: "In Advice on Political Life, Plutarch ignores the rest of the Harpalos affair and focuses on this detail because the Athenians' care in this matter illustrates by its very insignificance how all things in the community must be managed with constant regard and respect for the good of community, without exception."[80]

In contrast with this, I suggest that this example indicates like the others, that Plutarch chooses a snippet from the current examples of the contemporary rhetoric but changes the perspective. On the first layer they are not focusing the internal (as Cook thought) but the external relations of the polis. Furthermore, Plutarch said that the examples should mold the character (*êthopoiein*) and evoke prudence (*sôphronizein*). All examples are well known to the audience, but the masses should not imitate the military but the peaceful aspects. On the second layer they are dealing with disaster experiences and show how to handle them in order to prevent them of becoming cultural traumata for the Athenians.

Conclusion

The political reality of the Athenian *plêthos* in the Roman Empire was an antagonism to the instigation to imitate the deeds of the ancestors because now the *plêthos* was not the former democratic *dêmos*. Plutarch saw the contemporary weakness of Greece as the limiting factor for the Greek politicians in the Roman Empire against the backdrop of the Greek past. He wants to avoid senseless revolts against the Romans by the *plêthos* and also external interventions into the Greek *polis* by the Romans.

While Plutarch recalls the heroic Greek past in his writings or places it in the schools of the sophists, this martial and heroic past should not be mentioned to the masses in a political context. The sophist is somehow different than the politician and can therefore present the glorious Greek past in his speeches. While the Greek patriot may be proud of the martial past, the

78 E.g. Pausanias, *Descr.* 2.33.3–5 or Philostratus, *Vit. soph.* p. 542–43, who counts three of the most famous six speeches of Polemon about Demosthenes. One of them deals with his claim for death for himself after the Harpalos affair.

79 Cf. Plutarch, *Dem.* 25.8 who gives more details.

80 Cook, "Imitable events," 209.

masses should be proud of the peaceful part of the past. Therefore it depends on the addressee, which reference to the past can be made. As Alexander has stated, a cultural trauma changes the group consciousness, marks the memories forever and changes the future identity. Plutarch was aware of the struggle for freedom as one part of the Greek identity with its sources in the Greek past up to the Persian wars. Therefore he wanted to change the consciousness of the *plêthos* by emphasizing another perspective on the past. Plutarch's Greek present has to suffer from the cultural trauma of Roman rule (i.e. the struggle for freedom was no more possible) and he advises omission as a strategy of coping with it.

Bibliography

Aalders, G. J. D., and L. de Blois. "Plutarch und die politische Philosophie der Griechen." *Aufstieg und Niedergang der römischen Welt* 36.5:3384-404. Part 2, *Principat*, 36.5. Edited by W. Haase. Berlin: de Gruyter, 1992.

Aelius Aristides. *The Complete Works*. Translated by C. A. Behr. 2 vols. Leiden: Brill, 1986.

—. *Quae supersunt omnia*. Edited by B. Keil. 2 vols. Berlin: Weidmann, 1898. Repr. Hildesheim: Olms, 1964.

Alexander, J. C. *Trauma: A Social Theory*. Cambridge: Polity 2012.

Ángeles Durán López, M. de los. "Plutarco, Ciudadano griego y súbdito Romano." Pages 33-41 in *Plutarch's Statesman and his Aftermath: Political, Philosophical, and Literary Aspects*. Vol. 1 of *The Statesman in Plutarch's Works: Proceedings of the Sixth International Conference of the International Plutarch Society, Nijmegen/Castle Hernen, May 1-5, 2002*. Edited by L. de Blois et al. Leiden: Brill, 2004.

Apelt, O. *Plutarch, Moralische Schriften*. Vol. 3. Leipzig: Meiner, 1927.

Appian. *Roman History*. Translated by H. White. 4 vols. Loeb Classical Library. Cambridge: Harvard University Press, 1982.

Blois, L. de, J. Bons, T. Kessels, and D. M. Schenkeveld, eds. *The Statesman in Plutarch's Works*. 2 vols. Leiden: Brill, 2004-2005.

Blois, L. de. "Classical and Contemporary Statesmen in Plutarch's 'Praecepta.'" Pages 57-63 in *Plutarch's Statesman and His Aftermath: Political, Philosophical, and Literary Aspects*. Vol. 1 of *The Statesman in Plutarch's Works: Proceedings of the Sixth International Conference of the International Plutarch Society, Nijmegen/Castle Hernen, May 1-5, 2002*. Edited by L. de Blois et al. Leiden: Brill, 2004.

Bremer, J. M. "Plutarch and the 'Liberation of Greece.'" Pages 257-67 in *The Statesman in Plutarch's Greek and Roman Lives*. Vol. 2 of *The Statesman in Plutarch's Works: Proceedings of the Sixth International Conference of the International Plutarch Society, Nijmegen/Castle Hernen, May 1-5, 2002*. Edited by L. de Blois et al. Leiden: Brill, 2005.

Bowersock, G. W. "Some Persons in Plutarch's Moralia." *Classical Quarterly* 15 (1965): 266-70.

—. "Zur Geschichte des römischen Thessaliens." Pages 47-59 in *Studies on the Eastern Roman Empire*. Edited by G. W. Bowersock. Goldbach: Keip, 1996. Repr. from *Rheinisches Museum* 108 (1965): 277-89.

Bowie, E. L. "The Greeks and Their Past in the Second Sophistic." *Past & Present* 46 (1970): 3-41.

—. "The Geography of the Second Sophistic: Cultural Variations." Pages 65-83 in *Paideia: The World of the Second Sophistic*. Edited by B. E. Borg. Berlin: de Gruyter, 2004.

Civiletti, M. *Filostrato: Vite dei Sofisti, testo Greco a fronte*. Milan: Bompiani, 2002.

Cook, B. L. "Plutarch's 'Many Other' Imitable Events: Mor. 814b and the Statesman's Duty." Pages 201-10 in *Plutarch's Statesman and His Aftermath: Political, Philosophical, and Literary Aspects*. Vol. 1 of *The Statesman in Plutarch's Works: Proceedings of the Sixth International Conference of the International Plutarch Society, Nijmegen/Castle Hernen, May 1-5, 2002*. Edited by L. de Blois et al. Leiden: Brill, 2004.

Desideri, P. „Greek Poleis and the Roman Empire: Nature and Features of Political Virtues in an Autocratic System." Pages 83-98 in *Virtues for the People: Aspects of Plutarchian Ethics*. Edited by G. Roskam and L. Van der Stockt. Leuven: Leuven University Press, 2011.

Eckert, A. "Das kulturelle Gedächtnis von Römern und Griechen und die antike Erinnerung an Lucius Cornelius Sulla." PhD diss., University of Halle-Wittenberg, 2012 (forthcoming).

Habicht, C. *Die Inschriften des Asklepieions*. Berlin: de Gruyter, 1969.

—. *Athen: Die Geschichte der Stadt in hellenistischer Zeit*. München: Beck, 1995.

Halfmann, H. "Die Selbstverwaltung der kaiserzeitlichen Polis in Plutarchs Schrift Praecepta gerendae rei publicae." *Chiron* 32 (2002), 83-95.

Hutton, W. "The Disaster of Roman Rule: Pausanias 8.27.1." *Classical Quarterly* 58 (2008): 622-37.

Jones, C. P. "Towards a Chronology of Plutarch's Works." *Journal of Roman Studies* 65 (1966): 61-74.

—. *Plutarch and Rome*. Oxford: Clarendon Press, ²1972.

—. "Multiple Identities in the Age of the Second Sophistic." Pages 13-21 in *Paideia: The World of the Second Sophistic*. Edited by B. E. Borg. Berlin: de Gruyter, 2004.

Jung, M. *Marathon und Plataiai: Zwei Perserschlachten als "lieux de mémoire" im antiken Griechenland*. Göttingen: Vandenhoeck & Ruprecht, 2006.

Meier, C. *Das Gebot zu vergessen und die Unabweisbarkeit des Erinnerns: Vom öffentlichen Umgang mit schlimmer Vergangenheit*. München: Siedler, 2010.

Meier, M. *Das andere Zeitalter Justinians: Kontingenzerfahrung und Kontingenzbewältigung im 6. Jahrhundert n. Chr.* 2d ed. Göttingen: Vandenhoeck & Ruprecht, 2004.

Melchior, A. "Caesar in Vietnam: Did Roman Soldiers Suffer from Post-Traumatic Stress Disorder?" *Greece & Rome* 58 (2011): 209-23.

Meyer-Zwiffelhoffer, E. *Politikôn archein: Zum Regierungsstil der senatorischen Statthalter in den kaiserzeitlichen griechischen Provinzen*. Stuttgart: Steiner, 2002.

Nikolaides, A. G. *The Unity of Plutarch's Work: 'Moralia' Themes in the 'Lives,' Features of the 'Lives' in the 'Moralia.'* Berlin: de Gruyter, 2008.

Pabst, A. "Identitätssuche: Wie römisch sind provinziale Geschichtsschreiber der Kaiserzeit?" Pages 121-41 in *Studia hellenistica et historiographica: Festschrift für Andreas Mehl*. Edited by T. Brüggemann et al. Gutenberg: Computus, 2010.

—. "Mobilität und Stabilität in der griechischen Welt der römischen Kaiserzeit." Pages 257-65 in *Mobilität in den Kulturen der antiken Mittelmeerwelt*. Edited by E. Olshausen et al. Stuttgart: Steiner, 2014.

Parker, R. *Miasma, Pollution and Purification in Early Greek Religion*. Oxford: Clarendon Press, 1996.

Pekáry, T. "Seditio: Unruhen und Revolten im römischen Reich von Augustus bis Commodus." *Ancient Society* 18 (1987): 133-50.

Plutarch. *Lives*. Translated by B. Perrin. Vol. XI. Loeb Classical Library. Cambridge: Harvard University Press, 1994.

—. *Moralia*. Translated by H. N. Fowler. Vol. X. Loeb Classical Library. Cambridge: Harvard University Press, 1991.

Puech, B. "Prosopographie des amis de Plutarque." *Aufstieg und Niedergang der Römischen Welt* 33.6:4831-93. Part 2, *Principat*, 33.6. Edited by W. Haase. Berlin: de Gruyter, 1992.

Renoirte, Th. *Les 'Conseils politiques' de Plutarque, Une letter ouverte aux Grecs à l'époque de Trajan*. Louvain: Bibliothèque de l'Université, 1951.

Roisman, J. "On Phrynichos' Sack of Miletos and Phoinissai." *Eranos* 86 (1998): 15-23.

RYAN, F. X. "Phrynichos kommt vor Gericht." *Studia Humaniora Tartuensia* 6 (2005). Cited 7 January 2013. Online: http://www.ut.ee/klassik/sht/2005/ryan5.pdf.

SAÏD, S. "Plutarch and the People in the Parallel Lives." Pages 7–25 in *The Statesman in Plutarch's Greek and Roman Lives*. Vol. 2 of *The Statesman in Plutarch's Works: Proceedings of the Sixth International Conference of the International Plutarch Society, Nijmegen/Castle Hernen, May 1–5, 2002*. Edited by L. de Blois et al. Leiden: Brill, 2005.

SPAWFORTH, A. "Symbol of Unity? The Persian-Wars Tradition in the Roman Empire." Pages 233–47 in *Greek Historiography*. Edited by S. Hornblower. Oxford: Clarendon Press 1994.

SWAIN, S. *Hellenism and Empire: Language, Classicism, and Power in the Greek World, AD 50–250*. 2d ed. Oxford: Clarendon Press, 1998.

THERIAULT, G. *Le culte d'Homonoia dans le cités grecques*. Lyon: Maison de l'Orient Méditerranéen, 1996.

WERNER, R., and H. BENGTSON. *Die Staatsverträge des Altertums*. Vol. 2. 2d ed. München: Beck, 1975.

WHITMARSH, T., ed. *Local Knowledge and Microidentities in the Imperial World*. Cambridge: Cambridge University Press, 2010.

WOOLF, G. "Becoming Roman, Staying Greek: Culture, Identity and the Civilizing Process in the Roman East." *Proceedings of the Cambridge Philological Society* 40 (1994): 116–43.

Primary Source Citations

Biblical

Apostolic Fathers and Pseudepigrapha

Greek and Latin Works

Ancient Near Eastern Texts

Subject Index